Wits & S

Jack Anderson
Russell Baker
Erma Bombeck
Jimmy Breslin
David Broder
Art Buchwald
William F. Buckley, Jr.
Ellen Goodman
James J. Kilpatrick
Carl T. Rowan
Mike Royko
George F. Will

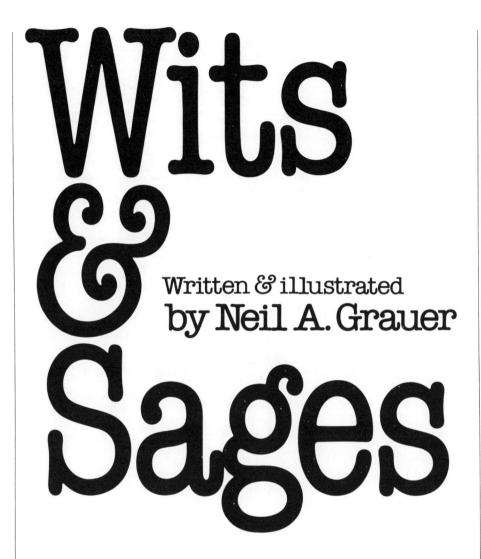

Wits & Sages

Written & illustrated
by Neil A. Grauer

The Johns Hopkins University Press

BALTIMORE AND LONDON

© 1984 by The Johns Hopkins University Press
All rights reserved
Printed in the United States of America

The Johns Hopkins University Press, Baltimore, Maryland 21218
The Johns Hopkins Press Ltd., London

LIBRARY OF CONGRESS CATALOGING IN PUBLICATION DATA

Grauer, Neil A.
Wits and sages.
1. Journalists—United States—Biography.
I. Title.
PN4871.G7   1984   070′.92′2   [B]   83–23891
ISBN 0–8018–3189–X

Permissions listed on p. 268 constitute a continuation of the copyright page.

For
Dr. William S. Grauer,
one of my better critics,
and
Miriam J. Grauer (1916–1974),
who was the best

Contents

Acknowledgments

With the insight indigenous to the breed, a *New Yorker* cartoonist once depicted a publisher saying to a prospective author: "Well, it's good, but people just don't write books all by themselves anymore." In writing this book, I have benefited immeasurably from the patient counsel, assistance, and encouragement of many friends and colleagues. High on the list of those to whom special acknowledgment is due are three friends, Thomas A. Cole of Chicago, Charles S. Fax of Washington, D.C., and Dan Rodricks of Baltimore, who read practically every chapter as it came out of the typewriter and offered invaluable advice that I endeavored to follow. Many fine points in these profiles are due to their perceptive analyses, and the failings that remain reflect my inability to meet their standards. Others who have read various chapters and offered valuable critiques include George H. Hanst, Robert Douglas, John Fairhall, Jonathan Acton II, Charles P. Goodell, Hugh Davis Graham, Stephen E. Ambrose, and Alice and Lou D'Angelo.

From the earliest stages of this lengthy project, I was fortunate to have the support and interest of Milton S. Eisenhower; the late Louis Azrael, a distinguished Baltimore journalist who spent over fifty years as a columnist; and Stephen H. Sachs, the Attorney General of Maryland.

In many ways, all of these people served on my personally selected "editorial board," but the official responsibility for the onerous editorial tasks associated with the completion of this book fell on Jack Goellner, the director of the Johns Hopkins University Press, and members of his staff. Gerard A. Valerio, the designer, and Joanne Allen, my meticulous copy editor, deserve special mention.

This book would have been impossible to write had not each of the columnists I chose to profile agreed to be interviewed, in some cases several times. I am indebted to them for the unique perspective they gave me on their work and how they perform it, as well as to a number of their colleagues who also offered me their time and views. In addition, thanks are due to William B. Dickinson, Jr., of the Washington Post Writers Group; Sidney Goldberg of United Features Syndicate; Lee Salem of Universal Press Syndicate; Allan Priaulx of King Features Syndicate; Leighton McLaughlin of Field Enterprises; and John Morton of Lynch, Jones and Ryan of Washington, D.C., all of whom spoke to me about the syndication business with cordiality and candor.

Wits & Sages

Introduction

A famous photograph of John F. Kennedy captured him standing silhouetted against a window in the Oval Office, his back to the camera, his arms resting on a table, his head bowed in apparent contemplation, the weight of the world on his shoulders. But as the photographer later recalled, moments after the photo was snapped Kennedy looked up from the table, on which was spread the *New York Times,* and muttered, "That goddamned Arthur Krock!"

Kennedy "didn't have the weight of the world on his shoulders at all," gleefully recounted *Times* columnist Tom Wicker, a Krock successor. "He had Arthur Krock on his shoulders." Such can be the power of a prominent newspaper sage to move the leaders of the land.

The importance of newspaper columnists is not usually illustrated by the fact that a single sage's column can anger a president or prompt him to adopt a certain policy. It is also unlikely that columnists persuade voters to pull one lever instead of another. Rather, columnists give our amorphous "press" its personality; they wade through the massive flow of news which swamps us daily and focus our attention on issues and events that otherwise might get lost in the deluge.

In tandem with the newspaper sages are the syndicated wits, whose social and political analyses are often as perceptive—and sometimes more devastating—by virtue of

the deceptively light manner in which they are presented. Their satires and witticisms subtly infiltrate our consciousness and color the way we think of ourselves. In the 1920s and 1930s, Walter Lippmann, Arthur Krock, and other sages wrote judicious commentaries on the issues of the day, but the droll, cryptic observations of Will Rogers and the orotund fumings of H. L. Mencken were the ones most relished by the general public (and are more often remembered today). The best humor deals with the immutable—human nature—rather than the transient—current affairs. Yet, ironically, humor is rarely given the critical attention it deserves. Over 40 years ago, E. B. White observed sadly that "the world likes humor, but it treats it patronizingly. It decorates its serious artists with laurel, and its wags with Brussels sprouts." In this book, wits and sages are accorded equal scrutiny and, when appropriate, nonvegetable adornment.

Recent surveys have indicated that the American public appears to want more than headline services and cotton-candy journalism. Respondents to one poll in 1983 reported that they found newspapers to be a more thorough source of news, and better at explaining it, than either television or radio. Despite the death of some once-major newspapers, the impressive expansion of television news operations in recent years, and the dazzling potential for an even greater explosion—perhaps glut—of information via various cable television and computer systems, daily newspaper circulation is rising. In 1982 it went up by one million—the largest jump in 16 years—with some 62.4 million papers now being sold each day. The educational level of the average American also has grown. Forty years ago it amounted to about 9 years of schooling; now it is the equivalent of the first year in college. "If a newspaper wants to survive," the Washington *Post*'s J. W. Anderson once wrote, "it adapts by widening the range of its interests and improving the quality of its writing." Columnists do just that, and perhaps in part because of them newspapers are surviving.

According to one industry guide, there are over 800 "major" syndicated columnists offering information and rumination in 24 different subject areas. They write about ecology and animals, medicine and science, decorating and antiques. Some 40 columnists write about food and wine, and over 50 write about hobbies. Over 230 columnists cover politics and other topics of general interest.

Selecting the columnists to profile in this book was not easy. On the advice of a colleague who had been in the newspaper business for more than a half-century, I began with the ones I like, which is, I suppose, as good a criterion as any. I wanted geographic spread, although a heavy concentration of Washington-based writers was inevitable because so many top columnists work there. Others were selected because they were widely read writers who offered something special in terms of either style or perspective. Finally, only a limited number of columnists could be profiled, since even the most insatiable readers—and the most indulgent editors—expect a book to end somewhere.

The dozen columnists whose lives and work I have endeavored to chronicle and analyze each meets one or more of these criteria. Taken alphabetically (again, as appropriate a means of listing as any), they are:

JACK ANDERSON—The acknowledged syndication king of columnists, appearing in an estimated 1,000 newspapers, including dailies, weeklies, and college papers, he is the Pulitzer Prize–winning, self-styled heir to the investigative reporting tradition of the turn-of-the-century muckrakers.

RUSSELL BAKER—Perhaps the most graceful and witty contemporary essayist in American journalism, he has won Pulitzer Prizes for his *New York Times* column and for his autobiography. His remarkably varied prose deftly delineates modern anxieties with humor and outrage.

ERMA BOMBECK—A genius at demonstrating that brevity is indeed the soul of wit, she addresses life's mundane annoyances and profound worries in the spirit of America's finest comic writers. Her column is syndicated in over 900 newspapers; her work has been compiled in several best-selling anthologies; and she appears regularly on ABC-TV's "Good Morning America."

JIMMY BRESLIN—A gritty, New York–born and based writer, he has had a significant impact on the present generation of journalists through his street-wise commentaries and books, all written with vitriol and insight.

DAVID BRODER—Chief political writer for the *Washington Post,* he is regarded by many Washington-based reporters as the keenest analyst of modern politics. Winner of a Pulitzer Prize for commentary, he is also among the most widely syndicated editorial-page columnists.

ART BUCHWALD—The Pulitzer Prize–winning clown prince of columnists, syndicated in over 550 newspapers, he has performed the astonishing feat of writing funny and perceptive columns for over 30 years.

WILLIAM F. BUCKLEY, JR.—Perhaps the most erudite conservative commentator among the most widely syndicated columnists, he manages to produce three essays a week while engaging in an incredible variety of pursuits ranging from magazine editor, television host, and novelist to amateur musician and painter, ocean sailor, and social critic.

ELLEN GOODMAN—Based in Boston and another member of the top ten editorial-page columnists in terms of syndication (and one of the few women in that elite group), she is a Pulitzer Prize–winning analyst who concentrates less on public policy than on individual inner turmoil, giving voice to the often unspoken concerns and anxieties of her readers.

JAMES J. KILPATRICK—Another of the top ten editorial-page columnists in terms of syndication, he was among the first—and he remains the most widely distributed—of the conservative analysts spawned in response to the Great Society. He also lectures widely and appears regularly on television and radio's "Agronsky and Company."

CARL T. ROWAN—The most widely disseminated of black columnists, he became a syndicated commentator following a career as a reporter, diplomat, and director of the United States Information Agency. He also writes magazine articles, appears weekly on "Agronsky and Company," and lectures widely.

MIKE ROYKO—A Pulitzer Prize–winning urban commentator, he is a modern exemplar of the brash Chicago school of journalism. Influential in his own city and respected throughout the country, Royko writes columns that are an admixture of tough reporting, tight prose, and biting humor.

GEORGE F. WILL—A Pulitzer Prize–winning commentator of unusual intellect and elegance who combines conservatism with compassion. He comments twice weekly in some 400 newspapers and biweekly in *Newsweek*, and he appears once a week on

"Agronsky and Company" and ABC-TV's "This Week with David Brinkley."

Syndication, the $150 million industry by which the work of these columnists is sold to the nation's 1,750 newspapers, is one of the nation's last great bastions of freewheeling, bare-knuckled entrepreneurship. One syndicate executive with whom I spoke balked when his business was described as "cut-throat," protesting with a weak chuckle, "We never kill." Nevertheless, as another syndicate chief put it, syndicates are "viciously competitive." It is a relatively small industry. There are about 200 syndicates, ranging in size from one-person cottage industries to megabuck operations with numerous offerings, but even the top 10 syndicates rarely have more than 6 to 12 salespeople. It is a highly secretive business. Most syndicates closely guard the list of clients for their various wares and will not reveal the price each paper pays for a particular columnist or feature. No more eloquent reflection of the competitive nature of the business can be found than the fact that the prices papers pay for syndicated columnists have not really gone up in over a decade—and at the bottom end of the scale they are astonishingly low. A small newspaper, one with a circulation of 4,000 or 5,000, pays $5 a week—or perhaps a little less—for columns bearing the by-lines of some of the biggest names in journalism. In the case of a commentator such as George Will, for example, that comes to a whopping $2.50 a column for his twice-weekly commentary. For large papers—those with a circulation of over 400,000 or 500,000 and a wide area of distribution—the same two columns may cost up to $70 a week or more. When two or more papers in an area are vying for a particular column, the price can be bid upwards to $150 a week.

Even at the lower end of the price scale, substantial sums of money can be made. "It's a matter of multiples," one syndicate director explained. Five dollars a week times 50 weeks is $250; 4 of those papers bring in $1,000, 40 of them pay $10,000, and so on. Add to that the number of papers paying much more than $5 a week—those paying $15, $25, $50, and up—and multiply the take from that. The "star" columnists, those with 250 to 350 papers, conceivably can clear $100,000 a year from their columns. Those columnists also are able to parlay their newspaper exposure into lectures, television appearances, and books, which in some cases earn them even more than they receive from their columns.

In general, the newspaper syndicate and the columnist split the proceeds from the column 50-50. Just how those proceeds are calculated can vary, however. Some split the "gross" income, others split the "net." As one syndicate executive put it, "There are probably a dozen different ways to define what's 'gross' and what's 'net.' "

Similarly, the hefty lecture fees some columnists receive—up to $15,000 an appearance in a few cases—are whittled down by their agent's percentage, usually a third, and taxes, which take half of what's left. All this should not suggest that highly successful columnists are reduced to penury by their syndicates, agents, and the Internal Revenue Service. They all earn a healthy, six-figure income and live well on it.

Most columnists, however, are hardly Croesuses. The majority appear in a relatively small number of papers—some 40 or 50—and earn anywhere from $15,000 to $25,000 a year. Still, having a syndicated column may open opportunities in other fields, and literally thousands of would-be columnists try to break into the business each year. As Richard L. Strout, the *New Republic*'s "TRB" for 40 years, put it, there is something more enriching than syndication proceeds: a "psychic pay" which every columnist enjoys.

Although most early American journalists resorted to pseudonyms out of a healthy sense of self-preservation, this nation prefers its commentary with an identifiable personal touch. People enjoy having a writer they can agree with—or despise. Readers look to the press to explain events and tell them what to think, and they prefer being able to react to another person rather than an institution. A society that gave the world town meetings wants to keep abreast of its governmental doings and likes to think that it personally knows the sources of its information.

For most of American journalistic history, newspapers were the personal product of the chief editors or publishers—the James Gordon Bennetts, father and son; Horace Greeley; Joseph Pulitzer; William Randolph Hearst. They were a hard-headed and opinionated lot whose journals reflected their personalities. Many modern newspapers, however, are simply a branch of some corporate behemoth, and most editors and publishers are unknown to the public. The personality vacuum has been filled by syndicated columnists. The superficiality of much television reporting—and the flabbiness of its occasional editorials—has given a boost to the forthright print commentators, who go behind the headlines and are not afraid to wield potent words.

There is some truth in the view expressed a century ago by Henry W. Grady, the legendary editor of the *Atlanta Constitution,* that "a good reporter who subsides into an able editor marks a loss to journalism," but when knowledgeable reporters "subside" into column writing, they can perform a valuable function. The freedom of the press guaranteed by the Constitution carries with it a concomitant duty on the part of the press to ensure the people's right to know and understand the complex issues facing them.

"We make it our business to find out what is going on, under the surface and beyond the horizon; to infer, to deduce, to imagine and to guess what is going on inside—and what this meant yesterday and what it could mean tomorrow," wrote Walter Lippmann, a unique public philosopher whose column was directed as much—maybe even more— at presidents and prime ministers as it was at the general public, whom he also served. "We do what every sovereign citizen is supposed to do but has not the time or interest to do for himself. This is our job. It is no mean calling, and we have a right to be proud of it and to be glad that it is our work."

In their role as editorial writers for a national audience, columnists who have extensive experience and sources in Washington and elsewhere can provide interpretations of current events based on a great deal more than the basic wire-service reports and slapdash research most locally based editorial writers employ in buttressing their viewpoints. The daily newspaper readers who pay serious attention to the editorial pages realize this. Devotees of editorials may be a minute fraction of the overall readership, but they include elected officials of local, state, and national governments, as well as those who make decisions and set trends of thinking in nongovernmental fields. Breadth of readership gives some cachet to a columnist, but a column's influence is measured less by how many read it than by who reads it.

Regardless of the number of readers who may be exposed to a Washington columnist's product through national syndication, his most important audience comprises the public officials who are his neighbors and sources, as well as the Washington-based reporters who sometimes take their cues from a columnist's informed observations. It is a small, very select and powerful group of readers whose proximity is sufficient to provide succor to even the most meagerly syndicated columnist's sense of importance and purpose.

Column writing also appears to encourage longevity. Columnists are to journalism as conductors are to symphony orchestras: they seem to last forever. It is a little astonishing to realize that several of the more prominent originators of the modern Washington column were still pecking away at their typewriters a decade or so ago. The profession may tax the brain, but the heart, lungs, and liver thrive on it. More than half of the writers profiled in this book have been columnists for 20 years or more, and none show any signs of slowing down or losing readers.

Occasionally a columnist's reports are an intricate shadow play, reflecting behind-the-scenes conflicts within the government. An axiom of political reporting is that it is much easier to get candid information from those who are against something than from those who are for it. Consequently, the losers in any hard-fought internal policy debate are the ones most likely to approach a sympathetic columnist in an effort to give their views a final shot at prevailing. Columns can be assayed in the same manner as smoke signals, tea leaves, or chicken entrails. They are, as press scholar and critic Ben Bagdikian observed over a dozen years ago, "an elite intelligence system of the highest order, and more effective than any memo. A subcabinet officer or member of Congress or ambassador who cannot get his message to the President through ordinary channels can do it through a column—and reach his target at breakfast time. Columns are often instruments of revolt, shooting rebellious messages directly into headquarters, the guerrilla protected by anonymity and the camouflage of the columnist's name."

"If you want to get to the largest number of people, you try to get on television," Ted Koppel of ABC told *Time* magazine in 1982, "but if you are trying to scuttle someone's program or get a hearing within the highest levels of the Administration, you go to a columnist."

Similarly, when the public's or a political party's response to a politician's actions can be influenced or gauged by the comments of a respected, syndicated observer, it often is prudent to determine beforehand how that observer may react. The columnists based in Washington may have their greatest immediate impact in the capital, but by virtue of their extensive syndication and their position as replacements for the offerings of many local editorialists, they also can help set the tone of citizen debates on major national issues. It is a role columnists have played since the birth of the republic.

Today's sages may trace their lineage back to a distinguished trio of Revolutionary leaders who in their spare time churned out more than 180,000 words of closely reasoned political analysis under deadline pressure and produced, for regular distribution in semiweekly newspapers, a series of 85 essays collectively entitled *The Federalist*.

This triumvirate of part-time journalists went on to scale greater heights: one, James Madison, became the fourth president of the United States; another, John Jay, became the first chief justice of the United States; and the third, Alexander Hamilton, was the first secretary of the treasury. Their collection of essays—all signed "Publius"—successfully promoted ratification of the Constitution, under which they later achieved these august positions. No journalistic endeavor since has been as effective. One historian called *The Federalist* the "most significant contribution that Americans have made to political philosophy" and ranked the articles in importance with the Declaration of Independence and the Constitution itself.

Today's wits may claim a similarly impressive progenitor, since it was, after all, through the homey wisdom of the aphorisms in *Poor Richard's Almanac*, as well as some anonymous literary hoaxes and parodies, that Benjamin Franklin gained his initial public recognition. He also earned the right to be accorded homage as the first, and certainly the best known, of America's early humorous commentators.

In the century following the Revolution,

few of the successors to Hamilton, Madison, and Jay could hope to match their learning and prose style. Instead, most of the journalists who achieved prominence as commentators attempted to follow Franklin's example and adopted the guise of homespun philosophers who wrote rustic letters to newspapers and magazines. The works of these supposed wits received wide currency through a rather haphazard method of distribution that featured more larceny than commercial enterprise. Early newspaper editors prided themselves on the care with which they clipped items from out-of-town papers for use in their own. One writer observed in 1876: "Papers which are made up entirely of original material are not, as a rule, very popular. It is a very common remark of shrewd newspapermen that they can steal better articles than they buy."

Nevertheless, the enterprising and facile forebears of today's syndicated columnists somehow managed to sell their material to papers in the hinterlands, sending "letters" containing items of interest from New York or Washington. One mid-nineteenth-century Manhattan scribe received a munificent $30 a week for his letter to the *Philadelphia Times*. A contemporary critic said that this prototypical column "certainly deserves the accusation of superficiality" but at least was "written in a graceful style and is very readable." Those still are marketable attributes.

Two writers whose works were both widely stolen and widely sold were D. R. Locke, editor of the *Toledo Blade,* who created "Petroleum V. Nasby," a rural satirist; and Charles Farrar Browne, city editor of the *Cleveland Plain Dealer,* who wrote a series of comic letters under the nom de plume "Artemus Ward," who was billed as the proprietor of a traveling sideshow featuring tame bears, a kangaroo, and "wax figgers" of prominent people. Both Nasby and Ward were favorites of Abraham Lincoln, who thought so highly of Ward's drolleries that he sought to lighten the somber atmosphere of one Cabinet meeting by producing an anthology of Ward columns and reading aloud an account of an attack by vandals on old Artemus's waxworks. Lincoln then adopted a graver tone and read a more sober document of his own creation: the Emancipation Proclamation. As latter-day columnists would find, association with the reigning chief executive enhances one's appeal, and Browne, in the person of Ward, made a great deal of money embarking on lecture tours to deliver comic talks based on his character's misadventures.

The human-interest letters from New York and Washington and the humorous ramblings of midwestern editors were not the only regular columnlike features of the ante-bellum and Civil War press. One impoverished, Prussian-born correspondent situated in London emulated the serious political analyses and philosophizing of Hamilton, Madison, and Jay, although from an entirely different perspective. Beginning in 1851, Karl Marx dispatched regular columns to the *New York Tribune* at the behest of its managing editor, Charles A. Dana.

Marx wrote reports and commentary on the developments in England and on the Continent, and by 1855 he reached an agreement with Dana to contribute biweekly, anonymous columns to the *Tribune* for ten dollars apiece. In time, he even found opportunities to comment passionately on the American Civil War. The *Tribune* was owned by antisecessionist Horace Greeley, and in November 1861, Marx wrote in a column from London, where many aristocrats sympathized with the Confederacy: "The South is not a country at all, but a battle slogan." Greeley undoubtedly was pleased.

Marx's heart belonged to different literary and political endeavors, however. (The first volume of *Das Kapital* appeared in 1867.) He complained to a friend: "This continual journalistic hack-work is getting on my nerves. It takes up a lot of time, destroys any continuity in my efforts and in the final analysis amounts to nothing at all. You can be independent as you please, nevertheless you are tied down to the paper and to the readers, especially when you are paid in cash as I am." Even right-wing columnists of today might feel a sense of kinship with the frustrated Marx.

One innovative form of private enterprise born during the Civil War and destined to play a crucial part in the development of column writing was the formal newspaper syndicate, which was aided in its growth by the strengthening of copyright laws. Syndicates were not spawned in the eastern mercantile centers of Boston, New York, or Philadelphia, but in an unlikely birthplace: Baraboo, Wisconsin. Ansell K. Kellogg, editor of the weekly *Baraboo Republic,* was bereft of his chief typesetter in July 1861, when the first call for Civil War volunteers was sounded. Unable to fill the paper's four pages without the typesetter's help, Kellogg arranged for the publishers of the daily *Wisconsin State Journal* in Madison to send him half-sheet, preprinted supplements chock-full of war news. These were inserted in his weekly as pages 2 and 3, leaving the outside for local items. Publishers of other small Wisconsin papers were enchanted by this labor-saving idea, and soon the *Journal* was kept busy supplying "ready print" or "patent insides" of war news and miscellaneous filler, complete with advertisements inserted between the articles, to some 30 papers. The cost for these features was kept attractively low by the expanded distribution.

By 1867, printers of patent insides were supplying their customers with political editorials—forerunners of today's syndicated columns—tailoring the partisanship of the articles to the particular client's ideological preferences. Other syndicates sprang up to fill the demands of a rapidly expanding market. Literary offerings such as serialized fiction, as popular then in print as it is now in soap operas, were added to the syndicates' lists of wares. During the 1870s, the ready-print concerns began marketing "boiler-plate," metal stereotype plate one column wide containing a complete selection of filler material, including children's stories, agricultural news, features, short fiction, and miscellany. By deftly wielding a hack-saw, the editor of a small, one-man weekly could render portions of the boilerplate suit-able for plugging any gap in the paper.

By the 1880s, the essential format of syn-dicated columns was established, although much of the material was unsigned. National fame was reserved for a select few among the widely disseminated writers. The American Press Association, founded by the publisher of the *Chicago Express,* distrib-uted the work of humorist "Bill" Nye, early Chicago columnist Eugene Field, and nov-elist Booth Tarkington. At its height, it sup-plied some sort of material to an awesome clientele of over 10,000 newspapers. Syndi-cates, then as now, were a ready and lucra-tive outlet for the work of well-known authors, politicians, and literati. Karl Marx's old boss, Charles A. Dana, having moved from the *Tribune* to the *New York Sun,* began syndicating the writings of Henry James. Samuel S. McClure, who founded the McClure Newspaper Syndicate to provide sophisticated fiction to city news-papers, was able to add Theodore Roosevelt, Robert Louis Stevenson, Mark Twain, Henry Cabot Lodge, Rudyard Kipling, Jack London, and Arthur Conan Doyle to his stable of contributors. Edward Bok, then editor of the *Brooklyn Magazine* and later long-time editor of the *Ladies' Home Journal,* organized the Bok Syndicate Press in 1886 to provide, among other fea-tures, a weekly New York letter written by the Rev. Henry Ward Beecher, the Billy Graham of his day, who also was the brother of Harriet Beecher Stowe, author of *Uncle Tom's Cabin.*

During the 1890s, syndicates sprouted

and withered with regularity. In 1895, the first Hearst Syndicate was founded by William Randolph Hearst, a press baron with an infallible instinct for circulation boosters. Its successor, King Features Syn-dicate (founded in 1915), remains one of the biggest operations in the business. Hearst syndicated the acerbic observations of Ambrose Bierce, as well as the shenanigans of early comic strip characters such as the Katzenjammer Kids, Happy Hooligan, and Alfonse and Gaston. Comic strips remain, at least in a financial sense, far more crucial to newspaper syndicates and their customers than columnists. The readership for comics exceeds that for columnists, and the mer-chandising spin-offs from cartoon charac-ters are incredibly valuable. No one has ever marketed a James Reston lunch box or a George Will stuffed doll.

The original Hearst Syndicate also dis-pensed the writings of Chicago columnist Finley Peter Dunne, whose barkeep charac-ter "Mr. Dooley" represented a significant departure from the tradition of unlettered cracker-barrel philosophers. Created by Dunne in 1893, Martin Dooley was a city dweller and street-wise political observer whose trenchant commentary always was delivered in a thick Irish accent. Dunne's review of an egocentric book Theodore Roosevelt wrote about his exploits in the Spanish American War ("If I was him, I'd call th' book 'Alone in Cubia,' " Dooley concluded) so impressed Roosevelt that he cultivated Dunne's friendship and would write him lengthy letters of self-defense if he thought an action of his might offend the columnist. Dunne was a tolerant humorist who often made allowances for the foibles of most politicians on the not unfounded assumption that people frequently get the government they deserve. His Dooley columns were reprinted widely, both in the United States and abroad, and were col-lected in a series of books.

Perhaps the last of the great populist wits was Will Rogers, whose determinedly ungrammatical observations were distributed by the McNaught Syndicate, founded in 1922. In a singular departure from its practice of never using outside columnists, the *New York Times* occasionally featured Rogers's column on its front page. His style may have been a throwback to the rustic wits of the nineteenth century, but his commentary was acute and timeless. He made a substantial contribution to the body of America's folk wisdom and is the only humorist (or as he might have put it, the only "official" humorist) honored by a monument in the U.S. Capitol's Statuary Hall.

As news reporting during the period preceding and encompassing the First World War began to assume an air of objectivity and uniformity, and the character of newspaper editorials changed from the heated, individualistic exhortations of proprietor-editors to the detached judgments of unidentified writers, efforts to maintain the personal quality Americans prefer in their journalism prompted the transformation of prominent reporters into columnists. Their work appeared regularly in the same spot in the paper and added that spark of personality that the rest of the publication often lacked. Columnists could comment on the news, recount humorous anecdotes, reveal their personal preferences and pet hates. The public responded enthusiastically.

The most sparkling early collection of columnists was assembled during the 1920s by Herbert Bayard Swope, executive editor of the *New York World*, who is credited with creating the "page-opposite editorial," or "Op Ed" page. Swope saw the page as a repository for the *World*'s best writers and as a rival to the paper's editorial page. Among the early columnists who appeared regularly on Swope's Op Ed page were Heywood Broun, later a founder of the Newspaper Guild and father of Heywood Hale Broun of CBS News; Franklin P. Adams, or "FPA," whose "Conning Tower" column was read avidly; and Alexander Woollcott, the rotund

and rococo theater critic. (The *World* was not the only paper engaged in column pioneering. Walter Winchell began his innovative Broadway gossip column at this time, appearing originally in a bizarre tabloid, the *Graphic*.)

The editorial page against which the *World*'s columnists competed was the private preserve of Walter Lippmann, a commentator of rare influence who also was a founder of the *New Republic,* a liberal bible. When the *World* expired in 1931, a victim of the Depression, Lippmann—once an assistant to the socialist mayor of Schenectady, New York; an aide to Woodrow Wilson; and a behind-the-scenes adviser to the Democratic opponents of Presidents Harding, Coolidge, and Hoover—moved to the Republican *New York Herald Tribune,* much to the surprise and shock of some of his liberal friends. It was there that he began a regular, thrice-weekly column entitled "Today and Tomorrow," which some journalism historians cite as the first modern by-lined column of opinion.

Actually, there had been earlier pioneers of public-affairs column writing, particularly in Washington, where Frederick I. Haskin began his daily "Haskin Letter" in 1909 and Sir A. Maurice Lowe, Washington correspondent for the *London Post,* prepared news summaries and analyses five times a week for the *New York World,* which distributed them nationally in the early 1900s. In 1929, Paul Mallon, a Capitol Hill reporter for the United Press, had his press gallery credentials revoked when he enraged many senators by uncovering the facts behind two closed-door votes in the Senate, which frequently resorted to secret sessions then. The brouhaha brought Mallon instant celebrity, and he left the United Press to set up his own syndicate and peddle "News Behind the News."

Others give the credit for creating the intrepretive column to David Lawrence, who began adding a tag end of analysis to his daily Washington dispatches for the *New*

York Post back in 1915. The *Post* began syndicating Lawrence's reports in 1916, on the strength of his performance during the presidential election that year. He was one of the few reporters to predict Woodrow Wilson's reelection, basing his forecast on a trip around the country. In 1920 Lawrence established a financial and feature news service that eventually evolved into the magazine *U.S. News & World Report*. He wrote a regular column for it in addition to five daily newspaper pieces, a routine he maintained for 57 years, until his death in 1973.

Nevertheless, Lippmann's columns—originally written from New York and only after 1938 from Washington—were unusual blends of practical analysis and philosophic discourse. When the *Herald Tribune* began syndicating Lippmann, other conservative newspapers realized that they could obtain the observations of an established writer of liberal credentials without having to adopt his views or pay his substantial salary. The safety—and economy—of this procedure appealed to newspaper publishers, who recognized the value of being able to offer readers a variety of well-known syndicated columnists for less than the salary of one good, and anonymous, editorial writer.

The Depression was hell for most industries, but it was a boom time for columnists. Just as a century earlier every moderately experienced reporter in Manhattan had thought that he could write a New York letter, the advent of the New Deal encouraged would-be pundits to flock to Washington, where government was a growth industry but insight was in short supply. There was no shortage of those willing to fill the gap.

Washington columns developed along two distinct lines. On one side were the serious ruminations of the contemplative representatives of large newspapers, such as Krock of the *Times* and Lippmann of the *Herald Tribune*; on the other side were the purveyors of behind-the-scenes information and gossip. The latter school was founded in

1932 with the publication of an anonymous book titled *The Washington Merry-Go-Round,* coauthored by Drew Pearson of the *Baltimore Sun* and Robert S. Allen of the *Christian Science Monitor.* Its inside scuttlebutt and debunking style, which included applying irreverent sobriquets to solemn institutions (the House of Representatives, for example, was dubbed "the Monkey House"), made the book an instant hit with everyone but Pearson's and Allen's employers. After issuing a second volume—*More Washington Merry-Go-Round*—the two reporters joined forces on their own to produce a regular column bearing the same title as their original blockbuster. The "Merry-Go-Round" still whirls under the proprietorship of Pearson's subsequent associate and successor, Jack Anderson.

Column writing, particularly the varieties practiced in Washington, flourished in the 1930s largely because there were so many complex and confusing developments which conventional reporting was unable to explain satisfactorily—much like today. The Washington columnists may not have been any more successful in unraveling the Roosevelt revolution, but at least they provided readers with personalized viewpoints they could identify with and adopt or reject. The popularity of Broadway and Hollywood gossip columns at the time also spurred the multiplication of Washington-based commentators. "It required no stroke of managerial genius to figure out that if this paid off for Broadway it also ought to pay off for Washington, too," wrote the late Cabell Phillips of the *New York Times.*

The ranks of Washington columnists swelled to include many who were more accustomed to appearing in news columns than writing them. In 1933 the McNaught Syndicate signed Eleanor Roosevelt, the new First Lady, to write a regular column entitled "My Day." Soon others with similarly barren newspaper backgrounds—such as curmudgeonly Interior Secretary Harold Ickes and Eleanor's waspish cousin Alice

Roosevelt Longworth—also were writing columns. The amount of vitriol in some columns became their hallmark. Westbrook Pegler's diatribes inspired a new verb; a recipient of his ire (Eleanor Roosevelt became a favorite target) was said to have been "peglerized."

Their lack of expertise or restraint did not affect the popularity of the columnists. The ultimate measure of their success rested on their "ability to write interestingly, not learnedly, not penetratingly, not even well; but in a manner to capture the emotional or intellectual interests of enough thousands of readers to make [them] a profitable 'property' to [their] syndicates," Phillips wrote over 30 years ago. That largely remains the case today, although syndicates now put a far higher premium on the ability to write penetratingly, learnedly, and well, not just interestingly.

There were more unsuccessful than successful columnists in the mid-1930s, but by then columns had become a journalistic institution. The widening scope of the issues the surviving writers sought to address may have placed an unpleasant burden on their abilities to be prescient, or even knowledgeable, about their subjects, but their popularity as a newspaper feature was undiminished. Despite any shortcomings, a syndicated columnist could become, as press critic Charles Fisher wrote in 1944, "the autocrat of the most prodigious breakfast table ever known. He is the voice beside the cracker barrel amplified to transcontinental dimensions. He is the only non-political figure of record who can clear his throat each day and say 'Now here's what I think . . .' with the assurance that millions will listen."

And that was long before columnists made regular appearances on television's weekly gabfests or taped half-minute commentaries for television. Who are these people, and how did they come to attain their lofty stations? How do they go about doing their job as interpreters, informers, guides, critics, and mockers of today's politics and mores?

The fierce competition among syndicates has led to a concerted effort to offer clients a broad selection of commentary and features. As in the days when McNaught recruited Eleanor Roosevelt, some syndicates raid the political arena for columnists. Ronald Reagan once was a star of the King Features line-up, and despite a denunciation of columnists following his unsuccessful 1964 presidential campaign, Barry Goldwater joined their ranks for several years. Andrew Young, the former United Nations ambassador and now mayor of Atlanta, was a columnist briefly, and Jimmy Carter's former press secretary, Jody Powell, now writes a column.

Other potential pundits have a rougher time making the grade. Of the thousands of submissions that the major syndicates receive each year from writers seeking syndication, only a tiny fraction—one or two per syndicate—are picked up. Syndicate editors also receive referrals from their client newspapers and instruct their sales personnel to comb the papers they serve, looking for possible offerings. Sometimes a syndicate decides that there is a market for a certain kind of column—on home computers, perhaps, or diets—and looks for someone to write it.

Little in the way of sophisticated market research appears to be done by the syndicate chiefs. Basically they use their instincts as ex-newspaper people—which most of them are—to divine what is in demand or may sell. "We put all the names in a hat," one syndicate chief joked. Another said that the selection procedure was performed "by guess and by gosh. It's a very subjective process. We try to determine what the industry wants. See, we don't sell to newspaper readers; we sell to newspaper editors. And for a columnist to be selected, the first thing he's got to do is get past *us*. Then we have to get him past the newspaper editor, and ultimately he has to find acceptance with the newspaper reader. So it's really kind of a three-step process."

For years, familiarity and frequency were key factors in the allure any columnist had for newspaper editors. After a half-century in harness, David Lawrence was considered tired and antediluvian by many of his Washington colleagues, but he wrote five columns a week, and editors could count on filling the same spot in the paper each working day with dependable Lawrence bromides. He remained a big seller until he died. As newspapers now seek to compete against television and other potential distractions, there is increased experimentation in the use of columns. Often a new feature is given only a 90-day test run to prove its appeal, much to the anguish of syndicate sales personnel, and the chronic reluctance of newspaper editors to take on a new feature now is compounded by a tendency to drop marginal items in order to cut costs.

Most of the columnists profiled in this book entered the field when it was a considerably more stable business, if no less competitive. They succeeded in an incredibly demanding profession and have survived in an era when newspapers are desperate for features that will help them in the battle to retain readers.

The personal backgrounds of the columnists are diverse, but their professional histories are somewhat similar. Most of them began as reporters, although their skill at that endeavor varied greatly. All of them have formidable reservoirs of energy, enterprise, and imagination. A student of the genre once observed that writing two or three "well-considered and original essays in seven days is a strain on even the most active spirit," yet most of these columnists have done this—and more—for years. They are disciplined and, in most cases, almost compulsive workers for whom column writing is just one enterprise. They read extensively, often travel widely, and usually have several other projects under way.

With a few exceptions most of these writers have a healthy ego, which is a necessary—perhaps essential—ingredient for anyone who addresses a national audience. On the other hand, most of them, again with a few exceptions, are not inclined to boast about their achievements or claim significant influence on politicians or the public. If they cite an example that may suggest the contrary, it usually involves some other columnist.

Few of them—or any of their peers—are ever found wanting in opinions, and it is against their nature (and contracts) to be at a loss for words. But each would probably admit that there are days when they wish they could emulate the late Bob Considine, an old war horse of the Hearst papers, who wrote a supremely succinct column in August 1973 which read in its entirety: "I have nothing to say today."

There are dangers—which I do not escape—in labeling any of these columnists "liberal" or "conservative." Even the ones who adopt such identifications for themselves reveal a greater subtlety of thought in their writing or conversations than the classification would convey. They all are reflective people and not easy to pigeonhole. There are more similarities than differences, for example, in what George Will has to say on the welfare state and what Art Buchwald thinks about it than either columnist probably realizes. For the most part, however, they all are distinctive public voices offering pointed, well defined, and diverse views with which millions of readers identify.

"Government and public issues are becoming complicated faster than the average citizen is becoming complicated," George Will said in reflecting on the role he and other columnists play. "We depend, therefore, to an unusual extent on journalism to not just communicate fact, information, and news, but to help produce a more complicated citizenry if we're to keep our republican institutions vital."

However large their following, enlightening their observations, and hefty their bank accounts, most columnists (including Will) recognize that their daily musings are essentially ephemeral. The lesson of "Ozymandias" was that little, if anything, endures; but journalistic writing tends to evaporate especially fast. Even the most quoted insights of Will Rogers or H. L. Mencken more often come from sources other than their newspaper work. Lippmann himself frequently expressed a jaundiced view of the task that has been compared to the labor of a journalistic Sisyphus, forever pushing 800 heavy words up a hill, only to start all over again at the bottom the next day. "I have never taken newspaper work very seriously," Lippmann confessed to his friend Bernard Berenson. "It is to me a livelihood, a means of practical influence." There is among the columnists in this book a shared appreciation for the difficulty of what they do and a lurking suspicion that its effects may be minimal.

Most readers probably read a column because the opinions of the writer confirm their beliefs; others may follow a column because they find it infuriating yet entertaining. Whatever influence columnists have is most likely general rather than specific, cumulative rather than immediate. "It's 'drip-drip-drip,' like water on a rock," said Richard Strout, the dean of Washington journalists.

"I think people do read columnists, and my general impression is that we have a marginal influence," said David Broder. "My own feeling is that sometimes columns may tend to confirm or strengthen a view. I think that sometimes, from the stories I hear, they are useful weapons to people who are involved in an argument, as to should you do this or should you do that. If they can say, 'Even George Will or even Jack Kilpatrick thinks that this is a dumb thing to do,' maybe that gives them one more argument inside the meeting."

Some of the columnists' working-stiff colleagues, perhaps out of envy, dismiss their efforts as claptrap. A former midwestern editor once grumbled: "I think the syndicated column is one of the biggest rackets ever put over on editors. . . . A page of these syndicated columnists is a perfect reproduction of the yackety-yack that fills the room after the third or fourth dry martini."

If that were entirely so, then few people would read them.

"As long as there's a market for newspapers there'll be a market for columns," Russell Baker said, "because unprocessed data is the great menace nowadays to the reader. There's so much of it you don't have time to synthesize it, and a columnist who does his job right helps with that. He points to something that's interesting, and you pause over that for a few minutes and you sort it out and it stands out from the mass."

For many journalists, command of one's own column is the honor most coveted, regardless of its frustrations. In the eyes of most of their professional peers and the public, columnists stand out from the mass of journalists. With a column, one still has an opportunity to become, as Ben Bagdikian once put it, "the voice of the government subconscious, viceroy of political kings, imperious controller of public emotion, proctor of public servants." (It is also possible, he added ruefully, to become a "shabby loudmouth unworthy of belief.")

For most regular readers of columns, these wits and sages are their friends in high places. Their writings illuminate our time, reflecting what we are and what we have been. Their work will also show future generations how well we saw where we were going. Theirs is a tremendously difficult job. They perform it with uncommon skill. They all would agree with the late Red Smith, the superb sports essayist, that the key to their success is simple: all one must do is sit down at a typewriter "and open a vein."

Jack Anderson

The Man with the Muckrake

Nothing in life is so exhilarating as being shot at without result," said Winston Churchill, recalling his tour of duty as a correspondent in the Boer War. It is a sentiment Jack Anderson appreciates and an observation he enjoys quoting. As the only columnist (one hopes) ever allegedly marked for assassination by peevish White House aides, Anderson knows the thrill of being an elusive target and the satisfaction of seeing his pursuers foiled.

Five feet ten inches tall, round shouldered, paunchy, with a pallid complexion and the remaining strands of his thin white hair combed in a neat arch, Anderson, 62, looks more like a benign grandfather of ten (which he is) than the merciless exposer of fraud and chicanery in government that his millions of readers—and he himself—consider him to be.

Although current fashion labels Anderson's brand of journalism "investigative reporting" (all reporting, in varying degrees, involves investigating), Anderson appears to adopt the new nomenclature only because of its marketability. He much prefers the less-sanitized, turn-of-the-century title for his job and those who practice it: he calls himself a muckraker and is proud of it.

The crusading reporters in the early 1900s who revealed the horrors of the meat packing industry, municipal corruption, and oil company monopolies were branded "muckrakers" by their early ally and eventual critic Theodore Roosevelt. In 1906, after a series of articles poked into the questionable finances of some powerful senators whose support he needed, T.R. denounced all investigative journalists with a typically Rooseveltian flourish:

In Bunyan's "Pilgrim's Progress"... the Man with the Muckrake is set forth as an example of him whose vision is fixed on carnal instead of spiritual things. Yet he also typifies the man who in this life consistently refuses to see aught that is lofty, and fixes his eyes with solemn intentness only on that which is vile and debasing. Now, it is very necessary that we should not flinch from seeing what is vile and debasing. There is filth on the floor, and it must be scraped up with the muckrake; and there are times and places where this service is the most needed of all services that can be performed. But the man who never does anything else, who never thinks or speaks or writes save of his feats with the muckrake, speedily becomes, not a help to society, not an incitement to good, but one of the most potent forces of evil.

The reporters themselves considered the new label their highest accolade. They also liked to point out that Roosevelt had become tangled in his own literary allusion—Bunyan's muckraker raked the muck in search of money; he was just the sort of person the journalists were out to skewer.

Jack Anderson is by no means as rapacious an entrepreneur as any of the malefactors he dredges up with his muckrake, but he certainly is as enterprising. He is not just a columnist; he is an industry with over $1 million in revenues a year. He is a seven-days-a-week mini-newspaper with 17 full-time employees, 13 of whom are reporters. He is a thrice-weekly radio program. He is a weekly television series, a weekly magazine editor, a circuit-riding speaker delivering over 50 speeches a year.

It is this latter endeavor, Anderson claims, that supplies his sole source of income. He receives a flat $250,000 a year from the American Program Bureau to travel the country from the middle of September to the end of May, declaiming before as many audiences as the agency can sign up. He says he doesn't know how much the speakers bureau gets per appearance for his services. (It averages $5,000 a shot.) "The agency charges whatever it wishes," he says with a touch of weariness and what might be viewed as an uncharacteristic lack of interest in details. "It's interested only in getting its money back, and they don't care how often I have to go, so I agree to give a speech a week on the average. I get my entire living from that. I take no money from my other operations. And one of the reasons is to force myself to get out into the country. I think too many Washington correspondents spend too much time talking to one another, and I think I would probably be lazy and do the same thing if I didn't force myself to get out. When I visit an area, I usually can come back with a pretty clear picture of what's going on in that area and what the problems are and how the people feel, what the mood is."

Unlike his predecessor and mentor, the late Drew Pearson, from whom he inherited the long-running "Washington Merry-Go-Round" column in 1969, Anderson does not

make an effort on his travels to drop in at the offices of the local newspapers to massage the egos of his clients or drum up business. "I write the column and leave it to the syndicate [United Features] to sell it. I don't look upon myself as a salesman."

That may be, but Anderson has demonstrated a sharp business acumen and a keen sense of salesmanship that sometimes borders on hucksterism. Since he took over Pearson's column, its roster of clientele has grown from about 600 newspapers to over 1,000, making it the most widely syndicated written feature in the world, with an estimated readership of 40 million. The staff has grown 5-fold from the 3 or 4 harried, overworked reporters Pearson employed (including Anderson himself) to 20 full-time and freelance workers. Anderson is not a philosophic crusader like Pearson, who set his investigative sights on ideological opponents, but like Pearson he is not above going up to Capitol Hill to lobby legistators, urging them to launch investigations into the targets of his exposés and thus provide both publicity for himself and future material for his columns.

Like any wise business manager, Anderson plows much of his proceeds back into his operation, spending an estimated $500,000 a year on payroll and office expenses, including a monthly telephone bill of "around $4,000." Anderson's wife of 35 years, Olivia ("Livvy") is on the payroll as his bookkeeper and handles all his accounts, so he is imprecise when dealing with such figures. "I've seen it [the phone bill] a couple of times," he says. "She's screamed about it."

With a taste for melodramatic characterizations that smacks a bit of press agentry, Anderson likes to describe his smoothly run news operation, which is situated—or "lurks," as he would prefer it—in a converted, nineteenth-century mansion in northwest Washington, as a "combination newsroom and spy cell." He portrays his staff as a raffish crew "of outcasts and boat-rockers, of the kind who would probably be turned down by the *New York Times* on the basis of their looks; the kind who, if they weren't turned down, would irritate, aggravate, and annoy the Ivy League editors." In fact, some Anderson associates have been or are Ivy Leaguers, and a cursory examination of several of the scriveners scurrying around his ten-room offices shows them to be no scruffier-looking than reporters inhabiting the city rooms of most metropolitan dailies.

But his us-against-the-world rhetoric suggests that Anderson is more than just a consummate salesman of his wares; he is an evangelist who knows how to create an esprit de corps for his disciples. It is not an unlikely role, one that Anderson would readily admit he takes to naturally, having once spent two years as a Mormon missionary preaching an unfamiliar and alien faith to unlikely converts in the Baptist country of Georgia, Alabama, and Florida.

Anderson was born in Long Beach, California, on October 19, 1922, and moved with his family to Utah when he was 2. He grew up in genteel poverty in Salt Lake City and one of its suburbs, Cottonwood. His father was a postal clerk, and his mother occasionally drove a taxi to help support the family. He landed his first newspaper job, with the weekly *Murray Eagle*, when he was 12, and he went on to become editor of his junior high and high school newspapers. He mastered both shorthand and touch typing because of their usefulness in reporting and worked part-time as a stringer for Salt Lake City's *Deseret News*, where he eventually became the teenage editor of the Boy Scout page. He was paid 15¢ for each inch of copy he got in the paper and sometimes earned more than the salaried reporters. (That was in 1937, when many reporters were lucky to earn $12 a week.)

By the time he was 18 and a freshman at the University of Utah, Anderson was a full-time reporter for the *Salt Lake Tribune*, but an early attempt at exposé dealing with the remnants of Mormon polygamy got him in hot water with church authorities, who directed that he drop out of college and fulfill his missionary obligations immediately by heading south. Anderson says that his two years as a missionary—preaching, resolving marital disputes, officiating at weddings and funerals—taught him more about human nature than all his years as a reporter. He also developed his fire-and-brimstone public speaking style on the missionary stump, "competing with a passing freight train" in rural southern towns.

After his missionary tour of duty ended in early 1944, Anderson faced the prospect of being drafted and sought an alternative to World War II combat by enlisting instead in the Merchant Marine. "I'm not proud of what I did, but I really didn't want to serve in the infantry," he once told an interviewer. After cargo runs to New Guinea and India, Anderson learned from some newspaper friends that it was easy to become accredited as a war correspondent, so he quit the Merchant Marine early in 1945, wangled accreditation from the *Deseret News*, and went to China, where he spent time behind Japanese lines with Nationalist guerrilla forces. He even struck up an acquaintance in Chungking with Chou En-lai, whose activities as the Communist party's representative there he covered briefly as a freelancer for the Associated Press. Anderson's draft board finally caught up with him in China, however, and he was inducted into the Army for a two-year hitch. He spent part of it as a reporter on the Shanghai edition of *Stars and Stripes*.

Completing his military service in 1947, Anderson headed for Washington and the Georgetown home and office of Drew Pearson, then one of the best-known syndicated columnists, if not the most notorious. A journalist friend in China had suggested that Pearson would be the swiftest, surest teacher of the reporter's trade in what had become the news capital of the world, and Anderson decided that that was where he wanted to be.

Anderson walked in cold and was hired immediately to replace a staffer who had just been fired after admitting Communist sympathies. (Even in those pre-McCarthy days, such political leanings were fatal and could have been especially embarrassing to an employer such as Pearson.) Anderson now thinks that Pearson may have been misled into promptly hiring him by reading his admittedly inflated résumé, which contained mention of his behind-the-lines tour with the Chinese guerrillas. He genially concedes that he probably was the least important—and least read—war correspondent of World War II. But it also is likely that Pearson was happy to have an eager, indefatigable, and inexpensive assistant who readily agreed to work around the clock for $50 a week. Pearson was, Anderson once wrote, "a bit on the close side as an employer, a trait I have come to appreciate." Anderson himself pays his top staffers considerably less than he believes they might earn elsewhere in Washington, saying; "I want as many eyes and ears as I can possibly get . . . sharp eyes and sharp ears . . . and so all of my people I think are underpaid . . . because they are highly qualified." The starting salary in the "Merry-Go-Round" shop is about $16,000, with Anderson's chief reporters earning about $25,000 a year—good by national journalistic standards but far below the $35,000 to $40,000 earned by top-scale Washington journalists, which he considers them to be.

Pearson was at the peak of his popularity when Anderson joined his staff. In a wartime poll of the congressional press corps by the *Saturday Review*, Pearson was picked as the best-known and most widely read, if not the most respected or believed, syndicated columnist in the country. He had, along with gossip-mongering and revelations of

trivia, scored some impressive scoops. According to Anderson's 1979 memoir of his work with Pearson, *Confessions of a Muckraker*, his future boss had uncovered massive corruption in the Louisiana state government; first reported Franklin Roosevelt's Supreme Court–packing plan and the lend-lease agreement between Roosevelt and Churchill; and broken the story of the wartime incident in which General George S. Patton angrily slapped a hospitalized soldier who was suffering battle fatigue.

Pearson, a Quaker with decidedly liberal leanings, was a crusader of sorts who conceived and carried out some grand—and some absurd—plans to foster world peace. He was the moving force behind a transcontinental Friendship Train that gathered $40 million worth of donated food in 1947 for war-torn France and Italy. He also led efforts to collect toys for European children; to urge Italian-Americans to write their relatives imploring them not to permit Communist takeover of that country; and to launch thousands of balloons near the Czechoslovakian border, each containing a message of goodwill from the United States, that would float over the iron curtain and—presumably—inspire the enslaved populace behind it. In addition, he engaged in behind-the-scenes diplomatic forays and obtained exclusive interviews with several world leaders.

Anderson became Pearson's top legman. According to his memoir, it was Anderson's gumshoeing (a verb which he likes to apply to government snoops but which serves just as well for his own labors) that helped Pearson expose the "five percenters" in high places during the Truman administration who demanded their cut of government contracts; the questionable largesse lavished on government officials during the Eisenhower years, in particular the liquor, furniture, and ritzy clothes—among which was an expensive vicuña coat—given to White House aide Sherman Adams by industrialist

Bernard Goldfine; and high living by Congressman Adam Clayton Powell of New York.

Anderson began his legwork on Capitol Hill, where he sometimes innocently identified himself as a Pearson assistant to congressmen who hated his boss. There he cultivated such potential sources as a couple of young congressmen named John F. Kennedy and Lyndon B. Johnson, among others. An unlikely early friend of the teetotaling, nonsmoking Anderson was the brash, boozing junior senator from Wisconsin, Joseph R. McCarthy, with whom he exchanged tips in the Red-hunting early fifties. He came to rue this association after McCarthy ran amok and began wrecking reputations and lives in his search for ever-bigger headlines. With the aid of Anderson, Pearson was among those who helped topple McCarthy by revealing his bogus war record, shoddy tactics, and empty accusations.

In order to support his growing family (which eventually numbered nine children, now ranging in age from the late teens to the mid-thirties), Anderson became the Washington correspondent for *Parade* magazine, the syndicated Sunday newspaper supplement, in 1954. In time, it would pay him much more than Pearson did—in 1963, for example, he received $28,500 from *Parade* and only $11,400 from the "Merry-Go-Round." It also provided him with a modicum of public recognition, which he rarely got otherwise. To many in Washington he was only "Pearson's Anderson," in the words of Arthur Krock of the *New York Times*, and to the general public he was unknown, even though they had been reading his stories for years. He was tired of being an anonymous supplier of material and told Pearson he was going to quit. Promising more recognition and offering the journalistic equivalent of the paternal pledge that "someday all this will be yours," Pearson convinced Anderson to stay on,

although regular Anderson by-lines did not appear until 1966. "For Drew, giving me a byline was like giving me a little bit of his blood," Anderson once told an interviewer.

One of the last great products of their collaboration was the 1966 exposé of Senator Thomas Dodd, an elderly Democrat from Connecticut who they revealed had pocketed campaign contributions. The revelations prompted the Senate to censure Dodd, and he was defeated in the subsequent election. Dodd, who some friends say was driven to his grave by the scandal, cried out that Pearson was "the Rasputin of our society [and] a liar. He is a monster. Those associated with him are thieves, liars, and monsters. . . . He is a devil. . . a molester of children." In fact, Dodd should have aimed his anguished barbs at Anderson; 98 of the 100 columns Pearson distributed on the Dodd case were written by Anderson.

Pearson died suddenly of heart failure on September 1, 1969. He had once asked Anderson to pay his widow a yearly stipend after inheriting the column, and Anderson quickly and cordially reached an agreement to pay her $12,000 annually. Realizing that the column needed bolstering, Anderson just as quickly hired two good reporters to assist him and switched his assistant on *Parade*, Joseph Spear, a one-time high school science teacher, to the column. He also signed a contract with the "Merry-Go-Round's" syndicate for less money than Pearson had been receiving in order to prevent papers from dumping it. Within three years he added 300 papers to his subscriber list and won the 1972 Pulitzer Prize for national reporting, something for which Pearson reportedly had been recommended in the Dodd case but denied.

Anderson's banner year of 1972 began auspiciously enough the very first week with a series of columns revealing the phony nature of the Nixon administration's public posture of neutrality during the 15-day war between India and Pakistan in late 1971.

Printing juicy excerpts from the classified minutes of discussions held by the Washington Security Action Group, made up of experts from the State Department, the Defense Department, and the National Security Council, Anderson quoted National Security Adviser Henry Kissinger asserting that Nixon wanted to "tilt" in favor of Pakistan. Both the *New York Times* (whose own "Pentagon Papers" on the Vietnam war had caused a furor not long before) and the *Washington Post* requested permission to print the "Anderson Papers" in full, which he graciously—and gleefully—granted.

In March, Anderson detonated more bombshells. He accused the International Telephone and Telegraph Corporation of greasing the skids for a Justice Department approval of its merger with the Hartford Fire Insurance Company by pledging $400,000 to cover the costs of the 1972 Republican National Convention. To back up the story, he produced a memo from ITT's chief Washington lobbyist, Dita Beard, to the company's vice-president in Washington, smugly advising him that the firm's "noble commitment has gone a long way toward our negotiations on the mergers" and had warmed the heart of former Attorney General John N. Mitchell, who then was in charge of President Nixon's reelection campaign. Shortly thereafter, Anderson charged that ITT had plotted with the Central Intelligence Agency in September 1970 to prevent Marxist Salvador Allende from assuming the presidency of Chile. Some commentators credited this scoop with temporarily shoring up the Allende regime, then on shaky ground.

In May 1972, Anderson won the national-reporting Pulitzer for his Security Action Group "papers," while the *Times* won the public-service Pulitzer for its papers from the Pentagon. Controversial as the award to the *Times* may have been, the prize given to Anderson clearly raised some hackles on the conservative necks of the bankers, businessmen, and lawyers who made up Columbia University's board of trustees, which under Joseph Pulitzer's will had to ratify the prize selections made by a committee of editors and publishers. A number of the trustees evidently found publication of pilfered government documents distasteful and objected vigorously to giving Anderson the award. They reluctantly voted approval but issued an unprecedented statement: "Had the selections been those of the trustees alone, certain of the recipients would not have been chosen." Grudgingly presented or not, the award was immensely satisfying to Anderson and recognized what he considers the absolute "right of the people to know what goes on in the back rooms of government."

Printing classified documents—or copies of them—which he may not have stolen but is glad to receive is not only a right, Anderson believes, but also a duty. "We think that the documents belong to the people, and that's who we're giving them to. We don't take anybody's property. We may see copies of them, and . . . so what we're accused of stealing, if anybody should so accuse us, is information. Every newspaper in the country, therefore, would stand condemned. There's not a newspaper in the country that does not 'steal' information from the U.S. government, if it's possible to do that.

"We insist on documenting our stories, if it's possible to do so. We think it's sloppy reporting to accept the word of a source when there is a document to back him up, and if a source tells us about some news event, we always ask for the documentation."

Ironically, Anderson's star descended in 1972 as rapidly as it had ascended, precisely because he violated his own rules. In July he reported on his program over the Mutual Broadcasting System, the nation's largest radio network, that he had "now located photostats of a half-dozen arrests for drunken and reckless driving" of Missouri

Senator Thomas Eagleton, the embattled Democratic vice-presidential nominee already under pressure to resign from the ticket of Senator George McGovern because of revelations about a history of psychiatric treatment and shock therapy.

Eagleton, who would quit the ticket within a week, branded the Anderson report "a damnable lie," and when reporters asked Anderson for the documents he claimed to have located, he awkwardly retreated and said he had traced but not seen the photostats of Eagleton's driving records. He said he had a "reliable" source for the story, but the source turned out to be Washington banker True Davis, a Missourian who had run against Eagleton in the Democratic primary for the Senate in 1968 and said he "tore up" the photostats without ever showing them to Anderson.

Anderson was forced to admit that he had made the broadcast without thoroughly checking the story because he wanted "to score a scoop." He ended up making an "unqualified" retraction of the report and an abject apology to Eagleton on nationwide television. "I have gone over every story, every scrap of evidence that I have, and I am totally satisfied there is no evidence," Anderson said at the time. "I think the story did damage to the Senator and I owe him a great and humble apology for that."

Although Anderson stands by that retraction and considers the Eagleton story "the biggest error" he ever made, he still has a curious reluctance to admit that the whole episode was an unmitigated disaster. "That's been exaggerated," he says, frowning a bit. "The error wasn't as large as it appeared. What we did was what the *St. Louis Post-Dispatch* also did on the same day—but I got the publicity and they did not—that is, to take the word of three or four traffic policemen and a story we checked out with . . . a Senator and the man who was running for the Senate, and they all told the same story."

Does he still think the story was true? "If you can't prove it, it's not true as far as I'm concerned. You should never run with a story that you can't back up. All I can tell you is that several policemen, one Senator and one man who was running for the Senate said they saw the documents. Most of the policemen said they saw the documents. No documents have ever been found that I'm aware of."

Joseph Spear, 43, Anderson's chief associate and a veteran of that turbulent period, puffs on his pipe and shakes his head over Anderson's apparent unwillingness to consider the Eagleton story an ignominious mistake. "I think Jack feels there was a shred of truth there. He cannot, I think, accept that [Davis] would just tell him an outright lie. Jack is convinced there *had* to be some truth to it. What bothered me about the incident at the time, aside from the fact that we had to eat maybe 350 plates of crow, was the self-righteousness of this son-of-a-bitch [Davis], when he went on television after all this broke, knowing he was the one who talked to Jack about it—I can see him to this day, hemming and hawing—and "assuming" that he was the source upon whom Jack was depending. Well he *knew* he had told him, he *knew* he was the source, and he played these games."

Spear offers the somewhat tempting theory—one to which Anderson does not subscribe—that their enemies in the Nixon White House, anxious to get even for the embarrassments the "Merry-Go-Round" had caused them, somehow engineered Anderson's sandbagging by planting the bogus Eagleton story. "That was the time of the Plumbers," Spear said, recalling the group of White House aides who tried to plug news leaks and perform political dirty tricks, and ultimately bungled their way into Watergate. "You'll notice, buried in Woodward and Bernstein's book *All the President's Men*, Deep Throat [says] at one point that the Eagleton thing was the work of the

White House Plumbers.* You realize where we were at that time? We had broken the Indo-Pakistani papers; Jack had won a Pulitzer Prize; we had broken the Dita Beard–ITT scandal; Jack Anderson's picture was on the cover of *Time* magazine. And right in the middle of all that, the Eagleton thing happened."

Perhaps the main flaw in Spear's theory, he concedes, is that it gives the Plumbers credit for more subtlety than they apparently were wont to employ. In October 1975, the Washington *Post* reported that ex-Plumber E. Howard Hunt had told associates that he had been ordered by a "senior official at the White House" in late 1971 or early 1972 to assassinate Anderson, preferably by using an untraceable poison supplied by the CIA. Hunt later denied that Anderson's murder had been contemplated but said that he had been urged by Nixon aide Charles Colson either to drug Anderson surreptitiously so he would appear incoherent on his radio program or at the very least to let the air out of his car's tires. Colson, of course, vehemently denied Hunt's charges.

"Those were hectic times," Anderson says with a rare touch of understatement. "We were under tremendous pressure, more so than any other reporters. . . . I was the only reporter in the Watergate era who really had everything in the book thrown at him. I was investigated by every government agency, just about. The Internal Revenue Service conducted a year-long investigation of my taxes. My accountant said my taxes were in the kind of order [that] they could have gotten all the information they needed in 24 hours.

*The passage in *All the President's Men* reads: "[The Plumbers] operation was not only to check leaks to the papers but often to manufacture items for the press. It was a [Charles] Colson-[E. Howard] Hunt operation. Recipients include all of you guys—Jack Anderson, Evans and Novak, the *Post* and the New York *Times*, the Chicago *Tribune*. The business of Eagleton's drunk driving record or his health records, I understand, involves the White House and Hunt somehow" (p. 133).

"The FBI got all my telephone records and went into them, and we found that out and went to court and got them to give them back. The CIA had 18 radio cars at one time keeping us under surveillance. They had an eavesdropping unit that was listening to our conversations and a photographic unit taking pictures of everybody going in and out of my office. . . . The Pentagon, according to their security chief . . . , ran 11 separate investigations of me that he knew about."

There was a Keystone Kops aspect to all this, Anderson recalled with a chuckle. "We knew we were being tailed, and I had my kids tail the tailers. I didn't have enough manpower to do otherwise. My kids would chase after the CIA cars."

But he says there is an unfunny footnote to the Watergate era harassment: Anderson suspects that the FBI still has its eyes on him. "We [have] found FBI agents outside our office. . . . I sent my reporters out to confront them. They produced their credentials and then claimed they were watching someone else. Maybe they were [but] we have been told by sources in the Justice Department that we're under surveillance. So I don't know. We found them, we confronted them, and they denied they were watching us." Be that as it may, Anderson promptly hired a suburban Washington security firm to conduct an electronic sweep of his offices in search of telephone bugs and hidden listening devices. They didn't find any.

The argument could be made that the government has good reason to maintain official secrets, that secrecy is an important tool in international—even internal—affairs. Anderson contends, however, that "secrecy is misused by the government. The government uses it to censor the news. The government [is not] careful with secrets; they are careful with the news. . . . They're trying to suppress the flow of news. There is a word for that, but it isn't *security*. The word is *censorship*. They use the 'secret' stamp to censor the news. Most of those stamps should properly read 'censored,' not 'secret.' "

Anderson's disdain for presidents, bureaucrats, and military commanders oozes from his speeches and drips from his columns. Self-important government officials often are characterized as "potentates" or "high muckamucks." Members of the military establishment invariably are labeled "brass hats." For recent presidents he expresses a special scorn: "When Jimmy Carter arrived in Washington from Plains, Georgia," Anderson tells audiences, "he had to ask the bureaucrats for directions to the bathroom. I think he learned that much before he left, but not much more."

Carter was a "Boy Scout," Anderson contends, who "did not understand how to run the government. By his own confession, he began making foreign policy for the United States by opening a geography book to find out where the hell the countries were. He knew where England was, and France, and a few others. He could find Canada and Mexico. Other than that, he did not know. And yet he presumed to make foreign policy for us.

"Ronald Reagan has come upon us equally oblivious to what goes on in Washington. He has brought with him simplistic solutions to complex problems. . . . You may have read that he works only three hours a day. I want in his defense to tell you that is wrong: he works five hours. And I think the only misfortune is that it isn't three hours."

Unfortunately, when Anderson proceeds to assure his audiences and readers that his command of intelligence matters has enabled him "to understand better than the President" numerous foreign policy developments and crises, he demonstrates as unsteady a skill with facts about his own work as President Reagan has often shown with statistics. As part of his standard speech, Anderson boasted to a university

audience in 1982 that in 1976 he saw secret intelligence reports from "our experts in Iran" which warned that there "was a revolution bubbling up under the Peacock throne that would catapult the Shah off [it]."

"I wrote in 1976 that this was likely to happen and that the Shah would probably be replaced by a viciously anti-American government. I wrote that in September 1976. In 1979, Jimmy Carter visited the Shah and pronounced Iran 'an island of stability' in the Middle East. He was wrong and I was right," Anderson tells his appreciative audiences in that unique blend of whine, whimper, and bellow that is his speaking style.

It would be a great story but for the fact that there does not appear to have been such a column. The *Washington Post*'s index of Anderson's columns in 1976 shows that he wrote 11 columns mentioning Iran that year, 2 of which appeared in September, but none of them predicted the Shah's ouster and replacement by an anti-American regime. A request to Anderson's office for a copy of the prescient column was made in vain. "I can't find the damn thing," said Anderson's chief of staff, Joe Spear. "Jack described it to me but I can't find it."

Similarly, following the death of Leonid Brezhnev in November 1982 and the ascension of former KGB chief Yuri Andropov as his successor, Anderson wrote: "For years, our intelligence agencies mistakenly thought no one with a KGB background could rise to the top of the Kremlin heap. At most, they believed, Andropov would have veto power over any would-be successor to Leonid Brezhnev. . . . Within the last year, however, Western intelligence began to rethink its assessment of Andropov's chances. In fact, as early as last May, I reported my intelligence sources' hunch that Andropov would be the one to grab the brass ring on the Kremlin merry-go-round."

There was no such Anderson column in May 1982, so it was not surprising that a somewhat embarrassed Spear was unable to find it either. All Spear could dig out of the legendary Anderson files was a "kind of vague" report that Anderson gave on his Mutual Broadcasting radio program in April 1982 repeating the intelligence assessments that Andropov would have the power to "pass on any successor" to Brezhnev, which is hardly the same thing as "grabbing the brass ring." The only column Anderson wrote that spring on Brezhnev's possible successor also appeared in April, not May, and did not mention Andropov at all. Instead, Anderson cautioned his readers against paying much attention to predictions emanating from "the cracked crystal ball files" at the Central Intelligence Agency.

I'd like to issue a mild warning about the spate of learned prognostications on what will happen if Soviet president Leonid I. Brezhnev recovers from his current illness or if he doesn't.

The truth, I'm sorry to say, is that no one really knows for sure. And I mean no one, American or Russian. So the best the CIA and other western intelligence agencies can do is offer an educated guess.

One popular consensus, for example, is that Brezhnev may announce his retirement at a meeting of the central committee that is scheduled for late next month. But even those who have come up with this theory emphasize that they don't know for sure. No one has ever gone broke betting against people who offer dead certainties on Kremlin succession, from Lenin to Stalin to Khrushchev and now Brezhnev. . . .

Eventually, of course, one of the myriad prognostications about Brezhnev is bound to come true. Until then, I'll buy the State Department's warning: "Experience suggests that the leadership rumors should normally be treated as speculation by knowledgeable, but not necessarily well-informed, political observers."

That would, with unintended irony, often serve as a good description of Anderson himself: "knowledgeable, but not necessarily well-informed." Certainly he has had his successes in using the arts employed by what he likes to call "the CIA palm readers" and other observers. Sooner or later, to use his own assessment of the CIA's track record, some of his myriad speculations come true. But with the cockiness of one who is reasonably certain that no listener or reader will go back and check, Anderson also apparently feels free to make unwarranted boasts about his supposed triumphs. He does it so compulsively, in fact, that he displayed the same sort of braggadocio before an audience of his peers and in response to a competitor who could easily refute him.

During a high-pitched 1982 debate with Robert W. Greene of *Newsday* about their respective coverage of the FBI's Abscam investigation, Anderson repeatedly told an audience of 200 reporters at a journalism conference in Arlington, Virginia, that he had been the first to publish excerpts from confidential Abscam tapes. Eventually he had to back down, however, and admit that Greene had scooped him.

Rather than emphasizing—and exaggerating—his coverage of headline-grabbers, Anderson could concentrate with more justifiable pride on some of his stories detailing government excesses and human distress, such as the case of a mentally impaired woman who lost her Social Security benefits because of a "mishandled" disability ruling or the potential pain caused by federal budget cuts to nursing homes and the National Center on Child Abuse and Neglect. Anderson often takes up the fight for individuals who have been battered or abused by bureaucracy or business. One of the few trophies in his office is an antique typewriter which he received as a gift from one of the people he helped.

"We get about 200 letters a day from people with pathetic stories to tell, and there's no way we can help them all," Anderson says. "But we try to help to keep people in Washington honest; and to remind them that they have to treat all citizens alike, we pick a case every now and then and write it up, some local case [such as] some widow who's been chiseled out of the widow's mite. . . . [We] did one [that] saved some mother who could have been chiseled out of her insurance. We just write stories like that occasionally and hope it'll cause insurance companies not to do that. This [typewriter] . . . just arrived with a note saying, 'I wanted to show my gratitude in some way and this seemed like something you'd like to have.' It's been here ever since, and I'm delighted to have it."

Bureaucratic waste, especially by the military, is a constant theme in Anderson's column. Self-righteous officials would be even more isolated and insufferable if they did not have the likes of Anderson and his reporters uncovering their abuses and nipping at their heels. Typical Anderson columns report how "the privileged poohbahs in the Pentagon . . . have a fleet of 9,000 aircraft available to chauffeur them around the country" at costs much higher than commercial flights or ground transportation; how legislators splurge on junkets; how the Navy, concerned about overweight personnel, made an unsuccessful request for a $300,000 appropriation to establish physical fitness programs "to flatten some of the bulging bellies that are popping Navy buttons"; how a Commerce Department official who broke his arm and shoulder had a $1,442 standing desk custom built for himself at government expense; or how a public relations man in the Navy set out to plug unflattering leaks:

Captain Queeg is alive and well and clicking his ball bearings in the Pentagon.

Recently I reported that Navy artists had been commissioned to paint landscapes, still lifes and portraits of bullfighters, belly dancers and brass hats' relatives to decorate the walls of VIP offices and rec rooms.

The Navy's response was immediate and massive. The embarrassed admirals moved not to correct the improprieties and illegalities, but to find my sources. They launched an investigation reminiscent of Queeg's hilarious effort to discover who had swiped the strawberries from the USS Caine's pantry.

A four-page questionnaire was distributed to graphics section personnel who might have been the source of my column. The covering instructions explained that the Navy is "conducting a preliminary inquiry relative to the content of Jack Anderson's column," and claimed that "the purpose of this inquiry is to gather the facts concerning the article in order to respond to official inquiries."

But the 25 questions—to be answered "to the best of your knowledge" and attested to before a witness—make it clear that the real purpose of the inquiry is to find out who blew the whistle. . . .

As it happens, the questionnaire was short-lived. Navy publications office director James Cherny called in all the forms and had them destroyed—but not before I had obtained a copy.

Cherny said he had the forms destroyed when he first found out about the questionnaire, implying that he had nothing to do with its issuance. "I'm not interested in who blew any whistles," he said.

Daniel Venor, a security officer in the printing office, admitted writing the questionnaire, but he said, "It was the supervisor's idea to ask the questions."

Who is Venor's supervisor? James Cherny.

There is enough backhanded humor in such pieces, perhaps, to warrant the decision of the *Washington Post,* Anderson's flagship paper, to put his column on the comics page, rather than on the Op Ed page with the other serious columnists who are supposedly his colleagues. (Anderson says he prefers having the comics as companions, claiming that he probably gets more readers that way.) But sometimes the *Post*'s editors have expressed doubts about Anderson's credibility, and on a number of occasions they have refused to print a column of his that they considered to be either unnewsworthy or unreliable. His penchant for the sensational, they believe, can lead to unfair or inaccurate reporting.

For example, in the wake of the Capitol Hill scandal in 1976 involving Representative Wayne Hays of Ohio and a buxom but stenographically inept secretary he had hired for reasons other than her typing, Anderson distributed a column suggestively billed as a "Capitol Hill Bedroom Survey." He claimed to have learned of several women, whom he did not name, who were supplying "secretarial and sexual services" to congressmen "dedicated to life, liberty and the pursuit of women." Perhaps "the most serious of the sex stories" Anderson claimed to have uncovered on Capitol Hill concerned the seduction of "one voluptuous Virginia constituent" by "staid Senator Harry Byrd."

"The *Post* editors responsible for preparing Anderson's daily column for publication had serious doubts and brought the column to me," later wrote the *Post*'s executive editor, Benjamin Bradlee. "It did not begin to meet the standards of relevance and reliability we try to follow at the *Post* in reporting on the private lives of public figures. . . . Here was no suggestion of payroll abuse, as in the . . . Hays case. There was no evidence of a crime, even if the allegations were true. No complaint had been filed with authorities at the time of the incident. And in addition, the accuser was unidentified, and thus immune from the normal journalistic checking processes.

"So I killed the column. . . ."

Bradlee also assigned one of his reporters to investigate the alleged seduction of Byrd's "voluptuous" constituent, correctly anticipating that the decision to kill the column would prompt criticism, as similar decisions had in the past. The reporter discovered that there was both less and more to the story than Anderson chose to report, Bradlee wrote.

It turned out that Byrd's accuser, who Anderson had said was described by acquaintances as a woman of "good character," was indeed a character—a lady "on the sunset side of 40 years old" who was well known to *Post* reporters and suburban Virginia police. They had investigated her earlier, unrelated complaints that "her husband had been killed or kidnapped by the Mafia, that people were sneaking into her back yard and digging random holes at five o'clock in the morning, that female neighbors were having homosexual affairs al fresco on the back porch of a neighboring house . . . but never a complaint about Sen. Byrd."

The woman admitted to the *Post* reporter that she was the one who had complained to an associate of Anderson's about Byrd's alleged seduction of her, but she had done so over a year before the column was written. Anderson apparently did not find the matter worthy of reporting until a week after the Hays scandal broke. The reporter also found that the woman's former neighbors did not exactly consider her of "good character."

"But the question isn't whether [the woman] is a nut or a saint, or whether Sen. Byrd seduced her. He says he didn't; she says he did," Bradlee wrote. "The question is whether newspapers should print such charges when the woman refused to identify herself, when no complaint was ever filed, and when no law was broken.

"I think they should not."

What Anderson likes to call his "spy cell" operates behind an unmarked door on the second floor of a huge red-brick mansion that once was the residence of James S. Sherman, vice-president under William Howard Taft and the only vice-president to die in office. For a brief period thereafter it was a high-class bordello, but for many years it served a much more mundane function as a dental hospital. Anderson and two attorney friends purchased the building, which is in the 1400 block of 16th Street NW, more than a decade ago for $350,000 and had it meticulously restored at a cost of some $240,000, returning to its former glory the Romanesque home's spectacular paneled vestibule with its rectangular staircase and skylight. But for an ornate crystal chandelier and a nonworking fireplace, Anderson's private office is modestly furnished and airy, with Oriental prints and a gold-colored muckrake, a gift from his staff, among the chief decorations.

Anderson lives in a five-bedroom colonial home set on four and one-half acres in suburban Bethesda, Maryland, and often works there. When he appeared on ABC's "Good Morning America" he arose at 5:30; now he gets up at 7:00 and grabs breakfast at his desk. If he goes into the office for the day, his long-time secretary, office manager, and "confidential assistant," Opal Ginn, 53, often prepares a large, elaborate lunch for him (sometimes featuring a complete roast turkey or roast pork), which he eats at a fully set dining table. He rarely returns home before 8:00 P.M.

Unlike Pearson, who was both an accomplished host and a sought-after guest at dinner parties, Anderson is a family man and homebody. He and his wife have never been members of the capital's social world. When his staff was smaller, he used to host "family gatherings" such as picnics, barbecues, or a Peking duck dinner at a local Chinese restaurant; now he rarely sees the entire crew assembled except for staff meetings once or twice a month to review projects and map strategy. He is, according to one former employee, an "incredibly good boss, a wonderful person to work for," a man who "doesn't run a very tight shop" and is really a "pussycat." Another former worker describes him as an "absent-minded

. . . very grandfatherly" employer who can be seen puttering around the office "deep in thought" and who is unaware of or unconcerned about the expenses entailed in sending reporters all over the country and abroad to look for stories.

In 1982 Anderson sent one reporter to India for a private interview with Prime Minister Indira Gandhi and went himself to the Middle East, where he had interviews with PLO leader Yasser Arafat, Lebanon's president Bashir Gemayel, and Israeli leaders such as then–Defense Minister Ariel Sharon.

To a visitor, Anderson appears open, candid, and friendly, although hardly gregarious. On particularly long days, as he reviews his schedule and rubs his eyes, he sags a bit and looks all of his 62 years.

To the accompaniment of the constant bleat of muffled telephone bells, Joe Spear, the editor and "chief of staff" of the Anderson news operation, describes how it works and defends it against accusations of slapdash reporting and inaccuracy. The "Merry-Go-Round" staff is expected to produce "copy of quality" in rather hefty chunks, Spear says. "I would expect from the average reporter somewhere around three or four major lead items [for the column] a month—that is, one, one and a half a week; I would expect them to do a television story every couple of weeks, on the average; and I would expect them to do two or three radio stories every week or ten days."

Since proceeds from Anderson's *Parade* articles also help pay the freight, each reporter is responsible for supplying magazine copy, too, Spear said. "That's quite a lot, but it isn't," he said. The reporters are encouraged to "spin off a little nugget for radio, a little nugget for television" while they work on their column stories, thereby fulfilling their broadcast responsibilities relatively painlessly. There is surprisingly little recycling of material, Spear claims, with most rehashed items appearing in a

"Weekly Special" sent out under his and Anderson's joint by-line to the column's weekly newspaper clients.

When Anderson is on the road lecturing, he keeps in touch with Spear by telephone and manages to visit the office two or three times a week to review and edit columns. "Every time I lay a column on his desk, I try to do it in a finished fashion, what I consider to be a column that could go out under the 'Jack Anderson' imprimatur and he would be proud to call his own," said Spear, who is slightly built, soft-spoken, and deceptively easygoing. "Sometimes Jack will look at it and be tremendously satisfied and make only a few changes. Other times he'll roll the paper in his typewriter and rework that thing from beginning to end. Mainly it's slant; he wants to put his particular point of view on a story, which we are permitted to do because we're columnists, and he'll rewrite it for that reason. Or, let's say, the writer . . . takes too long to get to the real news. Jack will run it through his typewriter and just boil her down."

During the summer months, when Anderson is free of lecture commitments, he still does a good bit of his own reporting and writing, according to Spear, but one former "Merry-Go-Round" reporter says Anderson has largely withdrawn from active reporting, devoting his days instead to his speeches, broadcasting work, and rewriting what his staff has dug up. (The clue to who actually did the work for a particular Anderson column can be found in his standard line of attribution, "[the source] told my associate . . .") "It's all a matter of how much time he has," Spear said. "Many times he'll get tips and not have time to pursue them, and he'll pass them on to me and I will assign them."

Anderson has well-placed sources, many of whom are veteran Washington bureaucrats he has known for decades and can tap with ease, according to several former associates. He has become too well known, however, for the kind of dogged legwork that he used to perform for Pearson and in the early days of his own regime. "When you get to be as famous as he is, you can't just walk down some corridor and talk with some secretaries," one former associate of Anderson's observed.

With so many hands now involved in the production of Anderson's columns, it may seem surprising that the final product has any coherent style, but the column's chief rewrite man, Dave Braaten, 58, once a columnist for the late *Washington Star,* has adapted his style to Anderson's, which at its best is spare and to the point and at its worst is appallingly hokey. "There is no combination of words in the English language that Jack Anderson regards as a cliché," a writer on the *New Yorker* once observed, "not 'boon companion,' not 'wine-dark seas,' not 'the story can now be told.' There is no vegetable he cannot press into service as a metaphor. . . . There is no lead paragraph Anderson considers too melodramatic."

Anderson apparently is not disturbed by such criticism. "I write for the Kansas City milkman," he once said. That is a modest literary ambition, and he has fulfilled it modestly.

A number of young reporters who have worked for him found the brief, "breathy" writing style of the column both unfulfilling and frustrating. "You'd report a complicated story [but] by the time it was rewritten in Jack's style any subtlety or notation of gray in it [was] gone. The column's all black and white, and that style tends to be misleading," one former "Merry-Go-Round" worker said.

Anderson sees his mission as one of writing for his legions of rural readers, to whom he is a "big hero," not for the people in Washington, according to another former associate. "He wants his writing to be colorful, jazzed up. He tries to make it entertaining, simple, and readable. He doesn't particularly care if people in Washington look down their noses at his style. But that style can make good, solid stories look trivial, and because of that some people take him less seriously."

As the *Washington Post* observed in 1983, Anderson's reporters dig up a mixed bag of stories that alternate between "gold" and "garbage," often rendered indistinguishable by the brazen style of the column. The impact of the column also has dwindled in recent years, many current and former staffers told the *Post*, partly due to the loss of Les Whitten, a former associate with whom Anderson used to share his by-line and who resigned in 1978 to write novels. In addition, many newspapers now are geared to do the exposés that once were Anderson's exclusive preserve, and he has seriously stretched his resources in order to meet the competition. The "Merry-Go-Round" still occasionally turns up a story that papers such as the *New York Times* and *Washington Post* later accord front-page coverage, but that is not a common occurrence.

What angers Anderson and Spear are charges that the column is padded with fluff, that it is a compendium of minor Washington peccadillos, marginal stories, and inaccuracies, all given unwarranted display because of the column's demanding, seven-days-a-week schedule. The "Merry-Go-Round," as one former worker put it, is "a furnace for copy."

"One of the things that rankles me most about our reputation is something that we inherited from Drew Pearson, and that's a reputation for recklessness, for gossip, for inaccuracy," said Spear with undisguised annoyance. "It simply is not true. We publish 365 columns a year. Fifty-two of those are Sunday columns that consist of one story. The rest, the daily columns, have a lead item, a secondary item, and usually a couple of tertiary items, i.e., three to four stories in every column. Add that up. In other words, you multiply 313 times 3.5, let's say, and that's how many stories we do

in the daily columns *a year*; add your 52 Sunday columns and you come up with God knows how many stories we put out in the column per year." (For the record, that's 1,147.5.)

"Obviously, we get complaints occasionally on comma faults, on name spellings, and that type of thing, but it is a rare day when someone catches us in a genuine misstatement of fact. It has only happened maybe three times since I've been here on major errors, and I mean *major* with a capital *M*. Maybe three times, one of which was the Tom Eagleton business. On a lesser scale, it might happen two or three times a year," Spear insists. He evidently does not consider Anderson's unsubstantiated puffery a "major" error.

In his 1979 book about his days with Pearson, Anderson wrote that "a nagging weakness of the understaffed 'Washington Merry-Go-Round,' then as now," was that it "could not, like a great newspaper or magazine, detach a reporter, or a team of reporters to one story and have them work on it concentratedly for weeks until it was broken."

"That's not a weakness today," he says now. "I have a backlog of 40 stories I look at. Each one is different in quality, but if I had to put out 10 columns right now, I could put out 10 columns. . . . They might not be as good as the columns I would like to put out, but they would be acceptable, they would be readable, they would be exclusive. I'm not under pressure to get material; I'm always under pressure to get good material. We operate like a newspaper, with an editor, a rewrite man, with assignments, beats. . . . I think in our daily conversations, the problem is deciding which good stories to use, rather than how we are going to get a column out today. That was a problem when I first took over from Drew Pearson. That is not a problem today. . . . With 18, 20 reporters, that's no problem."

That is a bit too rosy an assessment of his

column's strength, in the view of several former Anderson associates who still greatly admire him personally. In the late 1970s, they note, a number of Anderson's top staffers resigned, to some extent because they felt that he was overextended and they wanted to do more in-depth, quality reporting on their own.

"I thought then and I think now that he's spreading himself too thin," says one former Anderson reporter. "Now he's into everything. He's a conglomerate." In the view of another ex-employee, Anderson persists in taking on more and varied projects because he is looking for the one big financial "quick fix" that will enable him to support the column without difficulty.

The turnover of Anderson staffers—to some degree a natural process involving the desire on the part of experienced reporters to achieve individual recognition—"enables Anderson to revitalize himself," one former associate said. "That way he can bring in a new generation of reporters who will work like dogs for not much money."

Spear insists, however, that the "Merry-Go-Round" staff is not a kiddie corps. Although half of its full-time members are in their twenties, there are some 40-, 50-, and even 60-year-olds on the payroll, not counting Anderson. Spear also believes that the "Merry-Go-Round's" accuracy checks are as thorough as those employed by many daily newspapers, and better than most.

Once a reporter writes a story, it is turned over to Spear, who questions and checks it and may send it back to the reporter for double-checking. After Anderson sees the piece, it is given to Braaten, who also may quiz the reporter before and after he rewrites the story in Anderson's style. The reporter gets a chance to see the item at each step of the editing process, even after it has finally been turned back over to Anderson for possible editing and rewriting. The story gets a final going-over by Opal Ginn before it is dispatched by computer to the United Fea-

tures Syndicate in New York, where two other editors review it. "It then gets read back to us over the telephone line-by-line to be sure they have it exactly correct, and changes are made for accuracy at that point, if the editors in New York have caught anything we missed. I mean, that's a lot of checks," Spear says.

Fail-safe they are not, however, and Anderson is just as subject as other reporters—perhaps even more so, given the shadowy nature of much of what he reports—to manipulation by sources who have an ax to grind and can convince him that they have the goods on someone whose reputation they want to damage. Anderson's pride at having enough material for ten instant columns that would be "acceptable, readable, and exclusive" sounds more like the boast of a fast-talking salesman than the goal of a columnist more interested in covering substantive issues and stories than just sending out an endless flow of copy. It would be refreshing—and candid—if Anderson and Spear acknowledged that their seemingly inexhaustible supply of "exclusives" makes the "Merry-Go-Round" infinitely more marketable, especially to those small papers hungry for filler.

Rather than his column's accuracy, it is Anderson's judgment that has been questioned most strongly in recent years, with some of the sternest criticism coming from other members of the press. He has been involved in a few business enterprises that proved to be embarrassing, and his "disturbing, often cloying messianic streak," as one critic put it, causes others to accuse him of a "Boy Scout piety" with which he justifies some mean-spirited reporting.

Anderson is sensitive to the charge that the column's exposés under Pearson, such as the one revealing the mental deterioration of former Defense Secretary James Forrestal, who later committed suicide, sometimes had a heartless quality. He has admitted doubts over whether "these stories [were] worth the lives or sanity of people and the incalculable destruction wreaked upon their innocent families. . . . There are seasons when it seems a close call."

In his own affairs, there were close calls as well. In December 1975, Anderson became a founding director of the Diplomat National Bank, a predominantly Asian-American business in Washington, at the behest, he says, of old friends in the Oriental community who told him that they were the victims of discrimination and needed his assistance to found the bank. The minimum $2,000 in stock that he purchased was transferred to an Asian charity, he says.

The following November, the *Washington Post*, hot on the trail of the lavish gifts and cash allegedly given to congressmen by Korean businessmen, revealed that the largest block of stock in the bank actually was owned by Korean lobbyist Tong Sun Park, one of the chief suspects in the influence-peddling scandal, who had purchased it through three front men. The *Post* also reported that followers of the controversial Korean evangelist Sun Myung Moon controlled at least 46 percent of the bank's initial stock offering. Pak Bo Hi, Moon's chief aide, allegedly saw to it that other Moon followers invested in the bank, the paper reported.

When the *Miami Herald* subsequently cut half of a "Merry-Go-Round" column on South Korea and Moon followers, saying that Anderson was "now disqualifed" from reporting objectively on the subject, he promptly resigned from the bank board and also gave up his interests in four Chinese restaurants in Washington that also were partly owned by Koreans.

"That was one case where my colleagues in the press really blew things out of proportion," Anderson says now, still smarting a bit from a "Merry-Go-Round"–style petard. "I was the one who first exposed Tong Sun Park, two years ahead of the scandal. I told about his lobbying—I didn't go

into it in as much detail as later came out, but at least I was the first to do it. . . .

"I did not go into the bank for profit. I went into the bank to help the Asian community. While I was on the board, it came before the board—there are minutes to this effect—that one Tong Sun Park wanted to invest in the bank. Some of the board members said, 'He's got a lot of money, we could use his financial support.' I said, 'Fine, but he's a bad man, and I will not be able to serve on the board if he has any influence in this bank.' They then said, 'We'd rather have you than him,' and they voted him down. . . .

"He got an interest in the bank through strawmen. Question: Why would he have to go through strawmen? The answer was because Jack Anderson wouldn't let him in the bank. . . .

"As far as Moon is concerned, I never heard about his owning any interest [in the bank]. I don't think he did. There is no evidence that he did. Some members of his church did. And it never occurred to me—and it would not now occur to me—to demand to know the religions of people who invest in a bank."

Anderson says that because of the adverse publicity he received "on this bank thing," he "decided that I shouldn't have any interest in anything. All other newsmen do—not all, but I mean people in my profession do. Katharine Graham [chairman of the *Post*] does. She's on boards, banks. Everything the *Post* criticized me for, she does, except that I had no financial interest in the bank and she does have a financial interest in banks and other things. And that would be true of [other] publishers, and it's probably true of a number of editors, but it is no longer true of me. I've decided that if I'm going to be judged by different standards than other newsmen, then I will just give up my holdings."

While he may have abandoned outside business ventures, Anderson continues to pursue journalistic enterprises, sometimes with unfortunate results. In 1981, he and several other journalists joined forces with a smooth-talking private investigator from Texas to launch the *Investigator,* a magazine for investigative reporting. Jay J. Armes, the private eye, boasted an unparalleled record of successes in solving well-known crimes; proficiency in 3 languages (including 33 dialects of Chinese); James Bond–like equipment, among which was a smokescreen-spewing automobile and a pilot's license for jet helicopters; and a pair of weapon-equipped steel hooks for the hands he had lost in a childhood accident. One would think that the ever-skeptical Anderson would have scrutinized this proposed business partner with special care, but instead he found himself associated with a man of dubious veracity.

The *Washington Post* discovered that Armes had no airman's certificate, had not been involved in some cases he claimed to have solved, and had handled others in a highly questionable manner. Anderson quickly cut his ties with the flamboyant Texan, and the magazine, later called the *Investigative Reporter,* sputtered into limbo.

"I believed my fellow newsmen," Anderson says a little lamely. "They presented me with a Texas money man who had spent his career in magazine publishing [and] asked me if I would join in the publication of a magazine on investigative reporting. . . . He said his partner was Jay J. Armes. I'd never heard of him. He presented me with a book of news clippings, which included clippings from some of the greatest papers in the country. . . . I mistakenly assumed that they had done their reporting, and I accepted their appraisals of Jay J. Armes. I made one phone call to my paper in [El Paso], and they said, 'Well, he exaggerates,' but that's all they told me I had to be careful of. . . . On that basis I went into it, and . . . the moment I found out that he had been misrepresenting his background—

that's all he did, he's guilty of lying and exaggerating—I cut him out of the magazine."

All in all, it was not a sterling moment for the ace investigative reporter.

Anderson also does not have especially felicitous moments when he departs from his regular format and discourses in general on national issues or the frailties of our civilization. For example, in an October 1982 column he made a pallid attempt at explaining the economic situation. It was marshmallow analysis, gooey with clichés:

Party politics, with all its emotions and harangues and oversimplifications, has taken over the economic debate. The choice, if the political rhetoric is to be accepted, is between the Republicans' trickle-down theories and the Democrats' siphon-off practices. . . .

. . . Political solutions, invariably more expedient than efficient, have brought us to our present economic state. President Reagan's latest remedies—tight money, tax cuts and free-market measures, all wrapped up in a package called Reaganomics—started off in the clouds but lost altitude rapidly. . . .

Our conservative president rejected the "countercyclical stabilization policies" that past presidents have used for 40 years to maintain high employment and keep prices stable. What this profound phrase means is that Reagan's predecessors managed the economy by manipulating fiscal and monetary levers.

Reagan disdained the monetary machinery and decided to let the marketplace take care of itself. His theory was that the economy would run more smoothly if the government's monkey wrenches were removed from the machinery. But some of the wrenches, it turns out, were needed to repair the wheels.

It is the genius of the free economy that it does not require the innovator to secure the permission of organized society to launch his schemes. If he can get a few gamblers to bankroll him, he is on his way, free to create, if he can.

If he succeeds, the rewards can be spectacular, and society will share in the gain. If he fails, only he and his improvident backers are the losers.

But it has become increasingly difficult to get an innovative proposal, or even an old routine one, through the layers of bureaucracy that have accumulated in the past 40 years. Just about every private enterprise of any consequence has become ensnarled in government red tape.

The problem is this: how much government intervention is necessary to protect the public from the hare-brained schemes and grasping hands of private enterprise? But how much government interference discourages free enterprise and results in stagnation?

Even more than Pearson, who had no missionary training, Anderson is subject to an evangelical fervor that sometimes overwhelms his columns. Like many experienced journalists, Anderson visibly enjoys recounting his reportorial exploits. His blue eyes twinkle, and he almost smacks his lips and rubs his hands with satisfaction as he tells a visitor of his latest triumph in uncovering a story—the tawdrier the better. It is an engaging, even amusing, performance, but the occasional traces of tolerant humor he can display in private—and the dashes of waspish humor he uses in his speeches—are often absent in print. In his column, Anderson can become, as fellow columnist Nicholas Von Hoffman once wrote, "an honest Christian gentleman armed with an undisciplined and utterly mindless moral zeal."

In a 1978 article for *Parade*, Anderson let loose with the warning that "the nation's ideals are being sapped by permissive immorality. Never before has so large a share of the population indulged in an orgy of self-pampering, overdosing, loafing, sponging, looting, philandering, even mur-

dering. . . . Just about every vice is now on display in the temples of government. Members of Congress take bribes and put mistresses on the public payroll."

This view of the United States, Von Hoffman later observed, is "so distorted, so divorced from the daily experience of most Americans, that one can imagine reading it in *Pravda*. . . . A few politicians doubtless take bribes and put their girlfriends and/or mothers on the public payroll," Von Hoffman added, "but every bit of evidence suggests this kind of activity was far more prevalent a hundred years ago than it is today."

In the calm of the erstwhile bordello that now is his office, Anderson sounds a more restrained philosophical note about the nation as a whole and its capital city, a view he occasionally puts in his column as well.

"At no time have I ever thought that the majority of Americans engaged in vice and corruption, but you have one murder in a town and that's too many murders. You can have one whorehouse and that's too many whorehouses. It doesn't mean everyone in town is whoring. . . . I guess it's my orthodox Mormon background. I don't think there's much vice here. . . .

"I'm not an antagonist of the system. I believe in operating within it. And I've found that in Washington most of the people who serve in it are people of integrity. Even most members of Congress are people of integrity. They work hard. They have high standards. I think basically people in Washington are a reflection of people around the country. . . . The bad guys are a little worse because the temptations are greater; the good guys probably are a little better because the opportunities are greater. But the percentages, I think, are the same, so I suppose if you want to get a picture of Washington, just look in the mirror and you've found it."

The tendency of the government, consisting as it does of politicians, is to glorify its achievements, however modest, and hide its mistakes. The mistakes, the extravagances, the gaffes, and the inner machinations that the government doesn't consider newsworthy are what Anderson has made a career of reporting.

"We operate differently than most Washington correspondents. They cover the newsmakers, which might seem like a logical place to get news, but the newsmakers in Washington are *politicians*. Politicians have politics to play. We prefer to get our news, not from the politicians, but from the people the politicians go to. Those are the professionals. And the same professionals who advised Jimmy Carter now advise Ronald Reagan. We like to know what they're telling the President so we can better evaluate what the President tells us. . . . We tap into the permanent government. Some other correspondents do, but not nearly to the extent that we do, or if they do, they're not publishing it . . . , they're keeping it to themselves. . . . We don't have the obligations that other newsmen have of covering day-

to-day events. We don't have to worry about that, so we can concentrate all our attention and all our focus and all our investigative skills on getting the story behind the story."

Sociological or political analyses aren't Anderson's forte. What he does best is plain, hard-nosed reporting, unencumbered—for better or worse—by philosophical trappings. "Long before the current fad," wrote J. Anthony Lukas of the *New York Times* more than a decade ago, "Anderson was doing the investigative reporting that most Washington correspondents should have been doing and weren't. For that he deserves our respect and gratitude."

Propped on the mantelpiece of the fireplace in Joe Spear's large bay-windowed office is a small engraved plaque bearing Benjamin Franklin's observation: "Three may keep a secret if two are dead." The truth of that aphorism guarantees that the supply of muck Anderson rakes for our edification, benefit, and—whether he likes to admit it or not—amusement will never run out.

Russell Baker

The Observer

ussell Baker sits brooding before his typewriter, his hands clasped prayerfully in front of his mouth, his lower lip pushed forward in a slight pout. He is hard at work being funny. "Humor is only a fragrance, a decoration," Mark Twain wrote after thumbing through a "mortuary volume" of works by some long-forgotten contemporaries. "Often it is merely an odd trick of speech and of spelling . . . and presently the fashion passes and fame along with it. . . . Humor must not professedly teach, and it must not professedly preach, but it must do both if it would live forever," Twain observed. He then added dolefully: "By forever, I mean 30 years."

Much of Russell Baker's work will survive Twain's durability test. Some of it already is two-thirds of the way there. The best of his columns, collected in anthologies, and his Pulitzer Prize–winning memoir, *Growing Up,* surely will last even longer.

The number of American writers whose humorous works are capable of delighting not only contemporaries but also posterity can be calculated on the fingers of one hand. Maybe a hand and a half. There is Twain, of course; Finley Peter Dunne, creator of "Mr. Dooley"; Will Rogers; Robert Benchley; James Thurber; H. L. Mencken. The reason why this pantheon is so sparsely populated is that the only humorous writing that really endures is the kind that touches not just the absurdities of the moment but those that are endemic to humanity. The observations and witticisms must, of necessity, be garbed in the attire of their own day, but underneath that clothing should be a body of insight that readers long afterward can appreciate—and relish.

Baker is such a writer, perhaps the most graceful craftsman in American journalism. His "Observer" column for the *New York Times* incisively reflects the anguish, anxieties, and frustrated yearnings of late-twentieth-century America. Sometimes he is a coolly aloof spectator, not unlike the *New Yorker*'s emblem of urbanity, Eustace Tilley, commenting upon events with wry detachment. More often he is an exasperated urban man attempting to make some sense out of chaos. His writing, one critic observed, contains "a delicate balance of rue and self-mockery." Not surprisingly, there is much of that balance in Baker himself.

Six feet two inches tall, his slim, 172-pound frame beginning to bend and bulge in middle-aged fashion, Baker, 58, has the look of "a decaying boy," as he once put it, with sad, blue-green eyes, sandy hair flecked with gray, and a face creased with lines bespeaking both laughter and worry. A casual dresser, he boasts of having perfected the art of tying his necktie in a way that assures that his collar button will always be visible just above the knot. His weary, soulful expression often is brightened by a warm grin. He is devoid of cant or pretension and seems to enjoy sharing examples of what he considers his inadequacies and failings.

His absence of immodesty is not a lingering reflection of the insecurity that plagued him as a child, however. "I feel very self-confident," he says. "I'm at an age when a man tends to feel self-confident unless he's in difficult economic straits, and I've escaped that. I'm at an age when I'm not scared of many people or many things. I think what you might call immodesty is something I'd call a manifestation of insecurity."

"And I don't have a lot of weight to throw around," he adds, smiling. "When I speak the world doesn't necessarily jump."

Baker's conversation frequently is as rich as his writing. In a soft, sonorous voice, he spins sentences as discerning, entertaining, and smooth as those that make his columns so elegant. He may be the only modern journalist able to write columns featuring enduring epigrams:

Usually, terrible things that are done with the excuse that progress requires them are not really progress at all, but just terrible things.

The Congress is 535 people, mostly men, mostly white, mostly lawyers and mostly out when you need them.

The people who are always hankering loudest for some golden yesteryear usually drive new cars.

When he began writing his thrice-weekly column over 20 years ago, Baker says, his "intent was pedagogical in a way." Being funny was not his aim, only his avenue.

As a veteran correspondent at the White House and on Capitol Hill, Baker was convinced that "the vast percentage of the

Times's readership wasn't reading what I was writing," because they were bored—or intimidated—by the paper's "polysyllabic, Latinate" style.

"I wanted to change the language of the *Times* somewhat," he says. "I wanted to evolve a diction in which I could get people to read about these subjects that interested me so much but didn't necessarily interest them, and I thought if you could simplify the diction, simplify the language, approach it from an angle that would make them lift an eyebrow, you could hook them and get them to read. So I've always had a kind of missionary's purpose in mind.

"I thought that one way to get people's attention is to make them laugh a little bit, take a casual approach." In short order, he found himself labeled a "humorist."

"It had never occurred to me that I was doing humor. I just thought humor was a device for expressing what you wanted to get across to people," Baker says. Like Twain, he didn't professedly teach or preach. "My aim was really to sneak up on some pretty dense skulls and just insert a little needle in and let in a little daylight."

The world that Baker observes is not necessarily funny. His columns may make you laugh, but it often is the uncomfortable chuckle inspired by irony. "We live in an age of irony. I was born into that. Somebody said the twentieth-century tragedy is impossible, because tragedy is the result of one man's *hubris*; you have to be responsible for your own fate in order for there to be tragedy. But in the twentieth century, nobody's responsible. The complaint of the twentieth century is, 'The system is grinding me down.' Everybody is the victim of circumstances and position, so all you can have is comedy, really. And I think I was more aware of that than most people; I don't know why. Maybe because of the peculiarities of my own life, I was always impressed by the ironies of the world I was moving in."

Certainly among those ironies is the fact

that this gentle, cultivated man professes to lack intellectual inclinations but is profoundly philosophical. The son of an impoverished stonemason whose family was left destitute by the Depression, Baker spent his formative years in an isolated rural village and then in tough urban neighborhoods, not exactly the environments, one might think, for nurturing the kind of whimsical outlook that enabled him to win a high school essay contest with a piece entitled "The Art of Eating Spaghetti." Acutely aware of the irrational, random nature of modern life—and essentially attributing his career selection and development to luck— Baker nevertheless has a clear, uncompromised sense of who he is and what he ought to do. He has controlled his own destiny to a remarkable degree.

Baker was born in Morrisonville, Virginia, a Loudoun County hamlet that was rustic in the extreme, lacking plumbing, gas, electricity, and central heating. He had been conceived out of wedlock by an amiable, alcoholic father and a tiny, fiercely independent mother who married over the objections of his paternal grandmother, the matriarch of the town. Baker's early childhood was spent in an atmosphere more akin to mid-nineteenth-century America than to the mid-1920s.

"My mother and grandmother kept house very much as women did before the Civil War," Baker wrote in *Growing Up*.

It was astonishing that they had any energy left after a day's work to nourish their mutual disdain.

For baths, laundry, and dishwashing, they hauled buckets of water from a spring at the foot of the hill. To heat it, they chopped kindling to fire their wood stoves. They boiled laundry in tubs, scrubbed it on washboards until knuckles were raw, and wrung it out by hand. Ironing was a business of lifting heavy metal weights heated on the stove top.

They scrubbed the floor on hands and knees, thrashed rugs with carpet beaters, killed and plucked their own chickens, baked bread and pastries, grew and canned their own vegetables, patched the family's clothing on treadle-operated sewing machines, deloused the chicken coops, darned stockings, made jelly and relishes, rose before the men to start the stove for breakfast and pack lunch pails, polished the chimneys of kerosene lamps, and even found time to tend the geraniums, hollyhocks, nasturtiums, dahlias, and peonies that grew around every house. By the end of a summer day a Morrisonville woman had toiled like a serf.

It was, however, "a delightful place to spend a childhood," Baker wrote, especially in the summer. Then, on "a broiling afternoon when the men were away at work and all the women napped, I moved through majestic depths of silences, silences so immense I could hear the corn growing. Under these silences there was an orchestra of natural music playing notes no city child would ever hear." In the evenings, Baker would sit on his grandmother's porch and listen "to a conversation that had been going on for generations," replete with sturdy maxims. "Nothing new had been said on that porch for a hundred years," he wrote.

While his mother and grandmother despised each other and fought over him, his father, an undiagnosed diabetic unaware of the lethal effect alcohol could have on his system, was slowly poisoning himself with moonshine whiskey. He died in an "acute diabetic coma" at the age of 33, when Baker was 5.

"For the first time I thought seriously about God," Baker wrote in *Growing Up*.

Between sobs [I said] that if God could do things like this to people, then God was hateful and I had no more use for Him. . . . That afternoon, though I couldn't have phrased it this way then, I decided that God was a lot less interested in people than anybody in Morrisonville was willing to admit. That day

I decided that God was not entirely to be trusted. . . .

At the age of five I had become a skeptic and began to sense that any happiness that came my way might be the prelude to some grim cosmic joke.

Baker's mother, left penniless and with three small children, was determined to free herself of her overbearing mother-in-law and leave Morrisonville. She reluctantly "gave away" her youngest daughter to childless in-laws and moved with Baker and his other sister to Belleville, New Jersey, a suburb of Newark. There they moved in with one of his mother's brothers, a salesman for a soft-drink bottler who earned $30 a week. Baker's mother, who had once been a teacher, supplemented the family's income by going to work in an A&P laundry, where she earned $10 a week washing uniforms.

She was, Baker wrote, "a warrior mother fighting to protect her children in a world run by sons-of-bitches," and she was distressed that her only son lacked the "gumption" to "make something" of himself.

Fifty years ago parents still asked boys if they wanted to grow up to be President, and asked it not jokingly but seriously. Many parents who were hardly more than paupers still believed their sons could do it. Abraham Lincoln had done it. We were only sixty-five years from Lincoln. . . .

I was asked many times myself. No, I would say, I didn't want to grow up to be President. My mother was present during one of these interrogations. An elderly uncle, having posed the usual questions and exposed my lack of interest in the Presidency, asked, "Well, what *do* you want to be when you grow up?"

I loved to pick through trash piles and collect empty bottles, tin cans with pretty labels, and discarded magazines. The most desirable job on earth sprang instantly to mind. "I want to be a garbage man," I said.

Baker's elderly uncle was amused, but his mother was not. Soon afterward, when Baker was eight, she launched his career in journalism by getting him a job selling the *Saturday Evening Post* on street corners and door-to-door. He was a shy and singularly inept salesman whose attempts at an alluring spiel began and ended with the faint question: "Want to buy a *Saturday Evening Post*?" He spent three inglorious years trying to sell magazines, convincing his mother in the end that the business world was not for him. In school, however, he began to display a talent for writing, and his mother suggested that this might be the way he could make something of himself.

I clasped the idea to my heart. I had never met a writer, had shown no previous urge to write, and hadn't a notion how to become a writer, but I loved stories and thought that making up stories must surely be almost as much fun as reading them. Best of all, though, and what really gladdened my heart, was the ease of the writer's life. Writers did not have to trudge through the town peddling from canvas bags, defending themselves against angry dogs, being rejected by surly strangers. Writers did not have to ring doorbells. So far as I could make out, what writers did couldn't even be classified as work.

I was enchanted. Writers didn't have to have any gumption at all. I did not dare tell anybody for fear of being laughed at in the schoolyard, but secretly I decided that what I'd like to be when I grew up was a writer.

Baker even had a relative to whom his mother could point as an example of a writer who had made something of himself: Edwin L. James, a distant cousin, then an editor and weekly columnist for the *New York Times*. Baker's mother hadn't seen James in 20 years, and Baker never met him, but she would say, "Edwin James wasn't any smarter than anybody else . . . and look where he is today. If Edwin could do it, so can you."

Baker was unconvinced, being "consumed with timidity and a sense of my own incompetence," but he and his mother toiled together over his school compositions. One assignment required him to write about farm produce, and he chose wheat as his subject, "maybe because it seemed less boring than turnips and was easier to spell than rutabagas," he recalled in *Growing Up*. His mother laboriously reworked his feeble essay, and his unwitting teacher was so satisfied with the result that she mailed it to the *Belleville News*. In a few weeks it appeared under the simple heading, "Wheat," bearing the by-line "By Russell Baker." "It was my first appearance in print. It had been ghostwritten by my mother."

When Baker was 11, the family moved to Baltimore, where other relatives lived. They settled in an apartment above a funeral parlor that reeked of embalming fluid and, for some unaccountable reason, boiled shrimp. It was across the street from the rowhouse occupied by H. L. Mencken, but this lucky accident did not result in any memorable encounters, unhappily. The Mencken name meant nothing then to Baker, and he had no interest in meeting his new neighbor.

Baker says he was a political "dimwit" in high school, where his nomination for membership in the honor society was withdrawn because he "didn't know who Karl Marx was." Nevertheless, he had developed the beginnings of a basic—if somewhat contradictory—philosophy. At the center of it was, and remains, a devotion to the family, but it is from the conflicting principles of his maternal and paternal forebears that he draws his political beliefs.

His father's family were conservative southern Republicans from northern Virginia. Simple mountain folk of German stock, they had come to Virginia from Pennsylvania, were strongly pro-Union during the Civil War, and voted for the party of Lincoln

for generations. Baker's maternal ancestors were Tidewater Virginians, "quite a different kettle of fish," he says. They always voted the Democratic ticket and were "rabid for Roosevelt" in 1932, when Baker "became a Roosevelt New Dealer at the age of seven," he recalls wryly.

The dichotomy in his philosophic heritage still is apparent in Baker's columns, which suggest a political liberalism and a sociological conservatism. "In the crudest kind of terms, I have this old political liberal tradition that comes out of my Depression childhood," Baker says, "but in the family, I have this old conservative tradition that comes out of growing up among my father's people in the country. I tend to be very strongly in favor of the family, continuity of family relationships, like things the way they are, very slow to accept change."

"I think the most important thing in the world is to maintain a close family," Baker told Heywood Hale Broun on CBS's "Sunday Morning." The Depression taught him that principle even more than it nurtured his political liberalism.

"There wasn't any state relief to speak of. If you didn't have a family you were dead, and that's stayed with me. One thing I've always insisted on with my family is that we're the unit that counts, before the state, before anything else, we've got to stick together.

"I remember at one point during the Vietnam War [the *Times*] ran a remarkable piece on the Op Ed page by a father—I think from Mississippi—who was angry about kids not going off to the war, the resistance movement, and writing this letter to his own son, as it were, that said that any son of his that would not obey the call of the state he would just as soon see shot as he would a deer. And I thought that was one of the most outrageous things I'd ever seen, that anybody would put the state before the family, because the family is really your last defense, and in a family you forgive anything. If you don't, if you betray your own family, why will you not betray the country?"

Political theorizing, however, usually is not part of Baker's mental makeup. Twenty years in Washington convinced him that the intellectual process had little to do with the way politics really works. All the "talk of ideology didn't get to the point," Baker says. The Senate he covered and knew intimately was populated by men who represented clearly defined interests and constituencies rather than ideologies. In it were senators for the oil industry, for the aviation industry, and, in one case, for Coca-Cola. Politics means politicians, and politicians are people. People interest him.

"I've always been weak on political theory. I always boggle a bit at people like George Will, who has a political thesis that he developed, I suppose, at Princeton or wherever—maybe in the cradle—and has been refining it ever since. That's always seemed never to take me anyplace.

"To the extent I have any ideology, I'm pretty much on the side of the traditional liberal view, that is, the classic, nineteenth-century liberal view of let the individual decide his own destiny and don't impose something on him that can't fit.

"I don't believe that, politically, you can improve people's souls. People's morals are the business of the clergy; the government is the business of the politicians. To confuse the two of them I think is dreadful."

As a senior in high school, unaware of Karl Marx, innocent of Mencken, and uncertain as to what he wanted to do for a living, Baker was presented with a yearbook form which required him to fill out what his "Ambition" was. He turned to a friend and asked what he was going to put under "Ambition." The reply: "To be a newspaperman." Not wishing to plagiarize the idea completely, Baker instead wrote on his own form: "To be a newspaper columnist," even though he "hadn't the least interest in being a newspaperman, certainly not a newspaper columnist." But that is the ambition recorded in his yearbook for future generations to ponder. Was it a case of subconscious prescience or just irony? Baker would opt for the latter.

In view of the state of his family's finances, Baker had given no thought to attending college, which he then viewed as a place "where Bing Crosby and Jack Oakie sang songs about the fraternity."

Cinematic analogies pepper Baker's conversation and prose. The films of the 1930s and 1940s provide him with instantly appropriate, indelible images. He finds their simplicity amusingly ironic now, but somehow they manage to remain among the few welcome memories he has of the period.

"When I was a kid, movies were our television," Baker recalled during a chat in his brightly lit, tenth-floor office at the *Times*. "For 10¢ I could go to the movies and see a double feature, a cartoon, the previews of six coming attractions, a short subject with Ted Fiorito's orchestra, and a Robert Benchley three-minute comedy.

"People of my generation went to the movies to learn how to live our lives. You went there to see the proper way to dress; the proper way to kiss a girl; what to do with your hands. That's how I became a smoker," he says, puffing on one of his ever-present Kools. "I noticed everybody smoked. It seemed very sophisticated. Bogart smoked, everybody smoked. You look at those old movies, you can hardly see the actors for the gales of smoke rising up in front of the camera!

"And you dressed like them, you talked like them, you got off their wisecracks. They were your models, really, of how to live life in America. And I was down there, not on the bottom, but pretty close to the bottom, wanting to get up there," and the movies showed him how to act once he reached the top. "They were absolutely vital in forming the people that we became."

Baker could not see himself singing fraternity songs with Jack Oakie, but at the urging of a friend, he took an examination for a scholarship at The Johns Hopkins University and, to his surprise, won it. He entered Hopkins in the fall of 1942 and discovered to his discomfort that it was not like the colleges in the movies.

"It was quite a transition from high school—where everybody tells you what to do—into a rather high-flown graduate school where nobody gave a rat's ass whether you were there or not," Baker recalled in an interview with the Hopkins alumni magazine. He was an indifferent student and found the news from the battlefronts of World War II much more compelling.

"I was a great patriot, willing to die for my country," and so he enlisted in the Navy and left Hopkins in the fall of 1943. "I felt I was dashing. I was very disappointed when I got out after two years of training without getting overseas and without killing myself," he once told *Time* magazine.

When he returned to Hopkins in early 1946, his undergraduate classmates were a curious collection of teenagers and mature veterans. "After being away for two years, I felt I'd crossed some kind of line into manhood, and most of my peers felt the same way. So instead of sitting in awe of the professors and taking notes and playing them back like phonograph records on examinations, we were asking questions. We challenged everything, and that was fun, informal and very grown-up. The professors seemed to like it too—it was a lively time," Baker told the *Hopkins Magazine*.

Baker pursued a relatively unstructured course of study, concentrating on English literature supplemented by a dollop of history. He joined an experimental course known as the Writing Seminars, taught by Elliott Coleman, a sensitive teacher and poet who was masterful at encouraging young writers. "You'd give him something horri-

ble, and he would find a little pulse beat down in the right calf," Baker recalls. (One of Baker's contemporaries in Coleman's early writing seminars was John Barth, the future novelist.)

Baker got another taste of journalism on the Hopkins student newspaper, the *News-Letter*, but considered his activities there just a substitute for fraternity hijinks. His goal was to become a novelist in the Hemingway mold, and his immediate need was some source of income to subsidize the novel he was beginning to write. When Coleman told him about an opening for a reporter on the *Baltimore Sun*, he applied for the job. Assigned to the traditional apprentice beat, the police districts, Baker became a habitué of Baltimore's demimonde, and he was fascinated by what he found there.

"I was living in a night world of people who lived horrible, strange lives and died horrible deaths. . . . And I found I had a gift of imitating people on a typewriter. So I discovered that a journalist was what I was, and that the life I was living was so much more interesting than anything I could invent."

His novel was never published.

Just before he went back to Hopkins, Baker became acquainted with his future wife, Miriam Emily ("Mimi") Nash, whose first encounter with him was so unmemorable, he once told a friend, that "we don't even agree on how or when we met." Compelled to be more specific in *Growing Up*, Baker pinpointed the occasion as the shank end of a disastrous blind date, when his indifferent companion casually introduced him to one of her roommates—Mimi. What followed was a turbulent courtship, made more awkward by the subtle dislike Baker's mother had for a potential daughter-in-law she deemed unsuitable. But they persevered and were married in March 1950.

As Baker warmed to the journalistic calling, he made steady progress at the *Sun*. A fast, accurate, and artful reporter, he impressed veteran journalists there as a future star. Within 5 years, at the age of 27, he was given the prize assignment as chief of the paper's London bureau, where he blossomed even more in the competitive world of British journalism.

Arriving in London in 1953, Baker watched Winston Churchill "perform" in the House of Commons, eschewed conventional reporting whenever possible, and produced a colorful weekly feature called "Window on Fleet Street," which captured the flavor of the British capital.

England then was still subject to wartime rationing and shortages. Most American reporters avoided such austerity by shopping at U.S. Army bases. Baker did not: "I lived like an Englishman off the English economy, and I lost a lot of weight. I was hungry all the time," he once told an interviewer.

"I cut myself off from the American community. Most of the reporters hung around the foreign office to get the diplomatic poop. I felt the A.P. would provide that. I went to Parliament and wrote about the nature of British political debate. I wrote about what Sunday afternoon was like, and British eccentrics. I really was kind of a travel writer."

He even participated in one memorable royal event, winning "an invitation in the scribblers' lottery" to cover the coronation of Queen Elizabeth II. The directions for his attire were explicit: top hat, white tie, and tails. He was delighted. Now he could dress up like Fred Astaire. When he decided to walk the half-mile from his home to Westminster Abbey, he discovered, "for the first and only moment in my life . . . , what it was to be a star and strut upon a great stage," he wrote in a 1981 column on the eve of another great royal show, the marriage of Prince Charles and Lady Diana.

The sidewalks were packed with humanity, but the street was sealed against motor traffic. Most of the people had spent the night partying and sleeping on the sidewalks. They were drenched and should have been miserable in their sleepless waterlogged state, but their gravest problem seemed to be boredom.

When a magnificently briefed policeman, checking my assortment of passes, opened the barrier and let me stride down the center of the thoroughfare, the crowds rose from the sidewalk and began cheering. After hours and hours of wretched waiting in the downpour, they were getting their first glimpse of the great royal occasion, and they hailed me as happily as if I had been a Knight of the Garter in full regalia.

Fortunately the deluge did not abruptly resume to turn my great royal moment into high comedy, and as I proceeded up the long avenue to loud cheers and the waving of soaked newspapers I put aside timidity and, here and there, in a gesture I hoped was worthy of the great Fred Astaire, I lifted my top hat and tipped it to the crowd.

I had almost reached the Abbey before I realized what had put them in such good spirits. There I noticed that several persons at the curb were pointing at my hand and laughing. Then I saw the higher light. In that hand, quite forgotten, I was lugging my lunch of two sandwiches and an orange in a brown paper bag. The crowd loved it. Here this regular toff—top hat, white tie and all, mind you, at 6 o'clock in the morning—and he was brown-bagging the Coronation.

It felt quite wonderful to create such a stir with such democratic plainness and in an uncharacteristic seizure of stage presence I tipped my hat again, then lifted my brown paper bag and waved it, and was washed with the sweet thunder of applause. It was a sublime moment. The rest of the day was rather long.

Baker's articles from London caught the eye of James Reston, then Washington bureau chief for the *New York Times*. Reston offered Baker a job at the *Times*, but he turned it down and instead accepted reassignment by the *Sun* to its White House beat, which he thought would be exciting. He quickly came to detest it. He found the White House, then in the second year of Dwight D. Eisenhower's presidency, a boring place. Baker dubbed it "The Tomb of The Well-Known Soldier." His job consisted primarily of "sitting in the lobby and listening to the older reporters breathe," he complained.

Ironically, Baker now recalls those years with a tinge of nostalgia—at least for their aura of certainty and confidence. "It was probably as close to an Augustan Age as we'll have. It didn't seem that way at the time," he says. "But looking back, obviously that was the peak of American power and influence in the world. The country was comparatively rich, people were buying houses, having babies, there was immense optimism in the country, which began to come apart almost as soon as Kennedy was elected, and it has been shattering ever since."

When Reston repeated his offer of a job at the *Times*, Baker grabbed it after being assured that he would not be assigned to the White House. At first he was sent to cover the State Department, which bored him almost as much, but soon he was dispatched to cover the Senate, where the posturing and pomposities appealed to his taste for the absurd.

The Senate at that time contained John F. Kennedy, Lyndon Johnson, Hubert Humphrey, and Vice-President Richard Nixon, all of whom "were busy running for President." Baker saw them day in and day out on a professional basis, but he believes that "who you cover and who you know are two different categories."

"I never had social relationships with them. I always thought that was a bad practice, if you had to report from Washington, to go to their houses and eat their bread, or to have them to your house and share your whiskey. I just thought that once you had

done that with a man, it was very difficult to cover him with any objectivity. You tended to cut it then on tough stories."

At the time, Baker viewed John Kennedy "as sort of an office boy," handy for retrieving documents from the Senate floor. "He seemed to be about my age and somebody I could talk to as an equal. If there was a document on the President's desk down in the well of the Senate that I needed to get the text from . . . I'd go down and ask the doorman if he'd get Senator Kennedy, and Jack would come out, and I'd say, 'Hi, Jack, do me a favor? Would you get me the text of that amendment on the desk?' and he'd say, 'Sure,' and go in and bring it out and wait while I copied it and then take it back. So, in a way, I looked on Jack Kennedy in those days as my office boy. I was astonished when he announced he was going to run for President."

But Baker also maintained a healthy sense of skepticism about his own importance. He believes that many of the "Washington bigshots in journalism" are enthralled at being cultivated on a first-name basis by politicians. "You then begin to think you're somebody very important, and [the politicians] don't see you that way at all. They see you as the *New York Times* logo, or the *Washington Post*, or whatever."

When Lyndon Johnson was Vice-President, he once corralled Baker in a Senate hallway, dragged him into the ornate vice-presidential office, and launched into a long, intimate monologue about his political dreams. Baker had dealt with Johnson on a first-name basis for half a decade, but during the course of his confession, LBJ scribbled a note on a piece of paper and buzzed for a secretary, who took the note out of the office and soon returned with it.

Johnson continued his one-man show for awhile, then warmly ushered Baker out of the office. Another reporter later went into Johnson's office and spied the piece of note paper on the desk. LBJ had written, "Who is this I am talking to?" and his secretary had jotted in reply, "Russell Baker of the *New York Times.*"

"Johnson never had the least interest in me as a human being," Baker says with a chuckle. "I was just a vertical line of big Gothic type that said 'New York Times' from head to toe. I think it's salubrious for all newspaper people in Washington to realize that, and many of them forget it."

For Baker, reporting in Washington was "always a process of education. It was like attending the best graduate school of political science on earth, because whenever I wanted to know how something worked, I could go to the very top . . . like in the Senate, I could talk to Lyndon Johnson and say, 'Now why are you doing this on civil rights?' and he'd tell me. I covered the State Department and I'd say, 'Explain to me what's going on between Golda Meir and Abdel Nasser,' and somebody who really worked in it every day would explain it to me. And I was learning all the time. It was a great university experience."

After awhile, however, the lessons became repetitious. "After you've covered, say, the Senate for four years, the increment of learning becomes smaller and smaller. After you've covered the big foreign-aid-bill fight four years running, you begin to refer to it as 'the annual foreign-aid-bill fight.' And you get a little numb, you're not really learning anymore. And then it becomes dull."

Baker covered Kennedy's campaign for the presidency in 1960 and the early days of the New Frontier, but eventually the drudgery of reporting began to bore him. When boredom strikes Baker, as it has repeatedly during his career, he starts searching for something more challenging. He wrote a satirical guide to the capital, called *An American in Washington*, solemnly instructing the reader on "the supreme importance of lunch" and how to drop names with panache. His wonderfully appropriate characterizations of Washington reporters have received the highest compliment from other capital correspondents: they still quote them often.

The State Department reporter quickly learns to talk like a fuddy-duddy and to look grave, important and inscrutable. The Capitol reporter eschews the raucous spirit of the White House and affects the hooded expression of a man privy to many important deals. Like the politicians he covers, he tends to garrulity, coarse jokes, and bourbon, and learns to hate reform. The Pentagon man always seems to have just come in off maneuvers. . . .

The drab truth is that besides having the President call you up to say that he means to fire the Secretary of Something-or-Other, there are at least 3,000 other ways of gathering news in Washington, all relatively unexciting, some incredibly tedious.

His book was not enough to counter Baker's conclusion that he had reached a dead end. One day in 1962, while sitting on the floor of a hallway outside a closed meeting of the Senate Armed Services Committee, Baker "began to wonder why, at the age of 37, I was wearing out my hams waiting for somebody to come out and lie to me."

Not long afterward, the *Sun* sought to lure Baker back by offering him a column on any topic he wanted. Baker agreed and shook hands on the deal, but Reston wouldn't hear of it. He persuaded the *Times* to give Baker a column, and thus was born "The Observer."

Baker's column first appeared beside the *Time*'s editorials in a long, narrow stretch of type that for decades had held a dull, anonymous offering titled "Topics of the Times." "No one had read it for years," Baker says, and his column, employing simple sentences, "Anglo-Saxon root words," and a subtle, devastating wit, was a radical departure.

"What interested me in Washington were not necessarily the things that interest most Washington reporters. They're interested in details. Maybe I was not taking it as seriously as most of them did, but to me it was only part of a larger world environment. I'm sounding stuffy about this, but I was trying to make sense of the whole thing, and the only sense I could make of it was that it fitted into some grand pattern of irony. Now irony is not necessarily funny . . . , but the business of no individual really controlling his own destiny absorbed me."

People want to believe that the world is a rational place, but Baker thinks that the useless carnage of the First World War was "the beginning illustration, in fact, that the world doesn't work that way." All that has followed since then supports such a bleak assessment, he believes. Following the advice of that social commentator of an earlier age, W. S. Gilbert, Baker sought to make his fellow creatures wise by gilding his philosophic pill. Wielding parody, satire, and an astounding variety of stylistic scalpels, he sliced through the absurdities of American politics with surgical precision.

While many non-Washingtonians were entranced by Baker's clever dissections of the body politic, he was never convinced that the capital's power brokers bothered to read his observations. "My feeling always was that I didn't have much of an audience in Washington," Baker says. "People who read columns in Washington always seemed to me to be much more interested in being on top, or a day ahead, of whatever the news was, so they were reading the 'inside poop' kind of columnists. The kind of thing I was doing didn't have much audience.

"Also, Buchwald was writing very heavily for a Washington audience and he was in the *Post*, which gave him an immense circulation. I didn't have much of an outlet in Washington," Baker contends, the impact of the *New York Times* notwithstanding.

"There are only 1,400 people in Washington, really—the people who count. Maybe I'm much too high on the estimate. And when you're talking about who reads columnists, you're talking about a very small elite. Those people all read the *Washington Post* columns and discussed them, so far as I could make out. It was always astonishing to me, because columns probably have a higher bilge content than any other part of the newspaper. But very often that was the first thing they'd turn to in Washington," Baker recalls. "Washington just seemed like a dead town for me in terms of an audience. It still does."

Baker insists that few of his columns have any lasting impact on his readers, with one or two modest exceptions. "I did do a piece . . . which may have saved New York State from having the slogan 'I Love New York' imprinted on every license plate in the state," he says triumphantly. He believes former New York Governor Hugh Carey read the column and was persuaded to veto a bill that would have provided automobile-borne immortality for that bit of public relations hype. "If I achieved that, I will be very proud. That's worth a whole career."

Baker's supposed lack of audience or influence in Washington did not bother him as much as his own diminishing interest in the place. "I'm a very restless, mobile kind of person. I'd never lived one place 20 years in my life until I went to Washington . . . and I was appalled after awhile to discover I was staying in Washington longer and longer, although it was very comfortable.

"The explanation was that my children were growing up and I thought it important to provide the children with a stable place to grow up, rather than keep moving them around the world. And when the last one was grown and left home, I decided I just wanted to go, I wanted to go someplace else. I had 'done' Washington. I felt I wasn't learning anything there."

Baker chose New York as his next classroom and challenge. When he lived in

Washington, Manhattan gave him the willies. Now he has "discovered that I'm urban. Chevy Chase, where I lived in Washington, is like a small town in Indiana, full of people certified orthodox by the U.S. Government. New York is the way cities used to be," he once told an interviewer for *Time*.

Moving from Washington, the most atypical of American cities, to New York, the quintessential metropolis, greatly expanded the scope of Baker's column. The richness of his humor and the depth of his philosophical integrity were demonstrated with renewed conviction. Baker still can be magnificently funny, but he also shows pessimism, outrage, and melancholy. "I'm getting older," he told one interviewer. "If you're not melancholy at 58, there's something wrong with you." Since he left Washington, the subject matter of his columns has become almost as varied as his chameleonlike prose.

In 1979, five years after he moved to Manhattan, Baker won the Pulitzer Prize for commentary. The columns cited by the Pulitzer committee reflected his dazzling versatility, dealing in turn with the rapidly decreasing durability of trends, the distinction between "serious" and "solemn," inflation, loneliness, dying, and reminiscences of one of his childhood summers in Virginia.

And irony, the constant companion to Baker's muse, was present in his first Pulitzer, too. Six days before he won journalism's highest honor, a musical comedy on which he had labored for two years folded in Toronto, the victim of horrendous reviews just before it hit Broadway. "It was that kind of a week," Baker says.

While there is humor—varied and sometimes even surreal—in most of Baker's columns, there also is an artistry that sets some of them apart from the work of most columnists. But it is clear that there are days when he strains to be funny, and for some of

his readers, such as Jimmy Breslin, Baker's humor detracts from his writing. "If he would just write essays, and not humor, he'd be the best," Breslin says, "because he is the best essay writer in the country. . . . The humor is nice, but it isn't the compelling work that his essays [are]."

As far as Ellen Goodman is concerned, even Baker's failures are worth reading. "I like Baker's work because he's a risk taker. His stuff's very risky. He can bounce off the wall, and I like that sense of risk. . . . Sometimes when I read him I'm saying, Is he going to pull it off? And it's a thrill when he does."

Baker's columns now are syndicated in about 475 newspapers that subscribe to the Times News Service, but he doesn't concern himself with trying to address readers in the hinterlands. He writes for a New York audience—or at least an audience of urbanites who feel comfortable with references a New York reader would understand, he says. He also knows that the homogenization of the United States has blended a soupçon of sophistication—and an awareness of urban horrors—in even the remotest corners of the land. He may not exactly be the favorite writer of the New York Chamber of Commerce, but other readers feel he's got the city pegged:

W hen visitors from elsewhere start calling New York a sissy town I take them to the corner of Eighth Avenue and 42nd Street and point up toward Seventh Avenue and Times Square.

"Name any crime forbidden in any code of law written since the dawn of time," I say, "and at this very moment you can find someone in this block who has committed it, is planning to commit it, or is committing it right now."

. . . the block has never let New York down when challenged by an out-of-towner. A skeptical Chicagoan went home defeated one day when, in less than three minutes, I was able to introduce him to an arsonist, an ax killer, a jury suborner, a child molester, a receiver of stolen goods, four car thieves, eight violators of the Mann Act, 16 juveniles who'd stolen welfare checks from neighbors' mailboxes and three men planning the armed robbery of a nursing home.

Another time, challenged by a Texan, I even found a man who committed mopery. Actually, mopery isn't a crime, but only an old policeman's joke in which it's defined as displaying yourself in the nude to a blind person.

I reasoned that, whether mopery was a crime or not, if there were people in the world who thought it was a crime, those people would be on 42nd Street looking for a chance to commit it. I equipped the Texan with a white cane and dark glasses and, sure enough, a 42nd Streeter bounded out of a doorway, committed mopery and ran. . . .

He also remains as capable of taking Washington's measure from afar as he was when he lived there:

There is a natural affinity between a used car salesman and a congressman. Neither one wants you to know what's under the hood.

For that reason there is nothing surprising about Congress's rejection of new federal rules that would have forced used-car dealers to tell their customers about serious defects in their merchandise. Do congressmen advertise the cracks in their brains? Why should a used car salesman have to advertise the holes in his radiator?

I don't think it was all those campaign donations from the used-car lobby that made Congress toss out the proposed rules. I think a surge of natural brotherly sympathy would have been enough to carry the day for America's Honest Harrys, Smilin' Sams and Upright Ulrics.

Put yourself in your congressman's shoes. One of these days he is going to be out of office. Defeated, old, tired, 120,000 miles on his smile and two pistons cracked in his best joke. They're going to put him out on the used congressman lot.

Does he want to have a sticker on him stating that he gets only eight miles on a gallon of bourbon? That his rip-roaring anti-communist speech hasn't had an overhaul since 1969? That his generator is so decomposed it hasn't sparked a fresh thought in fifteen years?

You know and I know what he wants. When Happy Harvey brings a buyer over, he wants Happy to be able to say, "Now I've got to tell you this is a used congressman, but he's better than new. Had only one owner—a little old oil industry who never used him for anything except to go to church on Sundays."

On Sunday afternoons, Baker settles down to write his Tuesday column. On Monday afternoons he writes the column that will appear in the *New York Times Magazine* three weeks later. On Thursday afternoons he writes his Saturday column. He says his "glandular rhythms are attuned to that pace," and he has no desire to reduce his output.

He is engagingly modest about his craft. "My column is 700 to 750 words. I have to fit that space, like writing a sonnet. So a lot of my work is carpentry, avoiding ideas that run more than 750 words," he explains. "And I always finish at 6:00 in the afternoon. It's eerie. I can't explain it. I'm very rigid about scheduling. If I waited until I wanted to write, I'd never write. So I allot four hours, 2:00 P.M. to 6:00 P.M., to writing the column. And I don't think about it other than that. I don't hoard up ideas between writing periods—absolutely not. I *always* know I'm going to have an idea of some sort, I'm positive about that—although there've been times when 'It was a nice day out' became a 750-word column."

Baker insists that he has an illogical mind, befuddled by mathematical abstractions and philosophic theories, but the fanciful twists his thinking takes—the result, he says, of "a quirk of brain chemistry"—can convey the essence of reality more potently than any accumulation of facts and figures. He can take a building and turn it into a political party, as he did in a column just prior to the 1980 Democratic National Convention in New York:

The Democratic Party these days is a good bit like Madison Square Garden, which is not square, but round, and which is not a garden, but a *Sportspalast*. To compound the deception, it isn't situated anywhere near Madison Square either, which lies a mile or so to the southeast.

Like the Democratic Party, Madison Square Garden has drifted around the landscape for so many years and had its face lifted so many times that it has turned into something else. Madison Square Garden it ain't.

Still, Madison Square Garden is a wonderful old name and, Shakespeare or no Shakespeare, businessmen know there is plenty in a name. So the name lingers on, meaningless, confusing, deceptive, but charged with old New York emotions rooted in memories of great events that never happened there.

The Democratic Party is appropriately housed there for this year's convention. Though the name lingers on, evoking memories of a glorious past when the party was confident of itself and its importance in the country, the Democratic Party, like the Garden, has become a confused wanderer without much identity. It's something, all right, because there it is. But what is it? On what foundation does it rest?

Madison Square Garden rests atop the passenger station of a bankrupt railroad. The metaphor is arresting: politicians standing above a ruin, thundering about greatness past and greatness to come, while downstairs the trains fail to arrive on time.

A week before Christmas in 1982, Baker used the train station as the setting for a coldly furious commentary on the effects of the Reagan administration's economic policies:

The only Santa Claus I've seen so far this season was wearing a blue suit and a badge, and he was being interviewed on television in Penn Station where he works as a railroad cop. It was in the morning's wee hours, the time when Santa traditionally performs his ancient charities, and the station had a silent, abandoned look.

When the camera scanned the interior, though, you could see that while it was quiet all right, abandoned it wasn't. All around, down long corridors and against silent walls, people were snuggled—well, not deep in their beds, to be sure, but wrapped in their coats on floors of stone.

Sure, the cop said, if you went by the book you ought to throw them all out onto the street, but he didn't do that. Couldn't do that. Out on the street these late December mornings temperatures go down to 25, to 15 degrees. Sometimes lower.

Bedding on a railroad station floor might not be a heated water bed under eiderdown, but it was better than frostbite. His policy was to let them dream for a couple of hours, then wake them, tell them to move on and watch them shuffle to another corner, another corridor, and bed down again. . . .

If we had film of this sort of thing from Moscow, wouldn't it be widely screened as evidence of the failure of Communism? Does the juxtaposition on television of stone beds and gold coins for wrist decoration tell us something depressing about the failures of capitalism?

In a large part of the world outside the Communist zones, the message surely wouldn't be helpful to our cause, but we can always fall back on the explanation that while capitalism may not be perfect, it's still better than anything else on the market.

This may go down successfully in some countries struggling to survive, but it's embarrassing to have to settle for such faint self-praise here at home. Even President Reagan, the St. George of embattled capitalism, once thought he could rescue it without causing misery and desperation.

His famous "safety net" would see to that, he promised. It was a restful idea, the safety net. It suggested lying in a gentle hammock, secure until the great engines of capitalism recalled everyone to work. The reality is a patch of stone floor in a railroad station and a decent cop willing to let you dream for two hours before waking you up. Some safety. Some net.

Baker says there are days when his column is, at best, "marginal." But "unless one is really terrible, I never kill and rewrite," he says. He writes 140 pieces a year—totaling some 100,000 words—and the consistently high quality of the over-whelming majority of his work is reason enough to let an occasional clinker slip by. Tomorrow, he might observe with Scarlett O'Hara, is another day. The chances are pretty good that Baker will hit a bull's-eye then.

He says there is little of the missionary or pedagogical purpose in his columns now. "I'm so far along in it, I don't think about it anymore. Now I just survive. There's always another column to be done. I'm not interested in Washington particularly any-more. I'm interested in the public psychol-ogy, why the American mind has taken the direction it has. I'm always working on the fringes of that sort of thing."

Baker's fascination with how the coun-try's psyche has changed since his boyhood was in part the inspiration for *Growing Up,* which won the Pulitzer Prize for biography in 1983. It is a tour de force, by turns funny, poignant, and inspiring; "an American clas-sic" in the view of Baker's colleague at the *Times,* Anthony Lewis. In *Growing Up,* Baker achieves something few journalists, however fine, ever manage: he "surmounts the ephemeral," Lewis wrote.*

When he is in New York, Baker writes his column either in his office at the *Times,* where he performs his carpentry on an elec-tric typewriter that faces a window over-looking the theater district, or at his duplex apartment on Manhattan's West Side. He also has been dictating an increasing num-ber of his columns over the telephone from his 147-year-old house on Nantucket Island, where he and his wife spend up to a third of each year. They have two sons, a daughter, and three grandchildren. They are a close-knit family. One of Baker's sons has returned to his father's ancestral commu-nity, Morrisonville, where he is at work restoring a large log house that Baker bought there. In an unusually serendipitous coincidence, Baker was visiting his birth-place when he learned that he had won the Pulitzer for the memoir in which it plays such an important role.

A somewhat shy, private person who shuns the place in New York's celebrity cir-cus that would be his for the asking, Baker views the praise he receives—the Pulitzers, a cover story in *Time,* adoring mail—with bemused self-deprecation. "I get a lot of supportive mail, people telling me how

---

*Baker says he was "astonished" by the success of *Growing Up.* His agent and publisher were cool to such a "personal" book, and he shared their skepti-cism about its prospects. The book clubs ignored it; the major book stores bought few copies; the paper-back rights went begging. Only readers loved it. They kept it on the best seller lists for months. Eventually the paperback rights sold for an astro-nomical sum. "I can't sit back and sneer at how wrong the 'experts' were because I didn't think it was going to be a success either, commercially," Baker says. What sold it were excellent reviews, "word-of-mouth" raves, and small, independent bookstores, he says. "And then people read it. Most best sellers never get read. They just get best-sold."

great I am. Well, I don't know. Who looks upon you with awe? People who write letters to the editor," he says with a chuckle. "I used to have an English friend who said that writing a letter to the editor was prima facie evidence of insanity. It's not conclusive, but it's a good place to start the investigation."

He seems to be strangely delighted by the fact that the issue of *Time* magazine that carried his picture on the cover was the poorest-selling of the year. Notoriety is no blessing, he believes. "After my news agent on the corner began calling me by name, I had to begin walking two blocks to buy my copy of *Penthouse* or risk having it blabbed all over the neighborhood that I was reading trash."

As it is, Baker has the most enviable kind of fame: his name is known, but his face is not. He can stroll the streets of New York rumpled and unrecognized; he even can enter a bookstore that is displaying copies of his latest book, which features his photograph on the dust jacket, and browse undisturbed.

He doesn't go out to lunch very often, and when he does, he favors pastrami sandwiches or hamburgers. "I've always been a third-rate luncher," he once told an interviewer. "I never get the right table, and the captain never knows me, and as a result, people I invite to lunch are always embarrassed."

Baker and his wife don't dine out very often, either. They prefer quiet nights at home, and his taste in evening fare tends to be as simple as it is at lunch. (He is, however, partial to fine wines.) One of his most popular columns was a lampoon of the *Times*'s food specialist, Craig Claiborne:

T he meal opened with a 1975 Diet Pepsi served in a disposable bottle. Although its bouquet was negligible, its distinct metallic aftertaste evoked memories of tin cans one had licked experimentally in the first flush of childhood's curiosity.

To create the balance of tastes so cherished by the epicurean palate, I followed with *pate de fruites de nuts of Georgia*, prepared according to my own recipe. A half-inch layer of creamy-style peanut butter is troweled onto a graham cracker, then half a banana is crudely diced and pressed firmly into the peanut butter and cemented in place as it were by a second graham cracker.

The accompanying drink was cold milk served in a wide-brimmed jelly glass. This is essential to proper consumption of the pate, since the entire confection must be dipped into the milk to soften it for eating. In making the presentation to the mouth, one must beware lest the milk-soaked portion of the sandwich fall onto the necktie. Thus, seasoned gourmandizers follow the old maxim of the Breton chefs and "Bring the mouth to the jelly glass."

At this point in the meal, the stomach was ready for serious eating, and I prepared beans with bacon grease, a dish I perfected in 1937 while developing my *cuisine du depression*.

The dish is started by placing a pan over a very high flame until it becomes dangerously hot. A can of Heinz's pork and beans is then emptied into the pan and allowed to char until it reaches the consistency of hardening concrete. Three strips of bacon are fried to crisps, and when the beans have formed huge dense clots firmly welded to the pan, the bacon grease is poured in and stirred vigorously with a large screwdriver.

This not only adds flavor but also loosens some of the beans from the side of the pan. Leaving the flame high, I stirred in a three-day-old spaghetti sauce found in the refrigerator, added a sprinkle of chili powder, a large dollop of Major Grey's chutney and a tablespoon of bicarbonate of soda to make the whole dish rise.

Beans with bacon grease is always eaten from the pan with a tablespoon while standing over the kitchen sink. The pan must be thrown away immediately. The correct drink with this dish is a straight shot of room-temperature gin. I had a Gilbey's 1975, which was superb.

Baker says he received more requests for copies of the Claiborne spoof than for any other column. Claiborne even requested permission to reprint it in his next cookbook.

Before *Growing Up* elevated him from the field of journalism to that of belles-lettres, Baker was asked if he didn't find his newspaper work unfulfilling. He grew annoyed at the question, insisting that he already was overexposed in print. "The question implies that I should be doing something more than I am, and I always feel that I'm doing more than I could possibly do! I don't think any newspaperman confuses himself with Dostoyevsky."

It was a natural question, however, since Baker routinely has set new challenges for himself, spurred on, perhaps, by the memory of his mother's demand that he demonstrate "gumption." Some of his columns, in fact, served as preliminary blueprints for his more imposing edifice, which he wrote on the days when he didn't have to construct his 750-word pieces. Some of the columns that he is working on now may serve a similar function for a new book he is contemplating on how America's mood changed in the 1950s and 1960s.

"That's getting to be a time that's fairly remote now," he says. "A lot of the people I write for now weren't born in those years. One of the things about *Growing Up* that I wanted to do was to create the texture of a past era, a time that's dead. I was really dabbling in history a little bit. If I could find some way of doing that with the fifties and the sixties, I'd like to do that."

Although he grimaces and expresses boredom with his newspaper work on occasion—complaining that it has become "a habit, like smoking," and he is tired of hearing his own voice—Baker does not contemplate abandoning it. He does worry, however, about "aging out of the core of the population—demographically, I'm going off the curve. So there are millions of people coming along to whom I can't foresee that I will be able to speak effectively. What I dread is the day when people pick up my column and say, 'Why do they keep running this old fart?' "

Until that day arrives, he plans to continue putting together, brick by brick, board by board, his distinctive contributions to what he considers a basically insubstantial medium. "It's only daily journalism," Baker says. "The readers throw it away and forget it."

Throw it away, perhaps. Forget it? Not likely. And while he might dismiss the judgment with a soft grin and a wave of his cigarette, he has, without doubt, made something of himself.

Erma Bombeck

The Socrates of the Ironing Board

rma Bombeck is a serious woman.

"Don't let that get out," she says, sounding wounded, then breaking into a booming laugh.

Laughter, ranging from an easy-going chuckle to a window-rattling guffaw, punctuates Bombeck's conversation. It follows one-line cracks that are aimed only at making her listener laugh; it follows sad recollections and perceptive observations. It is both reflexive and defensive. The best way to make an audience like you, Bombeck believes, is to gain their sympathy by demonstrating that you are one of them—and an insecure one at that. If they nod in agreement as they laugh and later reflect on the thoughts behind the witticisms, that is even better. If all they do is laugh, and don't throw things at you, that is good enough.

Bombeck rarely laughs, however, when she writes. "Every once in a while I will. Every once in a while something right off the wall will come up, something so ridiculous I don't believe I'm going to say it. But I am. It's just insanity, and I think, My God, they *are* going to put me away."

But writing is so difficult for Bombeck, and humor so elusive, that she spends eight hours a day, sometimes six days a week, laboring over her 450-word columns, her two-and-a-half minute television commen-

taries and her books with hardly a giggle passing her lips. She also gets annoyed when people, especially critics or academics, try to analyze her humor or dismiss it as frivolous.

"One of the things [humorists] work heavily on is the spontaneity and the surprises; that's what humor is all about. Don't screw it up by saying, Now, why did that work? Who *cares*? That's one of the . . . phases of writing where you should never ask the question Why? *Just let it be.*

". . . You know what [reviewers] say about humor books? They say the same thing about Buchwald, they say the same thing about mine. They say, Well, this is a book about humor, but you can't read it all in one sitting. You shouldn't read *anything* all in one sitting, I don't care who you're reading. They say there's just too much laughter, and I think, My God, can't you figure that out? I mean, dummy, when you've had enough cupcakes, stop eating them and go on to something else. That's not a valid criticism of anything. . . .

"I think any humor, to be worth the space at all, has to have truth underlying it. . . . I guess you're inviting people to laugh at themselves, but also you're uncovering the truth that maybe they're seeing for the first time or they realize that someone else knows other than themselves.

"I think humor is just real, real personal. It just ferrets down and gets underneath. I make it sound so serious. It really is. I've done columns just for laughs. There's nothing redeeming about them at all. . . . Sure, you can get off a few of those. Most of them I like to think get down deeper and do tell the truth about people."

Bombeck, 57, is a tiny woman, only 5 feet, 2 inches tall, with light brown hair, green eyes, and a broad-lipped, toothy grin. For all her wailing in print about her weight problem, she carries her 125 pounds unobtrusively, with whatever she considers excess girth concentrated on her hips and upper arms. A writer for *Newsweek* once described her as looking "the way she writes: short, good-humored, somehow expectant—as if she's waiting for a pot to boil over."

Bombeck's tastes are middlebrow, and the expressions she uses—despite residing for years in a swank Western spa—relentlessly echo her native Midwest. Some people are "neat"; some experiences are "a real kick." Although Bombeck is warm, friendly, and unpretentious, she is not a Pollyanna—or perhaps she is, a no-calorie one without sugar or illusions. She is a knowledgeable businesswoman who reads every line in her contracts, is not ashamed to stump the country promoting her books, and scoffs at the syndication claims made on behalf of some other columnists. She will gladly show doubters the complete list of her own subscribers.

The only critics to whom Bombeck gives any credence are her readers, the ones who follow her thrice-weekly column in some 900 newspapers and who plop down cash for her books, which are given first-printing press runs in the hundreds of thousands and routinely hit the best-seller lists.

The admiration of her audience, which is reflected in her appearance (along with Ellen Goodman and advice columnists Ann Landers and Abigail Van Buren) on the annual lists of the nation's most influential women, is gratifying to Bombeck, but it

also is a bit embarrassing. It has done little to cure her painful shyness and chronic insecurity. "I think if I ever lost my insecurity I'd be scared to death, because I think the insecurity makes me try harder. It makes me look over my shoulder wondering if there's another little housewife back there with an IBM [typewriter] that works—real good. . . .

"I think everyone who has any measure of success has at one time or another thought, When are they going to find me out? Am I going to be able to continue? Every time you come back from a vacation, and maybe you've had two or three weeks off from writing, you think, Let me see, what was that formula again? Can I put the words together? Have I lost it? I think that's good. It's painful to live with all the time. . . .

"I always think I'm not going to be good enough. Maybe that's why I don't socialize more. I think I'm a big disappointment to people when I walk in a room and they expect something funny to come out of my mouth and it never does. And I have a *horror* of going someplace and having someone call on me to say a few words because, you know, I don't ad-lib a belch. Everything is planned. That's why I work so long with the columns. They don't just come off the top of my head. It's not easy."

Nothing has come easily for Bombeck. She lost her father when she was nine; worked her way through both high school and college; desperately wanted children but suffered two miscarriages before her first child was born; and battled her way out of a deadening world of household drudgery by setting up a secondhand typewriter on a table at the end of her bed and writing a column about the problems facing any woman who was "overkidsed, underpatienced, with four years of college and chapped hands all year around."

At first her column was just a comic chronicle of the woes of the suburban housewife—the endless cleaning, cooking, and washing; the frustrations of parenthood; the absurdities of communal cookie sales and Tupperware parties. "For housewives across the country, [Bombeck's] columns strike a responsive truth, the desperate truth made less desperate because it is universal," Ellen Goodman wrote in 1970, a year before she became a columnist herself and began mining a different vein in the same mother lode of problems and anxieties women find universal.

"When I first started writing the column, I thought I was mad, that no one would understand," Bombeck told Goodman. "I thought I was the only one with a washing machine that eats socks. The only one with a kid who could pretend he's a police siren—eeeeeeee—for 50 miles of traffic jams.

"One of the hazards of staying at home is the feeling of loneliness. The average housewife is lonely even if she has 15 kids. Sometimes all it takes is hearing there is someone else going through the same thing, that you're not standing there in your underwear all alone. Then you can put it in perspective. You can laugh instead of scream."

Unlike Goodman, Bombeck was not immediately enamored of the women's movement. She used to describe some of its early leaders as "roller-derby dropouts, or Russian pole-vaulting types" who were uninterested in the opinions or feelings of housewives. "When did a woman selling orange slices in the dime store become more impressive than a woman who did a darned good job raising three kids for twenty years?" she asked in a column.

But Bombeck readily acknowledges that the change in the role of women in our society—which she considers an even more revolutionary development than the civil rights movement—has benefited her both as a housewife and as a writer. As the women's movement grew, the vision of Bombeck's column also expanded and evolved. She began dealing with the frustrations of women other than housewives: "The woman with no children who made a career out of going to baby showers . . . , the older woman who gagged every time someone called her a senior citizen, and the career girl who panicked when she saw the return of the dress with the waistlines and belts. ('God only knows what I've grown under these shifts for four years.') . . . ," she wrote in 1968. And that was before the women's movement really got under way.

"I think probably this column . . . has gone through one of the greatest transitions ever because we were hit by a cyclone—the women's movement—and there's been no other group in this country that has [had] just total upheaval," Bombeck says.

"I think they've figured out that by 1990 there's only going to be one family out of 100 who will be 'traditional,' and we don't even know what that means anymore because they're just not there. This has been a break for me. There would be only so many years that I could go on talking about toilet training and seeing the school bus off. That gets a little tired. As it turned out, I've had 20 years with nothing but [change], which has been great. I've reacted to a lot of things that women never reacted to before, didn't know about before."

Despite her initial disdain for the "elitist" members of the women's movement, Bombeck campaigned around the country for the equal rights amendment and served on the now-defunct President's National Advisory Committee for Women. She has written columns that are touching, serious, and thought-provoking, which—because they are so rare and surprising—inevitably inspire a "fantastic" response from readers. She is not inclined, however, to travel the serious route often.

"If I did a serious column all the time, I think it would wear very, very thin. . . . I did all humor columns maybe for about the first five years and then when I put [a serious] one in, the editors were not crazy about it, but the response was so great because, as someone pointed out, 'Thank God there's another dimension to you. I thought you just went through life slapping your knees and tap dancing around.' You can't be this way all the time. . . . [But] I would prefer to be known as a funny writer."

Bombeck's politics and religion never surface in her column. She is a Democrat who should have "flaming liberal across my chest," and a Roman Catholic who is firmly opposed to abortion but thinks the church is wrong to ban birth control devices. She has not toured the nation advocating these beliefs as she did for the equal rights amendment, but even that and other women's movement causes are kept out of the column—at least directly.

"I'd never put the woman's movement in the column. I'm paid to write humor—and don't forget it. . . . I have 900 editors who have a lot of people on their staffs who can write serious, heavy stuff about women's goals and where they should be and where they're coming from and where they're going now and all this stuff. They don't need me to add to that. They buy Ellen Goodman for that. But if they want humor, then that's what they're buying from me. I assume that people buy syndicated columns because it's something that they can't produce at a local level. If they could, I would just be out on my ear in a minute, so I think it's wise to remember that and not stray from it."

Bombeck's genius lies in her ability to recognize a common experience, delineate it perfectly, and express a tight, punchy comic reaction to it that millions of readers can identify with instantly. She has an unerring eye for what she likes to call "the little things," the subjects once addressed by her idol as a humorist, Robert Benchley. "He's the best. He is so great. The gentleness of the man's humor—it was never really barbed, and it was directed at himself. . . . That's the kind of humor that I like."

Benchley was a sensitive, erudite Harvard graduate and one-time social worker who became drama critic for the *New Yorker*; a sophisticated comic actor in the movies; and the writer of brief essays that remain masterpieces of subtle wit. He died in 1945, but his name still evokes wistful sighs of reverence from devotees as disparate as Woody Allen and Walter Cronkite.

Many of Benchley's insights are timeless. A prolific writer with a well-deserved reputation as a bon vivant, he once postulated the great psychological principle that enabled him to do so much and still look so dissipated: "Anyone can do any amount of work, provided it isn't the work he is supposed to be doing at that moment." A corpulent man who periodically tried to sweat off a few pounds, Benchley sadly observed: "I can imagine no lower point of self-esteem than to find yourself one day the worst-looking exhibit in a Turkish bath." And it was Benchley, the father of two sons, who wrote: "In America there are two classes of travel—first class and with children. Traveling with children corresponds roughly to traveling third-class in Bulgaria. . . ."

While there is little doubt that Benchley is Bombeck's spiritual progenitor, her humor rarely has the subtle or rapier quality for which he and his luncheon companions at the Round Table of New York's Algonquin Hotel were renowned. Instead it is the humor of a suburban beauty parlor decorated with pink-poodle wallpaper on foil, and there are—for better or worse—a lot more of them than there are Algonquin Hotels. If, after more than half a century, we still can nod, grin, and laugh at the travails and neuroses Benchley endured as "the typical American Sap," there is reason to assume that fifty years hence similar Bombeck essays will strike a responsive chord:

Want a mother to fall apart before your eyes?

Just watch her when she asks a child what he is doing and he answers "Nothing."

Children usually do "nothing" in a room where the door is shut, a dog is barking, water is running under the door, a sibling is begging for mercy, there is a strange odor of fur burning and there is the sound of a thousand camels running in place.

Most mothers refuse to face whatever it is they're not doing so they simply yell, "Do you want me to come up and see what you're up to?"

Surprise! The answer is always "No!"

There are occasional belly laughs in Bombeck's column, but more often it inspires simply a knowing smile or a satisfied chuckle. It works, one critic wrote, "because it's not just wisecracks and one-liners . . . , but marvelously comic insights that grow out of [her] life as organically as fungus forms between the bathroom tiles."

Bombeck often depicts herself as the female of the species Mencken classified as *Boobus Americanus*. When she travels abroad, she once wrote, she must survive not only the rigors of continental breakfasts featuring hard rolls that "build a solid wall across the hips and the stomach" but also the terrors of "Montezuma II's revenge."

Few people realize this, but there were two Montezumas. Montezuma I is credited with lending his name to an urgency Americans refer to as the Green Apple Two-step. Montezuma II is generally known as the patron saint of gift shops. Both are unkind to foreigners.

With Montezuma II's revenge, I would be in the country no longer than five minutes before I got severe stomach cramps, my right hand would stiffen into the shape of a credit card holder, my step would quicken and I'd rush out into the street shouting "How much? How much?"

Bombeck has a perfect ear for parody. Her description of the sadistic—and humili-

ating—treatment of television game show contestants, who "run the emotional yo-yo from hysterical to rabid," is precise and devastating. Her readers have no problem recognizing the program Bombeck once described in a column. It was new, she wrote, and called simply "Coronary."

Hang on, Bernice," said the moderator. "Do you know what you have just won?" Bernice shakes her head numbly. "You have won one hundred and twenty-five thousand dollars."

As the band plays "Happy Days Are Here Again," Bernice jumps fifteen feet off the floor and throws her arms around the moderator's neck and begins to weep uncontrollably.

He holds up his hand for silence. "In Italian lira, Bernice. Do you know how much that is in American money? About forty-eight dollars and twelve cents. Too bad, Bernice, but wait! You are going to pick up the lira in an Italian bank. You have won three weeks in Rome!"

Bernice clutches her chest and sways dizzily as the band starts up again. She grabs the moderator's sleeve.

"That's Rome, New York." He grins.

Bernice slumps again, emotionally drained.

"But wait! Look what you'll be wearing to New York." The curtain opens to reveal a four-thousand dollar mink coat. The moderator helps her put it on. Bernice manages a weak smile and wave to the audience.

"Unfortunately, it's not your size. Too bad, Bernice, had it fit you, you would have walked out of here in a four-thousand dollar mink coat with a Swiss bank account for one hundred thousand dollars in the pocket."

Bernice faints dead away on the floor. The moderator bends over her. "You didn't stay conscious, Bernice. Those are the rules, but since you've been a sport, no one goes away empty-handed. For your consolation prize, we have a personalized pace-maker . . . let's hear it for Bernice."

"A lot of people think I write humor," Bombeck observed in one of her books. "But then I know a woman who thinks Marie Osmond and her relatives are depressed. As an observer of the human condition all I do is question it. I rarely find it funny."

Bombeck says she cannot explain the origin of her humor. Once she told an interviewer that "you have to dream to write humor. . . . It's a matter of looking at tragedy and dreaming up some humor in it. That way you survive. If you don't take yourself seriously, it's sure as heck you're not going to take anything else seriously. I always had a philosophy, even when the kids were little. They'd be bleeding and I'd take them to the emergency ward and say, 'Doctor, can this be fixed?' and as long as it could, I'd say, 'O.K., kids, it's no big deal.' That's the kind of person I am. Manic. Very manic."

Bombeck needed a somewhat manic psyche in order to survive a difficult childhood. She was born in Dayton, Ohio, the second child of a city laborer, Cassius Fiste, and his 16-year-old wife, Erma Haines. Her father had a cerebral hemorrhage and died in 1936, and the family was forced by poverty to split up. Erma and her mother went to live with her maternal grandmother, and her half-sister went to live with other relatives. Her perpetually sunny outlook, which she inherited from her mother, enabled the young Erma to weather the traumas, but she says that "stupidity" was a great help. She claims she was completely unaware of the bleakness of her surroundings and just "sloughed it off."

"We were poor, we truly were. I remember at my Dad's funeral, there was a great bustling of activity, and when you look back it was just like they were carting away everything there had been up to that time: the refrigerator left, the car left, all the furniture in the house. We owed for everything."

"My father was lying in the living room—

you know, a home funeral—and it just seemed the house of cards had come down. I was too stupid to realize it, you know. I thought, all these people have come, and there's all this neat food, and we're having a swell time. . . . And [our] whole life was uprooted. We moved in with grandma, and I went to a different school, and everything was changed and weird; and my half-sister left. The whole family fell apart. And looking back, I don't think there was any great sense of sadness about it at all. I think that's probably stupidity, the more I think about it. Really dumb."

As oblivious as Bombeck says she was to the abrupt destruction of her family, her father's death clearly left a scar that still aches, as she demonstrated in a memorable Father's Day column in 1981:

When I was a little kid, a father was like the light in the refrigerator. Every home had one, but no one really knew what either of them did once the door was shut.

My dad left the house every morning and always seemed glad to see everyone at night.

He opened the jar of pickles when no one else could.

He was the only one in the house who wasn't afraid to go in the basement by himself.

He cut himself shaving, but no one kissed it or got excited about it. It was understood that whenever it rained, he got the car and brought it around to the door. When anyone was sick, he went out to get the prescription filled. . . .

I was afraid of everyone else's father, but not my own. Once I made him tea. It was only sugar water, but he sat on a small chair and said it was delicious. He looked very uncomfortable. . . .

Whenever I played house, the mother doll had a lot to do. I never knew what to do with the daddy doll, so I had him say, "I'm going off to work now," and threw him under the bed.

When I was 9 years old, my father didn't get up one morning and go to work. He went to the hospital and died the next day. . . .

I went to my room and felt under the bed for the father doll. When I found him, I dusted him off and put him on my bed.

He never did anything. I didn't know his leaving would hurt so much.

I still don't know why.

The grandmother's home into which Bombeck and her mother moved was in Dayton's decaying Haymarket section, where winos made up a large segment of the population. Bombeck thought it was "a really neat" place to live. "No one in the neighborhood was doing much better than we were," she says with a chuckle. "That's the thing: live in lousy neighborhoods when you're broke. Then you don't notice the contrast."

As early as the eighth grade, Bombeck knew she wanted to be a writer and that what she wanted to write were humorous pieces. She had discovered the works of Benchley, James Thurber, H. Allen Smith, and Max Schulman in the library and devoured them. She cannot explain what drew her to them. "I don't know. You try to explain why you are the way you are and you come up with answers that sound great but don't make too much sense. . . . I always went toward those books and I loved them, I absolutely loved them, and I thought, God, what a thing that would be to just make people laugh, because I was laughing while I was reading. I just thought there was something real magic about that, where they could bring out an emotion which is really sort of hard to get."

Bombeck's mother was not impressed with her daughter's career plans. She thought then—and to some extent still does—that writing was "simple-minded," Bombeck once told an interviewer. Like some other Depression-era parents, Bom-

beck's mother thought Hollywood was the Emerald City and wanted her daughter "to sing and dance my way out of poverty, like Shirley Temple. It didn't matter that I had no talent and my hips were saddle bags. I had to go to dancing school. Mom still isn't impressed by the writing part of my job. But when I go on TV, she's happy. She thinks, 'Erma finally made it in show business.' "

Her mother got a job at the General Motors plant in Dayton, and Bombeck went to a vocational high school, not because she wanted to but because its program enabled her to alternate two weeks of classes with two weeks of work. She needed the money. "It was a deal: my mother bought my winter coats, and I bought the rest of the stuff. I bought the books; I bought the shoes; I bought the clothes; my lunch money, my carfare, all of those things."

Bombeck got a job as a part-time copygirl at the *Dayton Journal-Herald* and wrote a humor column for the school newspaper. A journalism teacher at the school was impressed with her writing and urged her to go to college. She got a night job reading proofs of technical manuals printed for the Wright-Patterson Air Force Base, and with that income, combined with her salary at the paper, she built enough of a nest egg to finance her education at the University of Dayton, which she entered in 1945. She was the only high school graduate in her immediate family and the only one of 28 cousins to go to college.

As a child, Bombeck—then a practicing Protestant—would go with her closest friend to one of Dayton's synagogues on Saturdays and a Catholic church on Sundays for entertainment. They had no money, and religious services were free. At the University of Dayton, a Catholic school, Bombeck found herself drawn to Catholicism for different reasons. "I was very curious, because I could see a deep sense of faith in a lot of these people that didn't seem to look that well on me, what I had. This is not to be critical of the Protestant faith, because for some it works. . . . I needed something real strong; I needed something with rules. I needed something that I could wear with pride and give some service to. . . . So I converted . . . and I've done that with Catholicism."

While she was at college, Bombeck earned money by doing public relations work for the YMCA, writing a column for a department store house organ, and handling a termite control account for a local advertising agency. She also continued her nonremunerative writing.

Bombeck graduated from college in 1949 and returned to the *Journal-Herald* as a reporter, performing the tasks then expected of female cubs: writing obituaries and compiling the radio listings. When she moved up to regular reporting, she discovered that she was not suited to it at all. "I was a terrible reporter," she says with a sorrowful expression. "Terrible, terrible. I couldn't stick to the facts. I was very opinionated about things. I knew there were five *W*'s, but I could only remember two of them. I think they would have fired me, really, if I hadn't moved on to something else."

She switched to feature writing and began a housekeeping column titled "Operation Dustrag," which she has referred to as "sort of a sick 'Heloise.' " "I told people to clean their johns, lock them up, and send the kids to the gas station at the corner," Bombeck recalled once in an interview. Most readers didn't know what to make of it. "In the 1940's, you didn't make fun of domestic chores. Housework was a religious experience!"

Not long after she rejoined the *Journal-Herald*, she married William Bombeck, a sportswriter at the paper who later became a teacher and then a school principal and administrator. During the early days of her marriage, Bombeck was bitterly frustrated by her inability to have children. "Without children, I became a person that even my

best friend was reluctant to tell when she was 'expecting.' I cried for a week," she recalled in a serious 1982 column on the plight of infertile couples.

I went through a who-cares period and lashed out with, "Thank God it's you and not me."

I wanted to physically hurt any woman who complained she had a bad day around the kids. I did physically hurt anyone who said, "How come you don't have kids? Don't you want them?"

I vacillated between grabbing every baby to my breast and shoving them away and saying, "You're a mess. Go to your mother."

Unless you have experienced the emptiness, there is no describing the pain. Unless you have held a baby and despaired at having to give it back, you cannot possibly know what it is like.

Finally, Bombeck became pregnant and quit the paper to give birth to her daughter Betsy in 1953. Then began a decade in which she had her two sons, Andrew in 1955 and Matthew in 1959, and "didn't do anything except blow up sterilizers" as a full-time mother and housewife. By 1964 she was bored and depressed.

She sat forlornly by the kitchen window, read articles about successful career women, and came to the conclusion that she did not feel fulfilled "cleaning chrome faucets with a toothbrush." At 37, Bombeck has written, she was "too old for a paper route, too young for Social Security, and too tired for an affair." So she decided to try newspaper work again.

She typed some sample humor columns about what she called "the utility room beat," titled them "At Wit's End," and convinced the *Kettering-Oakwood Times*, a small weekly in suburban Dayton, to pay her the munificent sum of three dollars a week for the privilege of publishing them. Within a year the *Journal-Herald* rehired her as a columnist, and in an astonishingly short time—only a matter of weeks—the Newsday Syndicate began distributing her columns nationally.

Bombeck's early columns dealt almost exclusively with subjects that housewives and mothers—people who she thought deserved a better press—could readily appreciate. There was a stand-up comedian's quality to much of her work, just one wisecrack after another: "My second favorite household chore is ironing. My first being hitting my head on the top bunk bed until I faint." "If [the oven] won't catch fire today, clean it tomorrow." "No one knows what her life expectancy is, but I have a horror of leaving this world and not having anyone in the entire family know how to replace a toilet tissue spindle."

"I've always worried a lot and frankly I'm good at it. . . . I worry about getting into the Guinness Book of World Records under 'Pregnancy: Oldest Recorded Birth.' I worry what the dog thinks when he sees me coming out of the shower, that one of my children will marry an Eskimo who will set me adrift on an iceberg when I can no longer feed myself. . . ."

But there also was a cutting edge to the humor, especially when she wrote about her children, the frustrations she felt about them, and, on occasion, how she thought they felt about her:

I will never understand children. I never pretended to. I meet mothers all the time who make resolutions to themselves. 'I'm going to develop patience with my children and go out of my way to show them I am interested in them and what they do. I am going to understand my children.' These women wind up making rag rugs, using blunt scissors.

I firmly believe kids don't want your understanding. They want your trust, your compassion, your blinding love and your car keys, but you try to understand

them and you're in big trouble. To me, they remain life's great mysteries.

I have never understood, for example, how come a child can climb up on a roof, scale the TV antenna and rescue the cat . . . yet cannot walk down the hallway without grabbing both walls with his grubby hands for balance.

Or how come a child can eat yellow snow, kiss the dog on the lips, chew gum that he found in the ashtray, put his mouth over a muddy garden hose . . . and refuse to drink from a glass his brother has just used. . . .

On the other hand, Bombeck gave her readers a glimpse at a school paper that one of her sons was writing entitled "Things My Mother Taught Me":

LOGIC
If you fall off your bicycle and break your neck, you can't go to the store with me.

MEDICINE
If you don't stop crossing your eyes, they are going to freeze that way. There is no cure, no telethon, and no research program being funded at the moment for frozen eyes.

ESP
Put your sweater on. Don't you think *I* know *you're* cold? . . .

CHALLENGE
Where is your sister and don't talk with food in your mouth.
Will you answer me?!

HAPPINESS
You are going to have a good time on this vacation if we have to break every bone in your body.

HUMOR
When the lawn mower cuts off your toes, don't come running to me.

She also wrote, in appropriately exaggerated fashion, about the feelings of inadequacy, boredom, and isolation felt by many women, not just the housewives and mothers:

Women were in a rut. At parties all the women retired to the living room to relive their birth pains and exchange tuna recipes while the men hovered around the kitchen and attacked the big stuff like strikes, racial differences, and wars. . . .

"The trouble with you," said my husband, "is you're just too cute for words. Coming over and grabbing my sleeve and insisting we leave this deathly dull group!"

"So I forgot we were the host and hostess. It's a perfectly natural mistake."

"You ought to get out more. Do something to make your day important. Give you something to talk about in the evening."

He had a point. What did I do all day? The only thing that had happened was I used the wrong aerosol can for my deodorant and I didn't have to worry about clogged up nasal passages in my armpits for twenty-four hours. No wonder he never talked to me. . . .

The rapid growth of her column's popularity and the burgeoning of her other projects—a regular column in *Good Housekeeping* and freelance articles in numerous other publications; her television appearances and lectures; even a record album entitled "The Family That Plays Together . . . Gets on Each Other's Nerves"—showed that Bombeck was reaching an audience that was as starved for attention as the women who were consigned to the living room to exchange tuna recipes.

"I think a lot of people thought that what I was writing about was maybe one woman who was sitting out there in the suburbs and she felt trapped and isolated and all those things, when in fact the Junior League people were feeling the same things; the women in New York in fine apartments were feeling

the same things; farm women were feeling the same things. It wasn't geographic, and it had nothing to do with economics. It's the way women feel, period."

The truth underlying Bombeck's humor—what makes it so funny and "real, real personal"—can be painful, especially to some of the subjects who inspired it. She used to say that neither her husband nor her children resented having their peccadillos publicized in her columns. They all have fine senses of humor, she would say, and they knew that the columns were "semifictional."

"I always knew there were limitations beyond which I would not venture," Bombeck told an interviewer in 1978. "I've never given their names, never said 'Little Betsy did this' or 'Matt did that.' I would never invade their privacy, never discuss their personal lives, their dating, finances, problems. I would never do that."

Bombeck now acknowledges that she was a little naive in believing that the "semifictional" columns about her family had no effect on her children, however good-humored they may be or proud of their mother's accomplishments. "I would amend that today," she says. "I'm sure I believed it when I said it. But . . . little things are beginning to come out. . . . And the reason I say that is because I begin to get it from . . . people who have said to me: 'I saw your son and I said to him, "Bombeck? Is your mother Erma?" And they said, "Yeah," like they really didn't want to go into that.' I'm kidding myself, I think, if I believe that kids grow up with an unusual name like Bombeck, plus all of the stuff that's been written about me, and [don't] have some feeling that they've got something to overcome here. I've taken a little bit of them away from them. I have."

Bombeck has no doubts, however, about her husband's ability to handle the reflected notoriety he receives from appearing in her writing. Her first column, in fact, dealt with his alleged reaction to her request that he put up Christmas lights. She wrote that all he did was replace the 40-watt porch light with a 60-watt bulb.

"Our relationship is a give-and-take thing," Bombeck says. "We are very blessed. We have been able to separate one from another, the fiction from the facts. That's not easy to do. I'm telling you the truth. We have never had one confrontation about 'Did you write this?' None of that. He knows what I do, and he understands what I do."

For many years, Bill Bombeck maintained his own career as an educator, and his celebrated wife bristled at any suggestion that her considerably higher income, which easily tops a half-million dollars annually, might cause friction between them. "I am overpaid and he is underpaid," she told an interviewer in 1978. "I equate it with calling in a babysitter. You're saying, 'I'm entrusting you now with my children. I went through 26 hours of labor with this kid, I have put $56,000 worth of vitamins in him, and now I'll pay you 50 cents an hour.' It doesn't make sense. If it's such a precious commodity to you, then why are you trusting it to a sophomore in tennis shoes? It is out of balance."

Her husband retired a few years ago and now manages "all of the investments and the business stuff, and keeps us out of the slammer with the IRS," Bombeck says. She thinks his is the sharpest sense of humor in the Bombeck family, a droll counterpoint to her zippy one-liners.

If a couple still can laugh together after decades of marriage, Bombeck once said, "they've either got something good going or they're demented. Please don't ask me to decide which."

As her column grew in popularity and became the object of fierce bidding from several syndicates (Field Enterprises won); as her books, now numbering seven, were purchased eagerly; and as her activities and affluence grew, Bombeck resisted the temp-

tation to become a housewife emeritus. She continued to do the shopping, cleaning, laundry, and ironing that previously had driven her to distraction. It not only helped her to keep in touch with her readers but actually served as a sort of safety valve, a way to unwind after a day at the typewriter. She often was photographed lugging hampers of clothes and wielding a plunger over a clogged sink. It was no act.

In 1971, however, the Bombecks moved from a 30-acre farm in Bellbrooke, Ohio, ten miles south of Dayton, to Paradise Valley, Arizona, a resort community outside of Phoenix, and as her children grew up and moved away, Bombeck gradually abandoned housewifery. Ironically, cooking, the only household chore she used to do indifferently—"I thought it was a fad," she once said—she now really enjoys and pursues as a hobby.

"I don't do as much laundry as I once did because I don't have any kids at home anymore, and my readers know that. I'm not going to snow them. The *National Enquirer* tried to come out with a thing that was bursting the bubble. There are no illusions about me. I have made a lot of money with what I do. I've never made any secret of it. They [the readers] are the people who did it for me, and if they don't like the product now, I can't help it. But they have bought my books, they've been very supportive, and they've put a lot of money into my till, and I really appreciate it. I got my kids' teeth fixed and that was wonderful. And I don't think they blame me for that."

In accordance with her policy of keeping politics out of her column, Bombeck's pieces of the late 1960s and 1970s contained few direct references to the Vietnam War, racial strife, Watergate, the women's movement, or any of the other traumas and changes of the period. Although she is a self-described "liberal," Bombeck's infrequent political statements in print fluctuate between Yankee Doodle Dandyism and despair over the nation's loss of trust in its institutions. In a late 1960s column, she said she wanted each of her children to grow up to be "a cornball, a real, honest-to-God, flag-waving cornball, who, if you must march, will tell people what you are for, not what you are against."

Please cry when school children sing "The Battle Hymn of the Republic," when you see a picture of the Berlin Wall, when you see the American flag on the silver suit of an astronaut. . . . It just seems that during the last few years the flag has become less symbolic to people. . . . Have some feeling for it and for what it stands for. Wear it on you as big as a conventioneer's badge.

Bombeck was hardly unaware, however, of the things that cast shadows on the flag, and by the early 1970s she felt moved to write:

We scream censorship when there is murder committed before our children's eyes on the tube. We can endure it when it appears on the six o'clock news with a dateline: Vietnam. My children in their short span on earth have seen Watts in flames, mothers with clubs protesting [integration in] schools, college students slain by national guardsmen, mass slaughter in California, and political conventions that defy anything they have seen on a movie screen. . . . I challenge you to protect a generation from violence that has seen the horrors of Kent, Dallas and Attica.

Sitting on a sofa in the living room of her home, Bombeck sighs and says: "I think all I'm talking about are basic values. We're 'Midwest'—I don't know what that means except the Fourth of July is a big deal—but I like to think [my children] would have basic values. . . . I do seem to go back and forth [between optimism and pessimism]. It depends on what kind of mood I'm in. I write as honest as I can, depending on how I feel that day. I'm afraid it shows."

While Bombeck still cheerily accepts the title *Life* magazine bestowed on her in 1971, "Socrates of the ironing board," by the dawn of the 1980s her ability to voice the concerns of millions of readers—whether they were "Midwest" or not—prompted *Newsweek* to ask her to write on the sober topic "Will America Regain Its Trust?"

It hasn't happened yet, but it's inevitable.

One night, Sandy Duncan will lean over the footlights of a Broadway theater and in the childlike voice of Peter Pan ask, "Will everyone who believes in Tinker Bell clap your hands?" And the theater will resound with silence. The silence will record the last Bastille of blind faith in America.

Who knows what triggered it? Maybe it began when Washington introduced a new dance to the nation, the evasion shuffle. (One step forward, two steps back, swing around the truth and change stories.) Whatever it was, the skepticism and mistrust filtered down into every part of our lives. . . .

Woman no longer trusted her male counterpart to vote on her behalf or act in her best interests. She began to wonder why she was 50 percent a partner in the marriage and only 10 percent at the divorce. By the end of this decade, there is virtually no one who is beyond question or suspicion.

We were all raised on trust. It was considered one of the better virtues. But it lulled us into apathy and down the path of blind acceptance. It has become a luxury we can no longer afford. Trust is what led 900 Americans in a little commune in Jonestown, Guyana, to toss down punch laced with cyanide. Trust is what struck horror in the town of Harrisburg, Pa., when Three Mile Island sprung a leak. Trust is what put a Chevy engine in an Oldsmobile body.

Out of this decade has emerged a new American who is questioning, skeptical and challenging. If you invited him down the Yellow Brick Road, he'd want to know who the contractor was, what the stress factor is and what is at the end of it before he sets foot on it.

Oh, we still have a few national institutions of trust left . . . Lawrence Welk, Walter Cronkite, Roy Rogers, penicillin, Mary Tyler Moore, Price Waterhouse and hot chicken soup. But everything is under scrutiny, including our own existence.

The question we face in the 1980's is not whom will America trust again, but more important . . . why?

Bombeck believes that a side-effect of the women's movement has been the expansion of her audience. With the demise of "women's pages" in newspapers and the transfer of her column to the features section—and sometimes the comics page—she has gained many male readers.

"Men have the security now to read more about women and find out who is this woman I'm living with, what is she feeling and why is she ready to walk, why is she so unhappy," Bombeck says. "I think women are doing the same thing. I think women are beginning to be interested in sports. The old football jokes don't play quite as well as they used to."

After 11 years in a nine-room, tile-roofed adobe home with a garden, swimming pool, and tennis court—all surrounded by a high wall, the Bombecks moved in 1982 to a half-million-dollar Mexican-style ranch home which they built on a mountaintop nearby. "You either clean a place or you buy another one," Bombeck says.

Now she has a "real office," not the partially converted garage in which she used to work, and a view of the mud-brown mountains that surround her plush desert community, which is a tribute to the triumph of air conditioning. The new home has neither a swimming pool nor a tennis court, since those were primarily for her children and Bombeck rarely used them.

Her mother lives not far away in Sun City, Arizona, and they see each other often. There is an instant rapport between them and a common sense of the absurd. "My Mom's only 16 years older than I am, so we're like sisters. . . . We're so close that it's hard to tell any more if she's taking from me or I'm taking from her."

Bombeck is a disciplined writer who follows a rigorous schedule. In addition to her three weekly columns, she must write two scripts each week for "Good Morning America" and work on her latest book. She has given up the lecture circuit but still delivers "benefit" speeches on behalf of battered wives, displaced homemakers, and similar causes. She has a part-time secretary who puts in 12 hours a week answering her mail.

Bombeck gets up at six every morning and drives her Mercedes to a fitness center a few miles away for an aerobics class. After exercising there for an hour while her husband is out jogging (an activity she considers ridiculous), she meets him at home for breakfast. An hour later, Bombeck hits the typewriter.

"I treat this like a job. I'm at my desk at nine o'clock, and I start to write either columns or scripts or book, whatever day it is, and I work until lunch, take 30 minutes off and go back and hit it until about five o'clock, and then I go out and shut it off. Everything shuts off. I don't think about it any more, I don't do it any more. I start cooking and then I'm a housewife. I'm a person. I do that five days, sometimes six days a week. I usually take Sundays off and do something. I like to needlepoint and stuff, but I don't get a lot of time off to play."

Bombeck thinks fast and writes on a typewriter, rewriting furiously and often. She purposely breaks down big words and writes as simply as she can "to make sure that everyone gets it."

"Ninety percent of the work is finding a topic that has common ground with the reader," she once explained, "and sometimes . . . you feel you've hit them all. Certain things are basic: husbands, rotten kids, diets, housework, styles. There are a million columns you can do on every one of those topics, but you have to have the new angle to hitch them to. But you do it. I've written a humor column immediately after attending a funeral. I've been able to write in the hospital with my kidneys driving me right up the wall. When I hurt, I don't cry. I write 450 words. They say you can't force humor. Well, you can. Sometimes it *sounds* forced. I'm the first to admit my shortcomings."

One of Bombeck's kinder critics, an editor of the *New York Times Book Review*, once observed: "There is truth in the best of her humor, as well as sanity; what it lacks is the lift and play of language. Sometimes she serves up a meat loaf extended with empty gags; even home cooking can pall, if not relieved by the occasional soufflé."

What Bombeck finds most difficult is to change gears and go from writing the column to doing the television scripts to drafting a book. "One of the things that I have trouble with—and it's a little unique with me—is that I do different mediums. I do a column, which should be short and terse and written very tight to fill my space, to establish what I'm going to talk about, to get in and get out. . . . After awhile you begin to think in 450 words. It's a page and a half, wide margins, and by the time you reach a certain point, you think, I'm going to wind it up now. I'm getting to the middle of the page and that's it.

". . . Then I do the things for 'Good Morning, America,' [with which] you can sort of be a little more Andy Rooney-ish, and you can write asides for yourself; you can relax a little bit; you can use a few more words, and you get a little more conversational with it.

"Then the third type, I turn another switch, and when I work on the book . . . I've got to remember the five adjectives that I know and use them, and then start expanding and filling in a bit more. Sometimes it's difficult for me to go from the column, the newspaper aspect, to the other two mediums. It's hard."

On a "bad day" it will take Bombeck "a day and a half" to write her column. On a "good day" she can do it in a few hours. "A 'good day' meaning I know what the idea is, I know what approach I'm going to take with it, and I've got a couple of funny lines going for it to begin with. It's an hilarious situation. 'Bad day,' I have no idea what I'm doing or how I can make it fit. The process is longer than people ever know."

Bombeck will set aside a full day to tape eight of her television commentaries—a full month's worth. Many of them simply are recorded in her home, but sometimes she goes "on location" to tape them. She readily admits to "some recycling" of her column material in her TV pieces but says that because her written work is fairly topical, most of it would be dated by the time it got on television.

"I'll tell you what I do steal from myself: I will steal an idea and I'll revamp it and redo it and I'll put some visuals to it, and that's understood [at ABC]. They knew that when they got me eight years ago."

Curiously, every other attempt Bombeck has made to transfer her material—but not herself—to television has been a disaster. Although her first three books sold briskly, her fourth book, *The Grass Is Always Greener over the Septic Tank*, was the runaway best-seller of 1976 and seemed to beg for adaptation to the tiny screen. CBS planned to develop it into a situation comedy series and in October 1978 aired a two-hour special based on it starring Carol Burnett, Bombeck's own choice for the lead. It was torn to shreds by the critics, and CBS took the advice of one of them "to mow *Grass* down at this early stage."

In 1981, ABC hired Bombeck to write a situation comedy called "Maggie," about a happily married suburban housewife. It received some mildly favorable reviews but was dismissed by most critics—and ignored by most viewers—as a dreadful piece of pap from the 1950s school of sitcom. It became the first new network program to be axed that season. "Twenty-three minutes of Bombeck one-liners apparently was a little much, even for ABC," observed the *Washington Post*.

Bombeck stoically accepts responsibility for the flop but thinks "Maggie" might have survived if she had followed her original instincts about it instead of the advice of the network experts. "I felt strongly . . . that you can't present a housewife and a mother without the irreverence. I mean, I always wanted to do the dark side of 'Donna Reed.' The way mine turned out, she was pitiful. And what it is is the mentality of the people in television, who want to play it so safe. They say, 'Hey, don't yell at the kids, people will think she doesn't like them; no, don't let her argue with her husband in the first segment. Put it maybe four segments down. Then they know that there's love,' you know.

"No-o-o, no-o-o, no-o-o. That doesn't mean any less love. They didn't understand what people are about. The irreverence in the column is one of the things that's made it. You *dare* to say that children are less than a religious experience in this life. You *dare* to say that your husband and you have never had this meaningful conversation in your entire life and have no intention of having it. And you *dare* to say some of these things because that's what people really need to hear. . . .

"[But] I had enough clout that I could have just held out and said, 'No, no, no, this is the way it's going to be or not at all.' But

this is a whole different medium. It was very strange to me and I was not used to it. I did not mind writing by committee, that wasn't a problem. In fact, it was fun. I worked with good people. The problem was their attitude. That's what I had control over and that's what I should have stopped. My fault."

Bombeck has no regrets, however, about giving up the exhausting weekly commute between Phoenix and Los Angeles and the enforced separation from her husband. She would fly to California Sunday nights and live in a rented apartment all week. She would get up at 5:00 A.M., write her column, and then go to the studio to work on TV scripts all day. "It was just miserable. . . . We'd never been apart. I personally hated it."

ABC offered her another shot at a series, but Bombeck recoiled at the thought. The schedule she keeps now is bad enough and leaves little time for any social life. When she lived in Ohio, Bombeck had a large circle of friends, women she had gotten to know before writing began to rule her life. Now she has few friends and sees them only rarely. She has complained about it for years. "I'm one-dimensional," she said in a 1978 interview. "I just sit here and work and work and work and I just hate that. . . . I've become a loner and it's got to stop."

It hasn't. "I just don't have time," she says wearily. "I love association with women. It's good and it's healthy for me, and it's a great way of complaining and getting it all out . . . I think relationships like that are great. I have lunch occasionally with the girlfriends that I have, but I treat them shamefully: sometimes I don't see them for six months at a time. I get myself loaded down, and I hate myself for it. I cut out the lecturing 'cause that was killing me, but still just keeping up is a problem. And I don't like to hurt people's feelings. . . . I still don't have any social life."

A small compensation for the loss of regular friends, Bombeck finds, has been the opportunity she now has to "brush elbows with the most fascinating people, people that if you weren't at this point you would just read about and want to meet," such as Art Buchwald, Judith Guest, Alistair Cooke, Anne Morrow Lindbergh, and Johnny Carson. After nearly two decades of prominence, Bombeck says she still is "astounded" at the popularity of her column and how it somehow qualifies her to be in the company of well-known people.

Bombeck also remains astounded by—but resigned to—the "sensitivity" of readers who find things in her columns she never intended. Some people not only can't take a joke, they don't even understand it. When Bombeck began her column, some editors actually objected to her using the words *bosom* and *bathroom* in her pieces, and a reader accused her of being sacrilegious because she once wrote that one of her sons was such a picky eater that he wouldn't have touched a thing at the Last Supper.

"The sensitivity just makes you gag," Bombeck says, "and you realize how many people you're writing for out there and what you're stepping into when they read [the column]. . . . Everyone gets a different perspective when they read it. That's what's scary."

Bombeck is also scared—and worried—about the future of newspapers. "I worry about it a whole lot. I'm not talking about tomorrow or next week. I'm talking about down the road. I really have some concern about the reading habits of people, and it's with a sadness . . . , not because that's how I make my living. I'll probably be dead and gone by the time all of this transpires.

"I have some concern . . . about the inertia, this lack of anything that people have to do any more. I mean, you don't even have to use your mind to tell what time it is. You push a button. . . . You're so passive. You *watch* stuff, you *watch* life, and this is driving me crazy. I feel like I'm out of sync with

the whole world. Really, I'm 55 and I feel like I don't *belong* to this," she says, making a sweeping gesture with her right arm to encompass the passive, timid new world.

"I don't have a computer. I don't even want a word processor. My mind is going so stagnant now that if I don't search for words and think, what's going to happen? I think newspapers have a very tough way to go. . . . Maybe all people want are the headlines. Maybe they only want to know what—I hate this expression—'the bottom line is.' I don't know. But it's just not the direction I want to be going in."

Bombeck thinks many other women don't want to go in that direction either. The wonders of computer terminals that will allow women to stay at home to shop, make bank deposits and withdrawals, teach their children, attend religious services, and plan menus threaten to turn them into domestic derelicts, she wrote in a 1982 column.

Where is it written that women want to spend more time at home? No one has been listening. It has taken us 200 years to get out of the house and now they want to put us back there.

Oh sure, talking chips are to be installed in our oven, range, refrigerator, dryer and dishwasher so we can establish some kind of rapport, but I did not come this far to sit around talking to my appliances. I already did that. . . .

Experts hammer on how much gas and energy we'll save by having everything at home. C'mon, I watch animal documentaries. Rats have no reason to lie. In some experiments they were jammed in an area with wall-to-wall rats every minute of the day. They became irritable and violent toward one another and could not reproduce.

One out of three reasons for computerized living is just not enough.

Bombeck has no immediate plans to reduce her weekly work load or retire, although she firmly declares her intention to do so every week. "I announce on Monday: 'I'm retiring. This is it. I don't need this. I'm not going to do this anymore.' I don't know. Every time a contract comes around I say I'm going to cut back . . . , and I don't know what keeps me going except there are a lot of things I haven't said yet, or another idea will come up. I suppose I'm a mild workaholic. I think I am because just when I think, No more, I'm not going to do this, then something will come up and I'll say, Oh, that sounds wonderful.

"So I can still get excited about things. And when you're still getting excited about something you've done for 20 years, then I don't think it's time to quit yet."

It is frustrating to Bombeck, who takes humor so seriously, that her sober pieces— the ones on the plight of infertile couples, the press's exploitation of the private grief of accident or crime victims, the challenges faced by mothers of handicapped children— are the columns that inevitably prompt the most mail from readers.

"With humor, people don't usually write to say 'I laughed,' 'My stitches came out,' or 'I cried,' or whatever. But they seem to react to something serious that touches them deep down inside. I just feel sometimes that humor is the bastard of the industry because it seems so easy and it's taken for granted. You know, you put all this time in on something that people will laugh at and say 'Oh, that is funny,' but you don't get the reaction like the serious stuff [does]. And the serious ones aren't that difficult to write, not nearly as hard as the humorous ones."

Hers is the lament of all comedians, whether in print or on stage, who know that the most difficult artistic task is not to make an audience cry but to make it laugh. It is the desire to achieve that "illusive bit of mystery that bubbles out of control for no apparent reason," as Bombeck once described laughter, that is the fuel that drives her engine.

"It's got to be an ego trip—and a challenge—to see how many people you can scoop in with it, how universal you can get, to how many people one column will play. I think that's the real challenge of getting people to laugh. You can write a column that teenagers are going to kill themselves over, or you can write one that the housewife will identify with and find memorable . . . , but you're trying to sweep 'em all in there. You're trying to get as many readers for that newspaper as you possible can."

It isn't enough, of course, to sweep in all those readers only once. The greatest challenge—which Bombeck has met—is to keep them. Bombeck does not believe that she has any special power or influence over her readers. "I give people more credit than that," she says. "My dream reader . . . is not one I can influence or manipulate [but] the one who will pick me up someday and maybe say, 'Oh, Bombeck, that's crap and you know it and I don't agree with you at *all*, I mean not one bit,' *but* will come back to me another time and read what I have to say that time. Don't write me off just because you disagree with something I say. . . . At least get an exchange of ideas."

And, with luck, a few laughs, too.

Jimmy Breslin

On the Sidewalks of New York

ostello's is a venerable pub on Manhattan's East Side that looks like a set decorator's conception of the favorite after-hours haunt of New York newspapermen. It is dark at midday despite a large window facing the street. It has a pressed-tin ceiling and a mammoth bar festooned with dusty mementoes of current and former patrons: press passes, cartoons, book jackets, a broken shillelagh. It has signed drawings by the late Walt Kelly, creator of "Pogo," and Charles Addams, the *New Yorker*'s master of the macabre. Two small, slightly cramped dining areas seem an afterthought, but the menu is respectable and the decor is entertaining. The wall of one section is covered with color caricatures painted by local newspaper cartoonists, while the other section is decorated with lovingly preserved doodles drawn on the wall decades ago by James Thurber. An ancient dumpling of a German named Herbie, celebrated as "the world's worst waiter," shuffles past the booths and tables, inquiring in a guttural mumble: "Vot do you vunt?"

Enter stage left: Mr. Jimmy (Himself) Breslin. As he rushes in, an untied necktie flaps around his shoulders, a rumpled, dark blue raincoat seems a pace or two behind him, and he offers a cheery salutation to the Greek chorus of bartenders and regulars who give him irreverent greetings. "Shad-

dap! Shaddap! Shaddap!" Breslin shouts as he whirls through the bar, tosses his coat on a hanger, yells at Herbie to bring him some coffee, and settles into a booth beneath a half-dozen samples of Thurber's graffiti.

At 54, Breslin looks trimmer and a bit more haggard than he appears in the grinning mug shot that accompanies his column. He has largely given up heavy boozing, is a frequent and energetic swimmer at the YMCA, and his hefty gut has evaporated in proportion to his abstinence and exercise. He has thick, dark eyebrows set in a permanent scowl but an engaging, almost boyish smile. His hair, once jet black and curly, still is unruly, but now steel gray is the predominant color. He runs his fingers through it constantly and rubs his eyes repeatedly with the heels of his palms. He quickly accepts the offer of a cigar and a light, shrouds himself in white smoke and converses in purple language.

Author Ronald Steel's observation regarding a renowned New York reporter of an earlier era, Herbert Bayard Swope, fits Breslin: he is "the kind of journalist that newspaper dramas are written about: a flamboyant, self-publicizing . . . promoter with a keen instinct for the news." Breslin is that, to be sure, but also much more. Now at the *New York Daily News* and syndicated in some 60 newspapers, he is a superb writer, an accomplished reporter, a provocative novelist, and a columnist who, while not

inventing a new genre as some have contended (and Breslin denies), has produced
such compelling work that a generation of
urban journalists has been influenced by
him.

Breslin has also been accused of inventing
himself. He is, some detractors contend,
"the tough-guy-with-the-heart-of-schmalz
bard of the little man and the big celeb"; a
"male sob-sister"; a phony "street-smart
tribune of the Queens working class" who
hates unions, crosses picket lines, and "is
an elitist who identifies with power and
ownership." He loves to puncture others'
pretensions with malicious jibes but hates to
be on the receiving end of needling pot
shots.

As a counterpoint to the boasts about his
abilities as a reporter and writer, Breslin
enjoys telling interviewers that he is "an
unlettered bum" who has read few books
and took five years to wade through high
school without ever obtaining a diploma.
Despite this small gap in Breslin's secondary education, a friendly basketball coach
somehow got him admitted as a student at
Long Island University, since the *Long
Island Press,* the first newspaper he worked
for, "only wanted college guys."

"So I went there and took a few courses
[and] now the Long Island University
claims I graduated from there!" Breslin
exclaims, rolling his brown eyes upward
and chuckling. "I mean, you could look it
up—I didn't take but four courses. They
want to list me as an *a-lum-nus,* whatever
you call it. They want my name on letter-
heads. I mean, it's a fucking gag. . . . I
don't know what I took."

Perhaps. Breslin's old friends James G.
Bellows and Richard C. Wald once wrote
that facts about his education "are hazy
because he lies so much about it," and he
himself has written that "reminiscences are
to be enjoyed, not authenticated." If he were
as uneducated, uncultured, and illiterate as
he claims, it would have required the kind

of miracle the nuns used to tell him about in
elementary school for him to have written
from London on the day Winston Churchill
died:

The rest of London was quiet and
empty in the wet Sunday morning. Lord
Nelson stood on his spire, high over the
black lions and water fountains of Tra-
falgar Square. The Duke of Wellington
glared down at the taxicabs and delivery
wagons moving around his plaza. Queen
Victoria sat grandly on her throne, surrounded by angels, her back turned on
Buckingham Palace. The water dripped
from Gladstone, who was stationed by
Saint Clement Danes Church. And at
8:05 A.M., on January 24, 1965, in the
rear first-floor bedroom of No. 28 Hyde
Park Gate, the old man in the green bed
jacket died with the curtains drawn
and a lamp turned on and he became
England's last great statue.

Sir Winston Spencer Churchill, who
saved his nation; saved, perhaps, the
entire English-speaking world, stepped
into history with its scrolls and statues,
and he will be the last who ever will do it
as he did because the world never again
can survive the things that had to be
done in the years he lived.

He died wordlessly. He was a man who
put deep brass and powerful strings into
words, and then built them up to a drum
roll to reach out and grab people and
shake them by the shoulders and in
their hearts. But he had not uttered a
word for ten days when he lay dying in a
coma, while his heart throbbed and
struggled to throw it off. . . .

Such is not Breslin's usual subject matter,
and his style more often is considerably less
lyrical. His regular beat is New York, a city
he still loves passionately despite the growing decay, inequities, and racism he finds
there; and increasingly the people he writes
about are the homeless, the unemployed, or
the troubled, not the colorful, famous, or

powerful who filled his columns 15 or 20 years ago.

But when he first confronts an interviewer, Breslin still projects the image of one of his own early characters: a sloppy, uncouth slob; an inveterate barfly (who nonetheless can go on the wagon cold in order to trim a few pounds from his bulky, five-feet, nine-inch frame); a writer whose style miraculously contains "a touch of Runyon, a touch of Hemingway, and a touch of the poet," as *Newsweek* put it 20 years ago in a description that Breslin adores.

Why, one wonders, if Breslin has the intelligence and sensitivity that his best writing suggests, does he play the gruff, hard-boiled braggart so relentlessly? Is it an act? "It isn't an act," he insists, shifting in his seat a bit and puffing on his cigar. "I don't know. . . . There's a way you talk on the streets, and a way you talk on a typewriter. . . .

"You get very tired of the strictness of writing," he says with a sheepish grin. "I do books; I'm doin' a novel, and I'm writing a column at the same time, right? That's a long time to have the way you think in words in a strait jacket, of trying to be as proper as possible. And when you have three drinks at the bar, then you say 'Fuck it,' it's a relief; you talk any way. . . .

"My life . . . is an open book. It's on the page. So anything you do after that at a bar is sheer fun. A little promotion, a little publicity. But I mean your essential character and your worth is on paper. Nobody has to say, 'What did you do yesterday?' It's there. I don't have to explain how I made my living yesterday. But I can tell some lies at the bar. That's fun. It's bullshit. Anyway, it's a dreary, fucking world. What do you want me to be, like a fuck in a bank who's playin' with other people's money all day?"

The way Breslin talks on the street—or in a bar—gives the impression that he was raised by a stevedore rather than by a mother who worked as a high school English teacher and social worker. Of his father, James Sr., he speaks reluctantly and then with smoldering eyes and bitterness. "He ran away when I was seven. I never saw him after that. He was a piano player. He died in Florida around 1975. There was a piece in the *Miami Herald* that said he died in a nursing home with a copy of the *The Gang That Couldn't Shoot Straight* [perhaps Breslin's most popular book]. I didn't even know he was there or dying or anything else, and they had a big fucking headline: 'Rich Writer's Father Dies Penniless.' I have a copy. I hadn't seen him since I was seven years old, the dirty son of a bitch. They were going to put him in potter's field till finally somebody got ahold of me and I got somebody to take care of it."

Breslin has written that most of the New York Irish have to go back three generations or more before they find a forebear who actually was born in Ireland. Breslin himself is a second-generation American. For many of a similar lineage being Irish "is more a toy than a reality. . . . A drink, a couple of wooden sayings, and a great personal pride, bordering on the hysterical, in being Irish. The bloodlines were present. But they were being thinned by time," he wrote in his novel *World Without End, Amen.*

Somehow undiluted in Breslin's Irish bloodlines was the love of words that he thinks is indigenous to the breed. It survived not only the indifference of his family but also the hostility of those who sought clumsily to educate him. In *World Without End, Amen*, Breslin described how the tentative flowering of a literary imagination in the mind of the main character, a bigoted New York cop named Dermot Davey, was crushed by insensitive teachers when he was in the seventh grade. Instead of dutifully writing a composition "of the 'My Trip to the Planetarium' type," Davey decides to write about an old, one-legged man who worked at the stables at Jamaica Race Track in Queens.

[Dermot] couldn't write fast enough to keep up with the things he wanted to put down. After a while his hand started to hurt because he was gripping the pen so hard. When he finished, he took the composition up and put it on the Sister's desk. He slid it right in front of her and stood waiting.

"Well," she said. She began reading. When she finished the second side, she told Dermot to take it to Sister Rita, the eighth-grade teacher. He ran it down the hall to Sister Rita's room. Usually he was nervous about opening the door and walking into another class, the whole room always looked at you, but this time he couldn't wait to get the composition onto Sister Rita's desk.

She took it and read the one side so quickly he couldn't understand how anybody could be that fast, and when she turned it over and only glanced at the second side, and when he saw she wasn't reading, the bottom fell out of him.

"Well," she said.

"Yes, Sister."

"Do you know why Sister had you bring this up to me?"

"No, Sister."

"Well. Come over here. Look at this handwriting. Just look at this handwriting. Do you call this penmanship?"

Breslin nods his head and mumbles assent when asked if that incident actually was drawn from his own boyhood. "Nobody paid that much attention to me because those were tough years, tough personally on the adults, so nobody paid attention to the kids too much. Certainly nobody helped me very much. I had one Aunt Harriet who helped me a little bit with the writing, but that's about all. I staggered through high school, did very poorly, failed everything, and went to work at the *Long Island Press,* and that's how I did it, really. A lot of people there helped me. . . . I wanted to work on newspapers. That's all I ever wanted to do."

From the now-defunct *Press,* then the flagship of the giant Newhouse chain, Breslin went to the *Boston Globe,* where he spent six months as a copyreader whom "nobody even remembers," then latched onto a position as a feature writer for Scripps-Howard's Newspaper Enterprise Association (NEA) Service, used by the *New York World-Telegram* and other Scripps-Howard newspapers. From there he went to Hearst's *New York Journal-American,* a paper whose readers, he later said, "couldn't even believe the weather report." He covered practically everything but showed a special flair for sports.

His "servitude" for Newhouse, Scripps-Howard, and Hearst was, he once said, hard time in "the Sing Sing, Leavenworth and Folsom of American journalism." He was poorly paid, always in debt, and frustrated. He married Rosemary Dattolico on the day after Christmas in 1954, and as the number of their children grew (eventually reaching six), Breslin turned in desperation to freelance writing in order to increase his earnings.

He quit the *Journal-American* in 1960 and concentrated full-time on free-lancing, by far the toughest and traditionally the least remunerative branch of journalism. But he was a hustler, and he was good. Within three years he had written one book, an affectionate biography of James "Sunny Jim" Fitzsimmons, the legendary horse trainer, and over one hundred magazine pieces, mostly on sports. His rat-ta-tat-tat, wisecracking, and intimate style was so arresting that editors were willing to indulge what they claimed was his chronic inability to make deadlines—a failing he now insists he never had, or at least overcame a long time ago.

It was a grueling pace he kept, sometimes juggling multiple assignments from two or three magazines at one time. In 1962, however, Breslin became one of the hundreds of thousands of New Yorkers who were enraptured by the birth of a new and incredibly inept National League team, the Mets. He wrote a book about them, and as he observed seven years later when the Mets won the World Series, it was the wonderful original team of rejects and retreads that had been his salvation. "The Mets," he wrote, "got me out."

The title of Breslin's book was taken from the anguished query of Casey Stengel, the Mets' first manager: *Can't Anybody Here Play This Game?* The book captured the rationale behind the seemingly inexplicable adoration so many hard-driving New Yorkers felt for a team that recorded the worst record in major league history, 120 losses and 40 wins.

The newspapers call the Mets fans "The New Breed." This is a good name, but there is more to it than this. It goes deeper. As the Mets lost game after game, for example, you heard one line repeated in place after place all over town. It probably started in a gin mill someplace with a guy looking down at his drink and listening to somebody talk about this new team and how they lost so much. Then it got repeated, and before long you were even hearing it in places on Madison Avenue.

"I've been a Mets fan all my life."

Nearly everyone was saying it by mid-June. And nearly everybody had a good reason for saying it. You see, the Mets are losers, just like nearly everybody else in life. This is a team for the cab driver who gets held up and the guy who loses out on a promotion because he didn't maneuver himself to lunch with the boss enough. It is the team for the guy who has to get out of bed in the morning and go to work for short money on a job he doesn't like. And it is the team for every woman who looks up ten years later and sees her husband eating dinner in a T-shirt and wonders how she ever let this guy talk her into getting married. The Yankees? Who does well

enough to root for them, Laurence Rockefeller?

Part of Breslin's rambling, anecdote-filled account of the Mets' first year was a glowing profile of a plutocrat he adored, Mrs. Charles Shipman Payson, the "helluva lady" who owned the team. She also happened to be the sister of John Hay Whitney, the erstwhile sportsman, movie producer, and diplomat who owned the *New York Herald Tribune*. Not surprisingly, Whitney loved the book, and after meeting its slightly intoxicated author in a tavern near the *Herald Tribune* one night in 1963, Whitney offered him a job as a sports columnist.

Soon, however, Breslin found relegation to the sporting news too confining and his place in the paper too obscure. He wanted to branch out and move into a more prominent position. "I feel much better when I am very big," he told the editors. He was moved to the front page of the local section, where he began providing readers with highly personal accounts of city scenes and quirky characters he knew, remembered, or, as some believed, invented: cops, thieves, bookmakers, hoods, even a professional arsonist—Marvin the Torch—whose work, Breslin wrote, was "building empty lots."

Breslin could be funny; he could be touching; some would say he could be maudlin at times. But he also could be unbelievably powerful. When John F. Kennedy was shot in Dallas, Breslin was on the first plane out there. He knew what part of the story he wanted to cover and how he had to go about writing it. "I just got off the plane and grabbed every single thing and kept moving and moving and moving and moving," he recalls. "I had to go 15 different ways. You have an idea before you go in and then go after it, but, boy, be ready to change on a phone call at any time."

What he wrote was called "A Death in Emergency Room One."

The call bothered Malcolm Perry. "Dr. Tom Shires, STAT," the girl's voice said over the page in the doctors' cafeteria at Parkland Memorial Hospital. Nobody ever called Tom Shires, the hospital's chief resident in surgery, for an emergency. And Shires, Perry's superior, was out of town for the day. Malcolm Perry looked at the salmon croquettes on the plate in front of him. Then he put down his fork and went over to the telephone.

"This is Dr. Perry taking Dr. Shire's page," he said.

"President Kennedy has been shot. STAT," the operator said. "They are bringing him into the emergency room right now."

Perry hung up and walked quickly out of the cafeteria and down a flight of stairs and pushed through a brown door and a nurse pointed to Emergency Room One, and Dr. Perry walked into it. The room is narrow and has gray tiled walls and a cream-colored ceiling. In the middle of it, on an aluminum hospital cart, the President of the United States had been placed on his back and he was dying while a huge lamp glared in his face. . . .

The President, Perry thought. He's bigger than I thought he was.

He noticed the tall, dark-haired girl in the plum dress that had her husband's blood all over the front of the skirt. She was standing out of the way, over against the gray tile wall. Her face was tearless and it was set, and it was to stay that way because Jacqueline Kennedy, with a terrible discipline, was not going to take her eyes from her husband's face. . . .

Here is the most important man in the world, Perry thought. The chest was not moving. And there was no apparent heartbeat inside it. The wound in the throat was small and neat. Blood was running out of it. It was running too fast. The occipitoparietal, which is a part of the back of the head, had a huge flap. The damage a .25-caliber bullet does as it comes out of a person's body is unbeliev-able. Bleeding from the head wound covered the floor.

There was a mediastinal wound in connection with the bullet hole in the throat. This means air and blood were being packed together in the chest. Perry called for a scalpel. He was going to start a tracheotomy, which is opening the throat and inserting a tube into the windpipe. The incision had to be made below the bullet wound. . . .

Then he started the tracheotomy. There was no anesthesia. John Kennedy could feel nothing now. The wound in the back of the head told Dr. Perry that the President never knew a thing about it when he was shot, either. . . .

Now, Malcolm Perry's long fingers ran over the chest under him and he tired to get a heartbeat, and even the suggestion of breathing, and there was nothing. There was only the still body, pale white in the light, and it kept bleeding, and now Malcolm Perry started to call for things and move his hands quickly because it all was running out.

He began to massage the chest. . . . Over in the corner of the room, Dr. Kemp Clark kept watching the electrocardiogram for some sign that the massaging was creating action in the President's heart. There was none. Dr. Clark turned his head from the electrocardiogram.

"It's too late, Mac," he said to Malcolm Perry.

The long fingers stopped massaging and they were lifted from the white chest. Perry . . . stepped back.

Dr. M. T. Jenkins, who had been working the oxygen flow, reached down from the head of the aluminum cart. He took the edges of a white sheet in his hands. He pulled the sheet up over the face of John Fitzgerald Kennedy. The IBM clock on the wall said it was 1 P.M. The date was November 22, 1963. . . .

It was an astonishing piece of reportage for which Breslin won the Columbia School of Journalism's Meyer Berger Award and the

Sigma Delta Chi journalism fraternity's General Reporting Award. What was particularly remarkable about this minutely detailed, painstaking, and heart-stopping story was, of course, that Breslin had not even been in Dallas when Kennedy died. He didn't actually get to talk to Dr. Perry until the day after the assassination. It was a prime example, some literati would have said, of a supposedly innovative method of reporting called "the new journalism," of which Breslin has been hailed as a founding father. He denies parentage and, in fact, scoffs at the name. "There's no such thing," he says.

The key feature of "new journalism," according to Tom Wolfe, another practitioner and modestly confessed pioneer of the method and popularizer of the term, is to "write journalism that would . . . read like a novel. . . ." "By trial and error, by 'instinct' rather than theory, journalists [in the early 1960s] began to discover the devices that gave the realistic novel its unique power, variously known as its 'immediacy,' its 'concrete reality,' its 'emotional involvement,' its 'gripping' or 'absorbing' quality," Wolfe wrote in an introduction to *The New Journalism,* a 1973 anthology of work in the field.

The four main devices that the new journalists employed, Wolfe explained, were scene-by-scene construction of a story, avoiding historical narrative, if possible; recording dialogue in full, thereby involving the reader completely in the story and defining the characters precisely; adopting the "third-person point of view," which gives the reader the feeling of being inside the mind of a character in the piece; and recording all the "symbolic details that might exist within a scene."

Wolfe and fellow New York writer Pete Hamill, a colleague of Breslin's on the *Daily News,* credit Breslin with using these techniques—plus his extraordinary skill as a reporter—to "reinvent" the art of column writing. "The idea of reporting breaking news as a column didn't exist before [Breslin]," according to Hamill.

"Breslin made a revolutionary discovery," Wolfe wrote in *The New Journalism.* "He made the discovery that it was feasible for a columnist to actually leave the building, go outside and do reporting on his own, genuine legwork. Breslin would go up to the city editor and ask what stories and assignments were coming up, choose one, . . . cover the story as a reporter, and write about it in his column. If the story were big enough, his column would start on page one. . . . "

There is hype, and a touch of hogwash, in Hamill's and Wolfe's descriptions of Breslin's achievement. They also tend to gloss over the potential problems when such a technique is employed by less skillful, or less scrupulous, writers.

Wolfe acknowledges that there were some historic predecessors to himself and his fellow new journalists. Figures such as Charles Dickens, whose magazine pieces, "Sketches by Boz," circa 1836, provide a vivid walking tour of pre-Victorian London and "immediate," "concrete" descriptions of its clerks, laundresses, kidney-pie sellers, hackney drivers, courtroom habitués, and slums—all reflecting the view of the man in the street; James Boswell, biographer of Samuel Johnson; Daniel Defoe; Mark Twain; Stephen Crane; even George Orwell. Wolfe argues that these eminences either were traditional essayists using little if any reportorial techniques, writing autobiographical works, producing fiction, or just "literary gentlemen with a seat in the grandstand" of life.

Curiously, Wolfe makes no reference to Damon Runyon as a forerunner of the new journalists, except to note that Breslin has been referred to disparagingly as "Runyon on welfare." If what Breslin wrote was often described as "Runyonesque," then there must have been a writer named Runyon who did some of the things that Breslin later emulated. (When asked if he ever read Runyon when he was a kid, Breslin replies with a wonderful *non sequitur*: "No, and he was terrible, too, by the way. He got away with murder.")

There was, of course, a Runyon—a "snap-brim merchant of marzipan and machismo," as Heywood Hale Broun once described him. He is best remembered for his Broadway stories, peopled with characters who are the direct ancestors of the "friends" who appeared three decades later in Breslin's columns and early books. Runyon knew, or contrived, the likes of Nicely-Nicely Jones, Dave the Dude, Sam the Gonoph, Harry the Horse, and Big Jule. Breslin has known the likes of Jerry the Booster, Klein the Lawyer, Bad Eddie, and others. Breslin, minus the snap-brim, may have written about a low-life behemoth such as Fat Thomas, a 350-pound bartender-bookmaker, or Big Jelly Catalano, an inept Mafia hitman, but Runyon was there first with a fellow named Earthquake:

Earthquake is a guy of maybe six foot three, and weighing a matter of two hundred and twenty pounds, and all these pounds are nothing but muscle. . . .

When he is in real good humor, Earthquake does not think anything of going into a night club and taking it apart and chucking the pieces out into the street, along with the owner and the waiters and maybe some of the customers, so you can see Earthquake is a very high-spirited guy and full of fun.

Big Jelly, a character from *The Gang Who Couldn't Shoot Straight,* was just as tall as Earthquake, weighed a lot more, and benefited from an easing of the rules of what was suitable in print:

Big Jelly . . . is 425 pounds slabbed onto a 6-foot-3 frame and topped by a huge owl's face with a mane of black hair. He looks at the world through milk-bottle eyeglasses. What he thinks the world should be has made him, at thirty-two, a legend in South Brooklyn. In grammar schools, with 280 pounds of him lopping over both sides of his seat and blocking the aisles, he spent his years with his hands covering his mouth while he whispered to the girls:

"Sodomy!"

"Period!"

"Come!"

Since that time he has done so many bad things that Judge Bernard Dubin, Part 2B, Brooklyn Criminal Court, one day was moved to observe, "If this man ever could have fit on a horse, he would have been a tremendous help to Jesse James."

When Breslin began his column, there was a spirited debate over whether the stock characters he used were real persons or fictional composites. The same questions could have been raised, but weren't, about many of Runyon's figures. A Runyon biographer, John Mosedale, provided some insight into how Runyon worked by describing a tour of New York he gave a young friend. While on the tour, Runyon introduced the new arrival to a seedy character he called Dr. DeGarmo. " 'I have deposited Dr. DeGarmo right here,' he said. And he tapped his brow with a well-manicured finger. 'Locked up tight, right here. Money in the bank. The Runyon Savings and No-Loan Bank.' " Breslin undoubtedly has opened up his own branches of a similar depository.

Runyon was not universally beloved, and neither is Breslin, but even as good a friend of his as Chicago columnist Mike Royko resents Wolfe's notion that what Breslin did gave birth to a "new journalism." "Well, I'm not a real student of the new or old journalism," says Royko, "but it seems to me these techniques were pretty damn old by the time somebody decided to call it the 'new journalism.' "

Breslin, who hardly is shy in other respects when citing his own achievements, agrees completely with Royko. "New journalism," he says, is the oldest kind of journalism there is. "Wolfe came out with that phrase 'cause he was writing something, so he comes up with a phrase. [Norman] Mailer came up with a thing, 'the novel as history,' 'history as the novel,' 'non-fiction novel.' Just when they're lookin' to sell a book they come up with a trick title, and the suckers believed them. 'New journalism' consists of going out and doing a lot of things and ringing a lot of doorbells and going around and seeing a lot of people and getting a column. And you talk to a lot of people a long time and get quotes and run it. I don't know where it all came in to [be] 'new,' 'old'. . . . There's no difference in the game. It's always been the same."

Whether new or old, the kind of journalism Breslin practices did not, and does not, appeal to everyone. He has been subjected to some wicked and bitter criticism, which he does not accept graciously, and some comparisons he considers both odious and unfair. The late critic Dwight MacDonald dismissed Breslin (and Wolfe) as "parajournalists" who produced something similar in form to the real thing but different in function. MacDonald wrote that in such highly personal pieces, "notions of truth or accuracy are irrelevant. . . . All that matters to anybody—subject, writer, reader—is that it be a good story."

There are other ways—in many cases better ways—of capturing the essence of an individual or event far more penetratingly than straight, this-is-what-it-looked-like and this-is-what-was-said reporting. But like all delights, the cutting of some traditional journalistic corners can be subject to abuse. For a less disciplined journalist, or one devoid of ethics, the temptation to palm off colorfully written fiction as fact may be too great. It may lead inevitably to the kind of bogus story Janet Cooke wrote for the

Washington Post, briefly winning for it a Pulitzer Prize for feature writing but ultimately earning it embarrassment and scorn; or to the kind of incident that resulted in the forced resignation from the *Daily News* of Michael Daly, a young writer whose column alternated with Breslin's and who was accused of fabricating a piece that he wrote from Northern Ireland.

Breslin defends Daly's alleged transgression as an "aberration." He has known Daly's parents for years, has known Daly since he was a child, and thinks his work before and since the Northern Ireland piece demonstrates his skill as a reporter. "Whatever happened on that other thing, I'll never know. It's something that happens when you're young," Breslin told one interviewer, confessing that he had not been above a little fabrication himself when he was a scrappy cub on the less than pristine *Long Island Press* and the *New York Journal-American.* "It never happened that bad [but] I would have to plead the statute of limitations ran out 15 years ago on those crimes."

He takes great offense, however, at the suggestion that any liberties he may have taken in the name of poetic license 20 years ago or now could be equated with the outright manufacturing of a news story. "As far as making up the stuff, I mean . . . , there's a big difference [between] a humorous piece, obviously trying to make you smile, [using] a little overstatement, as opposed to cold, factual reporting, at which I can do with anybody who ever lived. . . . I mean, c'mon. To say Janet Cooke is a derivation of anything I do with a Fat Thomas is nuts. That's nuts."

One of Breslin's colleagues on the *Daily News* thinks any liberties he cares to take should be—and are—granted willingly by both the paper and his public. "Breslin is an institution, and his stuff is always alive and worth reading. Some people you give liberties to. Maybe some half-literate subway worker in Brooklyn may take it all as gospel, but it doesn't bother me that Breslin may take some liberties. Everybody knows his columns sometimes are full of stock characters. But he's in a class by himself."

Wolfe wrote that the kind of criticism MacDonald leveled at Breslin and other "parajournalists" was a "literary tribute in its cash forms: namely, bitterness, envy and resentment." But there was another kind of backhanded literary tribute to Breslin that was more painful, perhaps, because it was so clever. In 1964, at the height of his popularity at the *Herald Tribune,* the *New Yorker* ran a critique of him in the form of a parody. The thought of it can still make him growl.

Y̲ou know that now there's a guy sitting behind a desk at the *Trib* who cares, a guy who knows that things matter. All kinds of things. You've just turned with a tremendous sort of urgency in your fingers to Jimmy Breslin, and in a moment you're with this one buzzing the traffic on Pitkin Avenue in a fire chief's red Dodge. You're suddenly right plunk in the middle of life, right there where things matter. You've been all kinds of places with Jimmy Breslin before. Like down on the Bowery the other Sunday, or out to the Big A or the trots, or digging up streets with the Sicilian Asphalt Paving Company. Anyplace there's life, life with its insignificant joys and pointless little tragedies. But now you're in the chief's red Dodge on Pitkin Avenue and you're counting the streets and the heartbeats of the city while you're whipped along the floors of Brooklyn's canyons to the sadness of a siren's electric screams. . . .

And you wonder if other writers on the staff might start to write like you did when you were a sophomore in college who dreamed about having your own obtrusive little column. . . . Back then, you knew you didn't have to button your shirt or quite begin sentences you'd just finished, as long as you realized in your big heart that it was Pitkin Avenue

and the little, dull things in life that really matter. You knew you could sprinkle magic on those little, dull things with your beatup Smith-Corona. You could *make* things matter. You were the big guy who wrote about little guys, and you did it in the second person singular most of the time so the reader got the feeling he was really the big guy. . . .

Breslin's reaction at the time to the *New Yorker* parody was typically calm and reserved: "I called Roger Angell, a *New Yorker* editor, and told him that I was going to have him killed and put in a trunk and thrown into Gravesend Bay."

Anyone capable of writing "A Death in Emergency Room One," or the moving accounts of the Selma civil rights demonstrations, or the searing pieces from Vietnam, or the columns about the people, places, and problems that no one else was covering in New York could survive a *New Yorker* parody, however sharp. What the *Herald Tribune* itself could not survive, unfortunately, was what Red Smith called "the spectacular immaturity, the complete childishness of labor-management relations in the newspaper business." In that battle, and in all subsequent ones like it, Breslin— the working man's friend—has been on the side of management. He suspected, correctly, that any newspaper strikes in New York would kill the *Tribune,* and he hated the unions for it.

The Newspaper Guild, he once wrote in a column, "is a union of elevator operators and accountants which has been kind enough to allow in it a small group of workers who are reporters and rewrite men and copy editors." Journalism, he wrote a friend, "still is a business of words, and words written by a reporter, whether he makes big money or not, still are far more important in life than the laborer who prints the words."

In the three years Breslin worked for the *Herald Tribune,* the editors refused to print only one of his columns—a furious attack on the unions. "If food companies packaged their stuff with newspaper methods, we'd all be growing broccoli in the windowsill to get by," he wrote. It was an "immoral situation," he declared, that permitted the unions to bring New York's newspapers to their knees in order to preserve "antiquated procedures and . . . antiquated machines." Others might have said that what the union representatives of the newspaper workers from Breslin's own Queens, Brooklyn, and the Bronx were trying to do—however pigheaded their tactics—was preserve their jobs and families.

Breslin eagerly agrees that his anti-unionism is paradoxical, to say the least. "Oh, of course," he says with a broad but not quite disarming grin. "Because it's whose ox is gored—it's the oldest story on earth. The unions were hurting the newspapers, that's all, so I'm against them. If they're hurting a department store, I'm for them. I got hurt."

After a lengthy strike that silenced all of New York's newspapers for 114 days between 1962 and 1963, and another record-breaking walkout that closed the *Herald Tribune* for 135 days in 1966, the badly weakened *Herald Tribune, Journal-American,* and *World-Telegram and Sun* tried to stay afloat as a merged mishmash called the *World Journal Tribune,* which carried Breslin's column until it, too, went under in May 1967, after only eight months of publication.

One of the jewels of the *Herald Tribune* in its closing days had been its lively, innovative Sunday magazine supplement, *New York.* The year after the *World Journal Tribune* folded, Breslin became one of the founding writers of *New York Magazine,* which soon inspired creation of similar "city" magazines across the country. (Breslin later severed his connections with *New York,* complaining that its concentra-

tion on trendy stories and conspicuous consumption "caused me to become gagged by perfume and disheartened by character collapse.")

He also spent about a year writing a column for the *New York Post,* then a liberal paper owned by Dorothy Schiff, a socialite publisher who could have passed for a prototype of Mrs. Pynchon in television's "Lou Grant." It was while he was with the *Post* that Breslin had to employ the techniques he had used after John Kennedy's assassination to cover the murder of Martin Luther King, Jr., in Memphis ("Here he was, trying to get dressed for dinner, and he had no tie.") and the doomed 1968 presidential campaign of his close friend Robert Kennedy. Breslin was just 20 feet away from Bobby Kennedy when he was shot in the pantry of the Ambassador Hotel in Los Angeles following his victory in the California primary, and Breslin wrote what many consider the finest eyewitness account of the slaying of a man he revered:

He was shaking hands with the kitchen workers who leaned across trays and cups and saucers and bins of ice cubes. Shaking hands with them and looking at them with those deep-set blue eyes and his teeth showed in a smile and photographers pushed around the work tables in the kitchen and skidded off the wet floor to make pictures of him and I guess he never saw the guy with the gun.

The gun did not make a very loud noise. Four or five quick, flat sounds in the low-ceilinged room and Kennedy disappears and a guy behind him disappears and people screaming and running and here is the guy with the gun.

People run from him through the kitchen. Run screaming and Billy Barry grabs the guy and Roosevelt Grier pounds on him and Rafer Johnson grabs him, and they are struggling with him and the guy still has the gun in his hand and they lurch against the table and now

you see what is on the floor behind
them.

Robert Kennedy is on his back. His
lips are open in pain. He has a sad look
on his face. His right eye rolls up in his
head and his left eye closes but still there
is this sadness in his face. You see, he
knows so much about this thing. . . .

Breslin soured on newspaper work for
awhile following Kennedy's murder. Complaining that his column in the *Post* "got
lost between the girdle ads," he quit the
paper in 1969. If Kennedy had lived, he
said, "they couldn't have gotten me out of
newspapers with a bulldozer. But with him
gone, who needs it?"

The main reason, however, for his departure from the daily press was that he finally
had hit the jackpot as an author. His first
novel, *The Gang That Couldn't Shoot
Straight,* a spoof based on mob gang wars in
Brooklyn, eventually earned him an estimated half-million dollars. It was made into
a film, distinguished mainly for the debut of
Robert DeNiro, and convinced Breslin that
his future lay in books, not newspapers.

He began work on his second novel, but
to amuse himself, to drum up the kind of
publicity on which he thrives, and to gather
material for another book, *Running Against
the Machine,* Breslin joined novelist Norman Mailer in a quixotic 1969 campaign for
office, with Mailer running for mayor of
New York and Breslin seeking the post of
city council president. Their campaign slogan was "Throw the Rascals In," and the
main plank of their platform was a call for
New York City's admission to the Union as
the 51st state. They alternated between
declaring how desperately serious the city's
problems were and demonstrating how
unserious they were about running. Mailer
would wave a whiskey glass at a fund-raiser
and curse those gathered to support him.
"You're all spoiled pigs," he once yelled.
Breslin would roll his eyes and tell friends:

"I knew I was crazy, but you got me running with Ezra Pound!" Breslin at least out-
polled Mailer in the Democratic primary,
coming in fifth in a field of six candidates
with 75,480 votes, compared with Mailer's
fourth-place finish in a field of five with just
41,136 votes. "I had a ton of money . . . ,
so I went with Mailer, just foolin' around,"
he says now. "But it was a great experience.
I mean, I can use politics on a different level
now [in writing]. I know what I'm doing."

A few years later, Breslin spent a summer
in Washington as a "writer in residence" to
help boost the circulation of the faltering
Washington Star. His months in the capital
reinforced his distaste for politics as a regular subject. "Politics is just dreadful. Lousy,
dreary, boring. To write about it over a year
would be boring. I couldn't do it. . . . I
know them too well. I know the business
too well. . . . It's so sleazy. What a business. You wanna puke."

He has remained more directly active in
politics, however, than many columnists
who write about it all the time. He was
selected to be a McGovern delegate to the
1972 Democratic Convention in Miami, and
he got so involved with Ulster rebels while
living in Ireland and researching his 1973
novel, *World Without End, Amen,* that Dub-
lin police paid a midnight call on his rented
home in Killiney, prompting him to
denounce their "Gestapo tactics" and get
out of the country fast. He wrote an entertaining behind-the-scenes account of the
congressional impeachment proceedings
following the Watergate break-in, *How The
Good Guys Finally Won,* and in 1976 he
served as a delegate for Arizona Congressman Morris K. Udall at the Democratic
Convention in New York that nominated
Jimmy Carter. "I didn't even get there honestly," he says proudly. "I was picked by
the bosses of Queens County." (Breslin
always has had an affinity of sorts for old-
time political bosses.)

Even without a regular paycheck from a

newspaper or syndicate, Breslin never had trouble making a buck, although he has had difficulty managing the money he earned and has had a few unpleasant encounters with the Internal Revenue Service over back taxes. He is a born entrepreneur, and in between books and free-lance writing he turned h.s hand to television commentary, at which he felt awkward; a motion picture role as a music promoter in a treacly 1972 flop called *If Ever I See You Again;* even endorsements for scotch, beer, coffee, and breakfast cereal. Some Breslin-watchers have observed that he has rarely been seen to drink the brands of scotch or beer he has peddled on TV, and Breslin himself once wrote a humorous piece describing how he threw up after being forced to eat bowl after bowl of a certain cereal during the daylong filming of an ad.

Breslin is happiest, however, when he is covering a breaking story for a newspaper, and in 1976 he returned to the daily grind as a columnist for the *Daily News,* then the largest circulation newspaper in the country and still the nation's most popular tabloid. Within a year he was embroiled in the most controversial—and some believe the most tawdry—episode of his career. It involved a gripping story, one that any reporter would pursue, but the manner in which it was covered offered examples of the American press at its best and worst.

On July 29, 1976, Donna Lauria, an 18-year-old girl with shoulder-length brown hair, was fatally shot while seated with a friend in a parked car in front of her home in the Pelham Bay section of the Bronx. She was the first victim of David Berkowitz, a 24-year-old former postal clerk, who used a .44 caliber revolver to kill six people and wound eight others over a 12-month period. Berkowitz, who was captured in August 1977, claimed that he was instructed to commit the murders by a 6,000-year-old demon that spoke through the dog owned by a neighbor named Sam. He called himself Son of Sam.

Although ruled legally sane—a classification that psychiatrists and courts have a tough time defining—Berkowitz clearly was, in laymen's terms, bonkers. He also was a fan of Jimmy Breslin's. Read him all the time in the *Daily News.* And he wrote Breslin some letters which, when printed under the inch-and-a-half-high headlines in the *News* and reprinted in Breslin's tasteless "fictionalization" of the Son of Sam slayings, *.44,* contributed mightily to the sensationalist coverage of the horrifying case and the subsequent criticism Breslin received for his role in it.

Nearly a year after Berkowitz's first killing, the *Daily News* received a hand-printed letter from "Son of Sam," addressed to Breslin. After photocopies were made of the letter, it was sent to police headquarters, and an excited editor telephoned Breslin to tell him he was the recipient of an unusual piece of fan mail. Breslin was, he has admitted, "delighted" to get the killer's letter, if somewhat chilled by its contents and apprehensive about its consequences. "The day that letter came, I told my wife, 'Boy, we're in a lot of trouble now,' 'cause nobody ever came out of these things in one piece," he recalls. "I mean, anyone who goes near a case like this is going to get dirty, that's all there is to it. We're all gonna look lousy, what can we do?"

Berkowitz had written:

Hello from the gutters of N.Y.C. which are filled with dog manure, vomit, stale wine, urine, and blood. Hello from the sewers of N.Y.C. which swallow up these delicacies when they are washed away by the sweeper trucks. Hello from the cracks in the sidewalks of N.Y.C. and from the ants that dwell in these cracks and feed on the dried blood of the dead that has settled into the cracks.

J.B., I'm just dropping you a line to let you know that I appreciate your interest in those recent and horrendous .44

killings. I also want to tell you that I read your column daily and find it quite informative.

Tell me, Jim, what will you have for July Twenty-Ninth? You can forget about me if you like because I don't care for publicity. However, you must not forget Donna Lauria and you cannot let the people forget her either. She was a very sweet girl but Sam's a thirsty lad and he won't let me stop killing until he gets his fill of blood.

Mr. Breslin, sir, don't think that because you haven't heard from [me] for a while that I went to sleep. No, rather, I am still here. Like a spirit roaming the night. Thirsty, hungry, seldom stopping to rest; anxious to please Sam. I love my work. Now the void has been filled. . . .

Breslin was impressed by Son of Sam's writing ability. "Whoever he is, he is probably the only killer I've ever heard of who understands the use of a semicolon," he later wrote.

The police asked Breslin to publish the letter, in the hope that it would prompt the killer to write again—perhaps even telephone—and somehow give them a clue that would result in his capture. Breslin and the Daily News were eager to comply, although not right away. They waited a couple of days, until a Sunday—June 5—when Breslin's column regularly appeared and the paper has a larger circulation. Then in huge black type the News's front page proclaimed: "Breslin to .44 Killer: Give Up! It's The Only Way Out." Inside, on page three, Breslin described the reaction of Donna Lauria's parents to the letter and wrote:

[Detectives] hope . . . that the killer realizes that he is controlled by Sam, who not only forces him into acts of horror but will ultimately walk him to his death. The only way for the killer to leave this special torment is to give him-self up to me, if he trusts me, or to the police, and receive both help and safety.

If he wants any further contact, all he has to do is call or write me at the Daily News. It's simple to get me. The only people I don't answer are bill collectors.

The time to do it, however, is now. We are too close to the July 29 that the killer mentions in his letter. It is the first anniversary of the death of Donna Lauria. . . .

Of course, Breslin's was not the only piece in the paper that day about Son of Sam. The Daily News and its rival tabloid, the New York Post, were engaged in a furious battle to outdo each other in covering the case. It became a "media event," Breslin later wrote, "like the death of a rock star or the emergence of a transsexual tennis player." (The city's third paper, the Times, covered the case as well, but in its own subdued fashion. The story about the killer's letter to Breslin appeared two days later—on page 28.) Printing letters from a homicidal maniac certainly gave the News an edge in the competition. It was an even better promotion than a bingo contest. The only thing the Daily News failed to do was adopt a new slogan: "Crazed Killer Prefers Jimmy Breslin."

Berkowitz did not reply in writing to the plea of Breslin or the police that he surrender. Instead he shot two more people on June 26.

As the July 29 anniversary of Son of Sam's first slaying approached, the tabloids "indulged in a frenzy of non-news," as the New Yorker put it, rehashing accounts of the earlier shootings and describing the lack of progress in the police investigation, the fears of residents in the neighborhoods where the killer struck, patrols of possible murder sites, and a beefing up of the police probe.

The New Yorker singled out for special opprobrium Breslin's column of July 28, headlined "To the .44-Caliber Killer on His 1st Deathday." He recalled Son of Sam's inquiry, "Tell me, Jim, what will you have for July Twenty-Ninth?" and responded:

I have this, a column about the .44 killer and his victims, particularly the first victim, Donna Lauria. Which is exactly what the killer wanted when he sent me the letter. He who would be God with the lives of young women can also use his great power to direct the newspapers to write what he wants and when he wants it.

And somewhere in this city, a loner, a deranged loner, picks up this paper and gloats. Again he has what he wants. Is tomorrow night, July 29, so significant to him that he must go out and walk the night streets and find a victim? Or will he sit alone, and look out his attic window and be thrilled by his power, this power that will have him in the newspapers and on television and in the thoughts and conversations of most of the young people in the city?

I don't know. Nobody else does either. For we deal here with the night wind. . . .

The *New Yorker* coldly observed that Son of Sam's letter had not suggested that he planned to kill again on July 29, but Breslin—the writer he was most likely to read—"saw fit to print the idea that the killer might go out the next night and 'find a victim.' . . . Journalism schools should use these paragraphs as examples of journalistic irresponsibility."

The *New Yorker* also noted that Breslin and Dick Schaap, a former colleague from the *Herald Tribune* (and now ABC-TV's chief sports reporter), were working on a book about the Son of Sam case and were reported to have received a $150,000 advance for it.

Berkowitz did not strike again on his "Deathday," but he did two days later on July 31, killing another young woman and critically injuring her boyfriend. Breslin spent time with the victim's families in order to write about their agony in his next column, but then he turned his fury on the *New Yorker.* He accused it of failing to do any reporting to back up its charges and of ignoring facts that conflicted with its view of his conduct as an "irresponsible" journalist.

Had it checked, Breslin charged, the *New Yorker* could have found out that he had printed his letter from Son of Sam at the request of the police, not to grab headlines. Regardless of that police approval, however, "every cell in your body tells you that this letter was news; legitimate news, important news, news that you publish as quickly and as prominently as possible," he wrote.

As far as his "Deathday" column was concerned, Breslin contended that "the notion that a column by me on Thursday, July 28, would send the killer out to destroy in Brooklyn two nights later could only come from someone who had not seen the complicated network of streets the killer had to learn in order to get away." (Later, and more succinctly, Breslin said that to blame him or his July 28 column for the subsequent shootings was "like blaming the Johnstown flood on a leaky toilet in Altoona.")

Breslin's last shot at the *New Yorker* was a dud, however. He noted with scorn that the magazine had cited—without attribution—an item in the *New York Post* about his book on the Son of Sam case and the hefty advance he and Schaap had received. "Again, a simple phone call could have cleared that up. I am writing a piece of fiction. The advance is not $150,000. Fine. But I do wonder why the New Yorker, which printed 'In Cold Blood,' is so interested in anybody doing a book about anything," he concluded petulantly.

To call *.44*—a patent re-creation of the Son of Sam case—just a "piece of fiction" is disingenuous in the extreme, as was the denial of a $150,000 advance. Had Breslin really wanted to set the record straight—as

People magazine did a year later—he could have written that he and Schaap had split a $350,000 hardcover and paperback advance for *.44.* The *Post,* for once, had been guilty of understatement.

"Doonesbury" 's Gary Trudeau joined in the criticism with a sharp, weeklong series of comic strips that the *Daily News,* in an incredibly stupid act of self-righteousness, refused to print. In the series, a would-be killer whose rather specific "nom de tabloid" is "Son of Arnold and Mary Leiberman" ("It's okay. They don't know where I am"), spends several frustrating days calling the promotion department of the *News* in an effort to get coverage of a murder he plans to commit. "Mine is a story of hopelessness and shattered dreams in the city they call New York," he tells the secretary who answers the phone. "Fine. That would be Mr. Breslin. Please hold," she says.

"Mr. Son" finds that Breslin is too busy conferring with his agent about Son of Sam book and movie deals to return the calls, so he angrily decides not to kill anyone. "I guess that's something we'll just have to live with, sir," says the long-suffering secretary.

Breslin says he was furious at the *News* for refusing to print the comic strips. "I tried to choke them to death when I heard they [wouldn't] run it. They said it's a personal attack; I said I'll buy *ad space* for it! A personal attack on me? I mean, how much more can you ask for in this world than someone attacking you?"

Instead of buying ad space, however, Breslin bided his time and got back at Trudeau three years later by writing a column—and drawing a cartoon—that ridiculed the Pulitzer Prize–winning cartoonist's work as a reporter at the 1980 Democratic Convention. "He can't write," Breslin says condescendingly. "He does clever little cartoons. . . . It's 'college clever.' It doesn't reach most people. . . . It's good for the *Washington Post–New York Times*–Central Park West brigade."

Berkowitz was arrested on August 10—as a result more of luck, as the *New Yorker* had predicted, than of any police dragnet—but the debate over Breslin's role in covering the case, and how it might affect the defendant's trial, continued. A lengthy article in the *Times* raised all the major dilemmas: the difference between exploiting the news and reporting it; the propriety of a reporter's becoming part of the story; the conflict between the public's right to know and an accused's right to a fair trial. Had it not been for Berkowitz's unexpected guilty plea in May 1978—the same month that *.44* came out—a defense attorney could have made quite an issue of the book's potential for prejudicing a jury not only in New York but anywhere else in the country. Part of the book contained verbatim quotations from Berkowitz's confession to police at the time of his arrest. Breslin already had written a full account of the confession, part of which he had witnessed, for the *Daily News,* and he has no qualms about possibly complicating an already tortuous legal process by printing it long before any trial.

"What am I supposed to do—be bound by the rules of the court?" he asks indignantly. "I have no rules. I'm a writer. My only rule is get it to the reader. I don't care about this other stuff. It's none of my business. That's the business of a law court. I heard the guy talkin' to them. I was satisfied with my own eyes and ears what was going on. That's my rule. If I was getting it second- or third-hand from some Irish detective I know, oh, fair game. . . . Let's start qualifying all over the lot, and let's start watching what's being said here. But what I see with my own eyes and ears, forget the number. My judgment must be the only thing that counts."

Breslin has nothing but contempt for the ethical ruminations of the *New Yorker* and the *Times.* The *Times,* in particular, failed to cover the story adequately, he contends, so "to make up for it, they had to run some bit of social criticism to take the heat off themselves. . . ." Apart from his involuntary receipt of letters from the killer—something for which he certainly cannot be criticized—does he think a reporter should become part of a story? "What, are you kidding me? I'll jump right in. You mean stay on the outside at all times if you can get on the inside and take over? Forget it! My first job is to the person who pays money to buy the newspaper. I don't know rules, I don't know ground rules, I don't know what ethics is, I don't even know how to spell the word. My first obligation is to the person who reads the newspaper. If I think it's a good story, I'll write it—in any form imaginable."

As for the question of exploiting the news he covers, wringing from it whatever publicity or money he can, Breslin has a similar response: "You exploit it. . . . All you can. Tell me somebody that doesn't. The *New York Times* gets its leaks from the government, and they don't exploit them? C'mon," he says, evidently referring to the quickie books the *Times* put out on its Pentagon Papers scoop and other stories.

The main problem about .44, in Breslin's view, is that it bombed. It was one thing to have critics skewer it; what was worse was that few readers bought it, and the motion picture industry turned thumbs down as well. Had .44 been a better experience financially, Breslin would not have had any second thoughts about it at all. "I have a regret it didn't come out a little later and sell more," he says now. "That's the only regret."

As his comments on the coverage of the Son of Sam story indicate, Breslin believes that the only truly free press is one that is completely unfettered, even by self-restraint. What some more philosophically inclined—or less anarchistic—people might view as an irresponsible press is what Breslin thinks is the only responsible kind of reporting. Print *everything*, he argues, even if some stories might be considered in bad taste or unnecessarily harmful to individuals.

"I think there is not enough bad taste in journalism. . . . I've got my own theory: most censorship is self-censorship in this business, and in television in particular, where they say, 'I better not put this in because "they" won't like it.' Nobody's ever told them not to put it in; nobody's ever told them not to report it. They just have some idea that the bosses won't like it, or someone won't like it, and you're going too far. They don't even know what 'too far' is.

"I think in this business we're not too smart and we don't have very much time, so therefore, if you have a guy who isn't very smart and he doesn't have much time, you're going to have him thinking, 'I better not say this, it's in bad taste; I better not say that.' You're gonna have a guy who's gonna start to forget to put in about Cambodia's being bombed [by the United States] someday.

"I would rather have the guy put in everything, and if there's a lot of bad taste—*abysmal* lapses of taste—I'll feel quite comfortable because then I'll know they're trying to put everything they see or hear in the paper, and out of all of this they'll make quite a few mistakes and things will be revolting, and maybe some people will get hurt—absolutely *will* get hurt—[but] all of a sudden out of it one day you will have [questions like] 'Why are we bombing this place?' or 'Why do we have troops on the alert here?' "

Breslin says there isn't enough of an adversary relationship between the press and politicians. He has his own guidelines when dealing with politicians, and off-the-record conversations are not a part of them. "I don't believe in working with [politicians]. I mean, I lie to them and tell them we're working together," he says with an impish grin. "Some politicians, we're together, I'll tell them anything. What the hell's the difference? He's going to tell *me* anything! If he has the right to lie to me, then I most certainly, over the third drink, will have a *license* to tell him: 'Don't worry, I won't put it in the paper.' If it's good enough, it'll go in. If it isn't good enough, I won't put it in. I'll honor my word."

As a sometime politician himself, however, Breslin has had favorites among his erstwhile confederates, and he has exempted them from the law of the jungle he imposes on other office holders. His oldest and closest political friend is New York Governor Mario Cuomo, with whom he grew up in Queens and whom he openly endorsed. Breslin could not contain his joy when Cuomo was elected governor in 1982, and he wrote two "insane" columns claiming full credit for the victory ("I am the boss," he boasted). He also claimed something infinitely more important: control over all patronage appointments. He printed his actual office telephone number and urged job-seekers to call. The response, he claims (holding up his hand in a Scout's honor salute), was the "North American world's record. . . . Five thousand phone calls in this area the first day. . . ."

"Sure it was insane," he laughs. "It was supposed to be insane."

Breslin finds few things to laugh about in today's world. In 1969 he felt free to write a comic novel about gang wars, although even then some critics found his account of bungled murders and inadvertent killings crude and unfunny. Now he would not attempt such a spoof. Mobsters, he finds, aren't funny anymore.

"It's all changed. It's changed dramatically for me. . . . It's all dope now. That's why 'The Godfather' was a fraud. All they do is sell dope; how the hell can you make heroes in a soap opera out of them? But they did, and the public loved it. I mean, it was wrong. . . .

"We're livin' in a world of change. . . . Television made it change ten times faster than it normally would. . . . Now it just changes with the flick of a dial. And if

you're doing . . . a column . . . you better adjust at all times to stay up with it. There are certain things that have just lost their humorous content. It's pretty grim, which is my loss. It's terrible for me."

With fewer of the things he once found funny to write about, Breslin has concentrated more on poignant themes. Politics and analysis are not really his turf; his specialty is the sidewalks. He puts as much determination and energy into covering what happens there as he once did covering headline-grabbers or recounting the adventures of wacky friends. He prowls the city's streets, shows up at major news events, casually asks questions, and listens more than he talks. He doesn't drive—"That's why I'm alive," he says—and he may be the cab companies' best customer, riding all over the city's five boroughs in search of column fodder. Quickly slurping a half-dozen tiny cups of espresso coffee, Breslin gives a rapid-fire description of how he works:

"I have over the years developed a rhythm to [column writing]. In other words, you can do a couple of serious [ones] and then you've gotta have something light. I just know certain days that I want to go to some place in Brooklyn, to something that's going on; certain things present themselves that you want to do. There's something going on and then you look for an angle on it. I always go to the other side of the street. If everybody's going to one side, I'll go to the other, you know, away from the crowd, against the grain at all times. . . . It's not as simple as I make it.

"I start out on a Monday, last week I guess, at 7:00 in the morning, I met a fellow here on Forty-second Street, who's a construction worker who's connected with the FALN [the Puerto Rican liberation movement]; there had been some bombings over the weekend. I talked to him till about 7:40—he had to go to work at a quarter to eight—and it was just too political, the conversation was too 'The masses shall arise and free the . . . ,' you know, and it wasn't—he wouldn't tell me anything—so that washed out.

"There had been a grandmother with a 4-year-old child, I guess it was a baby, walking across Second Avenue on Sunday, and a hit-and-run driver came along, and she threw the kid and saved the kid and got killed. And her son was living on Eighty-sixth Street and York Avenue or East End Avenue, way uptown, so I came back to the office, I made a couple of calls, I got him out of the reverse directory, had to look him up 'cause he wasn't listed . . . , I then got his number somehow, [and] once I found out where he was living . . . I went up to his house to talk to him, and he was moving. And he just didn't seem—I don't know, he was more concerned with moving, and he wouldn't answer any questions properly. He was her stepson, and he started to hem and haw, so he said, 'Gee, I guess I'm not helping you with the column,' and I said, 'Naw, it's not gonna make it as a column, and you're not gonna make it as a fuckin' stepson either to the woman who got killed,' and I walked out on him.

"So then I come back here, and I sat around and I started to make some calls, and they said a 13-year-old had been arrested in Brooklyn for the murder of a sailor at the Brooklyn Navy Yard. Shot him in the back. They didn't know the name. I took a cab over to the precinct handling the murder; they said the detective with the case has got all the files, he's in Family Court and we can't reveal the name. So they have the detective call the Police Commissioner's office from the Family Court while I'm sitting in the precinct. Then I have to call the Police Commissioner's office and try. I thought it was a deal and they would give it to me that way. And then some moron in the Police Commissioner's office says, 'No, we've got to wait for the deputy chief,' and I didn't have time, so I went to the Family

Court lookin' for the detective. I got to go way downtown Brooklyn from the neighborhood in Brooklyn, and he wasn't there, and finally in making another phone call from the lobby of the Family Court, I was told the 13-year-old had been acting with a 20-year-old, who also had been arrested, and I got the name of the 20-year-old and went to his home, which is in the same housing project where the 13-year-old lives. So I was talkin' to three or four kids in the project, you know; I then discovered the name of the 13-year-old—'Baby Rock'— and went to his apartment, and there were three young girls who should have been in school, and they were all saying that he carries a big gun and says 'Freeze!'

"And then from there I had to take a cab back to the office and write and make it. And I did make the deadline, and I think it was a very good column, I really do. I think it was a good, modern, urban newspaper column. But that's how the day goes to get those things. You try three or four different things."

Breslin's office is a cubbyhole at the *News*, where he spends so many hours on the telephone that the receiver seems grafted to his ear. He pounds his column out on a clattering, vintage Olympia typewriter. "I need the noise," he says. He can't stand the computer age's contribution to journalism, the video display terminal, on which reporters can make swift, clean, and silent corrections to their copy. He thinks it is a threat to good writing.

"It's very bad because it's too neat. I can't type that way anyway, but out of the neatness is the temptation not to do anything, whereas if you type, and then you have to cross it all out and you put the page in to retype it again so it's neat enough to read, as you're retyping—with that freedom of mind—some of your best lines come up. And that's how you write. With this other business, where it all looks neat, it's so neat that nothing can be wrong. You get fooled on one of those computer screens. . . . I would ban them from a newspaper."

With a pair of clear plastic designer half-glasses perched on his nose, Breslin often furiously reworks his column. Hunched over his typewriter, flailing away, he remains one of the finest reporters ever to come up against a deadline. When he is not writing his columns, Breslin works on his latest novel, which is about a construction worker in Queens.

In a 1982 interview, Breslin sounded a pessimistic note about the future of column writing: "What do newspapers want in a column? One, they want it ahead of time and two, they want it the same comfortable length so they can fill the hole and they don't have to worry every time. And they don't like it controversial, they don't want a lot of kickback from it. That to them is what a column is. Which is why so many big afternoon papers are folding."

He says he earns "close to $100,000" from the *Daily News* and its syndication of his column and commands "big, very big" advance money—"a quarter of a million dollars"—for his novels. He rarely gives speeches and has disdain for the lecture circuit. "Your life is dripping away on a stage at Colgate University or something when you're supposed to be home writing," he says.

In June 1981 Breslin's wife of 26 years, "the former Rosemary Dattolico," as he referred to her in many funny, affectionate columns, died after a long battle against breast cancer. Without his wife to run his life, Breslin had difficulty dealing with his three teenage children or handling his work. He briefly reduced the number of columns he wrote to one a week and fitfully worked on his novel *Forsaking All Others*, a gripping and brutal triptych of stories about the drug wars and ethnic animosities in the black and Hispanic South Bronx. He fought with his children often and developed a misanthropic view of his offspring that would

have put W. C. Fields to shame. "Kids are your enemy," he told one astonished television interviewer.

His three older children, now adults, responded well during the difficult period following the death of their mother, but his three teenagers "were a pain in the ass," Breslin says. "They're all selfish—not just my kids but all kids are selfish," he says grimly. "I was a single parent for 15 months, and I found out that given the chance to help you or betray you, the kids'll betray you every time."

He is uncomfortable with the question of whether his own failings as a parent may have contributed to what he finds deplorable in his children. "I was probably inattentive, sure," he says grudgingly. "I was in the newspaper business. How the hell you gonna be . . . it's been ever thus, hasn't it? I've never been that inattentive. I can't sit there and do homework with 'em. I don't have the nerves."

In September 1982 Breslin married Ronnie Eldridge, a 52-year-old Jewish widow with three college-age children who is a Democratic leader on New York's West Side and a long-time family friend. She now is the director of the women's division in the New York governor's office. Breslin sold his house in Queens and moved to an eight-room cooperative apartment on Central Park West, a swanky Manhattan neighborhood about which he enjoys making disparaging remarks.

Although Breslin is always prepared to enter the world of the Central Park West crowd—more often than not he is dressed in a suit, albeit baggy, and wearing a tie, askew or unknotted—he is more attuned to the ethnic, blue-collar neighborhoods in which he grew up and more concerned with the social and economic forces that are crushing those who live in them, or those who have nowhere to live at all. In September 1982, for example, he spent several days and nights with the street people living in a plaza in front of the Consolidated Edison building on First Avenue between Thirty-fifth and Thirty-sixth streets.

The weather was warm yesterday, but the sun was gone early and soon there will be more darkness and the wind will arrive with hawks' claws and we will have in the greatest city on earth, a city with wealth that cannot be calculated, people living on the streets in the cold; total wrecks whose presence at our feet convicts an entire city of neglect. . . .

. . . This is a great rough place, where throngs are so busy reaching for a part of life they think they want that much of the city runs by itself, and government is considered something best kept in a building someplace.

But at that time and in those places where you have human beings without shelter, it is a job for the government of the city, and anybody doing this work should have a flame inside him, a recognition that the helpless must come first, for all of us in the city will be measured by what is done for the least. If New York, in the year 1982, cannot get some 36,000 homeless off the sidewalks and out of alleys and into livable rooms, then we have become a city not worthy of its beginnings. . . .

Nearly a month later he returned to see whether any city agency had attempted to ease their plight. None had.

Breslin occasionally strays from New York's streets, commenting on such topics as the death penalty and its apparent failure as a deterrent to crime; the insanity of underground nuclear testing ("We were somewhere within a few hours of the anniversary of the first bomb falling on Hiroshima, and yet here we were, mindless as sand, trying our Big Boys out to make sure they can truly do the job"); the Middle East; and the immorality—or amorality—of oil companies that carry on business-as-usual with acknowledged international terrorists:

If our government in Washington sees [Libyan dictator Muammar] Khadafy as a man who wants to assassinate our president, have the nation's oil companies thought about giving up their business with him?

"I don't see why that has to be done," one man in the business said Saturday. . . .

Private enterprise always has much more balance in these matters, as the Khadafy situation shows. While a government shrieks, the nation's oil men once again honor their first principle: business before pleasure. While people representing the government are virtually rubbing their hands in public at the idea of doing something to Libya—killing Khadafy back, perhaps—the oil business plans something less delightful, more painstaking, but in the end much more rewarding: waiting the guy out and then taking his money.

Breslin also is capable of some cynical social commentary about Cape Cod or the Hamptons, the plush group of communities far out on Long Island where New York's beautiful people (and Breslin himself now and then) vacation. It is a far cry from Coney Island, he observed in one column:

There were no WASPs, with their skin barely stretching across their bones, at Coney Island yesterday. In places like the Hamptons or Cape Cod, all the people are either Protestant or striving so ambitiously to become one that cravings are subdued and the traditional Protestant meal, watercress and ice water, is a fixture.

There has not been a fat Protestant since Cromwell had an assistant named Stewart killed for obesity. Of course, these people are often victims of alcohol; in the Hamptons today, one can find lawns crammed with bony people who are stewed, but this is alcoholism by hostess, by schedule, within structure, and this is the worst alcoholism of all, for it is completely cheerless. . . .

What is happening in New York City, however, and by extension in urban America, remains Breslin's primary concern. He is fearful of what he sees.

Given Breslin's heredity, upbringing, and temperament, one would expect him to be a roaring bigot. The Irish are not especially known for their tolerance, and neither are the neighborhoods in which he was raised. He readily admits that he had a lot of prejudices to overcome. "So does everybody. There's no question about that. I mean, who grew up hearing nice things about blacks? We grew up hearing nice things about Jews because there was a Jewish chief inspector of the police department that my uncle worked for and they stole half of New York City, so they always said [in my family], 'God bless the Jews . . . !' So we didn't have anti-Semitism because of theft, because of grand larceny.

"But who the hell even heard of blacks? I'm cheatin' a little bit; we lived about three blocks from a black neighborhood . . . and I knew a little bit more than I'm saying. . . . [But] you didn't run into black people. You had to go out into the world and take a look. Newspaper work helped."

What he has seen in over 30 years of newspaper work convinces Breslin that racism remains this country's greatest curse and challenge. "The number one problem in this country, at least in the Northern cities, is the one that everyone's afraid of—anything to do with skin color," he once told an interviewer. "It directs all our lives. I mean, people are commuting three hours a day. Why? Because they like driving? There's no safety in hiding and I think it's a foolish exercise to ignore the problem."

Breslin did not ignore the problem in his last novel, *Forsaking All Others*, and he is serious enough about it to be satisfied alone with what he considers the lasting quality of that book and the critical acclaim it received. It did not sell well, but for once Breslin does not seem to mind.

"The central characters were not white, and the subject wasn't such a pleasant subject that anyone today wants to read about . . . , but over a long period of time it will become very well known, I think, as the best book done on the city, the best novel done on an American city this size, period. . . . So it didn't hurt me at all."

During his days on the *Herald Tribune*, his old friends Jim Bellows and Richard Wald recalled, Breslin was called "the animal" by those who disliked him and his work, and he was considered "a jolly, overweight pixie" by those who enjoyed his eccentricities and his column. "They were both wrong," Bellows and Wald said. Breslin is by turns boastful and sensitive; hard-nosed and caring; boorish and charming; anti-intellectual and intelligent; a joyful teller of lies and a tough reporter of truths. He appears to have as many faces as the city he loves has stories. They were made for each other.

David Broder

Political Science

There is a curious contrast in the words his colleagues use to describe David Broder. As the chief political reporter for the *Washington Post* and a twice-weekly columnist syndicated in some 260 papers, Broder is almost invariably characterized as "widely read" and "influential." In a 1972 poll his fellow scribes picked him as the country's "most respected political reporter." One columnist and reporter called him "the single most influential voice in American presidential politics," while another, more hyperbolically inclined writer once dubbed him "the high priest of political journalism, the most powerful and respected man in the trade." His columns have smoked campaigning but reclusive presidents out of the White House Rose Garden; detected the dry rot in the candidacies of prospective chief executives; and offered a passionate, recurring plea for the revival of a healthy two-party system.

Instead of the adjectives one might expect to be attached to such a powerful and influential journalist—*Olympian* and *magisterial* were applied unblushingly to some of his professional antecedents—the words routinely, and accurately, used to describe Broder are *self-effacing*, *plain-spoken*, and *modest*. He is not a flashy writer. His columns hardly ever sparkle and only rarely display any humor. A friendly fellow reporter once termed Broder's prose dispassionate, stately, even stodgy. It was a nice way of saying that he could be overly pedagogical stylistically and perhaps a trifle boring.

To some extent, Broder looks the part of an academician. Six feet tall and a lean 160 pounds, he is solemn and scholarly, poker-faced and chinless, with a domelike forehead, closely cropped, thinning gray hair, and large eyeglasses that obscure his eyebrows and shadow his eyes. He speaks precisely in a flat, clipped midwestern accent. But Broder is far from being aloof or forbidding; instead, he is easy-going and cordial, with a quick, often self-deprecating sense of humor and a keen appreciation, indeed fondness, for the absurdities in much of what he covers.

Characteristically, Broder dismisses the suggestion that his column may be extremely influential and accepts, with a touch of embarrassment, the notion that his writing may be less than scintillating. " 'Extremely influential' as compared to what?" he asks. "Is it as important as what Dan Rostenkowski [chairman of the House Ways and Means Committee] says he's got in mind for the tax bill? No. Is it as important as any suggestion that any Cabinet official makes? No. I think there is an order of things. . . . Anything that you write that is purely a matter of opinion I think is less important than what a reporter can lay out that was not generally known and then becomes a matter of general knowledge. I think that is very important. . . .

"I don't like to be called boring," Broder adds, looking pained. "I am envious of the stylists in our business. I mean, I wish I could write like Mary McGrory or Jack Kilpatrick or Safire on his good days or Bill Buckley. I think there are some wonderful stylists and I am not a stylist. But I hope [the column is] not always boring."

Notwithstanding Broder's demurrer regarding his influence as a columnist, his position as the top political correspondent for the *Post* guarantees that his work is followed closely by the politicians who he thinks have greater practical influence than he does; and the meticulous skill, judiciousness, industry, and insight he employs in his political reporting make it the yardstick by which his peers measure their own performance, even if they disagree with his judgments or in retrospect find his predictions flawed.

He is not unaware of his role as a bellwether for the nation's political reporters and a harbinger of future coverage for their subjects, but he says he cannot be preoccupied with the potential impact of what he writes. Just covering his continent-wide beat is challenging enough.

"It would be fatuous to pretend that the *Washington Post* is not part of a communications network that is very important in terms of the way in which this political-governmental system operates," Broder says. "I mean, the audience that the paper has, both among journalists and among people in government, does mean that what we focus on does tend to become at least a matter of conversation. Whether it's accepted as accurate and descriptive is by no means guaranteed, and the way in which people react to it is by no means predictable. For example, the Watergate stories [in the *Post*] were viewed with enormous skepticism by most of our colleagues for the first three or four

months that they were running. They did not, as far as I could see, change the behavior of the government. So it would be foolish to presume that in advance.

"Beyond that, as honestly as I can analyze my own thinking, it would be this: It's very hard, at least for me, to figure out what the hell I think is going on in a political or governmental situation, and then to find some way to summarize it and to describe it. If I added to that challenge trying to gauge in advance what the reaction to the process of reporting and writing was going to be, and then worry about whether I'm going to like or not like the reaction, I think you'd end up sucking your thumb and never being able to put your fingers to the keys. I don't think that in a job like mine you can afford to spend very much time worrying about the effects, if any, of what you write."

Broder's primary job is reporting. His column, he says, is "the tail," an appendage that literally came with the national political beat he inherited in 1966 from his predecessor as the *Post*'s chief political writer. "My basic work week is oriented around what I do as a reporter. Outside of Washington, people tend to see the column more than they see what I'm doing on the news side, so I'm typically identified as a columnist, but in fact my role at the paper is as a reporter." Tail though his column may be, Broder is quick to add that it is not an afterthought. He is constantly ruminating about the column, which deals almost exclusively with domestic politics, and gathering raw material for it.

When he is in Washington, Broder prefers to write the column at home, rather than in the cramped, glass-enclosed office that he calls his "Eichmann cage," deep in the center of the *Post*'s large city room. "I try to do it outside of the office, in part because I don't really want to take time away from the reporting and the newswriting to do it, and in part also because I just think it's psychologically easier if you're away from the phone and can sit down and say, O.K., think about this for a minute, what do you want to say? Much of the columns that I write fall very close to what we [at the *Post*] label 'news analysis.' "

In his double life as a hard news reporter and columnist, Broder scrupulously endeavors to keep his opinions out of his news stories. In many cases, that detachment carries over into his column as well. He prefers to use it to illuminate an issue, not to advocate a position.

"I think the column can do two things: First of all, you are not dependent on a news peg to start the thing. You can write about a situation just simply and say, an interesting situation has developed in which so-and-so and so-and-so, and while it may appear on the surface that it's this, underneath it's really that. . . . The other thing is that on those occasions when you want to express a very clear, personal viewpoint or advocate a side, I think you've got the freedom to do that in a column, which you certainly do not have in a news story.

"I've never gone back and done any kind of count myself, but I would suspect it would be a very distinct minority of the columns I've written in which you'd say, O.K., he is arguing for or against such-and-such a position. . . . I think that's largely a spin-off of the fact that I spend most of my time, and think of myself, essentially as a reporter. I would not urge that as being the best way to write a column. I think there's a lot to be said for somebody who just feels totally uninhibited and bangs away. But that's not what I feel comfortable doing while I'm basically making a living as a reporter."

Broder has strong opinions, of course. Although basically a New Deal–bred, middle-of-the-road liberal, Broder has called himself "an institutional conservative" with "essentially a very status quo view." In the opinion of some of his colleagues on the political beat, he has a nostalgic, almost

naive, pining for the days when party discipline was strong; newcomers went along in order to get along; and two-party politics wasn't fragmented by special-interest groups and obstreperous amateurs.

"Like a zealot in the cause of historic preservation, he has silently wept when the weapons of presumed 'progress' have shattered the curlicued facades of Tammany Halls and ground their smoke-filled rooms, still redolent of old-fashioned deals, into the lifeless dust of modern politics," wrote Broder's friendly adversary, the *Boston Globe's* Martin Nolan, in a 1979 article for *Washingtonian* magazine.

Broder chuckles over the quote, faulting Nolan for "a slight degree of Irish exaggeration," but he admits yearning for the old days of clearly defined party structures, loyalties, and cigar-chomping power brokers. "Yep. Because I think in many respects, particularly in the area of presidential nominating politics, they did a better job. I think it's a much tougher question whether the decentralization and diffusion of power in the Congress is, over the long term, going to be a good thing or a bad thing. I think it's something of both. But that's a much closer question. I personally don't think it's a terribly close question as to whether the [presidential] nominating system has deteriorated since the bosses were overthrown."

Nolan, who served as chief of the *Globe's* Washington bureau and now heads its editorial page, believes that a powerful party machinery that could keep the troops in line and minimize, if not snuff out, dissent would not strengthen the two-party system as Broder argues, but result in an even greater fragmentation of American politics. The United States might end up resembling the Fourth French Republic, Nolan contends, "with a party for every cause."

Broder says that is perilously close to the political situation in the United States today, precisely because party discipline has been shattered by "reforms." "I think the weakening of the party is what has permitted the kind of fragmentation we have now. It's a slight exaggeration, but we're at a point where you could almost say there are 536 federal parties, one for each member of the House and Senate and President . . . , and there are 1,000 parties in terms of platform, because each of the interest groups has its own particular agenda. I think that's the degree of fragmentation that we face."

In fact, Broder says, the efforts made in recent years to strengthen the structure of the Democratic and Republican parties have led not to factionalization, but to an increased degree of party cohesion. Broder adds that he is not as hostile to the development of special-interest groups as his strong-party philosophy might suggest. "In a lot of ways I am pro-faction. I defend the PACs [political action committees], for example, which everybody thinks are terrible. I think they are perfectly legitimate in a pluralistic society."

Broder doesn't know whether a debate of this sort is the kind that engages the interest of the average newspaper reader or only of the politically committed ones. He suspects the latter. "I have no idea what the audience measurement is for any of these political columns. But I assume that the people, for the most part, who read these columns are the people who have more than a normal interest—more than a *healthy* degree of interest—in politics. It's not Erma Bombeck and it's not 'Dear Abby.' They are writing about much more universal themes than most of us political writers are, and the people I see when I'm invited out to give a talk somewhere, the people that show up in those audiences, are people who are political junkies. Otherwise, why the hell would you come out to hear a political reporter talk about an election that's over or one that's a year away?"

There are countless political junkies, however, and Broder supplies them with the finest smack available, drawn from perhaps

the most extensive network of sources in the country. It is not just that he personally knows about two-thirds of the congressmen and practically every senator. By the time a presidential nominating convention convenes, he knows hundreds of the delegates by name, too.

Broder spends months on the road each year, and during presidential election years he travels up to 100,000 miles to attend party caucuses, rallies, barbecues, and banquets. His stomach seems impervious to the rubber chicken and bullet peas on the political fund-raising circuit, and his appetite for political gossip, strategies, and statistics appears insatiable. He is a political junkie himself, of course, a lifelong addict whose craving was nurtured by a steady diet of political talk around his father's dinner table in Chicago Heights, Illinois.

"I grew up in a middle-class Jewish professional family—Dad was a dentist—in an industrial town outside of Chicago, in the Depression and during the rise of fascism and Nazism and World War II. My parents were neither of them directly involved in politics. They never, as far as I know, worked for a candidate or a political party. But they were intensely interested in what was going on, both in terms of the domestic economy and in terms of the war. And so I listened to that. That was dinner-table conversation from the time I became aware of what the hell people were saying. I was an only child, which meant that I spent more time, I suppose, with my parents than I would have if I'd had brothers and sisters, and was very interested in [politics]."

Broder's interest in journalism developed at an early age as well. When Broder was about ten, his best friend got a primitive mimeograph-like machine called a hectograph for Christmas. "It was his, so he was very obviously the publisher," while another friend knew how to make it work, after a fashion, so he was the printer, Broder recalls. "There was only one job left, which was to be the reporter, and when we were all in the fifth, sixth, seventh grade, we put out this little kiddie newspaper."

The publisher and printer of the kiddie gazette later "went straight," Broder once told a friend, but he "was the only one who didn't believe that hey, this is a kid's game, you can't grow up and do it." Instead, he did "the whole *megillah*," working on papers in junior high school, high school, and at the University of Chicago, which he entered at a precocious 15, under a special accelerated program. He received his bachelor's degree at 18 and then obtained a master's degree in political science, further refining his political philosophy under the tutelage of the largely liberal faculty. His mentor was a professor "whose faith in the two-party system was such that he even ran for mayor of Chicago as a Republican," Broder once wrote.

As Broder told Timothy Crouse, the *Rolling Stone* correspondent who chronicled the press coverage of the 1972 campaign in *The Boys On The Bus,* he also learned a bit of practical hardball politics in college as leader of the group of liberal students who fought with a faction of Communist sympathizers for control of the student newspaper. "Both sides used the classic tactics," he told Crouse. "Come early, stay late, vote often, pack the staff with your own people, and always find an acceptable stooge to front for you. We had some incredible goddamn fights. You even had to worry about the political affiliation of the guy who was taking the paper down to the print shop on any given night, because if he was on the other side, he damn well might rewrite a lead or a headline to get the party line into the paper."

Broder and his followers won the fight for control of the paper, which heightened his appreciation for the mechanics of politics. "The people who were fronting for the Communists in that fight were very skilled political operators," he says, "and I saw what a few people who knew how to use the

rules and procedures could do, and I also saw the way in which certain kinds of slogans could galvanize people who were less sophisticated, more naive, than the people who were putting forth the slogans."

Broder made an unsuccessful application for admission to the Columbia School of Journalism, then spent two years in the Army during the Korean War, one of them working on a base newspaper in Salzburg, Austria. In 1953 he returned to Illinois and joined the staff of a small but widely respected local paper, the uniquely named *Bloomington Pantagraph*. His wife, Ann Collar, whom he had met at the University of Chicago and married in 1951, got a job on the paper as well.

"It was a family kind of paper, of a sort that is hard to find in these days of mergers and chain operations," Broder recalled in a 1982 column. It was owned for most of its 150 years by the descendants of the founder, James Fell, a friend of Lincoln's and maternal grandfather of Adlai Stevenson, the Democratic nominee for President in 1952 and 1956, and so the Broders were not the first husband-and-wife team to work there.

It was not, however, a "cozy-comfy" hometown sheet: "What distinguished the *Pantagraph* was the absolute professionalism of its journalism; it was as uncompromising in its standards as any place I have ever worked," Broder recalled.

The editors of the *Pantagraph* taught their cub reporters more than just accuracy and careful craftsmanship, Broder wrote; they taught them "the character of the relationship between a newspaper and its community." The editors "understood—and taught us—that journalists stand a step apart, that we are the observers, the monitors and—if need be—the critics of those who hold public responsibilities."

It is a lesson that has stayed with him. Although he enjoys the company of politicians, even describes himself as "squishy-soft" on them, Broder believes that all political reporters must maintain as much distance as they can from their subjects, as difficult as that may be while keeping company with them constantly.

"I don't think we have to be uncivil, but I don't think we have to be supine, either. I very much believe in the adversary relationship. I think there is, and properly ought to be cultivated, an adversary relationship between the press and politicians in the sense that we are the skeptics, and by asking the hard questions we make them present their *best* case for whatever it is they're doing, not the intellectually or politically laziest case. And I think that is our line of work. . . .

"You develop such close, personal relationships with the people you're covering, and particularly in a presidential campaign, where you're literally living with each other day after day, that the only way to kind of maintain any sort of detachment is to deliberately sort of lean against whoever it is that you're covering at the moment and hope who's covering the other candidate for your paper is doing the same thing. . . .

"I think if you've got that sense [of an adversarial relationship] in mind, then you can have a very civil kind of discussion because everybody understands what the rules of the encounter are going to be, and that it's not based on personal hostility, or even necessarily personal disagreement, but simply the professional requirement on our part to demand of them the best answers that they can give, and on their part the professional incentive to try to make the best case they can, because they're in the business of influencing public opinion."

It is not an easy assignment, as Broder readily pointed out in a 1969 article for the *Washington Monthly.* "Selectivity is the essence of all contemporary journalism. And selectivity implies criteria," he wrote. "Criteria depend on value judgments, which is a fancy word for opinions, preconceptions, and prejudices. There is no neutral journalism."

Many reporters can't manage the role of being both apart and involved, he noted. Some, overdosing on months of discussions about a candidate's strategy, tactics, and personality, go over the edge and decide to become "the Public Defender," alerting readers to the fact that "The Candidate Is Trying to Pull Something We Don't Like," when actually he may be doing nothing more than hedging his political bets. The opposite to the Public Defender, however, is "in every respect more obnoxious," Broder wrote; he is the "Assistant Campaign Manager . . . , [the] fawning lackey of the candidate, waiting on him with bits of advice, reveling in the supposed intimacy of his relationship."

He is a sad spectacle, but there is no blinking the fact that on every campaign I have seen, one or more of our colleagues have strayed from the paths of righteous skepticism and become avowed, active promoters of the candidacy of the man they are covering.

There is a subtle revenge, however, for the candidate who allows this to happen. Invariably, the advice that newspapermen give candidates is the worst claptrap imaginable. . . .

After two years on the *Pantagraph,* Broder went job-hunting, applying for positions at the major midwestern papers and most of the large dailies from Boston to Washington. He had no better luck than he did with the Columbia School of Journalism and was turned down by them all.

"There was no reason for them to take me at all seriously," he says now with a philosophic grin. "I mean, I hadn't done very much at that point that would have given anybody any reason to say, 'Wow, pull that application out of the pile,' rather than some other." The publication that did see merit in Broder's application was *Congressional Quarterly,* a highly respected but decidedly sober and unglamorous periodical devoted to dry, thorough, authoritative coverage of Congress.

The Washington to which Broder moved in 1955 was witnessing, largely unconsciously, what Broder believes was the subtle dilution of "responsible party government" under the deceptively detached leadership of Dwight D. Eisenhower. Broder believes that the two-party system has never been the same since. Ike's appeal "had little or nothing to do with his Republican party label," Broder wrote in *The Party's Over*, his 1972 book lamenting the decline of political parties. Ticket-splitting became a national habit because Eisenhower's personal popularity transcended previous party loyalties and it "was so easy to cast an 'I like Ike' vote, without worrying about what it was that Ike liked in the way of national policies," Broder wrote.

Although the Republicans gained control of both the White House and the Congress for the first time in 20 years when Ike was elected in 1952, he was unable to help the Republican party preserve its control of Congress in the 1954 elections. Nevertheless, with Eisenhower possessing "the almost total confidence of the American people," the Democratic leaders in Congress, House Speaker Sam Rayburn and Senate Majority Leader Lyndon Johnson, engaged the White House in a game of "legislative patty-cake," tailoring their programs "to whatever pattern they thought the President would accept," Broder contended. Voters re-elected Ike in a landslide in 1956 but also returned a heavily Democratic Congress precisely because "the public saw no sharp issues, no real policy choices" between the Democrats they had been in the habit of voting for and the man who had submerged partisanship in Washington, Broder wrote.

The popular belief at the time was that Eisenhower was politically unsophisticated, content to let subordinates run the show.

Historians now have questioned that view, a view to which Broder says he never subscribed. "I thought he was very impressive as a president. He was a hell of a politician. I don't think he was a party-builder for the Republican party."

In 1960, Broder joined the *Washington Star* as a political reporter and alternated between covering the presidential campaign of John Kennedy and the one of Richard Nixon. Even allowing for nostalgia, Broder still considers that contest, with its grand old bosses, bright young candidates, and gnat's-eyelash outcome, the finest he ever covered.

"You had two guys, both young, both very skilled campaigners, who knew from day one that they were in a very close race; they went flat out. We weren't at that point shadowed by the fear of somebody getting murdered in the middle of the damn campaign, which meant that there was much more real interplay with the crowds. I think the country was probably less cynical about its politics then, so there was much more natural and spontaneous public participation in the campaign, and in my mind I carry around more scenes, I suppose, from that campaign than from any of the others that followed it. And I'm sure in part that's nostalgia. The first is always special. But I really do think that was a helluva campaign, and I count myself very fortunate that I got to cover it."

Although Kennedy's victory once again put the Democrats in charge of the White House as well as Congress, Broder feels that JFK was unable during his short presidency to revitalize the two-party system, since he had too slim a mandate and had never really been an "organization man" in the Democratic party. He had an ill-concealed "contempt for most of the old-line organization Democratic leaders," Broder noted, a number of whom he had bucked in his drive for the nomination. After three years of battling as much with Democrats as with Republicans in Congress, Kennedy was on the threshold of building a stronger Democratic party structure when he was killed, Broder wrote.

Broder, who was riding in the Dallas motorcade behind Kennedy when JFK was assassinated, believes that with Kennedy's murder a "leader of magnificent potential" was lost. "The hope he represented, including the hope for a responsible party and governmental system, has not been recaptured," Broder wrote.

When Lyndon Johnson, the product of one-party Texas politics, became President and solidified the Democrats' control of the government with his mammoth 1964 landslide, he wasted his mandate by forcing congressional Democrats to follow him in a "half-mad, half-drunk Texas square dance" of domestic legislation and into a war "he entered by stealth, failed to win and let continue until it had fearfully divided the American people." He, too, was not able to restore responsible party government because he viewed the opinions of his fellow Democrats as "unwarranted intruders on the process of consensus government," Broder wrote.

"The root of Johnson's failure was not in Vietnam," Broder insisted, "but in his own flawed concept of presidential leadership and party responsibility in a democracy. Consensus government cannot work—because there are real choices to be made, choices of goals, choices of means, choices of values. . . . He did not so much try to run the government as to smother it . . . and he left behind a country divided, bitter, suspicious of its government and distrustful of anyone who even employed the rhetoric of strong leadership."

Of all the presidents he has covered, however, Broder says that Johnson was "the most fascinating. . . . I think the more he recedes into history, to me, he becomes a larger and larger figure all the time. He was larger than life in life . . . , just an incredible force of nature. I wish we'd had [pocket tape recorders] then, because there were some nights I was with Johnson in that [1964] campaign that were just unbelievable. He'd be up all night wanting to talk; he'd get wound up in a speech and couldn't sleep, so nobody else on the plane was allowed to sleep, and as a raconteur and a storyteller—and just as a political force—he was unbelievable."

In early 1965, Broder was offered the job as chief political correspondent for the *New York Times*. He loved working at the *Star* but decided to join the *Times*'s Washington bureau because "I did not have the guts to say no" to a call from the nation's most prestigious paper. He quickly came to regret the move.

As Gay Talese recounted in *The Kingdom and the Power*, his 1969 book about the *Times*, Broder was stymied by the paper's stifling bureaucracy and the rivalry between its New York headquarters and its Washington bureau. In August 1966, after only 18 months, he quit the *Times* and joined the *Washington Post*. He left behind an eight-page, single-spaced memo in which he detailed his frustration over the manner in which his stories were "raped" by the New York editors, who he felt had a preference for articles containing big names but little substance, as opposed to the kind of detailed political-trend stories and analytical pieces that are Broder's specialty.

When Broder was hired by the *Post*, he agreed to do a once-a-week column for the paper's Op Ed page, as he had done for the *Star*. He agreed to do it simply to fill a spot left vacant as a result of the decision of syndicated columnists Rowland Evans and Robert Novak to cut their weekly output from six columns to five. Then when a new White House correspondent for the *Post* declined to continue the once-a-week column his predecessor had written, Broder reluctantly agreed to pick up the slack and write two columns a week.

Born in this backhanded fashion, Broder's

column originally was sent out free to the subscribers to the Los Angeles Times/Washington Post News Service. It ultimately became the cornerstone of the *Post*'s own syndicate, the Washington Post Writers Group, which was founded essentially because Broder's four sons were approaching college age and he needed tuition money.

"We got into syndicating it out of sheer greed. When my kids reached the age when they were starting to go to college, I came to [Benjamin] Bradlee [the *Post*'s editor] and said, 'Look, is there any way I can make money out of this column? [Bradlee's] secretary [wrote] letters to a few editors saying, You can keep Dave Broder's column if you want to pay five bucks, or whatever the hell it was, and that is in fact how the Washington Post Writers Group got launched and how I became a 'syndicated columnist'. . . . I think we started with 10 or 12 papers . . . and I'm sure a lot of them [bought it] because they were pals of Bradlee's."

As he had for the *Times*, Broder continued covering the astonishing political resurrection of Richard Nixon, who was laboriously ridding himself of the "loser" image he had earned by virtue of his 1960 presidential defeat and his 1962 loss in the California governor's race. Nixon was campaigning around the country for dozens of local candidates, demonstrating that his name was still a draw and earning the various candidates' gratitude—and support. Broder logged at least as many miles as Nixon did in 1967 and 1968, interviewed scores of party functionaries, and reported what many political observers had a hard time believing: that in all likelihood, Nixon would win the 1968 Republican nomination on the first ballot.

Although Broder was not the only political writer to detail Nixon's strategy, he was the first to report the possibility that Nixon might pick Spiro Agnew, then the obscure governor of Maryland, as his running mate.

When the vice-presidential lightning struck Agnew at the Republican Convention, Nixon told startled reporters that they should not have been completely surprised: they needed only to have read Broder, who had spotted Agnew as a prospect three months earlier, Nixon said. Predictably, Nixon's praise led to articles in *Time* and *Newsweek* profiling Broder, calling him "a political reporter's political reporter." Broder viewed the lionization with bemusement, since his supposed scoop had been, to use his word, just a "plant" he had received from Nixon himself during the Oregon primary the previous May.

"We were on a plane flying from Pendleton to Portland, Oregon, and Nixon sent somebody back to the press section to get me to come up and talk to him," Broder later recalled, "and in about two minutes' time he had gone from the fact that he was confident of Oregon to the fact that Oregon would cinch him the nomination to the fact that he was now thinking seriously about what kind of person should be his vice-presidential running mate. He threw out a couple of obvious names that you would have to think about, and then he said, 'What would be the reaction to Ted Agnew? What kind of reputation does he have among reporters?' And so we talked about Agnew, and Nixon said, 'You know, he's quite an urban expert—he was a county executive, he's a lawyer.' And I said, 'O.K., I'm beginning to get the message.' "

Leery as always of being fed a story, even if it comes from a potential president, Broder dealt with the Agnew tip gingerly and reported his possible selection with an abundant array of caveats. "It never crossed my mind . . . that it was a serious prospect, and I was as astonished as everyone in that convention when it came to pass," Broder later said. Nevertheless, for awhile some of his colleagues considered him " 'a great confidant of Richard Nixon's' and 'the only reporter who knew he was going to pick Agnew.' "

Whatever prescience Broder has is based on his endless legwork and almost clinical detachment, and he will dutifully acknowledge cases when he has been dead wrong. "It would be very painful to reread the last story I wrote about the Illinois governor's race in 1982, because I thought [Governor James] Thompson was going to bury [Democratic candidate Adlai Stevenson III]; I thought Stevenson was going to be cut by the Democratic organization in many wards in Chicago, instead of which they turned out in large numbers," making it a very close race. "I could not have been more wrong—and that's my home state, my home turf, which is particularly embarrassing."

(He did no better assessing the 1983 Chicago mayoralty race. He reported in late January that the incumbent, Jane Byrne, was an odds-on favorite to win renomination in the February primary. She lost.)

Back in 1967, Broder unequivocally asserted that Minnesota Senator Eugene McCarthy's challenge to Lyndon Johnson over the Vietnam War would never knock the President out of the 1968 presidential race, and he underestimated the power and appeal of the antiwar movement.

In 1969, while on leave from the *Post* to accept a fellowship at Harvard's John F. Kennedy School of Government, Broder wrote an extremely controversial column—one by which he still stands—assailing the Vietnam Moratorium Committee and bitterly accusing the antiwar demonstrators of trying to "break" another president simply because they had proven they could do so before:

If there are any smart literary agents around these days, one of them will copyright the title "The Breaking of the President" for the next big series of nonfiction best-sellers. It is becoming more obvious with every passing day that the men and the movement that broke Lyndon B. Johnson's authority in 1968 are out to break Richard M. Nixon in 1969.

The likelihood is great that they will succeed again, for breaking a President is, like most feats, easier to accomplish the second time around. Once learned, the techniques can readily be applied as often as desired—even when the circumstances seem less than propitious. No matter that this President is pulling troops out of Vietnam, while the last one was sending them in; no matter that in 1969 the casualties and violence are declining, while in 1968 they were on the rise. Men have learned to break a President, and, like any discovery that imparts power to its possessors, the mere availability of this knowledge guarantees that it will be used.

The essentials of the techniques are now so well understood that they can be applied with little waste motion.

First the breakers arrogate to themselves a position of moral superiority. For that reason, a war that is unpopular, expensive and very probably unwise is labeled as immoral, indecent and intolerable. . . .

The students who would fight the war are readily mobilized against it. Their teachers, as is their custom, hasten to adopt the students' views (News item: The Harvard department of biochemistry and molecular biology last week called for immediate withdrawal from Vietnam.). . . .

There is still a vital distinction, granting all this, to be made between the constitutionally protected expression of dissent, aimed at changing national policy, and mass movements aimed at breaking the President by destroying his capacity to lead the nation or represent it at the bargaining table.

The point is quite simple. Given the impatience in this country to be out of that miserable war, there is no great trick in using the Vietnam issue to break another President. But when you have broken the President, you have broken the one man who can negotiate the peace.

Hanoi will not sit down for secret talks with the Foreign Relations Committee.

Nor can the Vietnam Moratorium's sponsors order home a single GI or talk turkey to Gen. Thieu about reshaping his government. Only the President can do that. . . .

Nixon's supporters gratefully duplicated the column and distributed copies, and Broder's students in the graduate seminar at Harvard argued heatedly with him about it. Broder says now that "The Breaking of the President" column stirred up more "ricochet, debate, and argument" than any other column he has ever written and that all of it did little to change his fundamental view, "which is that mass demonstrations are not the vehicle for deciding foreign policy in this country."

Broder would prefer that all policy debates, foreign or domestic, be conducted within the civilized confines of the two-party system, and following his year at Harvard he wrote *The Party's Over*, a book urging the restoration of the party structures as the key to resolving the nation's problems. Ironically, he thought that Nixon was "an advocate of party responsibility in government" and might be able to perform this miracle for the Republican party. Broder also sensed, however, that Nixon and his somewhat sleazy associates would never pull it off.

More than most Presidents, Nixon thinks of himself as a partisan, and he believes in the idea of responsible party government. His goal, often stated to associates, is to use his presidency to make the Republican Party the majority party, the governing party, in America. . . .

. . . because of the ineptitude of too many of his close associates, the actions of the Nixon Administration have more often contradicted than advanced the President's professed goals and long-term designs. As a result, his leadership has lacked a sense of coherence or even

of integrity. The prospects of America achieving responsible party government under Richard Nixon appear remote. . . .

Just how little integrity Nixon or his associates had was something Broder and most of his colleagues in the press could not begin to imagine as the 1972 campaign got under way.

With Broder as their leader, a *Washington Post* team canvassed several New Hampshire precincts in February and discovered that the impressive organization about which the supporters of Maine's Senator Edmund S. Muskie had boasted the previous fall was in fact "a facade," a paper bandwagon. Broder wrote a piece questioning Muskie's status as the presumed front runner for the Democratic nomination, and the rest of the press followed suit, much to the dismay and fury of the Muskie camp.

Broder then wrote that if Muskie failed to get 50 percent of the primary vote in New Hampshire, his presidential campaign would be seriously harmed. When Muskie later got 48 percent of the vote, the press considered it a "loss," and the frustrated senator angrily blamed reporters for setting a "phantom" goal for him and ignoring his plurality. His candidacy, however, never recovered.

Broder defends the press's performance in covering the Muskie campaign—up to a point. He and other reporters had not set an unreasonable, artificial standard for Muskie but simply had reported the goals that the senator's own followers expected him to achieve. What the press missed completely, he notes with a grim chuckle of chagrin, were the dirty tricks that Nixon backers used to destroy Muskie's campaign.

"The 50 percent figure was not something I pulled out of the air. . . . It came from . . . the coordinator of the Muskie campaign in New Hampshire. . . . Another reporter and I went to the Muskie headquarters at some point . . . and [asked] . . . 'How well do you think you can do?' and she said something like 'If we don't get more than 50 percent, I think I'll hang myself.' . . . That was the standard that was set, prudently or imprudently, by the Muskie coordinator in the state. It appeared in my copy in that form.

"So my own view of the whole Muskie campaign was that it was, with a couple of exceptions, well reported. Essentially what was happening there was the unraveling of a candidate and a candidacy. And there were many evidences of it, both in terms of his response to the pressures he was feeling, the way in which his organization reacted, and so on. I don't think we missed the story there in the sense of what was happening to him, nor did we misreport. The element of that story which we missed, which was a very important one, was that that campaign was being sabotaged by the Nixon people."

Broder cited as the most dramatic example of that sabotage the infamous "Canuck" letter, a scurrilous missive sent to the right-wing *Manchester Union Leader,* New Hampshire's largest paper, just prior to the primary. It alleged that Muskie had laughingly condoned an aide's use of the word *Canuck,* an epithet applied to the French-Canadian community in New England. The outraged Muskie people branded the letter a fake, but they were unable to uncover its source, and the political press, though intrigued, really didn't have the time or the inclination to try. The following October the *Post*'s Bob Woodward and Carl Bernstein reported as part of their Watergate exposés that the Canuck letter had been traced directly to White House operatives and had allegedly been written by a member of Nixon's staff.

"Now if [the political reporters] had known the origins of that letter," Broder says with a rueful laugh, ". . . that would have obviously put a *very* different context on the story."

Broder himself wrote little about the Watergate incident, but that October, fol-

lowing a frustrating campaign trip covering Nixon, he severely criticized the President for figuratively hiding in the White House and refusing to meet the press during the campaign.

There is a wall a mile high between Mr. Nixon and the press. Mr. Nixon travels in isolation—in his private compartment on Air Force One, in his helicopter or his limousine.

His major speeches on the trip—to Republican fund raising dinners—were watched by reporters from separate rooms, via closed-circuit television. . . .

Under these circumstances, the press functions more as a propaganda tool for the President than as an independent reporting group. The difference between a journalist and a propagandist is that a journalist can make his own observations and ask his own questions.

On the Nixon campaign, unlike the McGovern campaign, there is no candidate to question, and, really, no one authorized to speak for him. . . .

In every way possible, then, the Nixon entourage seems to be systematically stifling the kind of dialogue that has in the past been thought to be the heart of a presidential campaign. . . .

The press was accused—and I think, rightly—of being derelict in 1968 in not pressing Mr. Nixon to expound his strategy for ending the Vietnam war.

How does the press justify itself this year, if the man who is likely to remain President is allowed to go through the whole campaign without answering questions on his plans for taxes, for wage-price controls, for future policy in Vietnam and a dozen other topics?

An election is supposed to be the time a politician—even a President—submits himself to the jury of the American voters. As a lawyer, Richard Nixon knows that if he were as high-handed with a jury as he's being in this campaign, he'd risk being cited for contempt of court. . . .

The editors of the country and the

television news chiefs ought to tell Mr. Nixon, in plain terms, that before they spend another nickel to send their reporters and camera crews around the country with him, they want a system set up in which journalists can be journalists again, and a President campaigns as a candidate, not a touring emperor.

Four days later, Nixon—apparently stung by Broder's criticism—held a "surprise" press conference, his only meeting with reporters that fall.

But the following spring, in the wake of the Watergate-related resignations of Nixon's top aides and on the same day that Broder won the 1973 Pulitzer Prize for his 1972 commentary work and the *Post* won the public-service Pulitzer for its Watergate stories, Broder wrote a column noting that there was scant reason for boasting among the Washington press corps—himself included—over its coverage of the scandal:

N ot since last November has Washington witnessed such an orgy of self-congratulation as it has seen this past week. Back then, it was the members of the Nixon Administration and their political agents who were celebrating their own genius in producing the 49-state landslide.

Last week, it was the journalists of the country who were hailing each other—and graciously allowing politicians to praise them—for their splendid work on the Watergate story.

The suggestion here is that the journalistic euphoria is about as ephemeral . . . and is as ill-deserved as the White House euphoria last fall. We ain't as good as the returns make *us* look either. . . .

As press critic Ben H. Bagdikian pointed out . . . , "no more than 14 reporters" of the 2,200 regularly employed in this capital did any substantial work on the Watergate case, and the number of publications that pursued

it with any measurable vigor can be counted on one hand.

My own columns last fall, when reread, provide evidence for the observation by the Washington Post's ombudsman . . . that those of us whose supposed insights into the deeper meaning of events gain us editorial-page space in papers around the country did precious little to help readers understand the significance of this political crime.

I take some pride in the fact that a column I wrote last October, on the shielding of candidate Nixon from the press, apparently helped provoke the President into calling his one press conference of the fall campaign.

But anyone who makes a living as a Washington reporter must squirm at the realization that on the occasions Mr. Nixon met the press in the months between the break-in at the Democratic headquarters and the resignation of his top aides, only nine questions—most of them easily deflected—were asked him about the financing and conduct of his campaign aides. We have to do better than that.

Let us be modest in our moment of triumph, ladies and gentlemen of the press, for as the old saying goes, we have much to be modest about.

Broder did score a significant scoop covering the ancillary scandal of the Nixon administration, the investigation of bribe-taking by Vice-President Agnew. In September 1973, he broke the story that Agnew was seriously considering resignation as the investigators closed in on the allegations that he had taken kickbacks from contractors who sought to do business with Maryland while he was governor and later Vice-President. In May 1974, Broder received the top newswriting award from the Washington-Baltimore Newspaper Guild for his story on Agnew, which was praised as "a great newsbeat in a year filled with newsbeats."

At the height of the Watergate scandal in 1973, Broder saw in it confirmation of his oft-stated belief that the dilution of the political parties' structures would lead to disaster:

It is worth asking why the parties have been so impotent in this matter. Why was the Republican Party unable to prevent this sort of activity being conducted on behalf of its nominee? Why was it so difficult for it to persuade the President to undertake the kind of cleanup GOP leaders wanted and Republican office holders clearly thought necessary for their political survival?

Turning the question around, why was the Democratic Party unable to develop the evidence on the crime that occurred on its premises or to bring the issue of political espionage effectively to the public during the last campaign?

There are many specific reasons that come to mind, but they add up to the overriding fact that the parties have become weak, impotent institutions—incapable of exerting themselves even in the face of the most dangerous threats to their own integrity. . . .

In the last 20 years, the candidates have tended, more often than not, to keep the personal organizations, created in the contest for the nomination, as the main vehicles for their general election campaign.

Even though he was an incumbent assured of renomination, Mr. Nixon chose to set up a personal campaign committee (The Committee for the Re-Election of the President), rather than entrusting his campaign to the Republican National Committee. It was in the re-election committee, not the GOP national committee, that the scandals now coming to light centered.

What is wrong with these *ad hoc* groups is that they tend to be staffed either by mercenaries or single-shot sharpies. The mercenaries who comprise a modern campaign staff—the pollsters, advertising men, media advisers, computer whizzes, and direct-mail specialists—are people of great technical ability. But they operate as "hired guns," with no continuing commitment to party or principle and no responsibility for the behavior of those who employ them.

Even worse are the one-shot sharpies, men whose sole interest is in winning a single campaign for a single candidate. Often, they are ideological extremists, who run a candidate in order to justify a personal predisposition or political theory, and who leave the party in a shambles when he loses. . . .

It is time to reduce the role of the hired guns and the single-shot sharpies and to enhance the status of the political parties' permanent staffs. . . . Professionals know their party will pay a long-term penalty for any chicanery perpetrated in a particular campaign. It is time to put the professionals back in charge of presidential politics.

Nixon's successor, the amiable former Republican leader in the House of Representatives, Gerald Ford, was the president whom Broder knew the best and liked the most as a person. Jimmy Carter, however, was a party outsider, supported by yet another cadre of hired guns, who ran against the Washington power structure that had long been under the control of his own party and repeatedly pointed out that he had never even met a Democratic president.

Broder, who is as even-handed and nonpartisan in his observations as practically any political commentator in the business, did not think Carter was a responsible party leader and was perhaps the first to openly discern Nixonian tendencies in Carter's 1980 reelection campaign. In early February, as Carter confined himself to the White House, refused to debate his chief rival, Edward Kennedy, and cited the Iranian hostage crisis as his reason for supposedly remaining aloof, Broder wrote: "I am getting a queasy feeling. It is the same feeling I had in 1972, when the incumbent president of the United States treated his re-election campaign as a matter too unimportant for his notice." Broder urged Carter to "cast aside his protective cloak and face his duties as a politician seeking office in a democracy." He accused the President of using the White House "as a protective base from which [he] 'carpetbombs' his political challengers."

Other commentators, perhaps having harbored similar thoughts but not previously voicing them, followed Broder's lead—as Jeff Greenfield noted in his book *The Real Campaign*—and stepped up the criticism of Carter's Rose Garden campaign strategy. Carter never completely abandoned the above-the-battle stance, however, even after it became counterproductive.

Broder agrees with the main assertion in Greenfield's book, that what actually determined the outcome of the 1980 election was what Carter and Reagan actually stood for— their party labels, programs, and ideals—not how the print press and television covered the campaign. "I have never accepted the general thesis that somehow we in the press are defining the area or the terms of political debate or the political process," Broder says. "I think we are tag-alongs in that game, and that basically we deal with the campaign as it comes to us. If they choose to talk about issues, that's what we'll end up writing about; if they don't, then we can't."

As Greenfield pointed out, the Republicans had a specific message in 1980 and appealed to a specific audience: disaffected Democrats. If you don't like the way the Democrats have run things, Republican advertisements said, vote for us for a change. Such ads, Greenfield wrote, "helped turn voters away from personalized Presidential politics and into a realization that political parties and congressional power, rather than charismatic personalities, just might have something to do with poli-

tics." It was the kind of message Broder loves to deliver, even if he may not agree with the philosophies of its other bearers. It was also a message that impressed the voters in 1980. They gave Reagan and the Republicans a historic landslide, turning over control of the Senate to the Republican party for the first time since 1952 and evicting an incumbent Democratic president for the first time since 1888.

Broder had—and has—grave concerns about the views of the Republican right wing. Immediately following Reagan's election, he urged, without effect, that a concerted effort be made to "include black and brown leaders in the planning and staffing of the new government." But he saw in the Reagan victory the possibility of a realignment of political power in this country, perhaps a new era of Republican dominance, and he still believes that the 1980 election signaled a profound change in the basis of political debate in this country.

"Was there an ideological message in the 1980 vote? There sure was," he wrote shortly after the Reagan victory.

There was more ideological content in Ronald Reagan's campaign speeches than there was in Roosevelt's speeches in 1932. You had be be very shrewd to discern the shape of the New Deal in the rhetoric of FDR's 1932 campaign. But you had to be dense to miss the message of Reagan's campaign: a flat-out repudiation of basic economic, diplomatic and social policies of the reigning Democratic liberalism.

There is enough issue content in the Reagan campaign rhetoric to give shape and structure to a long-term political realignment if those policies produce the benefits Reagan and the Republicans promised their millions of new supporters this fall. . . .

The gains that the Democrats made in the midterm election in 1982 were not a repudiation of Reagan's policies, Broder believes, but more of a slap on the wrist, an instruction to keep trying but work harder. It was, he wrote, "a wonderful advertisement for democracy."

The voters used the election "to signal a course correction—adjustments in the basic Reagan plan that would reduce the deficit, shorten the recession, slow the pace of the military buildup, stretch out the tax cut and stop the cuts in lifeline support programs for those suffering from the economic squeeze." They performed this "democratic miracle," Broder wrote, by ousting 26 Reaganite diehards in the House—14 of them freshman members who had ridden in on Reagan's coattails—and preserving Republican control of the Senate.

They did not want to withdraw or cancel the mandate of the 1980 election, when they heeded Reagan's plea for a Congress that would work with him to slow the pace of federal spending and help curb the consuming cancer of inflation. Nor did they want to restore full sway on Capitol Hill to a Democratic Party that is still some months—if not years—away from thinking through and articulating its own economic program. . . .

Whether Reagan is wise enough to heed the message of the election is uncertain. But the voters have done their part by creating a situation where serious political and policy negotiations, involving the White House, the Senate and the House, can and should go forward.

Regardless of whether Reagan has that wisdom, doesn't run for reelection, or is defeated if he does, Broder does not believe the historic impact of the 1980 election will be negated. "The terms of the debate really have shifted in this country, for both parties," he says, "and [Reagan] defined what the new terms of the debate are."

Broder covers that debate by getting up

early and staying out late. He lives in a nine-room house in Arlington, Virginia—"the most unfashionable place imaginable," he often jokes—and commutes to work by driving a half-mile to a suburban Washington subway station and taking a 12-minute ride downtown.

Washington, he notes with resignation, is a city in which many bureaucrats and politicians are in the habit of conducting business, particularly interviews with the press, over breakfast. It is not unusual for him to have a 7:15 A.M. meeting with some administration official, legislator, or lobbyist. "That is not my choice of a time to do an interview, but it works out for [them]," he says.

If he doesn't have a sunrise interview scheduled, Broder arrives at the *Post* between 9:00 and 9:30. If he has a specific project to work on, he will call the sources he needs to discuss it and "go where that project is," perhaps to a campaign headquarters or congressional committee meeting. If he doesn't have a story in the works or a specific place to go, he visits Capitol Hill, "just simply because it's the best . . . listening post [for] political gossip, and I like that.

"My beat is such that I do not have responsibility for covering legislation on a day-to-day basis, or the President's activities on a day-by-day basis, but I'm in and out of the White House with some frequency, too, if I do not have some other specific place to go. But on a story that I'm working on, I will tend to head for Capitol Hill."

In a two-year cycle of off-year and on-year elections, Broder splits his time between Washington and the hustings. During 1980 he "was almost totally on the road; 1982 less so, but it roughly works out about 50-50," he says. "When I'm on the road, the schedule tends to be a very long day, either in terms of traveling with a candidate and the kind of routine they have, or if you're operating on your own in a state, doing a story on a governor's race or a Senate race. You tend to start with breakfast appointments and go on through late in the evening. Those days tend to be fairly long."

Broder and his wife avoid Washington cocktail parties and Georgetown salons, but they are not exactly homebodies. They are enthusiastic movie-, symphony-, and theatergoers, and Broder, who is especially fond of musicals, occasionally uses the lyrics from popular songs to humorously underscore a point in his column. Usually his memory for them is impeccable, but in a year-end *apologia* in 1980 he wrote that "the most embarrassing goof of the year" occurred when he tried to liken President Carter's habit of timing optimistic announcements for primary election days to "what I said was a lyric from 'Showboat'— 'Maybe Tuesday will be my good news day.'

"As several dozen of you were kind enough to point out, that line is from the George and Ira Gershwin classic, 'The Man I Love,' and not from 'Showboat.' When I checked with the Ultimate Quotation Authority, George Will, he even played the Ella Fitzgerald recording over the phone to make it perfectly clear I was wrong again."

Broder is proud, however, of his continuing fealty to the Chicago Cubs, unlike Will, another Illinois lad, who has switched allegiance to the Baltimore Orioles. He is a self-described "terrible left-handed hacker at tennis" and, like much of the rest of official Washington, a passionate fan of the Redskins.

Even if he did not have to spend so much time on the road as part of his job, Broder would be in and out of airplanes constantly just because he loves to travel. In order to keep up with the magazines and newspapers he feels he ought to read, on each trip he lugs along a large plastic bag stuffed with periodicals his wife has saved for him. He also has an assistant—one who is not a member of the *Washington Post* staff but whom he hires independently—to help him do research, handle the mail, and perform other chores. Unlike many columnists, however, Broder does not have a secretary screen his calls. If he is in his office, surrounded by foot-high stacks of press releases and yellowing newspapers, he will answer any call with a pleasant "This is Dave Broder." He gives few speeches—perhaps one a month out of town and two or three a month in the Washington area— because he finds the demands of lecturing "not compatible with doing a job on a daily beat."

He never seems to tire of the mind-numbing regimen or the politicians, a group traditionally—and some would say correctly—held in low esteem by hard-boiled reporters and much of the public. Broder instead finds much about them that is admirable.

"They're willing to put their reputations—and to some extent their livelihoods—on the line. I think there are few things in life, other than life and death itself, which are more final than the difference between winning and losing a campaign. And for people who are reasonably energetic, talented people, which most of the women and men I've met in politics are, that is a choice of vocation which I think [serves] a terribly important function at some considerable cost to themselves. . . . Now, obviously, you don't do it unless you've got a pretty healthy-sized ego, and most of them have that kind of an ego. So the good ones don't regard it as anything that is a terrible penalty on their lives, but I think it's one of the things I admire about them.

"Second, I think the ones who are good come to have a very balanced sense of their belief in goals and policies and programs, and their tolerance of people who on any particular issue are on the other side of them. They understand that it is a process in which they are involved in which all truth is not revealed to one side and all error and falsity on the other side, and they manage to keep that kind of balance in their approach even when they are fully engaged in the battle of the moment. . . .

"I enjoy the beat, and the cast of characters changes. You're not dealing with the same people all the time. . . . I'm not tired of it either physically or psychologically. . . . I enjoy the people I cover, with very few exceptions. I'm 'squishy-soft' on politicians as a group. And I enjoy the people who cover that beat, with very few exceptions. I don't think you could stay with it very long, or would want to stay with it very long, if that weren't the case, and most of the people who are good politicians and good political reporters do in fact get a lot of enjoyment out of just the human contact. They like each other. . . .

"One of the advantages that the people who work on this beat have is that we do tend to move back and forth, from people to people and party to party, so you don't have to hang around. I mean, occasionally you do get stuck with bores—there's no two ways about that. And there are parts of it where the routine *is* stupefying. You hear the same speech five times a day, with only a bus ride in between. At that point you fall back on your own resources, the frivolity of the group. There's generally enough ridiculous stuff going on offstage that makes those days bearable."

Regrettably, Broder rarely gives his readers a sample of his taste for the frivolous, partly because of his dedication to sober, no-nonsense reporting and partly because he simply feels insecure about trying to write anything humorous. "I guess I don't trust myself very much to be funny very often. I like to write [humorous] pieces, but I don't think of it as being my line of work. Maybe I ought to try it more often, 'cause there is a lot of wonderful, ridiculous stuff that happens in politics. . . . In fact, [in reporting] a lot of what happens in politics and govern-

ment, you lose a lot of the juice in trying to strain it into a fairly formalized, nonfiction format. I mean, almost every time I go to Texas to do a political story, I say there's no way to write this for a family newspaper, this is a novel. . . . It's always a mixture of money and lust and power, and it's all mixed in together, and it's talked about that way. So when you slice it out and say, Well, there's a campaign with so-and-so and so-and-so, you miss often the best part of the story."

Whenever Broder does attempt a humorous piece, it always is understated and straight-faced. He writes an annual devotional to the Cubs, the Harold Stassens of baseball, and at least one article each summer about his vacation retreat on Beaver Island, Michigan, perhaps as unfashionable a resort as Arlington may be as a residence. It is a place, Broder explained in a 1982 column, where an invitation to a "formal" party means "that both T-shirts and shoes must be worn. Simultaneously."

I take a lot of abuse from colleagues back in Washington who spend their summer vacations at fashionable places on Cape Cod, Martha's Vineyard or the coast of Maine. They insist that because they have cocktails with an undersecretary and cookouts with an ambassador, they are more "with it" than we are on this never-heard-of-it island at the top of Lake Michigan.

They are wrong, of course. I have known for more than 30 years that Beaver Island is the center of the real world, and this summer has proved it once again. Not since Bud's gas pump split its guts trying to recompute prices during the summer of the oil embargo have we had such dramatic evidence of the impact of outside concerns on this seemingly tranquil backwater. . . .

Deregulation—and particularly the change in the Environmental Protection Agency since Anne Gorsuch [Burford] took over—has helped the island. For a time, under what Interior Secretary James Watt would rightly call the environmental extremism of the Carter administration, the Beaver Island dump was threatened with closure. There were rumbles we would have to take our tax money and build an incinerator. Let me tell you, an incinerator would have been as out of place on Beaver Island as an All-Star on the Chicago Cubs.

But, thanks to Reagan, the dump is still in business, serving its dual function as a disposal point for old paint cans, etc., and as a place where neighbors can meet late in the day to exchange news and views (the equivalent of those snobby Vineyard cocktail parties).

There are nice new signs saying, "Please Don't Dump Here," and "Please Dump Here." It used to be, frankly, that any place within a quarter-mile was considered a good-faith effort. People are complying, voluntarily, and the seagulls don't have to roam as far in search of tidbits. James Watt and the Wilderness Society can both rejoice. . . .

Not surprisingly, these change-of-pace pieces get the most response out of Broder's readers. "Whenever I write a Beaver Island column, I think I hear from everybody who had ever lived on or vacationed on Beaver Island. There are some people I run into who say, 'When are you going to write your Cubs column this year?' And I always say, 'Well, I'm waiting for the big win streak.' " He even writes an occasional column stoically detailing his "howlers" in political judgment. It is a good device, Broder wrote in a 1980 New Year's Eve piece, "for letting you, the readers, know that I know that you know what a klutz I am. . . ."

Doubts about his abilities as a prognosticator aside, Broder—who once was considerably more pessimistic—now expresses optimism about the future of political reporting, the political parties themselves, and the nation as a whole. In his 1969 article for the *Washington Monthly*, Broder painted a less-than-complacent portrait of his fellow riders on the campaign press buses and airplanes, worrying at the end of the piece that he had probably exposed enough of their failings "to be expelled from the press bus for life." A decade and a half later, he finds future prospects more appealing. He even has kind words for those traditional pariahs of the pencil press, the television journalists.

"I think that the television people have learned to use their medium to do political stories, and they've developed an extraordinary skill for kind of capsulizing [the news]. I know there are criticisms made of the way they emphasize the horserace journalism and so on, but I think they do extraordinarily well in terms of the limits that they operate under.

"I think on the print side, as television has become the first and most relied-upon source of political news, we have as a group learned to find some more analytical ways of writing about the process. And I think two things in particular have helped. I think the technique of the exit poll has turned out to be an extremely valuable analytical tool for political reporting, which is something we did not have and did not know how to use [before] but which now gives you a much better basis for interpreting voting behavior in a contemporary setting than we ever had before.

"And I think in part thanks to Teddy White and others who followed in his path, there is a much better grasp of the techniques of politics, on a continuing basis, that is conveyed to people now than was the case before. I was looking back, for example, at the reporting on the [Wendell] Willkie draft [at the Republican Convention] in 1940. That was a very, very well-engineered, planned coup. You didn't find that out by reading the newspapers at that time."

Broder's view on the health of the two-party system is similarly upbeat, although it could not be characterized as rosy. Nevertheless, it is more positive than it was when he wrote *The Party's Over* in 1971. His outlook then was "not cheerful," to say the least, and he feared that further decay and fragmentation of the parties' structures might lead to the rise of "a plausible demagogue."

"That possibility sounds like scare talk," he wrote. "Some will dismiss it as apocalyptic nonsense. But things have been happening in this country that I would not have believed when I came to Washington . . . ," he observed, referring to the political assassinations; the urban riots; the sight of the U.S. Capitol, its dome enveloped in smoke and its base surrounded by soldiers defending it against civil disturbances; and all of the other frightening reminders of the 1960s. Still to come at the time Broder wrote that book was the spectacle of a president forced from office by his aides' wrongdoing and his own mendacity, as well as the further unraveling of the Democratic party in part because of the boss-busting "McGovern Reforms" which were adopted following the disastrous 1968 convention and which Broder, ironically, supported then.

Out of these calamities, however, have come positive developments for both the Democratic and Republican parties, Broder believes. "Both parties are in pretty good shape," he wrote in a column early in 1983.

There would be no news in this, except that we are accustomed to thinking every institution in America is either going to hell or is already there. Having written at considerable length on the weakness of the parties myself, I am personally delighted to see that the invalids are sitting up and taking nourishment.

Just how this came about is not entirely clear, but it is certain that for both Republicans and Democrats, catastrophe was the mother of recovery.

For the GOP, that calamity came in the form of Richard Nixon, who drove his party deeper than ever into minority status with Watergate and then cost it the presidency via the pardon he obtained from Jerry Ford.

The revival of the GOP organization . . . began only after everyone in the party had a vivid demonstration of the danger of letting it become a wholly-owned subsidiary of a particular president. When he wrecked, the party had no lifeboats.

Though his failings were political, not criminal, Jimmy Carter provided the same lesson to Democrats, costing them the White House, the Senate and a slew of House seats in 1980.

In both cases, the effect was to revive interest in the party machinery from officeholders, constituencies and interest groups which had deluded themselves into thinking they could make it on their own in Washington—or with just a friend in the White House to lend them a hand.

Since 1980, the Democrats . . . have been doing what the Republicans did . . .: raising money and pumping it back into party-building projects at the state and local level, while cementing relationships with mayors, governors, state legislators and members of Congress. . . .

The result is a healthy aura of competition, centering around not just the presidency but control of the Senate in 1984 and a multitude of state and local contests. . . .

All this comes under the heading of good news . . . , just what the White House has been begging us reporters to give you. So even if you don't buy a new car or house this week to celebrate the Reagan Recovery, at least send a few bucks to the party of your choice.

Ever since his days at the University of Chicago, Broder has subscribed to the late V. O. Key's "perverse and unorthodox argument that the voters are not fools," and despite his observation following the 1980 presidential election that voter turnout was continuing its 20-year decline, Broder believes that the pattern is on the verge of reversal and that our political system is healthy.

Between 1978 and 1979, Broder conducted over 300 interviews with members of the generation of political activists and politicians who now are "poised on the brink of taking power." His "private agenda" for undertaking this project was to ensure the continued vitality of his national network of sources, guaranteeing that it would not age and fade away as the current group of leaders begin collecting Social Security. The initial result was *The Changing of the Guard,* the 1980 book in which Broder exhaustively profiled and analyzed the individuals who he felt would direct this country's fortunes beginning during the 1980s and then well into the next century.

Although the election of the oldest man ever to seek the presidency may have temporarily postponed until the 1990s the transfer of the nation's leadership "from the World War II veterans . . . to a new set of men and women," there is little doubt—for actuarial reasons if nothing else—that "America is changing hands," as Broder put it. *The Changing of the Guard* contains echoes of Broder's earlier—and continuing—concerns about the two-party system, but it is a surprisingly optimistic book, especially considering Broder's previous "apocalyptic" forebodings.

He found that there is "a lot of talent coming along" in the new generation of nascent leaders and that while many of the problems he has bewailed remain, most of the young people he interviewed seemed dedicated to salvaging our political system, not junking it.

Much of what they seek to change is practices and policies that have cried out for alteration. It was surely no mistake

to take to the streets to protest segregation. If the Vietnam war was not immoral, as they claimed, it was surely unwise, and the protests they organized against it helped push American policy back toward sanity. It was not wrong for them to be affronted by the spectacle of a senile committee chairman's stalling needed legislation, simply because he had never had an opponent at home and the seniority system kept him in power as long as he had strength enough to hold the gavel. Nor were they in error in thinking that unreported, under-the-table campaign contributions came close to being bribes. . . .

What can be criticized is not the motivation on which they acted, but their inability to foresee the unintended consequences of some of the changes they managed to bring about. But that is a failing from which no one is immune, and it is particularly and historically the shortcoming of youth.

What is encouraging now is the extent to which they have begun to identify and correct their own previous misjudgments. . . .

The prediction I would like to make is that the next two decades will be as much a period of institutional rehabilitation and repair as the last two decades have been a time of disparagement and destruction of the machinery of our government. There is sufficient understanding of the task that needs to be done, among those same young people who were busy in their twenties and thirties with the crowbars and bulldozers, to make that prediction come true. Given leadership, the parties, the Congress, the presidency and the courts can be set up to work again—and state and local governments can attain a level of competence they have not shown before. To me, as a devotee of those institutions—a thoroughgoing conservative when it comes to the structure of our democracy—that would be the fulfillment of a dream. But whether it is realized or not, the exercise of writing this book has impressed on me a lesson of which others too may need reminding. Institutions are human artifacts. What is fundamental is the people who create them and lead them. They give life to the institutions and determine how well they function. The institutions cannot create their own leaders. But the leaders can create—or perhaps it would be more accurate to say re-create—the institutions the country needs.

For all his practical knowledge and experience of politics, Broder remains essentially an idealist, and while he believes that his optimism may be "somewhat out of sync in terms of the popular mood," compared with the recent past, the future looks promising indeed.

"The only time that I've really seriously thought the country might be shaken apart was in 1968," he says, recalling the murders of Martin Luther King, Jr., and Robert F. Kennedy, as well as the horrendous Democratic Convention in Chicago. "That was the worst year that I've ever witnessed in this country. From 1974 on, I've been increasingly optimistic about it. I mean, for all the pain that Watergate caused, I do think we learned a very important and positive lesson from it, which is the basic devotion of the American people to that fundamental proposition of the Constitution about the rule of law. I figured if we could deal with that kind of situation as well as we did, that the political vitality of this country was not really in question."

In *The Boys On The Bus,* Timothy Crouse wrote that Broder's reputation among his colleagues for thoroughness, fairness, and insight was such that if "he were to quit tomorrow and begin publishing a mimeographed tip sheet in his basement, Broder would still probably wield the kind of influence that can change campaigns in their course and other reporters in their opinions."

Although the thought of slowing down has crossed his mind, as it does for anyone reaching middle age, Broder, at 54, is not about to put his luggage in the attic and set up a newer version of the hectograph in his recreation room so that he can produce a senior citizens' guide to politics. He is looking forward to the 1984 campaign with as much enthusiasm as he remembers the 1960 contest or anticipates the political battles of 1988 or 1992 or even 2000.

He is shy, however, about handicapping the current race. (Given his performance in Illinois in 1982 and 1983, that is not surprising.) As the gears of the 1984 election machinery began their laborious, tortured grinding in early 1983, Broder smilingly refused to offer an informed guess on the outcome. "I don't know who the candidates will be, nor do I know who's going to win."

It was a pronouncement worthy of Calvin Coolidge, the president so favored by Ronald Reagan. Coolidge, garrulous in private but taciturn in public, knew that if you do not say anything, you will not be called upon to repeat it—or eat your words.

Art Buchwald

His Foe Is Folly and His Weapon Wit

As Edmund Kean, the great British actor of the early nineteenth century, languished on his death bed, his final words were: "Dying is easy—comedy is hard." For over 30 years, Art Buchwald has been the clown prince of American journalism, performing the death-defying feat of writing three funny columns a week for an ever-growing audience. At last count, his column appears in 550 newspapers in the United States and overseas, and in 1982 he received journalism's highest award, the Pulitzer Prize for commentary.

In the fiercely competitive marketing world of newspaper syndicates, Buchwald is said to have attained a unique status: his column is a "loss leader," an item his syndicate sells at a loss in order to attract clients to its other offerings. According to the *Masthead,* the journal of the National Conference of Editorial Writers, other highly popular syndicated columnists may receive 60–70 percent of their column's gross revenues, but the Los Angeles Times Syndicate pays Buchwald 105 percent of what his column earns, or about $250,000 a year.

The managing editor of Buchwald's syndicate told the *Masthead* that the customers for his company's wares have become increasingly choosey—and insecure—when it comes to deciding what mix of columns and other features will attract the most readers and serve their papers best. "Never has there been more sensitivity about 'space' or more selectivity. . . . They're increasingly resistant to long contracts for a feature—unless it's Buchwald, whom they'd kill for."

The amiable object of this potential editorial mayhem is a 58-year-old high school and college dropout who survived the traumas of a Dickensian childhood to parlay a remarkable sense of the absurd, and a genius for friendship, into a career now in its fourth decade. And he shows no sign of slowing down.

If the truth must be told, in 99 percent of his columns Buchwald is a rather pedestrian writer. There is nothing fancy or memorable about his prose. Its elegance is in its economy. He can take a complex or common situation, capture its essence, turn it upside down or inside out, and roast it thoroughly—all in 600 to 650 words. That he has been able to perform this journalistic magic with such a high degree of success thrice weekly for three decades is simply stunning.

It is also true that many of Buchwald's columns follow an almost painfully predictable formula. Conceding that Buchwald has a "brilliant" ability to come up with a premise and telegraph it to his readers in the first paragraph or two, a critic for the *Washington Monthly* found little else to praise about Buchwald's comic skills except his deftness at making so much of so little.

How did he think up his hilarious gag ideas? Looking over his columns I realized he either (a) exaggerated wildly or (b) stood a news event on its head. He also created funny metaphors from common figures of speech and well-worn, overused cliches. . . . One of his favorite devices, I noticed, involved the Expert with the Funny Name. It's a great way to win extra laughs. For many years, of course, our country's greatest humorists—among them, Buddy Hackett—have used funny names to punch up their work. But Buchwald was the true master of this technique. For example, in a column on Al Haig's business prospects after leaving office, he named the literary agent who immediately telephones Haig to offer him a book deal "Fast Fingers Dundy." Buchwald often went one step further, creating an imaginary expert with a funny name and then "interviewing" him about a particular topic. (The interview format, of course, allowed him to use plenty of dialogue filler.) So in one column he interviewed "Vladamir Gluck," the purported inventor of the junk telephone call. Sometimes Buchwald topped even that by attaching the expert to an imaginary agency or business that *also* had a funny name. In a column on the student shortage, an advertising executive, Mr. Honeybee, made a presentation to the board of Desperate Tech University. I'm forever grateful to him for teaching me such handy shortcuts to laughter. . . .

Buchwald readily admits that he is essentially a "dialogue writer" and that Art Levine, the writer of the *Washington Monthly* critique, scored some points about his methods. "Yeah, maybe he did. But, you know, in the long run it isn't what's behind it or how you do it, it's if it works or not. And if it doesn't work, there's nothing you can do about it, and if it does work, there's nothing you can do about it. I'm stuck with this formula; it's very easy for me to do, and it works for me. I admire

Russell Baker because he can write essays, and I couldn't write an essay to save my life. It's very hard for me. . . . But dialogue works for me, and it also works for the reader. I think readers like to read dialogue."

At least they like to read—and listen—to Buchwald's dialogue. His popularity as a columnist has never waned, and the demand for his services as a speaker now keeps him on the road twice a week from September to June each year, giving between 40 and 50 lectures that—at $12,500 a shot—earn him much more than his newspaper column. He also delivers about 20 "freebie" lectures annually, donating his services to worthy causes.

"The Speech," as Buchwald calls his standard spiel, consists of a series of one-liners and jokes neatly printed on well-worn three-by-five inch index cards, à la Ronald Reagan's all-purpose campaign bromides. The material in Buchwald's speech isn't new, either, but culled from his "vast and accurate memory of his columns," as a reviewer of a Buchwald performance once observed. The memory of his audience may not be as vast or accurate, and even if it is, Buchwald fans do not seem to mind the self-plagiarism. His round, bespectacled face and the whine of his nasal, New York accent give him the air of a mischievous, oversized elf, slyly popping the balloons of pretension and sham with the tip of his cigar.

But there is a core of anger—or at least annoyance—at the center of all of Buchwald's humor. "Well, some days you wake up madder than other days," he says. "I'm not sure how 'angry' I am, but . . . for example, in [the Reagan] administration, I haven't heard the word *peace* used once. Everybody's talking about war, everybody's talking about missiles. . . . And I get upset about that because this administration is trying to resolve every diplomatic problem militarily, and I don't know where that's going to lead, and my life's at stake and so's the world's. So that's the kind of stuff I get upset about. . . . I don't consider myself an angry man, but I do get upset about stupidity in government, about people lying, and [about] hypocrisy. We have it in all the government establishments [and] business."

What is fortunate for Buchwald is that he has a chance to let off steam regularly and get paid for it. "Everybody else is just as upset about things, whether it's the phone company or Three Mile Island, and they don't have any way to let their frustrations out. But here I've got this beautiful column three times a week, and there's this empty space, and I can *say* it. And that's the most perfect situation to have."

The ranks of Buchwald fans are not reserved for the hoi polloi. The late Dean Acheson, the former Secretary of State, thought Buchwald was "the greatest satirist in English since Pope and Swift"; Bill Moyers, the former press secretary to Lyndon B. Johnson and now a CBS commentator, once called Buchwald the capital's "court Jester in Residence"; and the late Walter Lippmann, as sober-minded a columnist as ever plied the trade, praised Buchwald as "one of the best satirists of our time." Russell Baker, who is not only Buchwald's idol as an essayist but a close friend, once succinctly declared: "Buchwald is incomparable."

He also, in Baker's view, is courageous. Buchwald bravely faces a blank sheet of paper and stoically endeavors to do something all serious artists in every field know is the toughest creative act: he tries to be funny. To do that consistently, without any change of pace or style, is especially difficult, Baker observed. "One example of the genius of Irving Thalberg at MGM was that he discovered you just couldn't run the Marx Brothers for 60, 70 minutes—it got boring," Baker says. "So he had this inspired idea: he'd get Kitty Carlisle and Allan Jones to come in and stop the Marx Brothers. They would have a love scene,

sing a dreadful song, till the audience was really screaming for relief, and in would come the Marx Brothers. You just cannot be continuously funny. That's the problem Art's set for himself."

Buchwald doesn't look on his effort to be funny as a problem, but as "part of my life. It's the way I survive, and, therefore, whether I was making a living out of it, or whether I was in the dress business, I probably still would use it as my way of getting through the world. I don't think of it as a job, I just think of it as part of living, being funny."

Buchwald's predilection for the absurd was nurtured and refined during a grim childhood against which humor was the only defense. He was born on October 20, 1925, in Mount Vernon, New York, a suburb north of Manhattan. His mother died when he was a baby, and his father, a Jewish curtain maker down on his luck, was unable to support Buchwald and his three older sisters. Instead, he placed them in the Hebrew Orphan Asylum in New York, from which they were farmed out separately to a series of foster homes.

"It was probably the most ridiculous situation of all the ridiculous situations I've been in," Buchwald told Mike Wallace during an interview on "60 Minutes." "What am I doing in this place? Who are these people? I'm different than everybody else. What happened to me? And if you say that at six or seven or eight years old, then you have to cope with it. And my way of coping with it was to make a joke out of everything."

Eventually his father raised enough money to reunite the family, but the scars from those repeated traumas remain with Buchwald to this day. "The world may look all right to you," he once told an interviewer, "but it looks crazy to me. My book—I tell you *my* book—is *Catcher in the Rye.*"

Life with his father and sisters was not

smooth, and school—except for the enjoyment and encouragement he got from writing classes—was even less satisfactory.
Suddenly finding himself the main preoccupation of three older sisters, all intent on
mothering him, and constantly being told by
unamused school authorities that his clown-
ing in class would lead to the penitentiary,
Buchwald ran away from home at 16 to join
the Marines in October 1942. Because he
was underage, Buchwald needed the consent of a parent to sign up. He found a drunk
in Greensboro, North Carolina, to pose as
his father, providing him with a pint of
whiskey for his trouble. "Most patriotic
thing anybody ever asked me to do," the
ersatz paterfamilias mumbled.

After three and a half years of wartime
service, two years of which he spent
attached to the Fourth Marine Air Wing in
the Pacific, Buchwald was mustered out as a
sergeant in 1945. Despite the lack of a high
school diploma, he slipped through the
admissions cracks at a veterans-besieged
University of Southern California and
enrolled as a freshman. When the university
discovered its goof, Buchwald was permitted to stay on as a special student, ineligible
for a degree.

Although he was able to pursue his interest in writing, becoming managing editor of
the campus humor magazine, *Wampus*; a
columnist for the college newspaper, the
Daily Trojan; and author of a variety show
called "No Love Atoll," Buchwald found
that university life suited him no better than
high school. When he received an unexpected $250 veteran's bonus from New York
State in 1948, he quit college and booked a
one-way passage to Paris on a student ship
called, appropriately enough, *Marine
Jumper*.

When he arrived in Paris, Buchwald
enrolled in the Alliance Française, ostensi-
bly to learn French, but instead he bribed
the girl who took attendance and never
showed up for class, preferring to sleep all

day and stay up all night. When his money
ran out, he began looking for a job and
landed an $8-a-week part-time spot as a
nightclub reporter for the New York-based
show business paper *Variety*. In a few
months he convinced the Paris office of the
New York Herald Tribune to hire him as its
nightclub columnist for $45 a week. His
first column, entitled "Paris After Dark,"
contained "offbeat scraps of information
about Parisian night life" and quickly
became popular with the large English-
speaking community in postwar Europe.
Buchwald soon added another column,
called "Mostly About People," in 1951,
featuring interviews with the celebrities who
regularly passed through Paris.

Buchwald says he never consciously
chose journalism as a career. His interest in
and penchant for writing just happened to
coincide with his immediate need for funds
and his familiarity with Parisian nightspots.
"It was a very natural thing for me. I always
loved to write. I didn't pick it; it picked
me."

He was, by all accounts, an abysmal factual reporter, but as a jovial habitué of
Paris's more glamorous restaurants and
watering holes (where he drank only wine),
Buchwald developed an extraordinarily
diverse group of friends among the famous
visitors to the French capital. He came to
know everyone—from Eleanor Roosevelt to
Zsa Zsa Gabor, from Humphrey Bogart and
Lauren Bacall to Elizabeth Taylor and Mike
Todd. Pablo Picasso even dashed off a portrait sketch of him, which Buchwald then
hung in his bathroom.

"I wrote a piece about a guy who wrote to
me; he wanted Picasso's autograph—he was
having a fight with his girl, and he thought
the autograph would bring them together
again," Buchwald recalls, lighting a large
Montecruz cigar. "And David Duncan [the
photographer] was with Picasso down in
Vence, and he showed Picasso the article
and read it to him in Spanish, and Picasso

was very moved and did a sketch for the guy. Duncan called me and said, 'I've got the sketch for the guy,' and I said, 'Screw the guy, what about me?' so Picasso did a sketch of himself and me having a drink."

(In recent years, the Picasso sketch has been displayed in a darker—and more respectful—spot in Buchwald's Washington home, since the crayon with which the master drew it was beginning to fade.)

Buchwald's engaging bonhomie captivated nearly everyone he met, including a young blonde named Ann McGarry, a publicist for Parisian dress designer Pierre Balmain. Despite an unconventional courtship and differences in religion—she is a devout Roman Catholic—they were married in 1952. Their three children were adopted from Ireland, Spain, and France.

In early 1952, the *Herald Tribune* decided to try marketing Buchwald's column in the United States and began syndicating it, picking up a meager six papers when the combined offerings of "Paris After Dark" and "Mostly About People" appeared under the new title "Europe's Lighter Side." It wasn't long before the column gained additional subscribers, however, and Buchwald himself attained the status of the celebrities he had been covering.

Even before his column was syndicated, Buchwald added a taste for the good life to his instinct for the ridiculous. Observing that no one was covering Parisian restaurants for the *Herald Tribune,* he decided to add them to his beat. He lunched regularly at Maxim's, happily accepting the management's courteous deduction of 30 percent from his check, and devised exotic exploits to enliven the contents of his column. Gently ridiculing Hemingway, he went on a Congo safari, taking along a professional hunter to bag his only trophy, a deer; he hired a chauffeur-driven limousine to take him to Moscow in order to show the Soviets "what a real capitalist looks like"; he marched in a May Day parade in East Berlin; went to Turkey to sample a Turkish bath firsthand; and crashed exclusive parties whenever possible.

The high life soon added to his waistline. As a young child, Buchwald suffered from rickets because of poor nutrition; as a gourmand on the Continent he carried close to 200 pounds on his five-feet, eight-inch frame. Fitful dieting occasionally has reduced his girth by 16 to 20 pounds, but now he is back around 190, he notes with resignation. Except for a passion for tennis, he scorns physical exercise. "I think exercise is dangerous. People should stay in the horizontal position as much as possible."

Buchwald's columns from Europe rarely were overtly political. More often, they were comedies of manners and social satires, written in the traditions of Robert Benchley and James Thurber.

Ever since I mentioned that I was a member of the International Set, I have received queries as to how the ordinary citizen can become a member. It is not as hard as a person might think. Anyone who has a string of polo ponies, a yacht, or an old can of caviar hanging around the house is eligible to join.

To be a member of the International Set is one of the most rewarding experiences I can think of and, in a world fraught with strife and striven with fraught, it is still nice to know there is a group of people in Europe who just don't care what is going on. . . .

There are no written rules concerning membership in our set. The basis for our friendship is built on mutual understanding. If you own a boat, a stable of horses, and you are a direct descendant of Louis XIV, it's understood that you are going to be invited to our parties. If you're beautiful and rich, or ugly and rich, your chances of making the grade are infinitely better than if you are ugly and poor. (Beautiful and poor girls do get in without much trouble, but they don't stay poor for long.)

These columns hold up extraordinarily well. Buchwald had a knack for capturing the eternal qualities of the nations and peoples he parodied. His description of the sales techniques of the Italians and French is a classic:

In Italy, when a customer walks into a store he is greeted like a long-lost brother.

"Welcome, signor; welcome, signor. Please come into the shop where it is nice and cool. You do not have to buy anything. You can just look."

"I would like a poplin shirt. Do you have any?"

"Do we have any? That's all we have is poplin shirts. Mama, give me the best quality poplin shirts for these nice people."

While Mama is dragging out the shirts the man says: "Are you from America?"

You say you are.

"I have relatives in Chicago. You know them. The Qualliteris. Look, here is their picture. My cousin has seven children. Please to look. That is Rosita, Antonio, Carlotta, Alfredo, Guiseppe, Charles and Thomaso. Rosita is seven, Antonio is, etc., etc."

The shirts finally come. The man says: "Beautiful Egyptian cotton. Notice the pearl-like quality of the buttons, how the tail of the shirt is rounded gently . . . the firm rich feel of the collar. Please to touch it yourself. . . . Take a dozen. In America you will thank me for selling you these shirts."

You are touched by his kindness. You buy a dozen. His wife gives your wife a bouquet of flowers. They both escort you to the door. You shake hands with them . . . they ask you to come back soon. They tell you not to miss a visit to St. Peter's, and they give you the names of a trattoria in Rome and friends in Florence. There are tears in their eyes as you walk away. Everybody is happy. . . .

But in France everything is different. You walk into a shop which is quite empty, with six or seven sales people standing around.

You wait fifteen minutes and finally someone comes up to you and, speaking in the tone that a Poujadist would use on a tax collector, he says: "What do you want?"

You tell him you want a shirt.

"What size?" he says sneeringly.

"Size 17."

"Ha!" he shouts. "We don't have your size. Do you think we can carry everyone's size? How much space do you think we have here? The largest size we have is 16 and ½."

You tell him you'd like to see it.

A look of disappointment comes over his face.

"What colour?" he says.

"White."

"Ha!" he shouts. "We don't have white. We only have them in colours. Do you think we can stock both white and coloured shirts?"

Another salesman comes over and asks, in French, what is the trouble. The fellow salesman tells him in French: "This idiot wants a white shirt. First he asked for a size 17 and now he wants it in a 16 and ½. What kind of store does he think we run?"

"These Americans are all crazy."

Despite Buchwald's withering lampoons of the French national character, he lived in Paris for 14 years and insists that he "had no problems with the French people," making as many friends there as elsewhere.

As his column grew in popularity, Buchwald sniffed his first whiff of controversy in December 1957, when a column of his that poked fun at the press conferences held by James Hagerty, the press secretary to President Eisenhower, sparked a display of the usually unflappable Hagerty's fearsome temper. Buchwald parodied the exorbitant minutiae Hagerty faithfully supplied the press corps covering Ike's attendance at a NATO conference in Paris.

I'm sorry I'm late, gentlemen, but I thought the show at the Lido would end at 11:30. I have a few things to report. The President went to bed at 11:06 tonight. . . . As far as I know he'll sleep until morning.

Q. Jim, whose idea was it for the President to go to sleep?

A. It was the President's idea. He was tired and decided to go to sleep.

Q. Did Sherman Adams, or Dr. Snyder or the President's son suggest he go to sleep?

A. As far as I know, the President suggested the idea himself.

Q. Jim, did the President speak to anyone before retiring?

A. He spoke to the Secretary of State.

Q. What did he say to the Secretary of State, Jim?

A. He said: "Good night, Foster."

Q. And what did the Secretary say to the President?

A. He said: "Good night, Mr. President."

Q. The Secretary didn't say: "Pleasant dreams?"

A. Not to my knowledge. I have nothing on that.

Q. Jim, do you have any idea what the President is dreaming of this very moment?

A. No, the President has never revealed to me any of his dreams.

Q. Are we to assume from that that the President doesn't dream?

A. I'm not saying he does or he doesn't. I just said I don't know.

When Hagerty saw the column, he publicly blasted Buchwald as a writer of "unadulterated rot." Buchwald cheerily contended that he only wrote "adulterated rot." (Ike reportedly found Buchwald's column amusing and later tried to soothe Hagerty's bruised feelings.) The minor tempest, gleefully reported by the journalists regularly assigned to the presidential beat, did wonders for Buchwald's reputation. His column gained 14 newspapers on the strength of Hagerty's backhanded endorsement, Buchwald later boasted.

By 1961, Buchwald was earning $50,000 a year (in *real* dollars), living in a seven-room apartment on Paris's Right Bank, and writing for 115 newspapers. Anthologies of his columns regularly sold more than 100,000 hard-bound copies. There even was talk that the *New York Times,* whose daily circulation in Paris lagged behind the *Herald Tribune's* by 13,000, was thinking of luring him to its staff. One Buchwald devotee said such a switch was unlikely: "I could as soon see Gypsy Rose Lee playing St. Joan."

Life in Paris was comfortable for Buchwald—too comfortable, he decided. A humorist, he believes, has to feel bruised and battered in order to produce good work, and all the years of easy living were being reflected in the column. It was becoming repetitious, he thought, and a lecture tour in the United States convinced him that it was time to come home. In this country, he notes, "you don't have to worry about getting too comfortable or happy."

When Buchwald's decision to return to the United States was announced, political gossipmonger Drew Pearson reported that the publisher of the Republican *Herald Tribune,* John Hay Whitney, was so furious at John F. Kennedy's much-publicized decision to drop the *Tribune* from the White House subscription list that he had decided to get even by plopping Buchwald into the middle of Kennedy's Washington. Buchwald denied that he was being sent on a rear-guard sabotage mission. "I made my decision to go to Washington before the White House canceled the subscription," he said. "In fact, I understood one of my duties was going to be to deliver the paper to the White House."

In fact, Buchwald chose to settle in Washington, rather than New York—and retitled his column "Capitol Punishment"—because "for my purposes, this was where the action is. New York is just a city now; Washington is the capital of the world. I have maybe 70, 80, or 100 papers overseas that carry my column because it's from Washington."

Most of Buchwald's friends advised against the move. In Europe he was *the* American in Paris, as much a tourist attraction as the Eiffel Tower. In the United States, they warned, he would become just another Washington-based byline. Buchwald, on the other hand, never doubted his ability to conquer the capital, and his confidence proved justified. In one year he added 75 newspapers to his syndication list and upped his income to $80,000 a year. He found plenty to write about on the New Frontier.

Everybody I talked to was impressed by Mrs. John F. Kennedy's television tour of the White House, and I believe Mrs. Kennedy has made a great contribution to the American home because she has made people conscious of their own surroundings and furniture.

Probably no one was more influenced by the program than my own sister who lives in Kew Gardens, Long Island. I went over to her apartment on the Sunday after Mrs. Kennedy showed the White House, and my sister was waiting at the door to give me a guided tour.

"Thank you for coming," she said. "I'd like to show you around because I feel that's the only way people can understand our heritage."

"Well, it's awfully kind of you to let us come here, Mrs. Jaffe. Where shall we begin?"

"I think we ought to start with the East Room," she said. "We call it the East Room because it overlooks the Eighth Avenue subway and Queens Boulevard—at least it did until someone built an apartment across from us and blocked the view. The East Room was originally intended as an audience room where we could meet our in-laws or

insurance agent, and our son's teacher when he got in trouble at school.

"But now it's gradually become associated with other events. Our large receptions are held here because, as you can see, this room can hold as many as twelve people at one time."

"Would you describe some of the furniture to me?" I asked her.

"I'd be delighted. That couch over there, the one with the stuffing coming out of it, is an early Franklin D. Roosevelt period piece donated to us by Aunt Molly, who said she was going to throw it out anyway. Aunt Molly used it all during the Depression and it has a great deal of historical interest.

"That lamp over there is a rare pre-Pearl Harbor Macy basement special. It was a wedding gift donated by Mr. and Mrs. Arthur Gordon, of Forest Hills, New York, and there are only 65,900 of them left in the United States."

"Is that the oldest thing in the house?" I asked her.

"No, the hot-water heater is the oldest thing in our house, but that's in another room."

The Buchwalds themselves settled into an ample, five-bedroom residence in the posh Wesley Heights section of northwest Washington. In time they added an oval swimming pool to their ¾-acre compound, which is surrounded on three sides by a high fence. Buchwald thoroughly enjoyed the sprightly spirit of the Kennedy years and became a confidant of Robert Kennedy.

His friendship with Kennedy was a rare exception to Buchwald's usual practice of eschewing social contacts with politicians. "When you talk to senators and congressmen, you get the impression they are working, and you know it isn't true. And people have a tendency to win you over with flattery. I'm a pushover. I figure a guy who likes my columns can't be all bad," he told an interviewer in 1963. Instead, many of Buchwald's close friends are fellow journalists, such as Benjamin Bradlee, executive editor of the *Washington Post;* David Brinkley of ABC; and Robert Novak, of the Evans and Novak columnist team.

Following his move to Washington, Buchwald clearly was at the top of his profession, but there was a down side to his fancy home, famous friends, and booming popularity. He had achieved all his childhood dreams of success, but he was not happy. He was, in fact, worse than unhappy; he was "suicidal." The humor may have sparkled in his column, but it began to ring hollow to him personally. He became depressed and confused and sought professional help, undergoing two and a half years of analysis. "One of the toughest things to handle in life for somebody who has had a tough life is success. That's why so many successful people are in analysis. You've been kicked around when you were a kid, so you get used to that, and you know that you *should* be kicked around," Buchwald observed some years ago. "To be on top is a very difficult thing—not to let it scare you, because it scares the hell out of you."

Buchwald's early experiences had taught him always to prepare for the worst and to try to make a joke out of it. "It worked for me for 30 years. And when it stopped working for me, I got into trouble," he told one interviewer. What he discovered in analysis was that, like many underprivileged children who become successful, he somehow felt guilty about his achievements. What he also learned was that he deserved the success he had and the amenities that came with it. "I have no problem now accepting all the things that I figure I got coming to me. When I was a kid everybody's telling me I was going to end up in a bad way. You know, the guy who's a funny kid is not well received by the grown-up population. They think he's a wise-ass; they think he's a troublemaker."

However secure he may feel now about his success, one of his colleagues as a columnist said that Buchwald is believed to feel habitually insecure about his column and fearful that papers may cancel it. Buchwald says that is not so. "I have a lot of insecurities about life, but not my work. Dealing with children, grandchildren, my wife— that's where all of my insecurities lie. When it comes to my work, I'm completely secure. . . . I'm very satisfied with the numbers [of papers] I have and also the circulation I have. . . . As a matter of fact, I sort of stay out of the business end of it because it really doesn't interest me that much. If I lose a paper or pick up a paper, I really don't pay that much attention to it."

The insecurities that began gnawing at Buchwald when he arrived in Washington were not reflected in his columns. John Kennedy reportedly enjoyed Buchwald's satires immensely, and when Kennedy was assassinated, Buchwald wrote one of his most memorable, and perhaps most poetic, pieces. In 21 spare sentences he captured the nation's anguish in a way that still can evoke the shock of that November day:

We weep for our President who died for his country.

We weep for his wife and for his children.

We weep for his mother and father and brothers and sisters.

We weep for the millions of people who are weeping for him.

We weep for Americans, that this could happen in our country.

We weep for the Europeans

And the Africans

And the Asians

And people in every corner of the globe who saw in him a hope for the future and a chance for mankind.

We weep for our children and their children and everyone's children, for he was charting their destinies as he was charting ours.

We weep for the Negro, who saw in him a chance for a decent life.

We weep for the working man for
whom he tried to find jobs.

We weep for the artist and the writer
and the poet.

For he cared about all of us.

We weep for the teachers and the
pupils.

We weep for old people whom he tried
to help.

We weep for the young people who he
believed in.

We weep for the soldiers and sailors
and airmen whom he commanded.

We weep for their parents because he
saved their children from being destroyed by war.

And while we weep, we weep for the
twisted mind that committed this horrible crime.

We weep for all the tortured and
warped people who could not accept the
decent things he stood for.

And we weep for all the hatred and
prejudice that fill the hearts of such a
small segment of our society.

We weep because there is nothing else
we can do.

Except curse those who would destroy
a man in hopes of destroying all of us.

The number of times Buchwald has
been deadly serious over a 30-year span can
probably be counted on the fingers of both
hands, and perhaps it is not surprising that
those infrequent detours down a somber road
inspire an even greater avalanche of reader
mail than usual. (Ordinarily, Buchwald
receives over 100 letters a week from
readers.)

"It's so out of character for me to do a
serious piece that when I do do one, it has
tremendous impact," Buchwald says. "It's
unexpected, for one thing, and secondly, at
the time I do them, people are rather grateful. I'm careful not to overdo it, and I prefer
to say something serious in a humorous
way, but there are times when you can't do
it, and you don't want to do it, and you're in
bad taste if you do do it."

Lyndon Johnson was not a Buchwald fan.
The richness of Johnson's character and his
overbearing manner provided ample fodder
for Buchwald, but LBJ's skin was notori-
ously thin when it came to humor derived at
his expense. Bill Moyers once recounted
how Johnson found him chuckling over a
Buchwald piece and angrily asked: "Do you
find him funny?"

"No sir," Moyers responded with a
straight face.

At the height of the Johnson reign,
Buchwald put the question of his impact on
the President in proper perspective: "Some
of my inside sources at the White House tell
me that President Johnson reads me and
chuckles. Other equally informed sources
tell me that LBJ does not read me. I suspect
the truth is somewhere in between; he reads
me but does not chuckle."

When the colorful Johnson was replaced
by Richard Nixon, a visitor to Buchwald's
cramped and cluttered office, which is in a
building just a block and a half from the
White House, heard him bemoan the loss of
a splendid subject. "What am I going to
do?" he wailed in mock panic. "At least
with Johnson you could make fun of his
accent, but Nixon has no accent. He's plastic, his wife's plastic, his kids are plastic!"

As things turned out, of course, the Nixon
administration proved an even greater boon to
Buchwald than Johnson had been. Buchwald fondly recalls the Watergate era as his
"Camelot." One of his most felicitous crea-
tions was the "Old Nixon," kept hidden in a
White House closet and only let out at night
to do the devious, underhanded things the
pious "New Nixon," surrounded by the majesty of the Oval Office, found beneath him.

It took the President's White House staff
all day to locate the Old Nixon. They
finally found him at Howard Johnson's
across the street from the Watergate,
eating a meat loaf sandwich.

"You'd better get back to the White

House right away," John Ehrlichman told him. "The boss is really steaming."

When the Old Nixon walked into the President's office, he found the New Nixon in a rage.

"I've just received information that you're behind the Dirty Tricks Department of the Committee for the Reelection of the President. What do you have to say for yourself?"

"I refuse to comment as I don't want to prejudice the rights of the defendants in the Watergate bugging trial."

"Don't hand me that stuff," the President said. "You've put me in a helluva spot! How could you do it to me?"

"Ah, come on. You're overreacting. We were just having a little fun with the Democrats. No one takes it seriously," the Old Nixon said.

"But we didn't need it," the New Nixon said. "We're ahead by twenty-eight percent in the polls. It makes us look cheap and unscrupulous."

The Old Nixon retorted, "Sure, you can say that now. But at the time we started the intelligence operation, no one knew what was going to happen. Suppose it had been real close? Our Dirty Tricks Department could have made the difference. You've been President so long you don't even understand politics anymore."

Nixon, either Old or New, was not Buchwald's only foil during those halcyon days. The exploits of Henry Kissinger—first as National Security Advisor and then as Secretary of State—were ripe for parody:

When the history books of this decade are written, they will refer to Henry Kissinger's trip to China as "The Tummy Ache Heard Round the World."

Using the excuse of an upset stomach, Mr. Kissinger managed to elude everyone and high-tail it off to Peking to have sweet-and-sour pork with Chou En-lai.

While it was a great ploy, Mr. Kissinger's "diplomatic illness" could backfire on him. Suppose he *really* gets a stomach ache at some future time. Who is going to believe him?

Our scene opens in the medical room at the White House. Henry staggers in, clutching his stomach, and says, "Doctor, I have this pain right here."

The White House doctor laughs. "Good old Henry. Where are you off to this time—the Suez Canal?"

"I'm not joking, Doc. It hurts terribly."

"I know," the doctor says. "The President is sending you to talk to Castro."

Henry is now writhing on the floor. "Believe me, it hurts. Right in the gut. . . ."

"You really can put on an act, Henry. I wouldn't be surprised if you turned up in Albania next week."

Henry crawls out of the doctor's office on his hands and knees [and] is rolling on the floor as Secretary of State William Rogers comes by.

"Hello, Henry. You going to the Cabinet meeting?"

"Mr. Secretary, my stomach. I have a pain in my stomach. It's killing me."

Secretary Rogers says angrily, "Well, no one has informed me about it. What are you up to this time?"

"I'm not up to anything, Mr. Secretary. Could you call an ambulance?"

"Hanoi," Rogers says. "You're cooking up something in Hanoi. I'll probably be the last one to know about it."

"I'm not going to Hanoi. I'm really sick."

"No kidding? Well, I'm sorry to hear that, Henry." And Rogers smiles and walks away.

With his last ounce of strength, Henry staggers into the Oval Room and falls down in front of the President.

"Henry," the President says. "You don't have to prostrate yourself in front of me. I know you're loyal."

Henry is in such agony he can't speak.

"What is it, Henry?" the President says. "Would you like to go to Morocco?"

Henry shakes his head.

"The Vatican? You want to see the Pope?" Henry groans.

The President gets up. "I don't have time to play games, Henry. Write me a memo telling me what you want. By the way, Mrs. Nixon said she would like you for dinner tonight. We're having meat loaf."

Henry screams and passes out, as the curtain falls.

Buchwald turned his facility for dialogue and scenes to advantage in 1970, when a comedy he wrote called "Sheep on the Runway" became a modest hit on Broadway. The play dealt with a befuddled U.S. ambassador and a globe-trotting, hawkish columnist bearing a marked philosophic resemblance to Joseph Alsop. The two manage to push the tiny Himalayan nation to which the ambassador is assigned towards disaster by hunting for nonexistent evidence of Communist subversion in the country.

The play got encouraging reviews from most of the tough New York critics. Clive Barnes, then the theatrical arbiter for the *Times,* called it "a rattling good first play," adding with uncharacteristic generosity: "It may not be perfect, but who is perfect?" Walter Kerr, in a subsequent *Sunday Times* review, was less kind, but gentle nevertheless. He called the play "all sheep and no runway" but termed Buchwald "one of the marvels of the age," who could not be expected to write plays as funny as his columns. "It would have made him too marvelous, and led to hubris, which all my friends tell me is a good thing to avoid."

Despite the play's success, and the urging of several critics to try again, Buchwald hasn't written a second comedy, primarily because such an effort is too time-consuming. "From the time you write one to the time it gets on Broadway, you're talking about two years. You're talking about going on the road for two or three months. It's very hard to be a part-time playwright [or] a part-time screenwriter. My first loyalty is to the column. Everything else comes out

of the column. I don't want the column to slide."

Not only does the column spawn The Speech, but an anthology sprouts from it once every two years. His books still sell upwards of 80,000 to 100,000 in hardbound copies.

Because of his loyalty to the column, Buchwald also rejects almost weekly overtures to transfer it to television. "Television makes you a personality. It doesn't do anything for your work. You just become a personality. I'm getting enough out of my speeches and my column as far as wanting to be a personality goes. I don't need extra."

Richard Nixon reportedly despised Buchwald's column, although an effort to obtain his comments on Buchwald's work—as well as on the other columnists in this book—was unsuccessful.* Gerald Ford was the only president to invite Buchwald and his wife to a formal dinner at the White House, and Buchwald has no idea whether Jimmy Carter and Ronald Reagan have ever read him. "I stay away from the White House," he says. I'm not the type of guy who goes around looking for stories or feeding off sources. I sit here in this messy office and I'm like a political cartoonist. If someone asked me what I did for a living, I'd say, 'I do political cartoons in words.' "

The subtleties of Buchwald's caricatures in prose either escape the Soviets or are used for their own purposes. They long have reprinted Buchwald's column (without permission and without compensation, of course), passing it off to Russian readers as factual reports from a troubled America. When American authorities occasionally complain to Buchwald about the nefarious ways in which the Soviets use his satires, he grins and gives them a two-word answer: "Stop them!"

The view that Soviet—and American—

---

*Similar letters to Gerald Ford and Jimmy Carter also were unsuccessful.

readers get of Ronald Reagan's United States, as seen through Buchwald's black horn-rimmed glasses, sometimes is not so jolly. In an especially pungent 1983 column, Buchwald funneled his anger over the decimation of the Environmental Protection Agency through a stinging parody of Thornton Wilder's "Our Town":

STAGE MANAGER: The name of the town is Seven Corners. It's a nice town, you know what I mean? Nobody remarkable ever comes out of it as far as we know. We're just plain simple folk here and we can't claim to be nothing more than just another town along Route 16.

I better show you around a bit. That nice white house for sale on the corner belongs to the Jorgensons. It's a real good buy if you don't mind living over a landfill of dioxin. Oh, I forgot to tell you. About 10 years ago a fellow came through and sprayed oil mixed with dioxin on the roads to settle the dust. The dioxin's all over the place. That's why you see so many "For Sale" signs on people's lawns.

"Over there is the school, and right behind it is where some chemical company dumped all its PCB in those big oil drums. The chemical company's out of business, and the stuff is now seeping into the playground. Funny, you don't ever see any kids playing there anymore.

Well, as I said, it's just about morning. Here's the mayor. How's it going, Charlie?

MAYOR: Not too good. I been calling the EPA for two weeks trying to find out what they're going to do about all our hazardous waste. They claim they still have no idea whether our soil samples are bad for human health or not. . . .

STAGE MANAGER: Well, have a nice day, Mayor. Here comes Doc Gibbs. You look kind of peaked, Doc.

DOC: Mrs. Henigen gave birth last night to a premature baby. That's the 14th premature baby I've delivered this year.

By the way, if you're still using well water, be sure and boil it before you drink it. . . .

STAGE MANAGER: Excuse me . . ., I want to have a word with Sam Peters. (To audience) Sam's our undertaker, and I guess he's about the busiest man in town. Sam, can I have a word with you?

SAM: Sorry, I don't have the time.

STAGE MANAGER: Don't let me stop you, Sam. Well, it's getting on to bedtime. Most of the folks are tucked in for the night after another uneventful day. Like I said, nothing much ever happens in Seven Corners. If it wasn't for the lead in the river which killed all the fish, Seven Corners would still be a real fine place to live.

In the early days of the Reagan administration, Buchwald confessed to finding himself sometimes agreeing—a bit uncomfortably—with some of Reagan's cherished beliefs. "I'm sort of like most people who grew up with Franklin Roosevelt, who thought government could solve our problems," he said early in 1981. "Since I live in Washington, I've become a little skeptical and I seem to find myself agreeing with Reagan more than I want to that government is not the answer to all our problems."

By 1983, however, Buchwald expressed a somewhat different view of Reagan's bureaucracy-busting policies. "What Reagan did was eliminate the government that was screwing up business, to the detriment of the public interest," he says, making no effort to temper his criticism with humor. "I agreed with the essential [idea] that government . . . does get into everybody's lives . . . and it's very bureaucratic and everything. The real problem is that when you start toying with it, you find all these sweetheart deals—the EPA is the best example of it—and suddenly you find [that] maybe [Reagan's] not eliminating government; he's just eliminating the parts of government that make life harder for his pals."

Buchwald has never been comfortable with the Reagan administration's military and foreign policies and says that Reagan "worries the hell out of me on defense and nuclear war and all this stuff." In a 1982 column, he suggested one way to view the administration's defense policies was as a macabre joke:

People are constantly asking me, "Who is the man with the most humor in the Reagan administration?" They're surprised when my response is "Cap" Weinberger, our secretary of Defense. Cap says things with a straight face that make you want to roll on the floor.

Just the other day he told newspapermen he is for a "protracted nuclear war." He doesn't want one of these hairtrigger wars which last 30 or 40 minutes. Cap said he has ordered everyone at the Pentagon to figure not only how to keep a nuclear war going, but how to make sure the U.S. wins one when the missiles start flying.

Half the people in the Pentagon took Cap seriously. But those who knew what a deadpan comic Cap is just laughed and went back to doing the crossword puzzle.

The material for Cap's "prolonged nuclear war" came out of a routine he did when he first took charge of the Defense Department and came up with a comic routine on "limited nuclear war."

... The only ones who didn't laugh were our NATO allies who figured out if a "limited nuclear war was going to be waged it would be on their turf," and even after Al Haig tried to explain to the Europeans that Cap was only joking, they still didn't find the secretary's war routine very funny. . . .

When he was asked if a nuclear war was winnable, Cap replied, again with a straight face, "I just don't have any idea; I don't know that anybody has any idea. But we're certainly going to give the armed forces everything they need to win one."

These are just a few samples of Cap Weinberger's humor. They may not sound as funny on paper, but when you see him standing up in front of the mike, looking like Woody Allen, delivering them, you could die laughing.

Leaning back in his office chair, Buchwald delivers an assessment of Reagan's abilities in foreign policy that is blunt and decidedly unfunny. "I think he's ignorant, and I think there're very few people in this particular government that have an overview of the world and how it works. And this is in contrast to Nixon and Kissinger, who I felt did have a strong overview of the world. I think Kennedy had an overview of the world; I think that was Johnson's weakest area.

"The point is that you need imagination; you need to have traveled; you need to have spoken with people. These are all things that neither Reagan or [William] Clark, his [then-] Security Affairs [adviser] do. They just don't. They have a Californian's view of the world. They don't know the suleties—this is all serious what I'm saying—but they just don't know the subtleties of different countries, how they operate, how they think. And this is something you can't learn when you've just become President of the United States. You know, Nixon read about the world like baseball. . . . That was his interest. Henry [Kissinger] made a lot of mistakes, but Henry at least has the concepts. I think [Secretary of State George] Shultz may have them, but I just don't know how much input he has."

Buchwald is not sanguine about the Reagan administration's domestic policies either. In a 1982 column he attributed some of them to the tenant he says replaced the Old Nixon in the White House attic: Bonzo, Reagan's old simian co-star.

It has been one of the best-kept secrets of the administration. When the Reagans first moved into the White House they brought Bonzo, the president's favorite chimpanzee, with them. Bonzo keeps to himself playing in the attic or down in the basement, and swinging on trees on the south side of the White House lawn at night when no one is around.

When the Reagans are alone in their upstairs living quarters, Bonzo might sit in the president's lap while they reminisce about their days on the old Warner Bros. lot.

Bonzo has never caused the president any embarrassment, until recently. . . . [He] managed to get out of the attic where he was locked up, and started exploring the West Wing, a place he had never been before. The West Wing is where the Oval Office is and where all the president's top administration officials work.

The chimp walked into an empty office and saw a computer in the corner. Bonzo hit a couple of keys and the words BUD-GET CUTS came up on the screen. This delighted him and he started to hit more keys. The word UNEMPLOYED came up on the screen and Bonzo clapped his hands and hit the keys again. The words TAX UNEMPLOYMENT BENEFITS appeared, and then Bonzo hit a communications key and the message was dumped into a computer that prints out White House press releases. The printer immediately went to work: THE WHITE HOUSE ANNOUNCED TODAY THAT IT WAS CONSIDERING TAXING UNEMPLOYMENT BENEFITS AS A WAY OF GETTING PEOPLE TO LOOK FOR JOBS. . . .

Larry Speaks, the White House deputy press secretary, didn't want to look ignorant, and he confirmed to reporters that the unemployment tax was being given serious consideration.

Ed Meese, one of the president's top aides, had a tough decision to make. He could either defend the tax that afternoon or wake up the president. He opted for defending the tax rather than interrupt the president's nap. . . .

Fortunately . . . a Secret Service man walked into the West Wing office and grabbed Bonzo . . . and gave him a banana.

The agent then called the Western White House and told them that he caught Bonzo [on the budget computer]. . . . When he reported what was on it, the pieces all started to fall into place concerning the unemployment tax announcement on Thanksgiving Day. . . .

But when someone on [Reagan's] staff suggested they move Bonzo out of the White House and send him to the Old Actors' Home in Hollywood, President Reagan wouldn't hear of it. "He's the best friend I ever had," the president said. "And just because he was in show business doesn't mean he can't come up with some good ideas."

Buchwald's preference for satirizing specific events and his frequent reliance on the comic dialogue form give many of his columns a rather short half life and often a numbing similarity. Even in the most recent anthologies of his pieces, there are many columns that require the reader to have a comprehensive memory of current events in order to remember the incidents that inspired various sallies. Similarly, his columns are better in small portions rather than steady doses. But as a reviewer for the *New Republic* observed over 20 years ago: "If you are stunned by the sameness of his columns (and you will be, upon reading them *en masse*), remember how good they looked when they appeared one at a time, three times a week, alongside gloomy headlines and the gloomier interpretations by the more serious pundits."

Although most of Buchwald's columns deal with politics, he still can produce some pieces of social commentary that are reminiscent of—and as timeless as—the best work he did in Europe:

Andy Rooney started it on CBS' "60 Minutes" by discussing one of America's greatest phobias, "Fear of Tipping." Rooney came out against tipping, but he admitted he didn't have the nerve to lead an anti-tipping movement.

Colman McCarthy, a columnist for The Washington Post, then wrote that Rooney didn't have to lead the anti-tipping movement in the U.S. because it already had leaders, including McCarthy, who not only "stiffs" waiters and cab drivers, but golf caddies as well.

I am happy to join in the discussion because in an earlier life I worked as a bellboy. While Rooney and McCarthy can cry about the inequities heaped on the tippers, I can talk about the joys of being a "tippee."

. . . In my day, those of us who always had our hands out could spot a deadbeat like McCarthy before he even got out of a taxi. He was easy to identify, because you could hear the driver curse him as he drove away. Another clue was a McCarthy-type always tried to carry his own bag in the lobby, and after checking in, attempted to lug it himself up to the room. . . .

An old bell captain from whom I had learned the profession told me, "When checking in a couple, there are two kinds you will be dealing with. The first will be married. Don't waste too much time on them because the size of the tip has already been established in the husband's mind. But every once in a while you will luck out and get an unmarried couple. At this moment money is no object, for them to get into the room and to get you out. Stall for time, checking the windows, the closets and the water in the bathroom. The longer you remain, the more nervous the man will become, and finally, in desperation, he'll shove a fistful of money in your hand if you just agree to leave."

"How will I know if the couple is married or not?"

"A married man usually flops on the bed first, and his wife always checks the closets to see if there are enough hangers."

"And an unmarried couple?"

"The unmarried woman usually starts combing her hair in front of the mirror, and the unmarried man always makes sure the bolt of the door is working."

My tutor gave me one other piece of advice: "If the couple is unmarried, wait 20 minutes and then bring them a bucket of ice. You'll gain the fastest five bucks you ever made in your life."

Buchwald takes a cab from his home to his office, arriving most mornings between 9:00 and 9:30. He reads the *New York Times*, the *Washington Post*, and the *Wall Street Journal* and clips or tears out articles that might provide subjects for his column, stuffing them into his shirt pocket. Some days he writes two columns in order to build up a reserve of material for the days when he is on the road making speeches and for the months of June and July, which he spends on Martha's Vineyard. He rented a home on the Vineyard for a dozen years and finally purchased one in 1980. A regular tennis partner of his during the summer is Walter Cronkite, who also has a summer home on the Vineyard. In a "Life of Walter" column written on the eve of Cronkite's retirement as CBS's anchorman, Buchwald "revealed" that Cronkite had established his reputation for trustworthiness at an early age: "He was the only boy that parents in Houston would trust with their daughters. Walter never violated that trust, and most of the girls he went out with reported it was the most boring date they ever had."

Buchwald does not like to build up too much of a column backlog, however, since he prefers to have his material as fresh as possible, preferably no more than a week behind the news event that prompts the satire. In a 1961 interview, he said that it took him around two hours to peck out a column on his typewriter; eleven years later, he told another interviewer that he could bat one out in 45 minutes.

"Let's settle for an hour," he says now, with a grin. He writes both at his office and at his home, where he has a computerized word-processor. With this new toy, he can make clean corrections on his copy, store it on small discs, and make printouts of it to be retyped for syndication.

While some of Buchwald's friends accuse him of having perfected the four-hour week, Buchwald once defended his apparently slapdash work routine by pointing out that he may spend two or more days thinking about a column idea before he'll commit it to paper. He writes swiftly and edits the final copy lightly. No one edits or alters his column once he sends it to the Los Angeles Times Syndicate by means of a telecopier in his office.

His office consists of a small reception area, where his secretary handles the flood of mail, and an inner office, piled high with books, newspapers, photographs, and other mementoes. Among Buchwald's treasures is a Washington Redskins helmet, a gift from his good friend, lawyer Edward Bennett Williams, the team's president. Buchwald is a devoted Redskins fan and attends most of their home games. The doors to both the outer and inner offices are never closed, and if his secretary is busy, Buchwald will nonchalantly answer his office telephone, the number for which is listed in the Washington directory.

For years, Buchwald jovially has displayed samples of his choicest hate mail in dime-store frames hung in the office's reception area. Some of it is clumsily amusing ("Smart Aleck; Sadist; Stupid," one addresses him); a few pieces are vicious. One regular correspondent, a virulent anti-Semite, signs a different name on each letter, "but the typewriter's always the same," Buchwald's secretary observed. "He's like one of the NRA people. They've all got nice typewriters."

The attempted assassination of President Reagan prompted one of Buchwald's rare serious commentaries. It revealed a sober view of his own role as a public figure and the strange hatred it can inspire:

Somewhere out in this country are sick people who, though complete strangers, harbor bitter grievances against well-known individuals who have never done them any harm. But for some reason, they have decided that a particular person is responsible for their pain.

The mail arrives and among the letters are the anonymous scrawls of anger and hate. The scrawls can be threatening, or they can make no sense at all. You tend to laugh them off, because you don't want to admit that somebody out there has chosen you as the target for his discontent.

The letters are either thrown into the wastebasket, or placed in the increasingly large "nut file" that you've built up over the years. Sometimes the mail continues for months and even years. Other times one letter is sufficient to relieve the person of whatever is bothering him.

The hate, anger and frustration are transmitted not only through the mail, but also over the telephone. The stranger tells you what you have allegedly done to him, and asks what you are going to do about it.

The trick is to talk calmly and assure him that whatever his grievance is, you will look into it. You try to persuade him that you are not responsible for whatever is hurting him, and you end the conversation as quietly and gently as you can.

For the most part, however, Buchwald's experiences with the public, especially on the speaking tours, are overwhelmingly favorable. "I don't think I've ever gotten a bad time from people. They like me and I like them. I think I've got a nice, personal relationship with the reader. He feels I'm a friend and reads the column. That's one of the reasons I've been staying away from television, because I just feel this relationship in print with the reader . . . is a very pleasant thing."

Buchwald is quick to agree with the assessment of one writer friend that most of his work is essentially transitory and will only engage the interest of Ph.D. candidates in American journalism 50 years from now. "In the back of my mind, I would like to do one or two things that would last. I haven't done 'em, but that's one of the things I've got on the back burner."

The work of most newspaper writers is unlikely to endure, he adds. "You read about 'Mr. Dooley,' you hear about some of the other newspaper greats, but nobody's reading them anymore. You get instant gratification, because what you write appears the next day or in a few days, but you don't get immortality."

The closest Buchwald thinks he may have gotten to immortality was the offer of a paper company in Appleton, Wisconsin—where he was giving a speech—to allow him to go out to its forest and select the trees to be used for his next book. "I'm not sure whether they used 'em, but I picked 'em. That's immortality."

In many ways, Buchwald has long been a member of the Washington establishment that he ridicules. Although he and his wife don't go out much in the evenings, rarely entertain and dislike the capital's cocktail parties and embassy soirees, it is more because Buchwald doesn't drink and already has "done it all" rather than because he wishes to remain a detached observer. "If it wasn't for the speeches, I'd probably be more of a recluse than I am," he says.

He used to be more visible socially. For years, Buchwald's annual Easter Party for the children of Washington's political and journalistic hierarchy was a major social event. He would greet the guests dressed in a large rabbit costume. (A photograph of Buchwald as Papa Bunny standing alongside a perplexed-looking Walter Lippmann—captioned "Lippmann's finest hour"—hangs in his office.) Similarly, Buchwald's regular table at the elegant Sans Souci restaurant was a focal point for oglers of Washington's lunchtime elite. He could be seen there often with Bradlee and Williams, who with him formed an exclusive "Club" that even mockingly rejected the application of Bradlee's boss, *Washington Post* chairman Katharine Graham. When the Sans Souci folded, Buchwald shifted his midday court to another fancy French eatery, Maison Blanche. "Wherever I eat lunch is the in place," he told one of the *Washington Post's* society reporters, with only a hint of hyperbole.

Now, however, he has even cut back on his long lunches, for both professional and personal reasons. "I'm not eating out as much as I used to, 'cause I'm on the road a lot and I find that I can get work done during the lunch hour. So I might have a turkey sandwich at home. I lose weight that way."

When Buchwald left Paris for Washington over 20 years ago, he did so largely because he felt he had become too comfortable and needed the challenges inherent in the complex problems facing the United States in order to keep his column fresh and vibrant. He has, of course, become comfortably situated in Washington, but the issues facing the nation now are, if anything, more intractable than they were when he first began satirizing them. Their complexity is reflected in the fact that while Buchwald disagrees vehemently with many of the specifics of the Reagan domestic program, he can still express some of the President's "anti-government" bias. He no longer knows whether to classify himself as a liberal or a conservative.

"I do feel that in a society as rich as ours, we can afford to take care of the people who are in trouble, and it's also an insurance policy to keep them from burning down our houses instead of their own. So I'm sympathetic to their problems only because I feel it's to our interest that everybody in this country gets as decent a shake as he possibly can. Now that may be liberal, that may be conservative—I don't know what. I can't put a name on myself right now. But I was brought up in the tradition of liberalism—Jewish liberalism, if you wish—and as you grow older, you see that a lot of things you thought the government could take care of, they screw up. They do a worse job than if they weren't involved. So you find yourself trying to figure out how you can take care of people without the bureaucracy screwing up."

He also finds himself trying to devise ways to describe how the government and society screw up that will make people laugh instead of cry. Humor has been the key to his own survival and prosperity, and he likes to think that it can help the nation survive and prosper, too.

"I consider it a challenge. I'm smart enough to know it isn't going to work every day. But the thing that saves you is that if it doesn't work on Tuesday, you always have Thursday to recoup.

"And if it doesn't work on Thursday," he adds with a broad grin, "you've got Sunday."

William F. Buckley, Jr.

Starboard Tack

These are heady days for William F. Buckley, Jr. The one-time *enfant terrible* of the Right is riding high, with an old friend and devoted reader in the White House, several of his favorite liberal nemeses expelled from public life, and many of the conservative dogmas he has preached for 30 years apparently triumphant.

He has cause to celebrate but not to rest. The conservative guard must never be relaxed. The Huns (or the liberals) are always at the gates; and those in power, even when sympathetic, must constantly be instructed. Besides, for Buckley, the joy of the battle is not in the victory, which may be temporary, but in the fight. He views conflict, whether political or philosophical, as great fun; one has the sneaking suspicion that even at Armageddon he would have a grand time.

Buckley is rich, but idleness is alien to his nature. He packs well over 24 hours' worth of activities into every day and plays as hard as he works. There are occasions, in fact, when the line of demarcation between his work and his play is a bit wobbly. For instance, twice he has sailed the Atlantic in a superbly equipped yacht and then turned the experience into a gracefully written, best-selling book.

In some respects, Buckley is like many professional athletes. He is the Eternal Undergraduate, neatly transforming his extracurricular activities and causes at Yale into his life's work. As a student editor and orator, he waged a crusade against the forces he believed were out to subvert Christianity and capitalism as espoused in New Haven. As a recent graduate-turned-author, he considerably widened his audience, if not his argument, by writing a book that drew heavily on his undergraduate pronunciamentos and outraged a large sector of the American educational hierarchy.

With *God and Man at Yale*, first printed in September 1951, Bill Buckley became a controversial public figure overnight, despised and revered with equal fervor. He remains as despised and revered today—although sometimes those who once revered him now froth at the mention of his name, and those who found, or find, much of his philosophy repugnant admit that there is something appealing about the way he expresses it. Unlike many ideologists, Buckley has never become boring, and at his best he is almost always entertaining.

Column writing is just one of the arrows in Buckley's quiver. He is the founder and editor of *National Review* magazine, which he calls "my number one love" and which consumes about 40 percent of his time; the author of 21 books, five of which are sprightly and highly acclaimed spy novels, and the editor of four additional volumes; the host, chief interrogator, and often the antagonist on his weekly television program "Firing Line"; a lecturer and debater who makes some 50 to 60 appearances a year across the country at fees ranging from $6,000 to $10,000 for college audiences up to $15,000 for non-collegiate listeners; a contributor of articles to periodicals other than his own, such as the *New Yorker, Esquire*, the *New York Times Magazine*, and even *Playboy*; an ocean sailor; an accomplished skier; a pilot; a musician adept at both the piano and—appropriately enough—its antecedent, the clavichord; a painter; and a seemingly tireless letter writer who endeavors to respond personally to the 600 or so letters he receives each week.

Buckley's frenetic schedule and baroque mannerisms often obscure his considerable achievements. He is, in the view of both philosophic soulmates and opponents, perhaps the chief ideological progenitor of the conservative movement that made Ronald Reagan President. "All great Biblical stories begin with Genesis," George Will told the celebrants at *National Review*'s 25th anniversary party in 1980. "Before Ronald Reagan there was Barry Goldwater, and before Barry Goldwater there was *National Review*, and before *National Review*, there was Bill Buckley with a spark in his mind, and the spark in 1980 has become conflagration."

As liberal writer John Judis observed in *Progressive* magazine, Buckley has been a leading figure in the postwar American conservative movement, helping to found the Young Americans for Freedom, New York's Conservative Party, and various right-wing foreign policy lobbies. In creating *National Review*, he "merged the competing and often discordant strains of the American Right into a powerful political force," Judis wrote, and by helping to de-fang and isolate the John Birch Society and similar conservative troglodytes, he enabled the conservative movement "to move into the American mainstream without having to face the usual charges of political extremism."

Buckley's most enduring achievement, however, may be his work as a talent scout for writers. He is a discerning editor with a keen eye for ability, and the list of *National Review* alumni and alumnae includes not only Will but novelists Joan Didion and Renata Adler, critics John Leonard and John Simon, and Gary Wills, now a conservative apostate and a liberal columnist. Buckley has been a seemingly impulsive mentor, quick to hire—often on the strength of a single article or just a letter—and generous with encouragement and praise.

There appear to be as many sides to Bill Buckley as there are activities in which he is engaged. In private, he is invariably gracious and accommodating, a courtly host, an easy-going conversationalist, and a lively companion. His blue eyes twinkle and his grin, containing, as he describes it, a "disconcerting sea of teeth," is ever-ready and winning. In the view of many who know him, Buckley is one of those rare individuals—a thoroughly opinionated person who will listen politely and thoughtfully to another's point of view. Some of his fiercest ideological foes are his warm, personal friends. Socialist Michael Harrington, who certainly is immune to Buckley's preachments, nevertheless finds him "a fascinating person . . . , one of the most liberal persons I've met. . . ." Harrington told an interviewer that Buckley is "not at all pompous or self-centered, and enjoyable to be with."

But there are those who have not been captivated by Buckley's charisma. They find him the prototypical preppy, a person whose icy interior is covered by a polished, friendly veneer. One acquaintance once described him as a "cold fish" who "has the charm of someone who is always saying 'Look how charming I am.' " Even his good friend Murray Kempton, as liberal a columnist as Buckley is conservative, once contended that Buckley "doesn't really have many feelings. He can say: 'I think you're a dangerous Communist agent but I love you,' and there can't be that kind of thing."

Another one of his colleagues doubts that Buckley has any grasp of how difficult life can be for many people. "I think Bill Buckley's problem is that nothing *really bad* has ever happened to him. Oh, he may have had an unpleasant day now and then. But nothing *really bad*." Others say that Buckley may be able to demonstrate genuine concern, even compassion, for those individuals whose personal or economic difficulties he encounters, but he is intellectually incapable of comprehending the plight of the poor.

He dismisses such criticism as itself shallow. "I tend to avoid, if I can, clichés—nobody can avoid them completely—but one of the ones that I tend to avoid is the cliché that suggests that one's feeling for the poor is measured by the frequency with which one states it. I've labored pretty consistently for the only system I know of that's ever done anything for the poor, which is the free system.

"The poor are as poor in India as they ever have been, and that's not true here. By measurement of constant dollars, 90 percent of the American people were poor in 1900. In 1980, that figure [was] under nine percent. So, therefore, the real income has removed from the poverty level the difference between 9 percent and 90 percent, or 81 units, of Americans, during a period when there was real population growth, too. Most of the people who ceased to be poor didn't cease to be poor because the people who talked about the horrors of poverty persuaded Congress to pass the Minimum Wage Act in 1901. I could very easily turn that particular criticism around to say I speak less about the problems of the poor and do more about the poor than any socialist I can think of."

With respect to the ingratiating private smile that often becomes a sardonic, even snide, leer in public or the clever wit that can draw blood as well as laughs when turned on an opponent, Buckley confessed in his book, *Cruising Speed*, published over

a decade ago, that his mannerisms and seeming flippancy are as defensive for him as they may be offensive to others.

"It is hard for me to appeal, without protective covering, directly to an audience," he wrote, "because the audience might turn me down; and as a conservative grown up in the knowledge that victories are not for us, I must not give the audience the power to believe that its verdict matters to me. There is my failure, as a public figure; and my strength."

Even though conservatism seems to have the upper hand now, Buckley does not foresee any diminution in his "hauteur." "I doubt it, because I think that one's style, when developed, tends not to change. . . . De Gaulle's style, for instance, was the same in all circumstances: in defeat, victory, retirement. That was the original 'hauteur,' no question about it."

He does admit to an increasing reluctance to go for his opponent's jugular, however. "It was sometimes a little bit necessary to do that in order to attract their attention, back 20, 25 years ago, so that in a public debate I would sometimes almost go out of my way to antagonize people. I still sometimes do that, in part to keep fit, in part to avoid boredom, but I don't think that contradicts what I said to you before. I think that one's relish of combat for the sake of combat diminishes as one grows older. When 22-year-olds play tennis, they tend to be more insistent on the competitive aspects of it than when they're 40, and are enjoying it as a game and as an exercise."

The overwhelming majority of Buckley's work involves writing, which he does at a breakneck speed, and one is a bit astonished to learn that it is an activity that he professes to despise. "If you disliked to write as much as I do, you'd write fast," he says, flashing both his eyes and smile. "I loathe it. It's so arduous. . . . Some people like to write. George [Will] likes it. He told me he wakes up in the morning and asks himself, Is this a day in which I have to write a column? And if the answer to that is yes, then he's happy. Mine is very much the reverse. . . .

"Writing is just agonizing work. I wouldn't dream of keeping a journal just for my own pleasure, which a lot of people who like to write do. For example, Ken Galbraith *likes to write;* John Chamberlain *likes to write;* my brother [Reid, a novelist] *likes to write.* I *don't* like to write."

Whether he likes it or not, Buckley writes just about anywhere and at any time: early in the morning or late at night in his elegant duplex apartment off Park Avenue in New York; in his rambling, 77-year-old home on the waterfront in Stamford, Connecticut; in his disheveled office at *National Review* on East Thirty-fifth Street in Manhattan; in the back of his customized, extra-long Cadillac limousine or on an airplane, en route to a speaking engagement; on board his 60-foot schooner while plying the Atlantic; at his rented residence in Switzerland, to which he repairs each February and March for serious skiing and composition of a book or two.

The objective behind most of his rapid-fire typing is the preservation and propagation of Buckley's conservative beliefs—social, economic, and religious. The role of *National Review,* enunciated in its premiere issue in 1955, has been to "stand athwart history yelling 'Stop!' "; and Buckley resolutely contends that the old verities, as he understands them, are eternal.

"Conservatives do not deny the existence of undiscovered truths," he once wrote,

But they make a critical assumption, which is that those truths that have *already* been apprehended are more important to cultivate than those undisclosed ones close to the liberal grasp only in the sense that the fruit was close to Tantalus, yet around whose existence virtually the whole of modern academic theory revolves. Conservatism is the tacit acknowledgement that all that is

finally important in human experience is behind us, that the crucial explorations have been undertaken, and that it is given to man to know what are the great truths that emerged from them. Whatever is to come cannot outweigh the importance to man of what has gone before.

While not denying that 10, 20, or 30 years in the life of an individual or a society can be instructive, Buckley believes that the lessons learned are merely cumulative, not new. His basic beliefs are the same as they were when he wrote *God and Man at Yale* a generation ago. "I don't think they've changed in any important respect. I hope I know a lot more than I used to, but my commitments are pretty much the same. I think that's true of most people. Gary Wills would be a very conspicuous exception, going from the radical right to the radical left . . . , [but] nothing has happened in the world that argues a substantial change in my position."

He cites "the amplification of the theory of supply-side economics" as a slightly new addition to his conservative canon, but otherwise "it's not easy to say what you know today that you didn't know ten years ago. Mostly it's an enhancement of the dimensions of a position you previously held."

Buckley is not offended by political or economic inequality, believing them to be "natural and desirable," John Judis noted, and "he supports such rights as freedom of speech and assembly only so far as their existence does not threaten the kind of government he deems best: a government that stays out of the free market at home and protects it abroad." He opposes the minimum wage, progressive income taxes, and inheritance taxes. He is against majority rule and universal suffrage.

"I think roughly speaking that there are 30 to 40 percent more voters than there ought to be," he told Judis. "Somebody once asked me who should not vote, and I said the 30 percent who don't know the existence of the United Nations. I think it is a travesty of democracy to assume that a vote is a congenital birthright."

In essence, Buckley believes that all efforts to achieve political, economic, or social equality are doomed. "Conservatives know you can't do away with Skid Row," he once said. Yet Buckley's positions on various social and moral issues sometimes are surprising. "I feel I qualify spiritually and philosophically as a conservative," he once said, "but temperamentally I am not of the breed."

For example, in a 1983 column he struggled with the moral strictures against suicide. "Of all the Christian commandments," he wrote, "surely the most taxing intellectually is that which prohibits suicide. The case against suicide in certain circumstances this writer accepts only as an article of faith. The rationale has always seemed to me beyond the reach of finite minds." A year earlier, he wrote a column urging passage of an amendment to the Controlled Substances Act which would permit doctors to give heroin to some patients dying of cancer. "It has been remarked that nothing is easier to get used to than other people's pain," he wrote. "This is unhappily correct, and perhaps necessarily so, because if one were as much involved in mankind as John Donne said we should be, there could be no happiness, ever." If the law were amended to permit the prescription of heroin for cancer patients dying in agony, "we'll be entitled to such happiness as is due to those helpful in relieving the misery of others," he wrote.

"On abortion, [Buckley's] Catholicism dictates strong opposition," Judis observed, "but on marijuana, prostitution, and gay rights his cosmopolitanism has won out. He is not above patriotic appeals, but he was unwilling to exploit the Panama Canal treaty, which he believed to be in the U.S.

interest. . . . And Buckley clearly despises the New Right's populism—its appeal to an anti-elitist sentiment, its demagoguery, and its glorification of direct majority rule through the initiative process."

Buckley's positions were formed as much by heredity as by inculcation and experience. The sixth of ten children, he is the son of a self-made millionaire attorney-turned-oil speculator from Texas and a gracious southern belle from New Orleans. Buckley's paternal great-grandfather emigrated from Ireland to Canada, and his grandfather, John Buckley, moved south to post-Reconstruction Texas, where he displayed the Buckley inclination to go against prevailing sentiments by assuming the anomalous profession of sheep rancher in cattle country (and maintaining his Catholicism in the heart of the Baptist belt). He also helped preserve law and order by getting himself elected sheriff—as a Democrat—in Duval County, just across the border from Mexico.

The sheriff's son, William F. Buckley, Sr., also took to the law and became counsel for some of the early major oil companies. He decided that he preferred being his own boss, however, and embarked on a somewhat checkered career as an international oil speculator. He had considerable success in Mexico but was booted out of that country in 1921 for fomenting an unsuccessful uprising against the then-ascendant revolutionary regime. He lost over $1 million in holdings—and was threatened with execution if he ever returned—so he had to begin rebuilding his career at the age of 41. His speculations and explorations in Latin America at first earned him the uncomplimentary sobriquet "Dry Hole Bill," but in relatively short order he once again was in the money—lots of it.

In time, he was able to purchase an eighteenth-century mansion, which he dubbed Great Elm, on a 40-acre estate in Sharon, Connecticut, as well as another ample lair he called Kamschatka, situated on an 18-

acre preserve in Camden, South Carolina. But business kept the elder Buckley overseas for most of the 1920s and early 1930s, and his offspring became world travelers at an early age. Although William Jr. was born in New York City on November 24, 1925, his first six years were spent mostly in Paris, where he learned to speak French and Spanish before English. When Buckley was seven, his father moved the family to London, and it was there that he finally mastered his native tongue, thus accounting for the British tinge to his pronunciation that some assume is affected and others find infuriating.

Buckley *père* placed his children in a series of exclusive prep schools and saw to it that their educational regimen never flagged, surrounding them at home with what one family chronicler called an "international menagerie of tutors in math, history, grammar, poetry, music and the languages." He also bombarded them with lengthy, cajoling, affectionate memoranda, instructing them on everything from the precepts of Catholicism to the evils of tobacco and mumbling. His expectations regarding his children were modest, one of his daughters later observed with droll understatement: "He brought up his sons and daughters with the quite simple objective that they become absolutely perfect." The Buckleys were a close-knit, proud family, united in their dedication to religion and economic individualism and in their antipathy to what they believed was governmental interference in private affairs.

Buckley Sr.'s precocious namesake developed multiple interests and an imperious manner which prompted his older siblings to nickname him "the young Mahster." When still in kneebreeches, Buckley Jr. wrote an outraged letter to King George V of England, demanding that Great Britain pay its war debts to the United States; when he attended Beaumont College, a Jesuit prep school in England, he lectured the school's

president on the institution's shortcomings; when he was a student at New York's Millbrook School, he appeared uninvited at a faculty meeting to chastise the staff about its inadequacies. And when he arrived at Yale in 1946, following two years of undistinguished stateside Army service (including duty as an instructor in sex hygiene in San Antonio, Texas), Buckley promptly gave a similar, unsolicited lecture to a faculty meeting there. It was not the last time they would hear from him.

Buckley became a star of the Debate Society and of the *Yale Daily News*, the nation's oldest student newspaper, of which he was unanimously elected chairman (editor in chief) in 1949. Although his father was "anti-Semitic in the same way as other men of his age and background," according to William Jr.'s older brother James, a former senator from New York and now an under secretary of state, the Buckley sons apparently did not inherit this paternal prejudice. Bill Jr. refused membership in Skull and Bones, Yale's exclusive secret society, unless it also accepted his Jewish roommate, Thomas H. Guinzburg, later president of Viking Press.

"This was rather bold," one Buckley biographer observed, "given the fact that the club had only recently begun to accommodate itself to Catholics." But both Buckley and his roommate were elected to Skull and Bones, with Guinzburg becoming perhaps the third Jew ever admitted to the society.

At Yale, Buckley studied history, economics, political science, philosophy, and literature and also taught freshman Spanish. In addition to his extracurricular activities on campus, he earned a pilot's license and flew a small airplane for recreation, once crash-landing on the campus of a boarding school that one of his sisters attended.

Buckley's editorials in the *Daily News* regularly excoriated Yale's faculty members for their alleged failure to promote capitalism and Christianity, which Buckley believed it to be their duty to do. In his senior year, 1950, Buckley was elected class orator, but the university administration requested an opportunity to review his proposed Alumni Day address, in which he elaborated on the basic theme of his editorials. He was denied permission to deliver it.

It was a decision that Yale presumably came to rue a year later, when Buckley published *God and Man at Yale*, a 232-page expansion of the speech, which was printed as one of the book's appendices. In his foreword to the book, Buckley said that he would "expose what I regard as the extraordinarily irresponsible educational attitude [at Yale] that, under the protective label 'academic freedom,' has produced one of the most extraordinary incongruities of our time: the institution that derives its moral and financial support from Christian individualists and then addresses itself to the task of persuading the sons of these supporters to be atheistic socialists."

Should there be, say, a socialist economist on Yale's faculty, Buckley went on to argue in the book, he should be barred from teaching "because he is inculcating values that the governing board at Yale considers to be against the public welfare." (Twenty-five years later, in an article for *Harper's,* Buckley asserted that he "still cannot come to terms with a university that accepts the philosophic proposition that it is there for the purpose of presenting 'all sides' of 'any issue' as impartially and forcefully as possible. I believe that a university *should* take sides, that it *should* be free to dedicate itself to . . . 'the training of spiritual leaders.' Without a sense of mission, a private university is incomprehensible.")

Buckley is not disturbed by the suggestion that the partisan educational advocacy called for in his seminal work might betray insecurity about the ability of the capitalistic and Christian beliefs he champions to triumph on the strength of their own attractiveness and logic. "I don't think they do," he says. "I think sometimes they do, sometimes they don't. But, after all, the same ideas have been available for years and they are rejected in Great Britain, for instance, [and] in France," where socialism is having a fling now.

"So that the notion that all you need is a quintessentially superior idea to defeat a contrary idea is a form of angelism. Society doesn't work that way. You've got to have laws, you've got to have constitutions. In this sense, I'm no different from Thomas Jefferson: 'Talk not to me about good men, but bind their wrists by the chains of the Constitution.' "

Buckley's restrictive view of higher education extends beyond what professors should be allowed to teach to the question of whom they ought to instruct. He once urged that the offspring of alumni be given preferential treatment when applying to Yale, and in a 1981 column he argued that many high school graduates are incapable of benefiting from a college education and shouldn't bother to get one. They can improve their minds later, he said, in an odd mixture of angelism and elitism:

Too many Americans feel they have to go to college in order to qualify as legitimate citizens. By the standards of France and Great Britain, about eight times as many Americans (including blacks and Hispanics) go to college.

. . . It is estimated that to profit from a college education you need an IQ of 110 or higher. About 25 percent of Americans have such an IQ. But about 40 percent go to college. The figures would then suggest that about 35 percent of those attending college aren't getting much out of it.

What they do get, often, is personal frustration and family indebtedness. The American community should stop looking for college degrees as prerequisites to useful and complete lives. Often these people who aren't ready to go to college at 18 develop intellectual interests later in life and can satisfy these by later learning. . . .

If there is a justification in state laws denying employers the right to inquire into an applicant's age, sex, race or religion, we might toss in a prohibition against asking whether there is a college degree, except where directly relevant. . . .

A college degree is an adornment of sorts, but the currency is debased by the prodigality with which degrees are handed out. It is no safer to assume that an applicant with a college degree is bright than to assume that the applicant without a college degree is dumb.

God and Man set off a firestorm of controversy in the American academic community that spread to the popular press and still smolders. To some, Buckley became "Yale's biggest mistake." McGeorge Bundy, later an aide to John F. Kennedy, wrote a withering review of the book for the *Atlantic Monthly,* saying: "As a believer in God, a Republican, and a Yale graduate, I find that the book is dishonest in its use of facts, false in its theory, and a discredit to its author." And in response to Buckley's introduction to the 25th anniversary reissue of the book, a Yale professor of historical theology wrote *Harper's* that Yale did, in fact, have a " 'mission,' though not an exclusivist, partisan" one, and provided " 'a place for the spirit' much more capacious than Mr. Buckley would prefer." The brouhaha made Buckley an instant conservative superstar. He was articulate, good-looking, witty—a distinct and refreshing departure from the dour, humorless, conservative spokesmen of the previous 30 years.

Shortly after his graduation from Yale, Buckley married Patricia Taylor, a statuesque former model and millionairess from Vancouver, Canada, who had been a roommate of one of his sisters' at Vassar. They have one son, Christopher, a talented writer

who is a regular contributor to *Esquire;* wrote a critically acclaimed book, *Steaming to Bamboola,* about his 78 days aboard a Merchant Marine freighter; and worked as a speechwriter for Vice-President George Bush.

For a brief period following publication of *God and Man at Yale,* Buckley was a "deep cover" agent for the Central Intelligence Agency, stationed in Mexico. His CIA boss was none other than E. Howard Hunt, who would earn notoriety and a hefty prison sentence 20 years later as one of the chief Watergate malefactors. Buckley and Hunt became close friends, and Buckley is godfather to Hunt's children.

As devoted as he was to the CIA's cause, Buckley found the work uninspiring and tedious, so he left the agency to return to the ranks of writers, co-authoring *McCarthy and His Enemies,* an apologia for the anti-Communist witch hunts of the odious Wisconsin Senator Joseph R. McCarthy. Buckley remains a defender of McCarthy, dismissing the senator's well-documented reliance on innuendo, half-truth, outright falsehoods, and large quantities of alcohol with a degree of tolerance that is a bit disconcerting in one who would vehemently denounce most philosophic opponents for similar failings.

(In recent years, however, Buckley also has displayed a surprising willingness to go to bat for several erstwhile radical left bogeymen. He wrote letters urging judicial leniency for Eldridge Cleaver, the one-time black revolutionary who became a born-again Christian, and Abby Hoffman, the former yippie, who repented his foray into drug-dealing and bail-jumping.)

Following the book on McCarthy, Buckley, seeking a wider, more regular forum for his beliefs, founded *National Review* with the aid of $125,000 in family funds and $300,000 that he raised on his own. The Buckley family fortunes, by then concentrated in the Catawba Corporation, founded by William Sr. in 1948, and Buckley's own income as a writer and lecturer were needed not only to help launch the new magazine but also to keep it afloat. They still are.

As a money-making enterprise, *National Review* is hardly a model of capitalism. In 29 years it has lost somewhere between $7 million and $8 million, with an average annual loss of $400,000 or $500,000, Buckley concedes. (In 1980, it had a whopping $750,000 deficit.) But Buckley, the magazine's sole stockholder, prefers to liken *National Review*'s role to that of a nonprofit educational or religious institution, and he rejects the suggestion that his cherished offspring hasn't "made it" in the tough world of magazine publishing.

"We *have* made it, because the fact that we've survived for 29 years means that we appeal sufficiently to people to do it. You would hardly say—or would you—that Harvard and Yale haven't made it. Of course they've made it. They're educational institutions. If you mean . . . you only make it if you have a positive cash flow, I would like to see the right-wing economist who draws that conclusion. He's got a lot of reading to do. We haven't 'made it' in the same way the Catholic Church hasn't 'made it.' The fact of the matter is that we've been able to stimulate enough people who, exercising no coercion by us, deem the operation important enough to ensure its survival."

In addition to receiving hefty transfusions from Buckley's six-figure income as a columnist and lecturer, *National Review* also benefits from a yearly fund-raising drive, which Buckley terms "absolutely crucial" to its continued existence. This appeal to readers to contribute over and above their annual subscription fee provides some 60 percent of the money needed to cover the magazine's deficits, he said.

Always something of a bible for the true believers in radical conservatism, *National*

Review's early years were marked by a number of internecine battles between members of its editorial staff, by nature a highly combative bunch. Now there is a more harmonious, even jolly atmosphere at *National Review*'s headquarters, located in a converted, turn-of-the-century residence. While "there have always been contrary positions advanced on practical matters, and certain ones on philosophic matters," Buckley says, "there has been no schism" sufficient to warrant a description of the *National Review* offices as a townhouse divided.

Buckley's proselytizing for the Right did not stop with his magazine work or his perpetual appearances on the lecture and debate circuit, where he honed the Oxford Union tactics he perfected while a member of Yale's Debate Society. He also served as a combination godfather and midwife at the birth of Young Americans for Freedom (YAF), a conservative student organization founded during a meeting at his home in Stamford in 1960. He also was a founder of New York's Conservative Party in 1961.

In early 1962, Buckley received a telephone call from the late Harry Elmlark, a feisty, independent syndicate entrepreneur and New Deal Democrat who suspected, correctly, that a column featuring Buckley's blend of conservative ideology and sophisticated wit would have broad appeal. In a nonstop monologue over the phone, Elmlark—whom Buckley had never met— succeeded in persuading him to attempt a once-a-week column beginning in April 1962. Elmlark then set out, again by telephone, to sell the Buckley column, sight unseen, to newspaper editors around the country. He corralled a modest list of 38 subscribers at first, but soon over 75 newspapers had signed on, and by the fall of 1964, when Elmlark's syndicate was absorbed by the mammoth King Features operation, Buckley began writing three columns a week. Buckley's column now appears in approximately 350 newspapers and is distributed by the Universal Press Syndicate.

His column is "a useful instrument by which to get things said and say things about current events and trends," Buckley says with a hint of indifference, and one gets the impression that he finds writing the column a bit tedious. He does profess to be a fan of other columnists, however. "I find, in my own reading, that I enjoy reading columnists. Occasionally they're cloying . . . , but I devote a fair amount of my newspaper reading time to reading columnists. I like to be up on what they're saying."

The cumulative impression left by Buckley's columns is one of a writer with awesome erudition who applies it brilliantly, if often casually, to domestic politics, international relations, social manners and morals, religion, personalities, and sports. At the core of his work is a passion for individual freedom. He once wrote:

I will not cede more power to the state. I will not willingly cede more power to anyone, not to the state, not to General Motors, not to the CIO. I will hoard my power like a miser, resisting every effort to drain it away from me. I will then use *my* power, as *I* see fit. I mean to live my life an obedient man, but obedient to God, subservient to the wisdom of my ancestors, never to the authority of political truths arrived at yesterday at the voting booth. That . . . is certainly program enough to keep conservatism busy, and liberals at bay. And the nation free.

Paradoxically, perhaps, he also finds that individual freedom is contingent in part on the ability of government to repress those whose exercise of it might harm others: "Each man's freedom extends only so far as it can extend without impinging on another man's; hence no rights can be absolute; hence there are occasions when, for the sake of freedom, government must repress certain actions that tend to destroy freedom."

Central to Buckley's devotion to freedom is an obsessive anti-communism, which has compelled him to find chimerical virtues in repressive, reactionary military regimes in Latin America and even to say kind things about a fascist dictator such as Spain's Francisco Franco, who he claimed provided more freedom for his benighted subjects than they would have had under the left-leaning Spanish Republic.

Buckley's columns remain interesting, largely because the fascinating voice behind them can be both infuriating and intriguing. The vibrancy of Buckley's mind is engaging, and the conversational tone of his writing never wanes, even when he uses etymological exotica that force the reader to resort to a dictionary in self-defense. One reads him in anticipation, almost hoping to be outraged. If you are, well and good; if not, and you find yourself agreeing with him, there is the delight of discovering that someone so superbly educated has the good sense to share your opinions.

In 1965, Buckley agreed to become the Conservative Party's candidate for mayor of New York City, despite the fact that his official residence is in Connecticut, where he always votes. He explained his willingness to serve as the party's sacrificial lamb by saying that it was his duty to support its right-wing principles and oppose the liberal Republican mayoral candidate, John V. Lindsay, then a congressman from a silk-stocking district in Manhattan.

Buckley accused Lindsay (who later became a Democrat) of "unsexing" the Republican party in New York, and with a breezy indifference—or ignorance—of practical politics, he believed that he would aid the campaign of Lindsay's opponents, chiefly Democrat Abraham Beame, by attacking Lindsay, whom he called "destiny's tot." In fact, he did just the opposite: he persuaded liberal Democrats that Lindsay was more their man than Beame was and drew away conservative Democratic votes from the hapless standard-bearer of their own party. By garnering 340,000 votes, or about 13 percent of the record 2.5 million tally, Buckley helped Lindsay squeeze in by a 136,144-vote margin in a city with a Democratic predominance in registration of more than three to one.

(Buckley's only other bid for elective office—an attempt in 1968 to win a seat on Yale's board of trustees—also ended in failure. He was beaten by Cyrus R. Vance, who later became Jimmy Carter's Secretary of State.)

But as a campaigner in Gotham, Buckley was entertaining. Asked what he would do if he won, he replied: "I'd demand a recount." He forswore the traditional appeals to New York's ethnic communities. "I will not go to Irish centers and go dancing. I will not go to Jewish centers and eat blintzes, nor will I go to Italian centers and pretend to speak Italian," he declared. He gave thoughtful, somewhat didactic lectures at campaign rallies. When he announced his candidacy, Buckley's address to the press was "like nothing so much as an Edwardian resident commissioner announcing the 39 articles of the Anglican establishment to a conscript assemblage of Zulus," Murray Kempton reported.

Buckley's campaign did contain some interesting proposals, including one for an elevated Second Avenue bikeway to cut midtown traffic and improve the muscle tone of Manhattanites. More than a decade later, New York Mayor Ed Koch tried establishing a bicycle lane on Sixth Avenue, with disastrous, traffic-snarling results. It was abandoned.

The year after his mayoral campaign, Buckley began a more successful venture, his weekly television debate and discussion program, "Firing Line." Originally an offering on commercial television, the program shifted in 1971 to the Public Broadcasting System, where there was no need to interrupt the hour-long dialogues with advertisements and ratings were not an obsession.

"Firing Line," which now is aired in about 250 cities, has done more to make Buckley a public figure than any of his lectures, books, or columns. In his 18 years on the air, he has become the talk shows' Erich von Stroheim, "the man you love to hate." When he is on the stump, whether in person or televised, Buckley's private charm is transformed into a brittle geniality. His quirky mannerisms and tics are intensified as he swings into action. He becomes a symphony of self-mimicry: constant fidgeting; quick, toothy grins; arched eyebrows and widening eyes; dramatic inflections; and a polychromatic vocabulary of rapidly spoken, often swallowed words. It is a captivating, and slightly terrifying, performance.

Buckley says he once kept a rough count of the number of people who stopped him on the street in a given day and found that out of 20 or so, about 12 commented on his television show, 4 made remarks about his columns, 2 or 3 mentioned *National Review*, and another 2 or 3 spoke of his books. The lopsided results of this informal poll hardly persuade him to abandon his column, magazine, or books. Television helps to make you known, Buckley observed, but it is less likely to make what you believe understood by the viewers. "You speak, numerically, to many more people on television, but the communication is much less orderly than when it's given out in written form, whether in columns or in magazines or in books. So I would say that television serves a role to create an impression, whereas the column is more useful to people who are given to analysis."

Buckley's most celebrated television appearance did not occur on his own program, but during ABC-TV's coverage of the fractious 1968 Democratic National Convention, where he was paired with writer Gore Vidal for a convention-related debate.

Their exchange grew increasingly ugly, and when Vidal called Buckley a "crypto-Nazi," Buckley shot back: "Now listen, you queer, stop calling me a crypto-Nazi or I'll sock you in your goddamn face!" The unpleasantness between the two continued in a series of articles for *Esquire* and a flurry of suits and countersuits for libel in which Buckley eventually prevailed, at least legally. Neither combatant emerged unsullied from the protracted nastiness, and Buckley has expressed regret over losing his temper in public.

In December 1971, Buckley and his column won what turned out to be a hollow victory for individual freedom when a convicted murderer named Edgar Smith, whose letter-writing campaign for a new trial had received Buckley's enthusiastic endorsement, emerged from the Trenton, New Jersey, State Prison after spending more than 14 years on death row, longer than any other prisoner in U.S. history.

Smith, a smooth, persuasive writer and articulate speaker, enlisted Buckley's aid in 1964 by initiating a correspondence that lasted seven years and consumed about 2,900 pages of Smith's prison stationery, by his own count. Buckley became convinced that Smith was improperly convicted in 1957 of murdering a 15-year-old girl and wrote about Smith's plight in his column. With the aid of Buckley's eloquence and the efforts of several dedicated lawyers, Smith was able to persuade both a federal appellate court in New Jersey and the U.S. Supreme Court that he had been tried unfairly. At a retrial, he reluctantly pleaded guilty to second-degree murder in order to be freed on probation after being given credit for time served. Buckley wrote:

A court of law is many things besides a truth-finding mechanism. It is a chamber in which subtle social and institutional conciliations are effected. The wounded pride of the State of New Jersey had to be healed, after the humiliation it suffered from the federal courts. How to do that?—except by insisting that however illegal the means by which the evidence was collected, in fact they had got the right man? Edgar Smith's claim to liberty had crystallized undeniably from his protracted struggle, at the low point of which he had left only a doting, proud mother and a fine, unhoned mind which became, after his dark night, a file by which, working at high sweat, he finally sawed through the bars that kept him caged in an 8-by-8 cell from the time that Dwight Eisenhower began his second term of office.

Well, he may not be in a mood for celebration [after the plea bargain]. But I cannot believe that his struggle will be uncelebrated in the annals of the human spirit. And it is always possible that the man who really did it will one day identify himself. Meanwhile, Smith can stop fighting. The knock on his door won't be the executioner's.

A moderately hostile reviewer of a Buckley anthology that contained this column observed: "This foe of the 'Warren Court' and its 'coddling of criminals' is also the man who spent years and a good deal of his own money to save Edgar H. Smith, Jr., from New Jersey's electric chair because Buckley was firmly convinced that Smith (a stranger to him) had been wrongly convicted—largely through the denial of many of those rights that Buckley assails the Supreme Court for having safeguarded. Those who have spent twenty years saying that Buckley is a stranger to human compassion might well read him on Smith."

Unfortunately, it turned out that the State of New Jersey *had* gotten the right man and Smith had bamboozled both Buckley and the appellate courts. He not only was guilty of the first crime but also tried to rob and murder another young girl in San Diego five years after he was freed from prison. When

Smith, on the lam from authorities, telephoned Buckley's office from Las Vegas and told Frances Bronson, Buckley's executive secretary, that he had been mugged, had lost all his money, and wanted Buckley to call him, Buckley instead telephoned the FBI, which nabbed Smith in his hotel room.

A wounded Buckley philosophized:

There is no mechanism as yet perfected that will establish beyond question a person's guilt or innocence. There will be guilty people freed this year and every year. But for those who believe that the case of Edgar Smith warrants a vow to accept the ruling of a court as always definitive, it is only necessary to remind ourselves that, this year and every year, an innocent man will be convicted. Edgar Smith has done enough damage in his lifetime without underwriting the doctrine that the verdict of a court is infallible.

Smith received a 20-year sentence in 1977 for the attempted murder in San Diego. When asked if Smith was still in prison, Buckley replied softly but emphatically: "I hope so."

Earlier in 1971 Buckley's column suffered a more immediate, and just as temporary, setback when 14 newspapers dropped it in retaliation for a bizarre hoax that he and his protégés at *National Review* had gleefully perpetrated.

Seeking some way to counter the impact of the *New York Time*'s publication of Daniel Ellsberg's purloined Pentagon Papers on the Vietnam War, *National Review* printed 14 pages of "the Secret Papers They Didn't Publish," outlining a "sharp knock" strategy to win the war by demonstrating a nuclear explosion off Haiphong Harbor, destroying North Vietnam's dike system, and "neutralizing" China's ability to intervene in the conflict. The "Buckley Papers" attributed these proposals to CIA operatives, former Secretary

of State Dean Rusk, and other high officials, almost all of whom were reluctant to deny that they had written the alleged memoranda.

For four days the supposed *National Review* scoop was accepted as fact, with its "revelations" distributed by the major wire services, reprinted in newspapers around the world, reported on the major networks, and broadcast over the Voice of America. One Pentagon official wondered whether there was a "counter-leaker" at work, endeavoring to undermine the importance of Ellsberg's selections from a 47-volume study of U.S. involvement in Vietnam that stressed disturbing differences between the public and private policies four administrations pursued there.

The bubble burst, however, when Buckley called a press conference and cheerily admitted that the magazine's "exposé" was a phony one which he and the other good-humored folk at *National Review* had concocted *ex nihilo* ("out of nothing") and "in something of a moral vacuum." Buckley said that the bogus papers had been contrived to demonstrate "that the Pentagon and the CIA are not composed of incompetents [and] that forged documents would be widely accepted as genuine provided their content was plausible."

He never suggested that the Pentagon Papers were forgeries but implied that if the *Times* could print stolen documents that leaned towards one side of the Vietnam debate, *National Review* was somehow entitled to print spurious ones that were equally biased. "The New York *Times* has instructed us that it is permissible to traffic in stolen documents, but they have not yet instructed us on whether it is permissible to traffic in forged documents," Buckley declared with an airy lack of logic.

An unrepentant Buckley still maintains that the purpose of the hoax "was magnificently fulfilled, namely, to demonstrate that intelligent analyses of the Vietnam situation between 1962 and 1965 were almost certainly made, as witness that we could duplicate what we were sure had been said, and that it would not be denied by people who were involved."

"Now, we didn't know how successful we'd be," he says with a sly grin. "We didn't know that Dean Rusk was going to say: 'I guess I did say that . . . ,' so we were too successful. We caused something of a journalistic scandal, and therefore a terrific backlash. But in terms of showing that the Ellsberg papers were tendentious, we proved that abundantly."

Buckley only regrets "that people were so incensed." "People don't have much of a sense of humor when they themselves are victimized," he adds, sounding a bit like a young prankster caught dropping a water balloon on the school principal.

Like the rest of the conservative community, Buckley was distressed when dirty tricks of another sort triggered the Watergate scandal and led to the unraveling of the Nixon administration. He was even more upset, however, when Spiro Agnew's star fell under the weight of white envelopes containing kickback boodle. The stupidity of Nixon, of whom he was never entirely enamored, and the bungling of the Watergate burglars apparently offended Buckley more than their malfeasance. He viewed the Watergate illegalities more as a lapse in good manners than as a series of impeachable offenses. But the greed and mendacity of Agnew, whom he admired, really hurt.

The Watergate felons "loved not wisely, if too well," Buckley wrote in *National Review,* "they forgot the restraints of civility; and they brought disgrace upon their own cause and ours." He was not as quick as George Will, then the Washington editor of *National Review,* to decide that Nixon had to go. When he finally did advocate the president's resignation in April 1974 (at the same time that his brother, James Buckley,

became the first conservative senator to urge Nixon to step down), Buckley characterized it as a noble course which a now-impotent chief executive could take to save the country further anguish.

A year earlier, the prospect of Nixon's political demise did not displease Buckley, since he clearly relished the idea of an Agnew presidency. When Agnew was forced to resign in October 1973 and plead nolo contendere to federal income tax charges, the editors of *National Review* lamented the "national as well as personal tragedy that his public career has come to an untimely end." "Mr. Agnew is a man of intellectual courage and political candor," the magazine's collective voice declared, and the "editors" wished him well "in his time of troubles, and in the future as in the past regard him as a friend."

Buckley personally was less forgiving. He feared that Agnew's disgrace would have harmful side-effects on conservatism in the United States. "Cupidity . . . was a factor in what we have come to think of as the great betrayal of Spiro Agnew," he told a dinner of the New York Conservative Party five days after Agnew's resignation. "The fault was substantially his. But the consequences of his weakness are substantially ours. Mr. Agnew, reaching for self-justification . . . , is no more plausible than Alger Hiss."

Six years later, Buckley himself ran afoul of federal regulators when the Securities and Exchange Commission accused him and three business associates of devising a complicated stock-fraud scheme to bail themselves out of possible bankruptcy stemming from unsuccessful investments in some Texas movie theaters. Buckley, who has written that business contracts make his eyes glaze over, professed ignorance of the allegedly fraudulent activities but avoided the personal and financial rigors of a lengthy court case by signing a consent decree agreeing to return some $1.4 million in cash and stock to the shareholders of Starr Broadcasting Group, a company which he headed for nearly a decade and which was the alleged victim of the purported fraud. Buckley's "time of troubles," however, was considerably briefer than that of the Republican party, and now both he and it appear more prosperous than ever.

Buckley begins his days early, often with a breakfast in bed that invariably includes peanut butter spread on whole wheat toast. "I have never composed poetry," he wrote in a 1982 column, "but if I did, my very first couplet would be: I know that I shall never see / A poem lovely as Skippy's Peanut Butter." (For all the columns Buckley devotes to substantive philosophic reflections, his confession of peanut butter addiction was the one that produced the most "extraordinary" reader response, including one letter from Charlton Heston that accompanied a case of Red Wing Peanut Butter, a brand to which Buckley is now a slave.)

Should it be one of those dreaded days on which he must write a column, Buckley may try to get it out of the way as early at 7:30 A.M. The initial research for his column, as well as for his books, magazine articles, and television shows, is done by a three-member staff of assistants who work in the *National Review* offices and occasionally are aided by outside consultants. After reading the material the researchers have prepared for him, Buckley quickly raps out his 850-word column in 20 or 30 minutes. ("And it shows," one of his columnist colleagues tartly observed.)

Buckley says that in over 20 years of column writing he has never had too much trouble finding a topic on which to write interestingly on relatively short notice, although the equanimity with which he approaches the task has been shaken on occasion. "Once, two or three years ago, I was doing a program with the amiable Gene Shalit of NBC," he recalled in a 1982 column. "Everything went swimmingly. Too swimmingly. Because he played me

like a cobra, undulating hypnotically this way, that way, as I gradually lost any sense of caution. He said then: 'How do you know what to write about, when you write a column?' I found myself saying, 'Gene, when you have been at the profession long enough, you can, if in a bind, close your eyes and point to the front page of The New York Times, and whatever story you are fingering when you open your eyes—you can write a column on that story.' 'Yes'—Shalit struck—'I think I remember that column.' "

Buckley composes his early morning columns either in his Manhattan duplex, which once was the home of Dag Hammarskjöld, the late secretary-general of the United Nations, or in his 15-room house in Stamford, where he writes on the 37-year-old Royal standard typewriter he bought when he was a freshman at Yale. His New York apartment is full of plush furniture, antiques, and glowing modern paintings, some of which are Buckley's own attempts at oils. The opulence of some of the decor his wife chose for their Stamford home makes sections of it resemble a "bordello the Shah couldn't afford," Buckley wrote in a 1976 article for *Vogue*. His refuge there is a less ostentatious music room which features a harpsichord and an exquisite view of a large garden and Long Island Sound. He works in what had been the mansion's fourth garage.

Buckley travels between his Connecticut retreat and Manhattan, as well as around the city from apartment to magazine office to television studio to nearby speaking engagements, in a Cadillac limousine that he had converted into a mobile office in a special body shop in Texarkana. It easily accommodates his six-feet, one-inch frame, as well as several bulging briefcases, piles of paper, and a portable typewriter. "I remember having no exact figure in mind when the garage manager asked me how long I wanted it to be," he recalled in a 1983 article for the *New Yorker*, "so I simply extended my legs from the chair I was sitting in and suggested that it be two feet longer than the current standard model. . . . The only problem is that people who get into the car will, unless they are warned, wheel about and sit down, allowing for the conventional interval. They land on the floor, because the back seat is two feet behind where it normally is."

While his driver, Jerry Garver, a former New York City firefighter, eases the limousine along highways or dexterously winds it through the potholes and double-parked delivery trucks in Manhattan, Buckley pushes the button that raises the glass partition that seals off the passenger area. He then catches up on his work, pulling out a small Dictaphone and dictating letters, memoranda, or notes. He keeps two secretaries busy transcribing his tapes. He also has a telephone in the car and can conduct other business while in transit.

Both in his 1971 book *Cruising Speed* and in the lengthy, two-part journal in the *New Yorker* that formed the basis for his 1983 book *Overdrive*, Buckley wrote about his daily and weekly activities, describing his hectic schedule and reflections in minute, exhaustive detail. He has a special skill for drawing the reader into his golden orbit: a world of ever-ready limousines and sailboats; spacious homes; solicitous, Spanish-speaking servants; a loving family; famous friends; glittering parties; and an endless stream of correspondence, speaking engagements, television programs, books, and columns. The underlying moral is unmistakable: This man may have inherited millions, but he *earns* his comforts, by God. The *New Yorker* articles came close to self-parody, an account of life among the rich, famous, beautiful, and conservative. They avoided that fate—at times—only because of Buckley's wit and entertaining writing. But real parodists, such as Prudence Crowther in the *New York Review of Books*, had a field day with them:

At 6 AM Carmina Burana, our serf, tiptoes in with my tray. She is small, mute, and as usual radiant with contentment, which we love. I nod warmly but say nothing, and sit up to read the telex from my wife, Jane, saying that I should go ahead and breakfast without her, as she has a 9:00 lunch in town. Dipping an unsweetened madeleine into my coffee, I begin dictating my column, due later that hour, on the recent encyclical reaffirming the doctrine of isostacy (I approve). I eat only a small piece, since I have more to do this afternoon.

When I have said *finis*, I slip into the clothes Jane has laid out for me, palpating the snack she always places in my right-hand pocket, and without which the day is practically graham-crackerless. I saunter on out to the orangerie and, pulling off some of the ruching she has attached to the trees, pinch one of the fruits with a calipers given to us by our old friend Luther Burbank.

Staring out across the lawn that Jane has so marvelously had mown, I am reminded of something Whittaker Chambers said to me once in this room: "Sometimes I just want to scream." And yet normally he was the least given to postprandial pronunciamentoes of anyone I have ever known.

I tug now on the bell sash and Junipera Serra, our Spanish-American duster, appears to carry me out to the car. I peek to see if Pete is driving. He is; he's always driving. I wave to him through the soundproof divider, but am careful to give no instructions. He throws the knucklebones on the upholstery, and soon (exactly right) we are tearing off to New York. Pete is a real *sine qua non*. His discernment is Olympian in everything but ornithology; he and I share an inability to distinguish between a prothonotary warbler and a right-wing blackbird, or whatever.

I open my briefcase now and spread out as much as I like. After my old limo was gathered to its maker, I discovered that the only way to duplicate its perfection was to design one myself. I reflect wryly on a letter I once wrote John DeLorean, saying that if he was looking for the maneuverability of a rickshaw with the capaciousness of St. Peter's, he could do worse than to conjoin the hulls of a trimaran and an old B-52, as I have done. (I have never heard from him and, well—*nolle prosequi*.)

What the parodists ignored—and rightly so, since their aim was to savage the articles' weaknesses, not highlight their strengths—were the bits of conscious, almost painful, self-revelation in the pieces. If the reader wonders why Buckley works so hard—and often to apparently neglible purpose (why all those letters, speeches, and empty debates?)—it appears that he wonders about it, too. It is not easy to explain:

Is it some aspect of a sense of duty that I feel? Moral evangelism? A fear of uselessness? A fear that it is wrong to suppress useful—here defined extra-morally, as merchandiseable—talent? I do resist introspection, cannot claim to have "guarded against" it, because even to say that would imply that the temptation to engage in it was there, and it isn't. . . . Why do I do so much? I suspect that the promptings to write issue from a subtle dialectical counterpoint. Of what? Well, the call of *recta ratio* and the fear of boredom. What is *recta ratio* . . .? We know that *recta ratio* translates to "right reason," and that the Scholastics used it to suggest the intellectual instrument by which men might reason progressively at least to the existence of God, at most to how under His aegis they should govern themselves in all major matters, avoiding the major vices, exercising discipline, seeking virtue. The search for virtue is probably best drowned out by commotion, and this my life is full of. It is easier to stay up late working for hours than to take one-

tenth of the time to inquire into the question whether the work is worth performing.

And then, as I say, that other—the fear of boredom. Thoreau is known for his compulsion to discover, day by day, more and more things he could be without. I have enough of everything material—measured by ordinary standards, at least—but not the self-reliance to do without distraction; so that I would not cross the street without a magazine or a paperback, lest the traffic immobilize me for more than ten seconds. The unexamined life may not be worth living, in which case I will concede that mine is not worth living. But, excepting my own life, I do seek to examine, and certainly I dilate upon, public questions I deem insufficiently examined. . . .

To expand the audience for his examination of public issues, Buckley tapes 46 "Firing Line" programs a year, 8 or 10 of which are recorded outside New York. The show has originated from locations as far apart as Jerusalem and London. When he is in New York, Buckley tapes the program at the Lower East Side studios of the Home Box Office cable television company. Guests are treated to huge platters of delicatessen sandwiches, potato salad, pickles, and cole slaw prior to their appearance before a studio audience that is made up mostly of local high school or college students, seated cross-legged on pillows.

Viewers of "Firing Line" have seen an astonishing variety of guests, ranging from Ronald Reagan to Groucho Marx, either do battle with Buckley (in most cases) or join with him in promulgating their common views. Buckley says he finds preparing for the program "moderately exhausting." "I'm not supposed to be an interviewer," he explains. "It's an exchange of opinion. If one were just an interviewer, then you wouldn't have to prepare so much; you could just ask questions and accept their answers. But I'm supposed to know at least enough about the field to hold my own, if it's a contest."

If preparation for the program is a perpetual cramming session, the actual taping of it is not particularly taxing, Buckley says, even though he often tapes several hour-long sessions in a row and has been known to do as many as eight programs in one sitting, with 10- or 15-minute breaks between each taping. "The television work itself I don't find exhausting. . . . I'm not the least nervous or uncomfortable in front of the camera. I shouldn't be, after all this time."

The strains of Bach's Brandenburg concerti open the program and are followed by Buckley's introduction of his guest, which either is congenial or combative, depending on the person. When he was editor of the *Yale Daily News*, Buckley confessed to having a weakness for the "fatal attraction of facetiousness, the compelling urge to jolt, to ridicule, to pound square on the nose." It is a tendency he still has.

But he also has "style," a *Life* magazine television critic observed over a decade ago, and he employs it in a carefully calculated way. Buckley "uses his formidable vocabulary as a weapon. Words like 'nugatory,' 'usufruct,' 'enthymematic,' 'asymptotic,' 'propaedeutic,' and 'endogamous' cast a spell over his readers and his viewers. Each word is used precisely and the cumulative effect is one of *routine*. . . . Buckley hits you between the eyes with a usufruct, and by the time you remember what it means, he has gone on to the next numbered paragraph and you never catch up with the transition in his logic. . . ."

Buckley defends his use of unfamiliar words by contending that popular motion picture and theater critics use "as many unusual words as I do, [but] probably I got the reputation for using them because I speak verbally pretty much as I write, and a lot of people are reluctant verbally to enunciate words they don't hesitate to use in their writ-

ing." That may be, but as Edwin Newman, the resident grammarian at NBC, has observed, the use of obscure language gives something "the overtone of profundity"; and the *New York Times* once contended that Buckley has "managed to cloak his Roman authoritarianism under heavy layers of convoluted verbiage."

Another, and certainly less linguistically complex, means Buckley has used in recent years to examine issues has been a series of spy thrillers begun in 1976 and featuring the exploits of Blackford Oakes, a CIA hero who in many respects suggests a younger, slightly handsomer, less weather-beaten Buckley. He once said flippantly—but undoubtedly accurately—that his decision to try fiction writing was motivated by three things: "Money. Hubris. And curiosity." He made his debut as a novelist after quickly reading a book on how to write a novel and then dashing off his first thriller, *Save the Queen*, in five weeks.

Finding, however, that his novels were well-received critically and eagerly read by the public (his third novel, *Who's on First*, sold 50,000 copies its first month), Buckley began to approach them with a more serious purpose in mind. The work of spies, while essential to national security, has fuzzy moral edges, he says, and it is best described—and justified—fictionally.

"The art of counter-intelligence and the art of disinformation is an ambiguity. I suppose I could put that most simply by giving you an example: (1) Are you in favor of assassination? Answer: No. (2) Should you therefore sanction assassination? Answer: No. (3) Is there anything worse than assassination? Well, yes, a world war. Question: Would you assassinate in order to prevent a world war? Well, then you would acknowledge from that succession of statements that you've got a syllogistic problem, and it's not one that can be solved, in my judgment, by a moral, constitutional declaration. It's got to be an artistic answer."

Hence, the Buckley novels.

Throughout his public life, Buckley has been criticized for being more of a performer than a conservative philosopher. He is, critics say, an entertaining speaker, a riveting television personality, a popular columnist, and a facile writer but essentially an unoriginal thinker.

"I consider myself an exegete," Buckley says, "[and] there's a certain amount of performing involved in any exegesis. If you get up on a podium and you're a preacher, you preach; if you're a writer, you try to write gracefully, alluringly, solemnly, depending on the situation. In that sense, anybody who writes is a performer. But I have steadfastly said that this is what I seek to be and what I am—an exegete. I don't pretend to know more philosophy or more history than [other] people . . . so that [criticism] bothers me not at all."

When he isn't traveling around the country or overseas, Buckley presides over the biweekly editorial conference of *National Review*, held in a book-lined meeting room which is more or less cater-cornered across a narrow hall from Buckley's own cubicle in the magazine's warrenlike office.

These days the early- to mid-morning conferences are jovial gatherings of a dozen or so editors and writers, including Priscilla Buckley, Buckley's older sister, who has served as *National Review*'s managing editor since 1956.

Buckley, ever fidgeting, leads a page-by-page critique of the magazine's most recent issue, bestowing praise for the parts he likes and cryptic expressions of displeasure at those he doesn't. His brow furrows and twitches; he hoists himself on the arms of his chair and quickly folds his legs under his rump; he reverses the contortion just as quickly and spreads his legs out under the conference table, then leans back and almost tips over his chair.

At a typical conference, there is constant banter containing jokes about New York's newspaper-, magazine-, and book-publishing worlds; political gossip; and pungent discourses on current affairs. Irreverent comments are made about foes and friends. There is a discussion around the table of suggested topics to be covered in "The Week" section of the next magazine. Buckley jots down ideas on a small, spiral note pad, then makes the "paragraph" assignments. "I'm trying to find somebody who's not totally illiterate in economics except me to write the Social Security piece," he remarks before matching up one editor and one subject. The pieces are due at 10:00 A.M. the next day.

The meeting ends and the participants scurry off to their offices, where they and Buckley labor with the satisfying knowledge that what they are writing will be read at the highest levels of the federal government, including, of course, the Oval Office itself. Ironically, Buckley's friendship with President Reagan—which is of much longer standing and intimacy than that which George Will enjoys—has never become the subject of debate among his associates in journalism. Perhaps it is a measure of the seriousness—or indifference—with which they view the impact of Buckley's column that his fellows in the field have never questioned the propriety of the dinners, vacations, and continuing correspondence he has with Reagan.

With such instant entry to sympathetic centers of power—and a secret method by which he is assured that his letters will be placed on the President's desk—the inevitable question is whether there is any need for Buckley to continue producing his political exegeses. He replies that his role as a popular explainer—and defender—of conservative principles is as essential now as ever. In a speech he delivered regularly at the height of the antiwar movement more than a decade ago, Buckley warned that "the allure of the revolution, and the importance of revolutionary attitudes in contemporary political and social affairs, are bound to grow." He now concedes that he isn't so sure they have, or will. But it would be a mistake for conservatives to become complacent.

"It's not plain at this point what the historical cycle will be," he says over a lunch of soft-shell crabs, asparagus hollandaise, and assorted fruits and cheeses in his Manhattan home. "It may very well be, conceivably, that the Reagan business will be a blip. I devoutly hope it won't be. [But] the revolutionary rhetoric hasn't changed much in those parts of the world that are susceptible to it. The United States is not susceptible to it.

"I remember six or seven years ago, Kissinger, when he was still Secretary of State, telling me that he thought that the vector of terrorism, almost necessarily, would pass into this part of the world. I think his analysis is correct, but his timing was wrong; it hasn't yet hit here. But I don't think there's any guarantee it won't hit."

And even with a friend of 20 years' standing, with whom he agrees on most subjects, in the White House, Buckley says that there remains "a continuing responsibility by people who are generally friendly to people in power to attempt to isolate the following differential: namely, the difference between how the President is behaving and how he could behave, while still taking into consideration the political requirements of consensus politics. That's one area in which he needs to be observed.* The other area of observation is the area between what a con-sensus politician can accomplish and what ought to be accomplished. As you can see, those are two different areas that need continuous exploration."

That exploration is something Buckley is compelled to pursue. He believes that "enough bite" remains in what he produces "to prevent the growth of tapioca" in his columns and his magazine. "It matters that one should understand exactly what is meant by 'bite'," he wrote at the conclusion of his 1983 *New Yorker* journal.

We suffer no lycanthropic illusions at *N.R.* We do not fancy ourselves out preying on innocent victims. I suppose it could be that, like wolves, we have biological needs that require satisfaction: if there were nothing to complain about, there would be no *National Review*. On the other hand, if there were nothing to complain about, there would be no mankind. But complaint is profanation in the absence of gratitude. There is much to complain about in America, but that awful keening noise one unhappily gets so used to makes no way for the bells, and these have rung for America, are still ringing for America, and for this we are *obliged* to be grateful. To be otherwise is wrong reason and a poetical invitation to true national tribulation. I must remember to pray more often, because Providence has given us the means to make the struggle, and in this respect we are singularly blessed in this country, and in this room.

---

*In his role as a friendly presidential observer and instructor, Buckley wrote two widely cited columns in December 1983 urging Reagan to withdraw the marines he had sent to Lebanon. "It is a matter of national pride Mr. Reagan worries over, not merely personal pride, although the two do sometimes get confused. . . . A misplaced pride can have [a] sui-cidal effect: Reagan can cut off Reagan's line of retreat, and that makes no sense. . . . On this one, the President is increasingly isolated." If a "peace-keeping" force was needed in Lebanon, "the composition of foreign troops is more plausibly made up of local and regional forces," not U.S. Marines, Buckley wrote.

Ellen Goodman

The Gardener

When Ellen Goodman went to work as a general assignment reporter for the *Detroit Free Press* in 1965, she found that women at the paper were allowed to be heard but not seen. "I was one of the very few women there. But the managing editor—who was a very nice guy—had a policy, literally, of keeping women out of the city room," Goodman recalls with a bemused smile. The writing of the women reporters went into the paper's news hole, she says, but their bodies were confined to a "plywood box" that surrounded the features section.

Then came the revolution, what Goodman has called the "greatest social change of our time—the evolving roles of men and women" over the past 20 years. As a reporter on the *Boston Globe* since 1967 and a columnist for it since 1971, Goodman has been one of the few journalistic chroniclers of the women's movement and among its most sensitive interpreters and persuasive exponents.

"The movement of women into the work force has come slowly, over many years," Goodman wrote in her 1979 book *Turning Points,*

but during the 1960s and '70s, it accelerated so greatly that it upset the sense of normalcy, the breadwinner and home-maker tradition on which . . . marriage had been based. . . .

At the same time, the political force of the women's movement touched and changed women's lives, as greatly as if they had enlisted in the Army. . . . Women's rights groups called upon women to look at their lives and their marriages, to question the traditional subservient role of women in the family and to change it.

Change, the central focus of that book, also has been a constant theme of Goodman's twice-weekly column, which is syndicated in 323 newspapers by the Washington Post Writers Group. She examines not just the change in male-female employment roles but also the changes in society in general and how they affect families and individuals. Although Goodman also comments on the latest news, as do most columnists, she tries to interpret how national and international developments affect—or reflect—the concerns of her readers. Her greatest skill, which verges on the uncanny, is her ability to articulate the unspoken, to express the often unformulated thoughts that readers have about social and political issues. Readers might agree with Goodman's views—which tend to be liberal—or disagree with them vehemently, but they recognize the vox populi when they read it. It is a viewpoint that is rarely voiced elsewhere in the press, perhaps because it is both ethereal and uncommonly sensible. As poet W. H. Auden once wrote, "A discovery about ourselves or the meaning of life is never like a scientific discovery, a coming upon something entirely new or unsuspected. I think it is rather coming to conscious recognition of something we really knew all the time, but because we were unwilling or unable to formulate correctly, we did not hitherto know we knew."

Goodman, who quoted this Auden observation in *Turning Points,* formulates many social issues "correctly," giving voice to concerns her readers have—however vaguely—and "did not hitherto know they knew." "What I'm trying to do is say, here is this issue," Goodman explains, using her hands to form a small oval space in front of her and then twisting the imaginary issue slowly. "This is the way people are looking at it. . . . Let's turn it around and look at it another way. And to the degree you can make people turn it around and look at it another way every time, and make them think of something a little differently . . . , that is the reaction I want people to have: 'Gee, I never thought about it that way.' "

This is a relatively modest goal, she readily admits. "My expectations aren't enormously high," she says with an engaging laugh. "I don't have an agenda . . . I don't have a ten-point program at all. What I'm interested in doing is observing, not in creating public policy, which is *different,* I know, than some other columnists."

Just as Carl Rowan believes that he has a special—although not exclusive—duty to serve as an outlet for the views of minorities, Goodman endeavors to serve as an advocate of the women's movement, even for the housewives who may not consider themselves a part of it or think it has ignored them. "One of the things clearly that I want to do is . . . lend a voice to people who haven't normally had a voice in newspapers—and who *don't* have a voice in newspapers. I mean, they don't even *die* in

newspapers. Try finding the obituary of a homemaker someday."

Her views, of course, do not represent "the viewpoint of every woman any more than Carl would say his is the voice of every black," Goodman is quick to add, and her constituency is not just the previously voiceless female reader. In a broader sense, hers is "the viewpoint of a person who looks at big questions from the point of view of private lives," she says. "There's almost no voice for private lives in the newspapers. Newspapers are very 'public issues,' " she says, wiggling two fingers on each hand to denote quotation marks, "and you often don't know how it affects a person—this giant 'public issue.' "

Public issues have always been a part of Ellen Goodman's life. Her father, the late Jackson Holtz, was a Boston lawyer and an unsuccessful Democratic candidate for Congress who tried twice to buck the Eisenhower tide of the mid-fifties in a heavily Republican district in Brookline, an affluent suburb of Boston. Goodman "learned the voting patterns of wards and precincts the way other kids learned the batting averages of the Red Sox and the battles of World War II."

"I learned how to 'work the polls' when I was ten," she recalled in a November 1976 column.

I discovered when I was twelve that standing in the cold from 8:00 A.M. to 8:00 P.M. felt good, the way fasting or mountain climbing does—the virtue of enduring, sticking it out. I learned about the crazy camaraderie of poll workers and the way cold unites political opponents over hot cider.

I also learned, when I was thirteen and my dad was running for office, that there are people in the world who would snap, 'I wouldn't vote for your father if he were the last man on earth.' . . . I learned that fathers could lose and feel awful. That, too, became part of growing up.

Except for the fact that she was the daughter of a man with a modest amount of local prominence, Goodman's growing up followed the conventional, upper-middle-class patterns of the fifties and the early sixties. Despite the demands of his law practice and political activities, her father, who died in 1966, was an attentive parent who always made it home for dinner; her mother, Edith, now 68, was a traditional homemaker and the kind of warm, supportive woman who "would listen to your problems until you were sick of them." Goodman's major adolescent trauma, she once wrote, stemmed from being "Tall-for-Her-Age." Now five feet eight inches tall and what one writer described as a "willowy" 130 pounds ("I loved that word!" she says), Goodman hardly seems an Amazon. Her height still remains a sore point, however. In a number of columns, she has jokingly bewailed the disadvantages of being what she now considers "Tall for Any Age."

Her childhood and adolescence were sufficiently secure that Goodman "wanted everything to stay the same," she wrote in the introduction to *Turning Points.* "I wanted to live in the same house, go to the same school, keep the same friends . . . forever."

Goodman remains fiercely devoted to the familiar underpinnings of her family, surroundings, and rituals. She still lives in Brookline—in the same zip code area, in fact, as most of her immediate family—and she feels best "when I've observed all my little neurotic habits" each morning: driving the 20-minute commute from her nineteenth-century brick rowhouse to the office; getting a cup of tea, perhaps a piece of toast or a doughnut, and reading through several newspapers and the reports from the wire services. She tries to have lunch every day in the *Globe* cafeteria with the same group of co-workers. "I'm just the sort of person who likes to have lunch with the same people I've had lunch with for ten years," she says with a shrug, breaking the cafeteria habit briefly over a bowl of mussels and a salad at a downtown Boston restaurant.

As an admitted creature of habit who finds many social changes liberating, decries others as disruptive, and seeks to encourage her readers to view public and private issues from unaccustomed perspectives, Goodman is, as she once wrote, "expert on only one subject: the ambivalence of life."

Goodman went to Radcliffe, where she majored in modern European history and, unlike most of her columnist colleagues, had no early interest in writing or journalism. Instead she was active in undergraduate theatricals, appearing in *Damn Yankees*, *On the Town*, and a 1961 production of *Guys and Dolls* that was memorable for casting alone: Peter Benchley, Harvard '61 and the future author of *Jaws*, sang his way through the part of Sky Masterson, the super gambler and ladies' man, while Goodman pranced in the chorus line as—believe it or not—one of the "Hot Box Girls."

There remains a touch of musical comedy timing in Goodman's conversation, which is punctuated with jocular asides and laughter. In her intonations and expressions—even her appearance—she is a bit reminiscent of the early Barbra Streisand, sort of a Fanny Brice with a Boston accent. Discussing the careers of two media stars who happen to be married, she will drop her voice an octave and remark: "God knows, between the two of them, they make a living," ending with just the proper roll of the eyes and upbeat cadence. She has long, brownish-blonde hair, which she cheerfully admitted to one interviewer was "not all natural"; large, blue-gray eyes; and a broad smile displaying a formidable set of teeth. She is quick to grin, but it can alternate rapidly between one that is friendly and warm and one that is frosty. It is with the latter that she turns away a number of personal questions, some innocuous, such as what her favorite foods are; some substantive, such as how the circumstances surrounding the collapse of her first marriage have been reflected in her writing on social change and families. "While I write a column that is personal," she says, "I do not write confessionals. There are real limits on privacy. . . . We have a very amicable divorce, and one of the reasons we do is that we don't talk about each other."

Goodman graduated from Radcliffe *cum laude* in 1963, and within a week married Anthony Goodman, a Harvard medical student. They soon moved to New York, where, "strongly motivated by poverty," she went job-hunting. Her sister, Jane Holtz Kay, now a respected architectural critic, had been working on the Quincy, Massachusetts, *Patriot Ledger,* "which was the only thing that ever gave me a remote idea that (journalism) was an interesting thing to do," she recalls.

Goodman "literally walked in off the street at *Newsweek* and got one of those underpaid, semi-slave jobs that they used to give to overeducated young women." It was a "dreadful, dreadful" $58.50-a-week position as a researcher in the television department, where the only saving grace was a renewed association with Peter Benchley, then a writer for the magazine. In 1965 her husband's work took them to Detroit, where she joined the staff of the *Free Press* and "covered everything that you could imagine; more features than hard news, but a lot of hard news, too." In 1967 they returned to Boston, where she hastened to get a job on the *Globe*—even as a features writer for the fluffy and despised "women's section"—before anyone noticed that she was, well, just a little bit pregnant.

She was determined, once her daughter Katie was born in May 1968, not to abandon her career "despite" motherhood. "I . . . decided to stay at home so my daughter could get a good start in life," she once told an interviewer, "so I stayed home six

weeks." To what she found to be the increasingly annoying question of how she could leave her newborn child to return to work, she adopted the reply: "Oh, I just leave her at home with the refrigerator open and it all works out."

Becoming a parent, she found, was "a passage into maturity, the final assumption of adulthood," and with full rank as an adult, she developed an even stronger commitment to her work. "Suddenly I was no longer, in some recess of my mind, working 'until' I had a child," she recalled in a 1979 column. "Whatever had been tentative about my commitment became solid. If I wasn't doing this 'until,' it was time to do it better."

As a reporter in the late sixties and early seventies, Goodman covered the civil rights movement, the antiwar movement, and the nascent women's movement, to which she was introduced in 1969 "in a stuffy meeting house on Charles Street in Boston where I had been sent . . . to 'cover what was happening' to some 'strange' women . . . ," she recalled in *Turning Points*. At some of the more heated feminist gatherings from which reporters were barred, Goodman and others from the *Globe* "went disguised as women." The issues raised at those meetings (the first one that she attended was on "self-esteem") found a receptive audience in Goodman, whose marriage and previous assumptions were crumbling.

"I went from high school to college to marriage to motherhood as if it were all a contract I'd signed. Through my twenties I defended the predictable life with security plans for the present and insurance programs for the future. I drew up more Five Year Plans than the Kremlin," she wrote in *Turning Points*. "I first began to think seriously about change when I was being buffeted by it. . . . While I am hardly an advocate of Creative Divorce . . . , it was a time of heightened vulnerability, a time when I was most aware of the weaknesses of my plans and most sensitive to how disruptive change can be."

The final break with her husband—which did not feature any "dramatic exodus" or histrionics, she says—came in 1971, the same year that her subjective, opinionated pieces finally were given an opportunity to make the jump from the features section of the *Globe* to the Op Ed page.

Not only did her early columns address subjects that had not previously been topics of editorial comment, such as feminine hygiene sprays, lesbianism in the Army, and whether women should shave their legs, but Goodman approached them in a manner that even prompted the woman who edited the *Globe*'s editorial page to describe her work as "rather shrill." Some of her male colleagues found her arrogant and combative.

By 1974, however, Goodman had tired of what she called "the eye of the hurricane," so she drew up a proposal—"It was bullshit," she chuckles, "but aren't they all?"—to study the dynamics of social change in America as a Nieman fellow at Harvard. She emerged from her year-long sabbatical with the beginnings of *Turning Points*, her first book, and a greater tolerance for the tendency of others—and herself—to resist changes that can be seen as logical yet threatening.

"At one time I was much quicker to make judgments, and to impose my own sense of certainty, like a grid, over someone else's life," she wrote in the introduction to the book. "I was much less patient with my own conflicts and those of others. I couldn't accept the part of me that resisted what the other part of me labeled reasonable, rational change."

She is more at ease now observing, not judging, people and developments; and perhaps it is as much a measure of the changes wrought by the women's movement as it may be of Goodman's mellowing that many of the book's humorless case histories of emerging social discontent among women,

marital disruptions, and personal growth sound a bit commonplace now, even boring.

Her column could not be accused of being either. When she returned to it and the *Globe*, she had, as one male colleague told the *Washington Journalism Review*, "abandoned her confrontation politics [and] become very adroit at persuading people to her point of view."

Goodman is not certain how much her altered image among some of her co-workers reflects her own change or that of the times. "It's really hard to know to what degree people's perceptions of what was new information that seemed quite radical . . . changed and to what degree my presentation changed. I think it's probably more perceptions changing over time. The first time you hear something it sounds pretty 'strident,' and when it becomes part of everybody's consciousness [it doesn't]. . . . Even the words *sex discrimination* sounded 'strident' in 1969."

The tone of Goodman's column now is comfortably conversational: a sensitive, 750-word bit of kaffe-klatsch rumination spiced with the humor and intelligence of someone whom many readers consider a friend. Her subjects are not the traditional ones found on editorial pages—and in fact, some of the subscribers to her column place it (mistakenly) in the features section. She deals with the evolution of the family unit; the concerns of parents, children, husbands, and wives. She also writes about topics that transcend the sometimes artificial gap between public issues and individuals: court rulings on abortion and child custody; educational policies; nuclear war.

In 1976 the Washington Post Writers Group began syndicating Goodman's column, and it picked up papers rapidly. *Turning Points*, the product of 150 interviews around the country, appeared early in 1979; the first collection of her columns, *Close to Home*, was published six months later; and in 1980 Goodman received the

Pulitzer Prize for distinguished commentary. A second collection of columns, *At Large*, came out in 1981.

After she won the Pulitzer, Goodman told an interviewer that what made the award most gratifying was that it meant that the subjects she wrote about now were taken seriously by newspapers; to a friend she joked that at least she now knew what the first line of her obituary would be. Otherwise, it hardly made her task easier. "You win it on a Tuesday and then on a Wednesday you have to get up and do it all over again," she told an interviewer. "In this business you can never rest on your laurels. Journalism is always work in progress. You're only as good as your next column."

Goodman says she cannot begin drafting her next column until she has done some basic reporting: researching her subject, interviewing people familiar with it, traveling to conferences and the sites of news events. She keeps a file of clippings on a variety of topics and has a part-time assistant who does additional research in the *Globe*'s library and also answers Goodman's telephone, which rings "incessantly." Despite her wide range of subjects, she tries not to shoot from the hip. "Hopefully, you don't have a formulated opinion until you've done the research," she says. "You may have a *response* to the issue. You can look at some things and say, 'Oh, yuch!' But there's a difference between 'Oh, yuch!' and a 750-word column—hopefully something more significant than 748 more words!"

Her reading is "pretty eclectic. There're some things I read regularly, and there are times when I fault myself for being too eclectic. I'll go through all the magazines, basically; I won't read every word, but I'll go through almost all of them, from the newsweeklies to the monthlies. I won't necessarily go through some of the more obscure ones. . . . I read history for pleasure, to the degree that I can. And I read a lot of novels." She took a course in family

law during her Nieman year and finds what she learned in it handy for researching and commenting on legal issues.

The reading portion of Goodman's morning rituals is the most important. "I definitely have to read before I write. I just have to read, have to ingest words." If Goodman has completed her background research by the morning when she is due to write a column, she turns to a Video Display Terminal computer beside her cluttered desk around 10:30 and tries to get at least 20 of the 75 lines of her column written before she takes a break for lunch and goes upstairs to the *Globe* cafeteria with her regular noontime companions. She loves the VDT.

"I think [VDTs] are *wonderful*. You're working with clean copy all the time. It's amazing, particularly for someone like me. I pick, pick, pick, pick, pick. It's the perfect machine for a truly 'picky' writer. I take one word out or two; I mean, I'm constantly fiddling with the last words. And it also gives you a line count, and columnists write to space so. . . . If you know you're on line 24, you know where you are [and] you can sort of work it [out]. You know when it's time [to say] Jesus, I better start working on getting out of this!"

The "dead, flying, on-deadline minimum" for completing her column is three and a half hours. On the average it takes her six hours to write it.

Although John Leonard, the *New York Times* book reviewer and cultural mavin, likes Goodman's columns, he once criticized her for a stylistic habit of limiting practically all of her paragraphs to just two sentences. Goodman says, "That's journalism," at least the way she and some other columnists practice it. "I'm very careful not to have long paragraphs. I find that people don't read blocks of print. Even if something could fit in one paragraph, I usually do it in two."

To the mild complaint that her columns sometimes contain painful alliterations and puns ("In this, the year of backlash and

Bakkelash . . ."; "In the world of Movie-tone and muscle tone . . ."; ". . . it is no longer chic for a sheik to marry a veiled woman . . .") she closes her eyes, grins, and laughs: "I know, I know. You don't know how many of them I take out! I like them, obviously, or I wouldn't do it. Sometimes when you're writing, some pun will appeal to you; but sometimes you can run a meta-phor into the ground, and then occasionally I will edit out half of them as I go along. I like them. I have a penchant for them."

In addition to her column and occasional magazine pieces, Goodman gives about 25 speeches a year. Her standard fee is $4,000 if she can make the round trip to the lecture site in one day and $5,000 if she has to stay overnight. She also gives speeches "for borscht," she says, lecturing free of charge to women's and student's groups. Goodman tries to limit the number of speeches she gives for several reasons. She finds that long tours on the speakers' circuit make it more difficult for her to write the column; she loathes air travel; and she thinks that there are more important things than raking in as many lecture fees as possible.

"I think in my case I've been very careful not to get myself overextended, partially because I have a family and I'm more inter-ested in spending time with my daughter as she grows up than in milking the last three speeches, you know. But a lot of it, too, is that I need a certain space to work in, and you need time for the 'non-work,' for the reading that becomes part of [it]; for think-ing, living your own life."

It is the life that Goodman leads, as well as the lives of her family and close friends, that provides the context for many of her columns. To the extent—which undoubtedly is great—that the experiences, anxieties, and perceptions of this small group of East Coast, middle-class, college-educated, white-collar individuals reflect those of an increasingly uniform American society, Goodman's commentary is sharp, meaning-ful, and on occasion poignant.

"He worked himself to death, finally and precisely, at 3:00 A.M. Sunday morning," she wrote of a "company man" in 1976.

The obituary didn't say that, of course. It said that he died of a coronary throm-bosis—I think that was it—but everyone among his friends and acquaintances knew it instantly. He was a perfect Type A, a workaholic, a classic, they said to each other and shook their heads—and thought for five or ten minutes about the way they lived.

This man who worked himself to death finally and precisely at 3:00 A.M. Sunday morning—on his day off—was fifty-one years old and a vice president. He was, however, one of six vice presidents, and one of three who might conceivably—if the president died or retired soon enough—have moved to the top spot. . . .

He worked six days a week, five of them until eight or nine at night, during a time when his own company had begun the four-day week for everyone but executives. . . .

He is survived by his wife, Helen, forty-eight years old, a good woman of no particular marketable skills, who worked in an office before marrying and mothering. She had, according to her daughter, given up trying to compete with his work years ago, when the chil-dren were small. A company friend said, "I know how much you will miss him." And she answered, "I already have."

. . . By 5:00 P.M. the afternoon of the funeral, the company president had begun, discreetly of course, with care and taste, to make inquiries about his replacement. One of three men. He asked around: "Who's been working the hardest?"

Goodman takes dead aim against those "with the moral perspective of a mush-room" who are "encouraging us to feel good about what we should feel terrible about, and to accept in ourselves what we should change . . . ," such as selfishness, greed, and duplicity. She also can effectively challenge even as august a critic of American society as Alexander Solzhenitsyn, who berated the West "for materialism, legalism, a shallow and powerful press, and—more than anything else—a vital loss of will."

"The author of *The Gulag Archipelago,* of *The First Circle* and *The Cancer Ward,* spoke as an exile rather than an immigrant, a scourge rather than a reporter, a better historian of Russian society than chronicler of America," Goodman wrote after attending the 1978 Harvard commencement at which Solzhenitsyn delivered his dreary condemnation.

Through his own necessity of seeing the world as right and wrong, black and white, he now scorns our uncertain grays. He calls our sense of complexity, weakness. To this man, anti-communism is a holy crusade to which he has dedicated his life. Anything less, he says, is capitulation. . . .

He was neither an ingrate nor a prophet that Commencement day. But he sounded like an out-of-town journalist who comes in with his own preconceptions and neglects to do his legwork, his homework. As a reporter, he was afflicted with the precise disease he attributed to the American press: He looked at America in the seventies with "hastiness and superficiality."

Goodman worries that the "communications gap between the sexes" continues largely unbridged, especially among young women who discuss among themselves their aspirations for families as well as careers but "maintain a kind of conspiracy of silence with men." The silence stems in part, Goodman wrote, from "the old female fears—can I be ambitious and feminine? Can I be 'liberated' and loved?" and it is compounded by the fact that the college classes and guidance sessions dealing with "women's issues" still remain essentially for women only, she observed in a 1981 column. The silence, she insists, must be broken.

The job of communicating with men, changing their ideas, again falls onto women. It falls heavily into the middle of all other issues raised in that emotional world we call a relationship. . . .

We may graduate a whole new generation, sadly unprepared to live together. We may graduate another crop of men who will be stunned and saddened at middle age, to discover that their wives do not, did not, want the life plan they thought was mutual.

In her column, Goodman does what she can to educate her male readers, pungently writing about the double standard she sees being applied to women, who she says are accused of further stratifying America's social structure by increasing their family's income or of unfairly using their feminine wiles to boost their business careers.

"I've grown weary of hearing some economists exercise their social conscience in public by worrying about whether [working] couples are responsible for a growing gap between the rich and poor," she wrote in 1978.

It seems to me that there is a rather subtle and updated version of Blame the Working Wife going on. Long accused of every social ill from juvenile delinquency to male impotence, she is now being held responsible for the class structure of America. . . .

Few of the working couples I know raise polo ponies. . . .

It is true that adding a woman's high income to a man's could further solidify the class structure. Yet I find myself suspicious of the undertone of these arguments.

It seems to find the working wife guilty of the evils of capitalism when she's just had her first bite of the fruit. I don't think it's a coincidence that the family with two incomes totaling as high as $50,000 is considered a serious problem, while the family with one worker earning $50,000 is considered a success story.

Two years later she wrote:

As far as I can see, every promotion to the executive suite is based in part on a personal relationship. Bosses promote the people they like.

It's no news bulletin that the ambitious will jockey for casual friendship in the steamroom, the golf course, the private club. These are precisely the places often closed to women. Men don't consider that "unfair advantage."

The other informal path to success is to stop for an after-work drink, or sign on for the out-of-town trip. This is the way a man convinces his leader that he is charming, intelligent, and a good business hustler. This is also the easiest way for a woman to convince her boss that she is another sort of hustler.

The after-work drink and the road trip work for men, but not for women. Men do not consider this an "unfair advantage."

When you come down to it, a woman who wants to diffuse the sex issues had better be plain, happily married and talk about her husband incessantly. At that point, of course, she will probably be passed over for promotions because she doesn't *need* a pay raise. . . .

If women can sleep their way to the top, how come they aren't there?

A battle-scarred veteran of the women's movement's consciousness-raising sessions of the late sixties and early seventies, Goodman does not see such columns as an effort at consciousness raising for her male readers. "*Raising consciousness* are not words that trip lightly off my tongue," she says. Rather, she suspects—and hopes—that these and similar observations, such as a polite but damning column that labeled Walter

Cronkite and I. F. Stone as "ancient, honorable and hopeless" male chauvinists, help make men more aware of their own prejudices and presumptions, even at the risk of making them self-conscious. "Self-consciousness is better than no consciousness," she says.

Goodman's word portraits of individuals, sometimes as reflections in memoriam, are gems—lean, sensitive, insightful. For example, in June 1976 she wrote:

A Crazy Lady died last Monday, or so we're told. The obituary described her as a woman who "once refused to bow to Queen Elizabeth, asked a newspaper to 'crucify' a senator, and hit a reporter on the head." Yes, a genuine Crazy Lady died last Monday and here's to her.

Here's to all the Crazy Ladies who ever wanted to be Somebody and settled for being Outrageous. May they rest in peace. Here's to all the Crazy Ladies who were patted on the head while they were harmless pets and were ruthlessly punished when they became serious. Yes, here's to Martha Mitchell.

Similarly, two years later, she gave substance to the work of a man many sophisticates scorned as superficial.

Now he's gone, the tall skinny man with a shock of white hair who always looked like a Norman Rockwell portrait as he bicycled across the small-town of Stockbridge, Massachusetts.

Now, for a few days his fans and detractors alike suddenly feel a kind of nostalgia . . . for his nostalgia.

There were, of course, critics who called him the Lawrence Welk of the art world, insisting that bubbles floated off the ends of his brushes and that his work was sticky with sweetness. There were others who adored him, saying that he was the artist among con artists. But now they can both be heard calling him an artistic link to our past, a visual historian.

Norman Rockwell was a craftsman, an artist who insisted upon being called an illustrator, and a gentle, sophisticated man. But no, not a historian. His folksy vision of this country was no more accurate than the bleak world of Edward Hopper. His magazine work was no more a total reflection of our society than the photographs of Walker Evans. . . .

He knew that he didn't portray America. He portrayed Americana.

I suppose that every society carries in its soul some collective longings, some common spiritual values. We invest these back into our history and then hold them aloft as a standard of comparison for the present. For most of his eighty-two years, through 360 magazine covers, that was what Rockwell recorded: our ideals and our common myths. . . .

Well, consciously or not, he painted America as we would like to think it was. As we would like to think it is at root. His legacy is an interior landscape . . . of our very best side.

Just as her conversation is sprinkled with chuckles and guffaws, Goodman's column also has an abundance of humor in it—enough, in fact, to prompt one West Coast editor to call her "The Thinking Woman's Erma Bombeck," a characterization that embarrassed her. "I wrote a note to Erma Bombeck about that saying I didn't say this and don't think this. *You* are 'the thinking woman's Erma Bombeck.'"

There is an unquestionably Bombeckian flavor in some of her pieces. There are the occasional odes to the pleasures and pains of her career as a vegetable-growing fanatic: "There was a summer or two during which zucchini surprises lurked in everything from soup to bread to the Cracker Jack box. When she was six, I found my daughter picking distrustfully through peppermint-stick ice cream, asking, 'Is there any zucchini in here?'

"She was right to be suspicious. I learned to make everything out of zucchini with the possible exception of a lamp."

There was the exasperated description of the smoke detectors she bought that went off at the first whiff of a reheating pizza but slept through the clouds belching from a clogged fireplace. "Is there any reason to keep my home safe from a broiling lamb-chop?" she wondered.

There are the straight-faced escape plans that she has formulated should her complete lack of faith in all mechanical things prove correct: "I have an escape plan for the elevator. I will escape Certain Death if the elevator drops twenty floors suddenly—which I fully expect—because I will be jumping up and down. I read once that if you jump up and down while the elevator is crashing you have a 50 percent chance of being up while it's down and softening the impact.

"Don't tell me if it's not true."

Goodman falters sometimes when she takes the experiences and observations of the "sources" among her friends and relatives—which may be just a glitch on society's calibrator—and projects them upon the entire nation, perhaps giving them undue importance. She also repeatedly asserts that her work is not something that it is unable to avoid being. She is not, she often says, a "trend" writer—as if being one somehow connotes superficiality—when practically all social commentary is, at least on deadline, "trend" reporting. It cannot be otherwise, as she acknowledges, sometimes with her tongue in her cheek and a tone of disparagement, in her column. She reports, albeit sarcastically at times, all sorts of trends. She wrote in late 1980:

Here we go again. No sooner do we end one Me Decade than another one comes peeping around the corner . . . armed to the teeth.

Goodbye to the Era of Self-Improvement, hello to the Era of Self-Preservation. Good-bye to Hedonists; hello pessimists. The Me People of the seventies were learning to actualize themselves, but the Me People of the eighties are learning to defend themselves.

Yes, indeed, fellow trend watchers, the true religion of the decade is not going to be est or evangelical, it's going to be Survival. Already 50,000 self-proclaimed Survivalists from coast to coast are hunkering down for the Apocalypse. They aren't preparing their souls to meet doom, they are preparing their bunkers to escape it.

What the hot tub was to the seventies, the bunker will be for the eighties: the emotional escape hatch.

She has written about the political evolution of the children of the sixties—at least those who were "activists," in college or out. She wrote in 1976:

In the late sixties it seemed that every human act was a heavy political symbol. You couldn't eat a head of lettuce, or lie on a redwood chaise lounge or open a door for a woman without your politics showing. . . . You couldn't get into a women's liberation meeting in a skirt (let alone a tie) or into a student radical meeting with a crew cut, or into a black power session with processed hair.

The generation of the late sixties was raised on television and was adept at using visual symbols. They chose to wear their politics on their sleeves. They literally "looked" different to those in the mainstream who watched them on the six o'clock news. The young self-defined radicals separated from Middle America and identified each other as compatriots by these symbols.

While the point of this column is that these sartorical and tonsorial political statements were superficial, and have been rendered meaningless since their adoption by "the moderate mainstream," a strong argument can be made that to a large segment of

the population these symbols meant nothing to begin with.

"My friend Cassie is the sort of trend-setter they ought to hire over at *People*," she wrote in 1977.

Ever since she was eighteen, she's been a year or two ahead of the times.

When everyone else arrived at college with Villager blouses and circle pins which had to be discarded by Thanksgiving, Cassie came with black turtlenecked sweaters and tights. Cassie was married before anyone else, and divorced before anyone else. She had a Cuisinart and a schefflera when everyone else had a crepe pan and a philodendron. . . .

Anyway, about a year ago, Cassie moved out of the last in a series of Meaningful Relationships and announced that she was now Into Being Alone. At the time, we both happily assumed that, at long last, Cassie was finding her own independent way through the world. But the fact of the matter is that, once again, she was just a bit ahead of things. This year, everyone who is anyone is Into Being Alone. People who were formerly "lonely."

. . . I am now quite convinced that Being Into Being Alone is this year's Alternative Lifestyle, having replaced Communes, the Soil, and Living Together. . . .

Later that year, another friend who serves as a handy "neighborhood touchstone" gave Goodman a different set of insights on "the Mood of Our Time."

I had just finished another one of those articles about the seventies that made me feel guilty for not being depressed [and] I . . . asked her if she thought that everyone was really all that depressed.

"Not everyone," she yelled in her abrupt fashion into one of those horrible little telephone boxes on her desk. "Just the men."

Well, I started ambling down the list of people I know—this was not a scientific poll, you understand—and it seemed to me that she was more or less right. While the women I know seem energized and even a touch manic, depression is running through the male half of the species like an Andromeda strain.

"Ellen Goodman is at her weakest when maundering on about the state of the nation in one generalization after another," wrote Molly Ivins, a Rocky Mountain correspondent for the *New York Times* in 1979.* "America is a country signally ill-suited to generalizations. She also has a tendency to generalize on very little evidence. It is an old joke among national reporters that it takes two to make a trend. Miss Goodman has a tendency to seize on the travails of one or another of her friends and see them as universal. It is not that Miss Goodman's friends are any less representative than the rest of us, it is just that this is a big country."

"I like Ellen Goodman's column," says Mike Royko, with a wry grin. "But if I was a friend of hers, I sure as hell would never say much at a dinner party because, you know, two days later, there I'd be," he chuckles, spreading his hands apart to form an invisible headline.

Goodman herself has expressed suspicion "of instant revivals, of critical retrospectives of the immediate past, because we seem to cannibalize our history, gobbling it up as fast as we live it." Yet as the late Philip Graham of the *Washington Post* observed, journalism is "the first rough draft of history," and Goodman—the amateur historian—recognizes its pitfalls as she practices it and tries to avoid them.

"I think I'm pretty conscious at this stage—at least in certain fields—of what's a glitch and what is a pattern. And, in fact, as many columns as may go for the glitch

*Ivins now is a columnist herself for the *Dallas Times Herald*.

[there are others where] I'm probably as aware of countering a trend, or saying this is not the first time this has happened. . . .

"Probably every single thing should be qualified, and very often I do go through and qualify everything, and sometimes I don't. And sometimes when you're writing 750 words on general themes you generalize. I think it's a real risk of the business, because we *aren't* doing double-blind crossover studies. And the fact that I might begin a column talking about something that happened to my small acquaintances is often an entryway to something I've thought of as much larger, because obviously there are a lot of things that happen to me or my small group that don't make the cut.

"Every time you generalize about anything, you hear about it. But there are points to which if you qualify everything, you can't say anything. There are limits to how cautious and how qualified you should be. . . . What kind of shortcut language is permissible? You do need some. And what is generally enough agreed on that you can do? I don't know the answers to those questions, but I think they're real interesting problems with the nature of the business."

Goodman is impatient with criticisms, probably because she is as stern a critic of her work as anyone. "I'm a very hard grader of my own work. If I see someone reading my column on the streetcar and they don't finish it, it's terrible, terrible! If I have three columns in a row that don't meet my standards, I sort of envision people yelling: 'Give her the hook!' "

She is just as tough—even cold-blooded—about some of her colleagues in the press. Told that a local columnist in another city was a great admirer of her work, her reflexive reaction was not to accept the compliment at face value but to curtly ask: "Is he any good?" Assured that her admirer was an award-winning writer, she deemed the compliment acceptable, smiled, and said: "Oh, that's nice."

Columnists, as Goodman observed in the introduction to *Close To Home*, "need the egocentric confidence that your view of the world is important enough to read," and ego—not to mention jealousy—plays a part in the backbiting against Goodman at the *Globe* that has surfaced on occasion in the past. Other writers there have described her as "forbidding" and "the least popular columnist around here."

Goodman, unlike many other nationally syndicated columnists, does not have a private office. She works in the *Globe* city room, surrounded by some less celebrated Boston-based columnists and workaday reporters, and it is clear that the vibes from the association are not always harmonious. She discusses the working atmosphere at the paper somewhat hesitatingly at first, then with a flash of annoyance.

"I have a desk in the corner of the city room, which is sort of a concession to—it's a very, very comfortable place for me. . . . It's always an issue when you become more well-known, etc., etc., than your colleagues who you started with. I think there's always an undercurrent, a recognition of that, and dealing with it daily. But I think it's about as minimal as it could be in this case. . . .

"I could see why somebody who didn't know me or chat with me might think any of those things. I'm not responsible [for it]. It's a little like asking Jews why anti-Semitism exists. I don't feel compelled to explain why somebody doesn't like me. They're entitled. I think . . . you could find somebody to make the same remarks about [any *Globe* columnist]. And in my case, I'm making more money, frankly."

Of course, some of Goodman's closest friends also are at the *Globe*. Her husband, Bob Levey, whom she married in 1982, is a national reporter for the paper. It is an extension of her family—and there are tensions in all families.

As an observer and participant in the women's movement, Goodman has wit-

nessed and felt the conflicts inherent in the desire of many women to be both a mother and a wage earner, a Supermom and a Superwoman. She rejects the image of the Supermom—the woman who "was your better basic, devoted, selfless Total Mother whose children never had runny noses because she was right behind them, wiping. Her children were the ones in the school lunchroom with sandwiches cut in the shapes of turkeys at Thanksgiving and bunnies at Easter."

She also finds the effort to be a Superwoman—to "have it all"—harrowing and bleak. The Superwoman, mother of 2.6 children, she says, not only prepares a nutritional breakfast for the kiddies—with raisin faces in the oatmeal—but wears designer clothes to her $25,000-a-year job "doing work which is creative and socially useful."

Then she comes home after work and spends a real meaningful hour with her children, because after all, it's not the quantity of time, it's the quality of time. Following that, she goes into the kitchen and creates a Julia Child 60-minute gourmet recipe, having a wonderful family dinner discussing the checks and balances of the United States government system. The children go upstairs to bed and she and her husband spend another hour in their own meaningful relationship, at which point they go upstairs and she is multiorgasmic until midnight.

In saying "no to Superwoman" in a 1979 column, Goodman said women "are no longer willing to look inside themselves for all the answers and all the energy. At the turn of the decade, they don't want a Superwoman peptalk any more. They long for something more precious and more realistic: a support system—of families, the workplace and the community—to fend off this cultural kryptonite." In essence, Goodman advises other women to do the best they can—either as full-time homemakers, mothers, working women, or all three—and not feel guilty if they can't meet impossible standards.

Goodman herself says she handles the multiple demands of motherhood, column writing, and lecturing the way "porcupines make love: Carefully. I think that I probably do a tremendous amount of figuring and balancing and weighing. That's very typical of working mothers. . . . Of course, I have a teenager, so it's not like having a baby. But a teenager needs a whole other kind of time. When they're little, there's this pressure to get home because the babysitter's going to leave and they can't be alone for a minute. . . . As they get older . . . , there's that sense of wanting to have an easy, private time in which [to discuss] whatever arises naturally, where you don't have pointed moments of 'Let us now talk about teenage sex,' you know; it doesn't work."

Goodman says her home has always been a mecca for her daughter's friends, and—contrary to accepted wisdom—she finds teenagers delightful. "I know I'm not supposed to, and I know they're supposed to be obnoxious and dreadful, but I just find them fun. . . . Maybe it's because I've had one child or whatever, [but] I have had much, much more pleasure than pain out of mothering."

Single parenthood also was a bit less burdensome for Goodman, she quickly points out, because she has been making a healthy income and is surrounded by a supportive family, one which in turn requires her support. "You know, it's all very well if I get the Pulitzer Prize, but if I don't show up with dessert for the family holiday, I'm in the, you know, not the doghouse—it wouldn't be that overt, it wouldn't be that judgmental in my family—but there are expectations, not just of that servicey kind of thing, which isn't really important, but of being there to talk, to be supportive."

The conflicts and anxieties that bedevil many American women during this time of transition confront Goodman no less tellingly, which perhaps is why she is so accomplished at expressing them. During a 1981 appearance at Corning College in upstate New York, Goodman found herself asked two familiar questions, unexpectedly posed in tandem. Why, one woman wanted to know, do homemakers always act as if women who go to work are lousy mothers? Moments later, a second woman asked why working women always act as if homemakers are somehow inferior.

With practically equal numbers of young mothers in the work force and at home, women are finding themselves forced to choose "sides" when addressing these conflicts, Goodman later wrote.

The mother working outside the home still feels most vulnerable to questions about her children. Are they getting enough of her time, energy, caretaking?

The mother working inside the home still feels most vulnerable to questions about herself. Is she doing enough, earning enough, proving enough?

. . . I suspect more women feel judged than actually are being judged. After all, the women I met . . . complained about being criticized but denied being critical. I suppose we all project our ambivalence outward, defending against our own reservations about our lives.

But it is still remarkably hard for any of us to make a critical life choice in this unsettling time of "equilibrium," to weigh all the complex values, all the uncertainties and then make a decision without defensiveness.

The toughest question is, finally, the one I was never asked. Why is it always so difficult for any of us to simply say: "I am choosing this way, not because it's right or wrong, but because, on the whole, it seems best for me, for mine, for now"?

For now, Goodman feels confident and secure—the "last of my peer group" to avoid psychoanalysis, she says with a laugh. She is convinced, as she wrote on the eve of her 40th birthday in 1981, that "these are my good old days."

"At 20, I wanted to know who I would become. By 40, willy-nilly, ready or not, I've become. I have a web of commitments, a history. I've survived some things, hardened to some and opened up to others. . . .

"Middle-age is responsible. Middle-age is busy. Middle-age is overcommitted. Middle-age asked for it."

Middle age might not always want it, of course.

"The [column-writing] business requires enormous energy," Goodman says. *"You're always working,* at a certain level, because you're always thinking about what you're doing next, and you're just always working. And if I felt that I just didn't want to, or I just wasn't up to doing that any more, or wasn't pleased with the work I was doing . . . , I will do something else at the paper. I wouldn't be able not to write. I think writing is a lifetime profession, and I can't imagine not writing, but there are lots of other ways. I'd also like to spend some time studying American history in an organized way."

Goodman will continue tending—perhaps even begin expanding—her gardens, both literary and actual, cultivating questions, raising consciousnesses, and, probably, wondering what she's going to do with all that zucchini.

James J. Kilpatrick

The Sage of Scrabble

The Sage of Scrabble actually lives in Woodville. When he purchased land in that tiny Virginia town of 14 homes in 1966, James J. Kilpatrick could have adopted Woodville's somewhat innocuous name as a dateline for the columns he writes there. "Woodville?" he says with mock distaste, wrinkling his nose as if he were caught downwind of some unpleasant barnyard odor. "What a prosaic name. Scrabble's just two miles on down the road past Woodville [and] I wasn't going to use *Woodville* if I could just appropriate *Scrabble,* which is a very real place. It's not any Yoknapatawpha County or Camelot. It's identified on official maps."

True, but it has no post office. That has caused the postal people in Rappahannock County many a headache. Kilpatrick, whose thrice-weekly column reaches a potential 35 million readers in 450 newspapers and whose pungent conservative pronouncements enliven public television's "Agronsky and Company," gets a lot of mail. "Correspondents will write to me in 'Scrabble, Virginia,'" he says. "I don't know how many letters have been returned marked 'No Such Post Office.' But I'm not going to give it up."

Some fastidious subscribers to Kilpatrick's column are not as interested as he is in the lilt of a place-name. They date-line his columns from the country "Woodville." "Shame on them," Kilpatrick says. "That's carrying the desire for literal presence too far, I think."

In some respects, Kilpatrick may find his literal presence in the twentieth century infelicitous as well. In many ways he is an eighteenth-century man, well versed in history, literature, etymology, and the law. He is capable of rich, congenial conversations embracing poetry, Shakespeare, Gibbon, and Mark Twain or of splitting constitutional hairs with a debating opponent whom he graciously addresses—in fine appellate court fashion—as "my brother" or "my sister."

Kilpatrick, 63, who is called "Kilpo" or "Jack" by his friends, is a courtly but unstuffy country gentleman, five feet ten inches tall, weighing 168 pounds, with a slightly pixyish appearance enhanced by thin gray hair, light blue eyes, rosy cheeks, and a finely veined button nose that has been burnished by rubbing the rim of his daily glass of "therapeutic bourbon and water."

In times past, many of Kilpatrick's opinions also had a somewhat eighteenth-century cast. As the young, fire-breathing editor of the *Richmond News-Leader* three decades ago, he was a tireless enemy of integration, an advocate of states' rights, and a champion of white supremacy. Naturally, he has mellowed, come to recognize

179

what he now calls "the moral wrongness of segregation," and otherwise modified his views on many subjects.

"I don't go around using *ad hominem* arguments—very often—anymore," he says, "and in a good many of my political views I think I certainly have mellowed. But this is a natural process of maturing, aging, whatever. When you're the editor of a major newspaper at 30, I think you have pretty clear, crisp, black-and-white views on *everything*. Then the older you grow, the more you find that the world is composed of half-tones. There's an awful lot of gray in things."

In fact, the shades of gray Kilpatrick perceives in several controversial issues cause him to adopt positions that amount to heresy in some right-wing quarters. He is opposed to any ban on abortion; he is against the efforts to return prayer to the public schools by means of a constitutional amendment; he has ridiculed the "gun nuts" and their opposition to gun control; he thinks that some of the Reagan administration's cuts in social programs have left a few painfully large holes in the so-called safety net; for many years he even supported and wrote kind things about the federal Legal Services Corporation, the courtroom advocates for the poor.

Kilpatrick is hardly a closet liberal, however. He is an unwavering conservative who finds most of the Reagan administration's handiwork satisfying to behold. But he is not an ironclad ideologist. He approvingly quotes James Fenimore Cooper's observation that "principles become modified in practice by facts," and he has little patience with the members of the radical New Right, who now complain that Reagan has betrayed them.

"All of them worked like sled dogs in the Republican campaigns. But they tend to forget that others also worked hard for the dear old GOP," Kilpatrick wrote in a column not long after Reagan took office.

More critically, they tend to forget what the presidency of the United States involves. Mr. Reagan cannot be president of the New Right only. If he is to govern effectively, Mr. Reagan must rally support on Capitol Hill from various quarters. And some of these other quarters also have political claims upon him.

One trouble with my far-right brothers—with some of them anyway—is that they cannot get used to the idea of governing. They have been out in the cold for so long that they feel uneasy about being warm. With them ideology is everything. . . . But if the problem is to get Mr. Reagan's tax bill through the House and Senate, ideology isn't everything. Votes are everything.

Let me speak bluntly to my disconsolate brothers. I was fighting for the conservative cause before some of them were born; I was in the trenches while some of them were still in knickers. Out of that experience I would say to them: You're doing pretty damned well.

Kilpatrick's ideological tolerance extends to personal relationships as well. He sees no reason why philosophic foes cannot be cordial, even warm friends. He counts among his chums former Democratic Senator Eugene J. McCarthy, with whom he co-authored *The Political Bestiary,* a 1978 satirical dictionary of political terms, and writer Shana Alexander, his erstwhile opponent on "60 Minutes"'s now discontinued "Point, Counterpoint" segment. Even fellow columnist Carl Rowan, with whom he does battle each week on the Agronsky program, nominated Kilpatrick for membership in Washington's exclusive Gridiron Club. The appreciative Kilpatrick called Rowan's gesture "an act of generosity . . . for someone whom he disagrees with just about constantly." There also was a touch of irony in it, since Rowan was the first black ever invited to dinner at the previously segregated Gridiron Club back in 1962, when Kilpatrick still was fighting integration in Virginia.

One also might be tempted to consider ironic the fact that Kilpatrick—the one-time editorial voice of Richmond, the quintessential Virginia squire, the rhapsodic bard of the Blue Ridge—is not a native of the Old Dominion or even of the Old Confederacy. He actually was born in Oklahoma City, Oklahoma. The place of his birth is of little consequence, however, since the spirit of the South is in his genes.

Kilpatrick was the eldest son of James Jackson Kilpatrick, Sr., scion of a prominent, old-line New Orleans family of Scottish descent and himself the son of a captain in the Confederate Army. (In the dining room of his home, Kilpatrick proudly displays a pair of silver spurs that his maternal grandfather received when he was crowned Rex of Mardi Gras in the early 1900s.) Kilpatrick's father moved to Oklahoma in 1910 to set up a lumber business specializing in fence posts and railway ties, but Kilpatrick visited his New Orleans kinfolk often and relished his southern heritage.

Kilpatrick displayed a bookish and literary bent at an early age, and his mother Alma, to whom he was extremely close, encouraged this inclination. When, at the age of six, he wrote a poem extolling Lindbergh's triumphant flight to Paris, she mailed it to a children's magazine, which accepted it and sent a "shiny new dime in payment." "I had lost my amateur status," Kilpatrick reminisced in a 1981 column. "Then came a copy of the magazine itself. Byline! It was a thrill that comes once in a life time."

He was hooked for life. At 13 he got a summer job as a copy-boy at the *Oklahoma City Times,* and in high school he became editor of the student newspaper, learning how to set type by hand and run the proof press. He found the smell of printer's ink "intoxicating," and throughout high school he devoted all his spare time to "writing, writing, writing."

He spent a "perfectly normal, middle-class childhood . . . , not marked by any traumatic incidents at all," until his first year in college at the University of Missouri's journalism school in Columbia. Then his parents were divorced, destroying the supportive family unit he had known. His father's lumber business had failed, a victim of the Depression, and "he was having an affair with his secretary," Kilpatrick says quietly. "I was 15–16. . . . I didn't understand it at the time. It was a bad situation." For many years after the breakup, Kilpatrick was estranged from his father, who married his secretary and became one of the countless Oklahomans who migrated to California in the 1930s. "We established some correspondence after a time, but I never saw him again," Kilpatrick says, his eyes reflecting a sense of sadness.

After the collapse of his father's business and his parents' divorce, Kilpatrick no longer could afford to live in the house of the fraternity that he had joined at Missouri, so he moved into the first of a series of boarding houses and tried his hand at "anything you could do to pick up a little money." He waited on tables both at the boarding houses and at the Tiger Hotel in Columbia; he tutored American history; he edited other students' term papers; he wrote free-lance pieces.

Then he got "lucky" and learned how to use the cumbersome Speed Graphic cameras used by most newspaper photographers in the thirties and forties. Armed with this new skill, he got a job at Stephens College, the all-women's school in Columbia, "as a staff photographer and sort of general flunky in their public relations office."

"That was the most desirable job in the whole city of Columbia," Kilpatrick says, assuming an air of adolescent pride. "There I was, 18 years old, taking pictures of all these beautiful girls, getting paid for it. That was really how I put myself through college—with my camera, working at Stephens."

When he accumulated enough credits to take his bachelor's degree in March 1941, Kilpatrick, "a southerner by inheritance," sought employment on southern papers, preferring the early morning to midday schedules of afternoon dailies because he was—and still is—"day people," prone to fade once the sun has crossed over the yard-arm. He applied to the *Richmond News-Leader,* among other journals, and when the city editor there asked in reply whether Kilpatrick would be interested in a $35-a-week job, Kilpatrick aggressively interpreted that inquiry as a firm job offer and wired back: "Will report Monday, March 31. Kilpatrick." The editor always insisted thereafter that he never really offered Kilpatrick a job—Kilpatrick simply appropriated it.

Kilpatrick was similarly aggressive as a reporter, eagerly seeking assignments on a wide range of beats and producing prodigious amounts of copy. "I swiftly discovered what all my brothers and sisters of the newsroom come eventually to know—that if you love newspapering, nothing in the world beats the business of going out on a story in the morning, and covering that story, and writing against the deadline, and seeing your work still warm and smudgy from the press. Nothing comes close," he wrote on the eve of his 40th anniversary as a reporter. He still considers reporting his main role, even after two decades as a columnist.

Early in his journalistic career, Kilpatrick also became infatuated with another discipline—the law—and his ardor for it has never cooled. Not long after he joined the *News-Leader*, he took the train to Washington, walked up the hill to the Capitol, and, "for some reason, I really can't tell you why," he crossed the street to the Supreme Court building and went inside. He identified himself as a reporter and was directed to a seat off to the side, behind some latticework, where he listened enthralled to the presentation of arguments in several cases.

"It was just love at first sight, it was just head-over-heels love for the thing. I was so impressed by it—the demeanor and the formality of the argument before the Court. And that was the beginning of a love affair that continues to this day. I suppose I write more about the Supreme Court than any of the other columnists," he says, gesturing with pride towards his "modest little law library," consisting of a complete, bound set of all the Supreme Court's cases, which he keeps on eight or ten shelves in his office library.

Not long after he arrived in Richmond, Kilpatrick also met Marie Pietri, a tiny, slender painter and sculptress, to whom he became engaged after a courtship that lasted precisely four days. "It was just one of those things," he once told an interviewer. They were married in September 1942, and now have three sons and three grandchildren.

A former colleague of Kilpatrick's in Richmond told an interviewer a decade ago that Kilpatrick arrived in the Virginia capital a liberal but soon learned that both the town and his newspaper were conservative and trimmed his sails accordingly. Kilpatrick disputes that recollection. "I was as apolitical as a reporter could be. I came out of college with no political convictions really one way or the other. At that time I couldn't even vote—that was before they had extended the vote to 18-year-olds—and I was never involved in any ideological battles at the University of Missouri," he says.

Kilpatrick does not deny another old colleague's characterization of him as an "ambitious" young reporter. "I was ambitious—and hungry," he says, observing that neither he nor his wife "had two nickels to rub together" when they were married and "started out as real 'po' folks.' She was working in a department store selling hosiery. I was just on a newspaper reporter's salary, which wasn't much in those days, even in 1941–42 dollars. So I was working my tail off as a correspondent for all kinds of trade publications. . . . I did all kinds of free-lance things. Lord, I was working six, seven days a week to supplement the income that I had from the *News-Leader*. So I guess I was ambitious, no question about it. I wanted to move on up in newspapering."

Move on up he did—rapidly. Because of bronchial asthma he was stymied in several attempts to enlist during World War II, so he soon became the war-depleted *News-Leader*'s star reporter, a one-man investigative platoon who terrorized city politicians and bureaucrats. In addition, he expanded his free-lance work, becoming the *New York Times*'s man at the U.S. Patent Office, which was moved down to Richmond during the war. He got $25 a week for a 1,000-word piece on whatever patents had been filed.

He also began developing a colorful, witty, and savory writing style, flavored with dashes reminiscent of Westbrook Pegler and H. L. Mencken—especially Mencken. Early in his career, Kilpatrick wrote at the time of the Baltimore Sage's centenary in 1980, "I fell boozily into Mencken and wound up drunk as Bacchus. For a time, I affected the devices that came naturally to my mentor and went about whacking at boobs, quacks, reformers and other such montebanks. The style can be imitated . . . but the imitations fall short of the real thing. Mencken was in a class by himself."

(Kilpatrick remains a Mencken devotee, however, and is not above posing for photographs in a Menckenesque mien, sitting in front of his old Underwood typewriter and peering quizzically over horn-rimmed glasses perched on the tip of his nose. All that is missing is the stub of an Uncle Willie cigar protruding from the side of his mouth.)

Kilpatrick's enterprise, energy, and stylish writing quickly impressed the *News-Leader*'s venerable editor in chief, historian Douglas Southall Freeman, and its scholarly general manager, John Dana Wise. Wise, a "very highly principled and self-educated, but brilliantly self-educated, conservative," according to Kilpatrick, became his political tutor, and Freeman, a biographer of George Washington and Robert E. Lee, began to groom Kilpatrick as his successor. Freeman made Kilpatrick the paper's chief editorial writer in 1949, and on June 30, 1951, he simply announced that he was "going home now" and designated Kilpatrick—then only 30—as editor in chief in his stead.

Kilpatrick was not an officebound or ivory tower editor. He remained an habitué of the state capitol building, as well as the city and state courts and the bureaucratic labyrinth. He viewed the editorial page almost as another news hole to fill and dictated new commentary for each edition over the telephone from the state capitol. He remained a prolific writer, producing up to 43 column inches a day for the editorial page and cranking out book reviews, magazine pieces, and lectures as well.

He also remained an investigative reporter, directing a two-year probe into a decade-old murder case in which a black defendant had been convicted and sentenced to death for murdering a policeman. Convinced that the death-row inmate was innocent, Kilpatrick assumed the roles of an appellate lawyer and sleuth, reviewing the entire trial transcript for inconsistencies in the evidence, which he found in abundance, and uncovering new facts. Witnesses had claimed that the defendant had driven to the murder scene, smoking cigarettes on the way. Kilpatrick found that the imprisoned man did not know how to drive and did not smoke. One witness, a patient in a hospital near the murder site at the time of the killing, had said that he had looked out the window in his room just after the murder and seen a black man running down the street. Kilpatrick went to the hospital, lay down on the bed, and determined that it was impossible for anyone to look out the window and see the sidewalk. The lengthy editorial campaign based on Kilpatrick's findings eventually paid off: the governor of Virginia granted the inmate a full pardon and freed him.

Kilpatrick's longest and most tenacious editorial crusade, however, is considerably less inspiring in retrospect. When the U.S. Supreme Court ruled in *Brown* v. *Board of Education* in 1954 that segregated schools were inherently unequal and therefore unconstitutional, Kilpatrick denounced the high court's "tyranny" and pledged "massive resistance" to integration. He latched on to a creaky, nineteenth-century constitutional theory propounded by John C. Calhoun and his followers that the states have the right, even the duty, to "interpose" their sovereign principles against any Supreme Court decision to which they object and, if need be, nullify it. He seemed, in the view of William S. White, the *New York Time*'s chief congressional correspondent at the time, to ignore all "the ineluctable facts of history since the day of Calhoun and of Lee's surrender at Appomattox." Instead, he apparently wished to refight the Civil War, this time in the editorial columns of the *News-Leader* and in a sharply written book entitled *The Sovereign States,* published in 1957. Although Kilpatrick endeavored, he has said, "to elevate the issue away from race," his arguments inevitably took on a racist tinge.

"The Negro race, as a race, has palpably different social, moral and behavorial standards from those which obtain among the white race . . . ," he wrote in *The Sovereign States.*

After years of exposure to the amenities of civilization from which the Negro might profit by example, one out of every five Negroes in the South today is the product of illicit sexual union. . . . The undisciplined passions which find one outlet in sex, find another in crime. . . . Often as not, the evidence discloses no reason—no white man's reason—that conceivably might justify murder.

What is it that the court, in effect, has commanded the South to give up? It is no less than this: The basis of the South's society, the vitality of her culture. The Southern States are ordered . . . either to abandon their schools or to breach the immutable law by which the South's character has been preserved. And the law is this: That white and black cannot come together, as equals, in any relationship that is intimate, personal and prolonged.

Kilpatrick does not look back on his anti-integration campaign with any pride, but neither does he apologize for it. "I was born, bred, and brought up in a southern milieu," he says. "I was born . . . and grew up . . . in an absolutely segregated society. When I went to the University of Missouri it was a completely segregated, all-white institution. I had accepted this as just one of the realities of the world around me without ever giving much serious thought to the moral implications of it.

"At the time we were caught up in *Brown* v. *Board of Education,* I was still, I think, pretty much a southern boy, with all of these acceptances, prejudices—in effect bigotry— that I had accepted all of my life, without clear thinking about them. And it was after that, when we really began to get into the fight over the desegregation of tearooms and theaters and so on, that I began, I think quite slowly, to understand the moral implications of it, the moral wrongness of racial segregation, and very steadily abandoned the views that I had had that segregation per se was a good thing.

"I've never, for one minute, relented in my criticism of *Brown* v. *Board of Education* as a piece of constitutional law. I think it was very bad constitutional law. I've thought that ever since the opinion came down in May of 1954. But morally I think it was sound and wise, and I have been pleased to see the changes that have resulted out of *Brown* and its progeny."

(Carl Rowan, for one, finds Kilpatrick's tortuous conversion to a belief in racial equality only partly praiseworthy. "Jack will say, 'Yes, I used to be a racist but I'm not one anymore,' and I'll say, 'I don't give a damn about that. You still support [economic and social] policies that are inimical to black people.' ")

However misguided, Kilpatrick's eloquent campaign against integration gave him a national reputation. "It may be the far right wing has found . . . its ablest literary voice of late years," observed the *New York Times*. "Mr. Kilpatrick is a talented writer, whereas William F. Buckley, Jr., . . . , for example, is only an educated one."

The praise for Kilpatrick's writing abilities, as apart from his beliefs, was voiced by others. Television newsman Roger Mudd, a reporter on the *News-Leader* when Kilpatrick was editor, once told an interviewer that he then considered Kilpatrick to be "one of 10 best stylists in the country," and the late Harry Elmlark, chief of the *Washington Star*'s syndicate and the man who had persuaded Buckley to become a syndicated columnist, began to woo Kilpatrick in 1964.

Kilpatrick, comfortable as "a rather substantial frog in a small puddle," was not inclined to leave Richmond. In the year that would witness Barry Goldwater's trouncing by Lyndon Johnson, he was not sure there was a national market for his conservative views. Later in 1964, however, *Newsday*, the Long Island daily, offered him a much safer option: a minimum $5,000 a year for columns it would syndicate, plus a guarantee that he could remain in Richmond, keep his editorship, and drop the column if it proved to be a flop.

As it turned out, Kilpatrick's column was immediately successful, and Elmlark, ever persistent, renewed his overtures, persuading Kilpatrick to join the *Star*'s syndicate line-up and move to Washington in 1966. Even though he shifted his perspective largely from the local scene to a national one, his columns retained the basic hard-news flavor of his old editorials, and he also continued his magazine writing, turning out commentary for the *Nation's Business* and Buckley's *National Review*, to which he was a contributing editor.

Kilpatrick is a delightful writer and sharp observer who possesses a facility for simile that can be both comic and poetic. A 1968 account he wrote for *National Review* of Senator Eugene McCarthy's antiwar campaign in the New Hampshire Democratic primary is a model of colorful political reportage, full of deftly drawn physical descriptions and humorously accurate analyses. In it, he characterized one key McCarthy aide as "a dough-faced lad, white as a dinner roll taken too soon from the oven; he was smoking, unexpectedly, an eight-inch cigar. It stuck from his face, when he leaned back in a chair, like a creosoted pole in the snow."

McCarthy, who from this encounter would become a good friend of Kilpatrick's, was described as moving "uneasily among the reporters, looking like a bridegroom on his way to dinner at the in-laws, saying the things one says to his dentist." When McCarthy smiled, Kilpatrick observed, it "was nothing to compare with Ike's grin or Romney's Pepsodent ramparts; it was a modest smile, the smile of a man reading Thurber in bed by himself; but it was not a politician's smile." When the diffident presidential candidate entered a reception room at a fundraiser, he did so "as inconspicuously as a rowboat docking on a millpond," and when he addressed the assembled faithful, he perversely violated all the "statutes" dealing with fundraising speeches.

The statutes make it clear that a candidate may not appeal to the intelligence of the audience before him. He may properly appeal to patriotism, to partisanship, or to pugilistic instincts; he may dwell upon the necessity for preserving the Republic from the depredations of the Administration in power. Other appeals should be reserved for smaller occasions. A candidate is expected to speak not less than 45 minutes and gesture not fewer than 128 times. Poetry must be limited strictly—two passages from Shakespeare and one from Edgar A. Guest; no other authors are allowed. If a prepared text has been distributed to the press, at least a substantial part of the text should actually be delivered.

McCarthy, he reported approvingly, "paid no heed to these rules."

As luck—or practical politics—would have it, 1968 was not McCarthy's year, but the election of Richard Nixon pleased Kilpatrick mightily. He had first met Nixon during the Alger Hiss affair in the early 1950s, and over the years they had corresponded casually and gotten together for long conversations and interviews. "I liked him. I like him still," Kilpatrick says.

Once Nixon became President, quotes from Kilpatrick's column appeared regularly in the White House press summary, and he was invited to state dinners and prayer breakfasts. He was a faithful exponent of most of Nixon's policies and appointments, even gritting his teeth (and "holding my nose") and supporting the doomed Supreme Court nomination of Judge G. Harrold Carswell. "We wish Carswell towered, and he doesn't," he said at the time. "But he is the President's choice, and if I were a Republican on the floor . . . I would, a little sadly, vote 'Aye.' "

When the Watergate scandal engulfed Nixon's presidency, Kilpatrick at first rallied to Nixon's side, but by early 1973 his presumption of Nixon's innocence began to fade. "The paranoia, the secrecy, the abuse of power!" he lamented in a 1973 interview. "You begin to wonder if the things you've supported all these years aren't rotten all the way down. . . ."

His growing uneasiness notwithstanding, Kilpatrick remained a Nixon defender, and as the crisis reached its crescendo, Nixon summoned Kilpatrick to the White House in May 1974 for what turned out to be the last exclusive interview he would give as President. In a rambling, one-and-a-half-hour monologue in the Oval Office, Nixon vowed to fight any impeachment in the Senate. He said that to resign would weaken the presidency, and Kilpatrick left the interview convinced that Nixon was innocent of complicity in the Watergate cover-up and that he would fight to the bitter end to prove it.

Three months later, when White House tapes revealed the extent of Nixon's involvement in the cover-up, Kilpatrick, close to tears, wrote a bitter column for *National Review*:

I have been covering politics and politicians for more than 30 years and have seen enough of duplicity to be immune to shock. Nixon's duplicity is almost beyond bearing.

The thing is: I believed him. Millions of other Americans believed him also. When he said, over and over, looking us squarely in the eye, that he had known nothing of the Watergate coverup until March of 1973, we believed him. "Your President is not a crook," he once said. I believed him. It no longer greatly matters. My President is a liar. . . . The lies, the lies, the lies!

. . . The swearing in of Gerald Ford can't come one hour too soon.

Although Kilpatrick still considers Nixon's obstruction of justice in the Watergate case "indefensible," he insists that subsequent revelations show that the types of illegalities and questionable activities that

Nixon tried to cover up were old hat in Washington. Eavesdropping, second-story jobs, and use of the Internal Revenue Service to put the squeeze on political opponents all were practiced to one degree or another by Nixon's predecessors, Kilpatrick contends. With a touch of weary cynicism, he sighs: "Poor old Nixon, what he needed was better burglars."

"The things that Nixon did by way of abuse of power were by no means unprecedented, and they have to be kept, it seems to me, in some sort of perspective in that regard. . . . I think one of these days history will be a great deal kinder to him than it has been in these past ten years since Watergate."

As far as his own fleeting role as a conduit for Nixon's assertions of innocence while the Watergate noose tightened, Kilpatrick says he doesn't feel that he was used by the President. "It was a reportorial job," he says, although one might observe that he was—and is—not always so compliant a journalist. Nixon "wanted to get these ideas out, and I faithfully transcribed exactly what he said, which seems to me is one of the duties a reporter has. He puts the questions as best he can, and then he provides the answers the President gives and that's it."

Kilpatrick considers Watergate to have been both inexplicable politically—given Nixon's certain reelection against a "phenomenally weak Democratic opponent"—and personally a "manifestation of Nixon's deep insecurity . . . [his] excessive, obsessive desires . . . to be absolutely certain and to get everything that he could" on political opponents. "I think we all of us probably have a screw loose somewhere," Kilpatrick reflected sympathetically, and Nixon's "obsessive desire . . . for absolute political security probably was a manifestation of some abnormality up there somewhere."

Kilpatrick can display similarly benevolent tolerance for some of the failings of a president he deemed an unqualified "disaster," Jimmy Carter. He refused, for example, to join the "hungry catamounts" in the press who licked their chops over the "Billygate" scandal involving the former President's brother and his friendly financial dealings with the Libyans. Chiding his colleagues for a "conscious or subconscious desire to demonstrate that [they] can be just as rough on Democrat Jimmy Carter as [they] were rough on Republican Richard Nixon," Kilpatrick observed in a July 1980 column that

Brother Billy's wrongdoing, by Watergate standards, is trivial.

Whatever may be said of Billy's judgment in dealing with the contemptible regime of a Libyan dictator, the only allegation of illegal conduct against him is that Billy failed to register soon enough as an agent of the Libyan government. . . .

It is preposterous to equate Billy Carter with Gordon Liddy, Benjamin Civiletti with John Mitchell, and Jimmy Carter with Richard Nixon. The equation will not compute. Billy is no Watergate plumber. He is a bumptious good ole boy.

Kilpatrick's sufferance of what he termed the Carter administration's "well-intentioned ineptitude" only went so far, however, and he rejoiced, albeit cautiously, at Ronald Reagan's election. Ten days after Reagan's landslide victory, Kilpatrick noted with gleeful hyperbole that his old liberal opponents in the press were "still in shock."

James Reston, Tom Wicker, Carl Rowan, the Washington Post, the New York Times, The New Republic, The Nation—all of them are down with the spavins and heaves. In the garden of liberalism they see only crabgrass and thistles. Civil liberties will vanish. Women will be relegated to the kitchen. Blacks, if permitted to speak at all, will be reduced to crying massuh, massuh, massuh. It is all too terrible to behold.

Recalling his own and other conservatives' "conniption fits" following GOP disasters in 1960, 1964, 1974, and 1976, Kilpatrick paternally assured his "brothers and sisters of the liberal press" that "they will recover." He also advised Republicans to temper their jubilation. "They have won a victory and lost their excuses. They must now take on the burden of forming a government and governing. . . ."

Of Reagan, Kilpatrick wrote in another post-election column: "He won a glorious victory. The millennium it ain't." He advised the incoming President that "government is only in part the art of politics. It is chiefly an exercise in the art of communication." Despite Reagan's subsequent billing by others as the "Great Communicator," Kilpatrick finds the President's performance with the press "one of the relatively few areas in which I've been disappointed in Reagan.

"I wish he would meet more frequently with the press. He doesn't handle press conferences as well as I had hoped that he would, whether for want of adequate briefing or some personal inability on his part, I don't know. But he's one of the least effective presidents I can remember in terms of the formal, stylized press conference. And he's been much less accessible to the press than Carter was."

Although Kilpatrick thinks his own attendance at presidential press conferences would be essentially pointless, if not counterproductive, and he has seen Reagan only rarely, he can be certain that his views are known at the White House, if only because the President calls him up occasionally to complain about a column. "He calls every now and then. He'll get wound up at one of my columns, and out of the clear blue sky the telephone will ring and it'll be the President on the other end." Their exchanges have been cordial—and haven't changed either man's mind about whatever point was in dispute. Kilpatrick, in fact, has a healthy

skepticism about the impact his column—or anyone else's —has on the general public or political leaders.

"It's awfully hard to measure (influence)," he says. "The only survey that I recall that was done on it was done some years ago in Toledo, and it had to do with the influence of the *Toledo Blade*'s editorials on a local election; and as I recall the findings of that study indicated . . . that perhaps 1 or 2 percent of the voters were influenced by the *Blade*'s endorsements of . . . particular candidates, which doesn't sound like much until you remember how many elections are decided by one or two percentage points.

"The same thing, I suppose, is true of editorial columns. They probably don't have much influence, but here and there they may have a decisive influence. . . . I try to write for a national audience, and to some extent my conservative views may influence people back in Peoria or Dallas or Salt Lake City or wherever to write their congressmen or their senators or to work on their own local movers and shakers. It may have that effect. It's hard to say."

In general, Kilpatrick believes that his columns "serve multiple purposes, if they serve any at all. They inform. . . . There is an aspect of information in it outside of what the wire services provide or the ordinary run of the news, little obscure things that come along in government or politics or court decisions that I think are of general interest and provide some useful information. And sometimes the column is intended merely to amuse. The columns I write under the 'Scrabble' dateline really have no other purpose except to amuse."

In fact, these finely crafted "country columns" of Kilpatrick's—the lyrical odes to the Blue Ridge countryside, the humorous accounts of rural annoyances and joys, and the warm descriptions of family blessings—can convey deeper meanings. Of all of his columns, these are the ones that "give me the most pleasure and . . . produce so much delightful mail," he says.

"I'm gradually tending to write more of these offbeat pieces. I think there's an audience out there for them. The editorial sections of papers are *so* filled with serious, somber, sober stuff, much of which I think is probably unread, or read very lightly, whereas the mood pieces, the offbeat pieces, the light pieces, I think are widely read. And to the extent that some conservative philosophy or conservative ideas can be woven into the country pieces, I think I'm serving my philosophy and my readers and myself all at the same time."

In these short essays, Kilpatrick is benignly tolerant of the skunks that waddle around the fields of his 37-acre spread; perpetually annoyed at the rabbits that savage his garden; and infuriated by the groundhogs, who dig large holes to no purpose and then "sit on the front porch in their undershirts and baggy pants," as he put it in a book-length country column, *The Foxes' Union*, published in 1977.

The cagey foxes in the book (wickedly portrayed in illustrations by political cartoonist Jeff MacNelly) exhibit modern traits that Kilpatrick doesn't admire. In recent years, he relates, they have left the tough bargaining over the hours and benefits involved in riding to hounds "to an international vice president who comes down from Westchester.

"When the hounds' spokesman mildly objected to this novelty, the union negotiators responded that they were, after all, 20th-century foxes."

He describes the flora of his country haven: "Dogwood are like teenage daughters: They cannot wait. One afternoon the big dogwood on the knoll is a sober, respectable green. The next morning it is cheerleader red, waving its arms for attention and calling, Oh, look at me, look at me!" He reflects on blessings most Americans take for granted: "Do we really understand—

deeply understand—how fortunate we are? I doubt it. As a people, we are the biggest bellyachers on the face of the earth. We complain of racism, of discrimination, of rights unfulfilled; we complain of traffic jams, of perfidy in public office, of poverty, of ill-housing. Well, I have seen Soweto in South Africa, and smelled the stinks of Rio, and looked in the faces of Leningrad, and I have come home to my mountains and wept." For Kilpatrick, "to cultivate a love for one's own land . . . is to forge the first link in the chain that leads from a love of one's own community to a love of country and thence to a love of all mankind."

The thoughts are not new or unique, but they are expressed with enduring wit, grace, and charm. "I think I do [the country columns] pretty well," Kilpatrick says. "They're hard things to write. I'll throw several of them away rather than send them into the syndicate."

Kilpatrick purchased the land for his Rappahannock County estate, which he named White Walnut Hill, in 1966, but he lived in Old Town Alexandria, just across the Potomac River from Washington, until 1973, when he and his wife completed their modest but elegant home. The gray clapboard house is set on a gently rolling hillside surrounded by farm country that is ringed by the Blue Ridge Mountains. The home is decorated largely with American antiques, which the Kilpatricks began collecting shortly after their marriage. It also has a spacious studio for Mrs. Kilpatrick's painting and sculpture work. Adjacent to the home is the property's old farm cottage, which has been expanded to accommodate Kilpatrick's library and office. (Officially, Kilpatrick is a corporation, Op Ed, Inc., and a neatly painted, formal business sign bearing that name adorns the front of the cottage.) The Kilpatricks also have a combination greenhouse and indoor pool, lushly decorated with their carefully tended orchids; a caretaker's cottage; and a tennis court flanked by four flagpoles, which fly a rotating assortment of banners drawn from Kilpatrick's 150-flag collection. He selects the flags each day to commemorate whatever occasion, guest, or event he deems worthy of special notice. Two more flagpoles stand by the entrance to the main house and usually fly the Stars and Stripes and the Virginia flag.

Inside Kilpatrick's office, plaster busts of Dante and Marcus Aurelius stare across an Oriental rug at each other, while a steely-eyed portrait of William T. "Alfalfa Bill" Murray, the crafty, red-gallused country lawyer who was governor of Oklahoma when Kilpatrick was a teenager, gazes down from the wall behind his carved Spanish desk. The eyes in the portrait, which was painted by "one of those old billboard artists," have a disconcerting way of following the viewer around the room, Kilpatrick likes to note with a grin. In addition to warmly inscribed photographs of William F. Buckley and Shana Alexander ("from your devoted fan, foe and friend"), Kilpatrick also displays an ornately lettered membership certificate from the Sons of Confederate Veterans Society and a needlepoint escutcheon of the Black-Eyed Pea Society of America, of which he is the proud founder and "Number One Pea Pro-tem." (He once wrote an entire column about the joys of this "noblest legume of them all" and fried catfish, both of which he says suffer unjustly from a poor image.) Not on display is any certificate or reference to his citation by *Washingtonian* magazine as among the top 20 "male chauvinist pigs" in the capital, although it is an honor he cheerfully accepts.

Kilpatrick prefers to write at home, keeping in touch with his sources in Washington by telephone and banging away on an old manual Underwood typewriter. He has no assistants or researchers to aid him, just a secretary to help with the mail, all of which he tries to answer personally. He still turns

out occasional magazine articles and books, the most recent being the texts for lavish photographic studies of the fourteen states south of the Mason-Dixon line and the major cities of the South. But his column is his major preoccupation.

"Sometimes writing comes easily, sometimes it comes awfully hard," he says, lighting up one of a steady stream of filter cigarettes.* "Ordinarily, if I've done all the work in advance on a column, it comes pretty quickly. It takes me about two hours, on the average, after the research is done, to write the column. . . .

"I write on a long lead time, because a number of my papers—quite a number—are still served only by mail. They don't have the high-speed wires. So we have to mail, and the Postal Service is thoroughly unreliable a good deal of the time. . . . Everything's gone to the bow-wows. . . ."

Kilpatrick writes on Monday for Thursday release, Tuesday for weekend release, and Thursday for release the following Tuesday. He has a telecopier machine on his desk for forwarding the finished column to the Universal Press Syndicate headquarters in Fairway, Kansas, just outside of Kansas City. There it is processed, placed on the speed wires, and mailed to the subscribing newspapers.

Kilpatrick tries to get up to Washington two or three days a week, usually making the 80-mile trek on Wednesday or Thursday morning and returning home on Friday night, following the mid-afternoon taping of the Agronsky program at the CBS network affiliate in northwest Washington. When he is in the capital, Kilpatrick works out of either the Supreme Court press room or the Senate Press Gallery, where both typewriters and telephones are available.

"I cover the Senate more than I cover the House. I can try to keep up with about 15

---

*Following emergency triple bypass open-heart surgery in August 1983, Kilpatrick quit smoking.

committee chairmen in the Senate, but trying to keep up with the House is more than I'm up to. But I'll go by the Justice Department or the Federal Trade Commission—it just depends what the news is."

He has sources "just as any other reporter would have," he says. "You have key sources and people you've worked with over a number of years down in the lower levels of the administrative hierarchy. I work with my sources just as anybody else would."

Kilpatrick finds it difficult, however, to maintain an orderly schedule because he is on the road fairly constantly from September through May, harvesting the fruits of the lecture circuit, as do so many of his column-writing colleagues. He gives "somewhere in the neighborhood of 40 or 50" speeches a year, including a dozen or so "freebies" to journalism schools, press associations, and the like. (He is a director for the Society for Investigative Journalism; a fellow of the national journalism fraternity, Sigma Delta Chi, and a former chairman of the National Conference of Editorial Writers.) A former assistant, Sheila Geoghegan, represents him on behalf of the Washington Speaker's Bureau, charging "whatever the traffic will bear" for his services, plus expenses, Kilpatrick says. Fees range "anywhere from $5,000 to $10,000, depending upon the audience, the size of it, how long it takes to go [there]." For the faraway speaking engagements, "Sheila holds them up pretty good," Kilpatrick says with an approving grin.

As a matter of principle, Kilpatrick has "made it a rule to turn down every invitation I get—and I get two or three a month—to speak at Republican rallies and dinners—that sort of thing. It just seems to me wrong for me to be publicly associated as a partisan with the Republican party. There isn't any question in anybody's mind, I suppose, about my rock-ribbed Republicanism. But to make that public by open participation in

that sort of thing I think is a mistake." (When asked what his party affiliation is, Kilpatrick invariably replies "Whig.")

Kilpatrick also has avoided any overseas junkets since a 1972 trip he took to Greece at the expense of some Greek bankers. It earned him a bit of uncomplimentary twitting by Jack Anderson, who accused him in a column of cozying up to the Greek junta then in power. Kilpatrick still goes abroad at least once each year "to have foreign datelines" and get "a little better perspective on foreign affairs," but "every foreign trip I take now is absolutely at my own expense." He says he had "qualms" about the Greek trip at the time, and "no matter how independent you are on these things in what you write afterwards, there always is going to be an appearance of impropriety, of being hired out to write these things up."

Kilpatrick used to tape three radio commentaries and three television commentaries a week, but he has abandoned them because they "got to be just one more thing that had to be done every week, and it was more than I wanted to do, and I didn't feel it was my best work." The electronic commentaries were ineffectual, he thinks, evidenced by the fact that they prompted little if any mail. In their place, he has started a once-a-week column called "The Writer's Art," attempting to compete—so far only modestly—with William Safire's etymological commentary "On Language." A collection of these columns is due out this year.

The television and radio cutbacks do not appear to have harmed Kilpatrick financially. He grins with satisfaction and says the proceeds from Op Ed., Inc.—the columns, speeches, Agronsky appearances—provide "a very comfortable income, well up in the six figures."

Although his individual work on television had little effect on viewers, Kilpatrick is somewhat awed by the seemingly permanent impact of some television programs on the public consciousness. He and Shana

Alexander have not appeared on "60 Minutes" since September 1979, but he "cannot go into an airport lounge anywhere in the country without some total stranger giving me a curious look and very often walking up and saying "Aren't you 'Point, Counterpoint'?" It is remembered after all this time. It's remarkable."

Also well remembered—probably even more that anything Kilpatrick or Alexander ever said on "Point, Counterpoint"—is the devastating parody of it on NBC's "Saturday Night Live," in which Dan Aykroyd's Kilpatrick curtly dismissed Jane Curtin's Alexander as an "ignorant slut." Both Kilpatrick and Alexander enjoyed the parody, he says, and sometimes mimic the mimics in a "dog-and-pony act" they occasionally take on the lecture circuit, reviving "The Jack and Shana Point, Counterpoint, Show."

Kilpatrick also disputes the view of one Washington-based journalism critic that "Agronsky and Company" cannot possibly be watched closely by the capital's policy-makers and press and could only influence "blind shut-ins who do not read newspapers, who have no contact with the outside world, and who are incapable of making even the most elementary political appraisals of their own." According to Kilpatrick, that put-down of the Agronsky show's audience "demonstrates nothing more than the ignorance of that particular critic, because it is *widely* watched by the most influential people in Washington.

"The President gets a tape of it; Carter watched it regularly, would often call up somebody to complain about it. I think there probably is a difference between being widely watched on the one hand and greatly influential on the other. But I know that Reagan has been pained—I know this to be a fact—by George Will's criticisms of him on the 'Agronsky and Company' show."

As comfortable—and memorable—as Kilpatrick may be as a television performer,

his medium—his love—is the written word. "From time to time, when I undertake to lecture journalism students on the writing art, I am asked about the writers they should read," he said in a 1980 column. "My response embraces the names you would confidently expect: Gibbon for the majestic cadence of his prose; Chesterton, for the gift of antithesis; Macaulay, who could double a sentence into a fist and land a devastating blow. I recommend Twain, for the love of laughter; Shakespeare, Pope and Housman for economy of phrase; Burke for elegance; E. B. White for clarity; and finally, H. L. Mencken."

Kilpatrick is convinced that the stylistic lessons to be learned by sampling this journalistic version of Dr. Eliot's five-foot shelf (not to mention the conservative flavor in some of these writers) are invaluable, and he is certain that newspapers, particularly as an outlet for good writing, are eternal.

"They'll always have a future. I'm not apprehensive about these marvelous new developments and technology, the things that will print out something in your living room—zap, zap, zap. I think we have problems ahead, that the television and cable and all of these things will exacerbate . . . , but there are . . . aspects of newspapering I think will always survive.

"We are, as impermanent as we may seem, a hell of a lot more permanent than television. We can be clipped and photo-copied and filed and mailed to Aunt Susie, pasted in family scrapbooks—all those things that you can do with a newspaper that you can't do with some of these electronic feeds. And it will always be possible to read a newspaper selectively, in the order of your interest, in ways that you can't follow a television program. . . .

"We have all kinds of advantages over television. I'm encouraged by this column I started writing on the language to believe that there is going to be an audience out there always for writing. Television will never be able to take that away from us. The quality of writing—the kind of humor writing that Buchwald does or Russell Baker does, the real artistry of one of George Will's columns. There *is* an audience out there. There's a demand, a market, for that kind of writing as writing. Television never on this earth will be able to serve that market."

Kilpatrick also is optimistic about the future of the First Amendment's guarantee of a free press, on which he can sound as liberal as any *Washington Post* or *New York Times* editorialist. He does think it is ironic, however, that most journalists do little to keep the public informed about the developments affecting this preeminent constitutional safeguard.

"I write a good deal about First Amendment issues, and I have a feeling that those of us in the newspaper business don't write often enough about the newspaper business. We're supposed to be the greatest communicators who ever came along—that's our profession, for God's sake—but somehow we came up with the notion years ago that nobody was interested in newspapers. . . . I don't think that's true. People *are* interested in the media—how it works and how the First Amendment works and what the dangers are in gradual encroachments on First Amendment freedoms.

"Actually, I don't think the First Amendment's in bad shape these days. You win a few, you lose a few. I was pretty disappointed in the Supreme Court's opinion in some of these closed court cases. I wish there was a little better state of the law on the matter of protecting our sources. But the First Amendment's not in bad shape. We can live with the libel laws the way they are now."

In assessing his own status as a columnist, Kilpatrick is modest but (with reason) not humble. "I don't think I'm in the same league with Dave Broder, for example, in terms of political analysis. I don't approach Joe Kraft or George Will in terms of erudition on foreign affairs. I have had a lot of political experience, though, and I think on a great many domestic political questions I don't have to apologize for my background, insights, or whatever. On constitutional amendments, especially, I think I have something to say that's reasonably informed and knowledgeable. But as to political analysis, I'll leave that to Dave and some of the others. . . ."

"I'm more of an opinion writer than an analyst," he says, breaking into a grin and chuckling softly. "Lots of opinions."

Carl T. Rowan

The Ambassador

orty-five years ago, Carl Rowan spent the twilight hours of the sulfurous summer days in McMinnville, Tennessee, standing on the rough wooden porch of his family's small, tin-roofed house on Congo Street. He looked over the junkyard across the dirt road and gazed towards the far-off Cumberland Mountains, waiting for the daily thunderstorm—and more.

"As the downpour rode across the distant fields like a wind-driven silver wave," he wrote in his 1952 book *South of Freedom,* "we young dreamers would pretend that this was the magic puff of rain that would cleanse McMinnville of junkyards and privies, pave Congo Street and give it a new name, and transform our frame house into a stone mansion with a huge brick chimney."

Today Carl Rowan lives in a 10-room fieldstone house atop a hill in a northwest Washington neighborhood of half-million-dollar homes, private swimming pools, and manicured lawns. He still yearns for forces that will purge the United States of poverty and racism, but he is no longer a dreamer or an optimist. Although he once was the highest-ranking black in the federal government and has made the most of the opportunities this nation affords, Rowan does not believe that racial animosities here—or elsewhere—can be eradicated or that progress towards social justice is inevitable.

"I've gone back many a time and read my foreword to *South of Freedom,* and I think I was probably a bit naive when I made the declaration that 'man was not born to hate,'" Rowan says. "I have since come to conclude that there is an awful lot of hatred that is ingrained in the very basic nature of mankind. There is a lot of fear, and fear generates hatred. And when you separate people, the fears are intensified and the inclination to hate is even greater."

His is a weary message, one that he has expressed so often that his delivery of it borders on recitation. "I am not as optimistic as I was when I wrote *South of Freedom,* although . . . the level of racism was a lot greater [then]. I say particularly to black audiences: You must give up the illusion that the federal government, or any other government, can deliver you to first-class status, because what one president gives, another can take away, and you're only going to have permanently what you work for and fight for and what you can cling to through the political power that you exercise, and the economic powers that you develop, and the other techniques of struggle that you're willing to employ. And I believe that fervently."

Rowan, 58, knows a lot about struggle. He was raised in abject poverty in McMinnville, where his father, Thomas D. Rowan, was a $2-a-day laborer in a lumberyard. A World War I veteran, the elder Rowan built the family's tiny home—and its outdoor privy—with a $400 veteran's bonus. The house had no electricity or running water, and Rowan, along with his brother and three sisters, would fetch water from a nearby spring while fighting off black gnats and other insects. His father was often without work, and Rowan frequently went to bed with "hunger-borne stomach aches."

The all-black school he attended was housed in a small brick building that accommodated every grade from kindergarten to high school. It had such a small library that "if two students were inside and one turned the page of a book, one had to leave," he recalls with grim humor. Its sole recreational facility was a weed-filled field, and its athletic equipment consisted of worn-out, discarded uniforms from the town's all-white high school.

Rowan earned spending money (and part of his family's income) by hoeing bulb grass for 10¢ an hour, and as he grew older he hung around the corner by the town's First National Bank, where black youths waited for white men "to offer 25 cents an hour to mow lawns, dig ditches, cart 100-pound bags of cement, or do the myriad dirty jobs that were the black man's only lot," he once wrote.

No one in Rowan's family had ever graduated from high school, but he was determined to do better, inspired largely by several perceptive teachers who sensed his potential for achievement. One, Bessie Taylor Gwinn, "somehow, through one of those 'arrangements' secretly effected by decent whites . . . , got enough books out of the 'white' library to put me on reading terms with the Brontë sisters, and Liz and Bob Browning, Byron and William Cullen Bryant, Coleridge and Keats, Tennyson and Thoreau . . . ," Rowan wrote in a 1980 column eulogizing "Miss Bessie."

I f you don't read, you can't write, and if you can't write you can stop dreaming," she said to me. . . .

She had me writing beside the kerosene lamp in my small frame house late at night, proud to know about iambic pentameter, believing that I was writing sonnets as good as any ever written by Shakespeare, pentameter that put Alexander Pope to shame.

Another teacher, Frances Thompson, asked the students in her art class to write down what grade they expected to get. "I put down a *C*," Rowan told an interviewer once, "and she read me a saying: 'Make no little plans. They have no power to stir men's blood and probably in themselves will not be realized. Make big plans.' " He did.

Rowan graduated from high school in 1942 as class president and valedictorian. He was accepted at the Tennessee Agricultural and Industrial State College and left McMinnville that summer with 77¢ in his pocket and his clothes in a cardboard box. He headed for a custodial job at the State Tuberculosis Hospital in Nashville, where he earned tuition money by washing dishes, sweeping floors, and carrying food to patients for $30 a month.

While he was at the State College in Nashville, Rowan passed examinations for naval officers' school and was given an opportunity to compete for a Navy commission, something that the strictly segregated Navy had never yet granted a black. Sworn in as an apprentice seaman in Nashville, he dropped out of college and returned home to await his wartime assignment. He found that his "year outside of McMinnville, and my status as a Navy man, created a revulsion within me and an air of haughtiness not designed to make me popular with the white citizens of my home town," he recalled in *South of Freedom*. In the parlance of the time, he became "uppity."

Wearing hand-me-down suits he had gotten from doctors at the tuberculosis hospital, Rowan shunned the grubby 25¢-an-hour jobs and instead set up his own business repairing cane-bottom chairs, employing a skill he had learned in high school. He spent the brutally hot summer days reading or strolling through the town and the cooler nights weaving new bottoms and backs on the chairs brought to him by the town's "antique furniture set."

Most of McMinnville's young blacks had been drafted, and many potential white employers looking for manual laborers would drive by his home early in the morning, just as he had gone to bed, and have him awakened so they could "half-demand" that he do some chores for them. "I had begun to love independence, and it pleased a part of me that I could not name, or even place, to be able to say that 'Tom Rowan's boy' didn't have to do the job," he wrote.

Fortunately, the Navy ordered Rowan to active duty in Topeka, Kansas, in October 1943, and he left McMinnville before he got himself beaten up or arrested for being the best-dressed vagrant in town. But McMinnville would hear from "Tom Rowan's boy" again.

At the naval training center at Washburn University, Rowan was the only black in a 335-man Navy V-12 unit. In 1944 he became one of the first 15 blacks in the country to earn a commission as a naval ensign, and he spent the rest of World War II as a communications officer in the Atlantic. After the war he went to Oberlin College, in Ohio, where he had done some additional naval training, and obtained a B.A. degree in mathematics in 1947. He then went to the University of Minnesota to get a master's degree in journalism, earning credits by working part-time on two black weeklies, the *Minneapolis Spokesman* and the *St. Paul Recorder,* and doing public-opinion surveys for the *Baltimore Afro-American* during the 1948 presidential campaign.

In November 1948 he got a job on the copy desk of the *Minneapolis Tribune,* and two years later he became the paper's first black reporter.

Although Rowan and the *Tribune*'s editors agreed that he would be a general-assign-ment reporter, not just one who would cover "Negro news," a pledge he says he made to a wartime buddy haunted him. He had become friendly with a young Texan who had grown up in a completely segregated environment and was astonished to discover that blacks had no special odor, actually had last names, and were pained by the indignities they were compelled to endure. Aware that Rowan was planning to become a writer, the Texan urged him to sit down after the war and "just . . . tell all the little things it means to be a Negro in the South, or anyplace where being a Negro makes a difference."

In December 1950, Rowan wrote a three-page memo to his editors requesting an opportunity to return to the South and describe it from a black perspective. They agreed to this then-unique proposal, and early in 1951 Rowan embarked on a 6,000-mile trip through 13 states in his native region, trying (mostly in vain) to see whether he could avoid consignment to dingy Jim Crow train cars and the roach-infested hotels in black ghettos from Washington, D.C., to Miami. He wanted to see whether progress was being made in race relations since he had left eight years earlier. McMinnville was one of the first stops on his trip, and he described its segregated public park, movie theater, town library, and drugstore—where blacks were unable to get a drink of water unless the counter attendant could find a paper cup—in blunt, unflattering terms.

His reports on the poverty, despair, and struggle for equality by blacks in the South, entitled "How Far From Slavery?" prompted the largest outpouring of mail in the history of the *Tribune* and earned Rowan the Sidney Hillman Award for best national reporting, the Service to Humanity Award from the Minneapolis Junior Chamber of Commerce, and an award from the University of Minnesota's chapter of Sigma Delta Chi, the national journalism fraternity.

The series, which subsequently formed the basis for *South of Freedom,* had not been written to "expose" the South, Rowan wrote in the book.

You do not expose racial hatred and social and economic injustice any more than you expose a fresh dunghill; you tell Americans it exists and wait until the wind blows in their direction.

In a world that rolls on the brink of disaster, it is easy to say that the Negro should subordinate his fate to that of his country and democracy. But there are no separate fates. Negroes are Americans: they are fused into the country's hillsides by the sweat of generations, by ages of toil and bloodshed. The destiny of the American Negro is also the destiny of America and democracy. To protect its own permanent fate, freedom must cease to be a sometimey, color-conscious thing.

Those were potent words in 1952, and in a review of the book in the *New York Times,* the late Hodding Carter, Jr., nationally regarded as a voice of southern moderation as editor of the Greenville, Mississippi, *Delta-Democrat Times* (but denegrated in Rowan's book as a "so-called" liberal), observed pointedly: "If someone were to write a book on the Northern scene and entitle it 'North of Decency,' the ordinary reader would conclude that such a study would hardly be objective, impartial or balanced. Carl Rowan has entitled his book 'South of Freedom.' "

Carter concluded, however, that Rowan's book was "a vivid reminder that changes which a white Southerner thinks are swift seem snail-like and indecisive to a Southerner who is not white and who suffers from color barriers."

Rowan grins wryly when reminded of Carter's critique. "I was really angry when the *Times* picked Hodding Carter to do that review. I was outraged. I wrote the *Times* a nasty letter. And years later I would sit

down and read that review again and say, 'Old Hodding wrote one hell of a perceptive, fair review of my book,' and it took some years of growth and understanding for me to realize it."

Rowan pursued the story of the fight for racial equality in the courts, spending much of 1953 covering the school-desegregation cases then pending before the U.S. Supreme Court. In 1954 these stories won him Sigma Delta Chi's award for best national reporting; a National Education Writers' Association prize for best educational reporting, and designation by the U.S. Junior Chamber of Commerce as one of America's "10 outstanding young men of 1953." He likes to note with a laugh that one of the other outstanding young men that year was future Texas entrepreneur and swindler Billy Sol Estes.

In 1954, Rowan went overseas for the U.S. State Department's International Educational Exchange Program, spending three months in India lecturing on the role of newspapers in social change and then another five months traveling through India and eight other countries in Southeast Asia as a foreign correspondent for the *Tribune.* His reports from India, describing the appalling poverty in the countryside and accusing the troubled new democracy there of "strolling on a bitter road named Racism in Reverse," sparked heated denunciations of him by some Indian leftists, who charged that he was just an "American parrot propagandist."

Among the stops on Rowan's itinerary was South Vietnam, then in a lull of "an eight-year-old war marked by indifference, some gallantry and much despair," he wrote in a 1956 book based on his journey, *The Pitiful and the Proud.* In Vietnam Rowan found a handful of U.S. military advisers and civilians engaged in a quiet, gunless "battle between democracy and communism . . . at odds in favor of communism." He felt that their cause was just, but in an eerie harbinger of millions of words yet to come from American reporters, Rowan wrote that "we were involved in a gang war, in bloody fratricide, in conflict with our consciences, in disagreement with our allies, and although the vast majority of my countrymen knew nothing about this dilemma, or of these faraway, remote places where all these things took place, much of their future and the future of Western civilization was at stake."

Rowan's prescience was hampered, however, by the assurances of the U.S. foreign policy makers then in power. "If the battle gets tough, according to the State Department in Washington, the United States Cavalry will not rush to the rescue—Hollywood style or otherwise," he wrote.

Rowan's reports from India for the *Tribune* won him his second consecutive Sigma Delta Chi award, this time for international reporting, and in 1956 he became the first—and only—reporter to win a third consecutive Sigma Delta Chi award for his coverage of the political turmoil in Southeast Asia and of the 1955 Bandung Conference, a gathering of 23 underdeveloped "colored" nations held in Indonesia.

In 1957, Rowan wrote a controversial 15-part series on the plight of the American Indians, as well as a third book, *Go South to Sorrow,* about the South's response to the emerging civil rights movement and the U.S. Supreme Court's rulings against segregation. He collaborated with Dodger great Jackie Robinson on a fourth book, a Robinson biography titled *Wait 'Til Next Year,* published in 1959.

Rowan became an important figure in his adopted community, serving as president of the Minneapolis Urban League, and he lectured extensively, giving about 100 speeches a year. He and his wife Vivian, whom he married in 1950, had two sons, Carl Jr., and Geoffrey. (Mrs. Rowan's daughter by a previous marriage, Barbara, now is a correspondent for NBC News.)

They were prosperous, with Rowan earning about $40,000 a year by 1959.

At the outset of the 1960 presidential campaign, however, Rowan received a reporting assignment that altered his life. The *Tribune* sent him to Washington to do a series of articles about Vice-President Richard Nixon, the GOP nominee, and Massachusetts Senator John F. Kennedy, the Democratic candidate. He considered it a routine job and was astonished when he received a telephone call on New Year's Day, 1961, while he was in Pasadena, California, covering the Rose Bowl, informing him that President-elect Kennedy wanted him to become the Deputy Assistant Secretary of State for Public Affairs, in charge of the State Department's press relations.

Kennedy had been wary of Rowan at the beginning of the campaign. He had received advance word that John Cowles, then publisher of the *Tribune,* and Johnny Johnson, publisher of *Ebony* magazine, planned to endorse Nixon, and he was convinced that Rowan had been sent to do a hatchet job on him. When the articles turned out to be "eminently fair," Kennedy later told Rowan, "I never forgot your name."

The Washington, D.C., to which Rowan moved in early 1961—at the considerably reduced salary of $18,000 a year—was more integrated than when he had visited it ten years earlier for *South of Freedom.* It still was very much like a southern town, however, and a perfectly plausible site for a story that Rowan invented to describe how his family "broke" a previously all-white neighborhood.

"I mowed the lawn in those days, and I'd laugh as all the whites would come by, because I could tell they were wondering: was I mowing the lawn or had I 'broken the neighborhood,' so to speak," he says. The curious glances inspired him to concoct the story, which quickly made its way around Washington, of how he had been mowing the lawn one day when a "gorgeous blonde" drove up in front of his home and called: "Hey, boy!" He ignored her, Rowan told friends, but she persisted: "Hey, boy, you with the lawnmower. Tell me, how much do you get for mowing lawns?"

"Well," Rowan said he replied, "the lady here lets me sleep with her."

The joke took on a life of its own, Rowan says with a pride that is tempered a bit with chagrin, was quoted—even printed—widely, and soon was accepted as fact.

A grimmer fact in the Washington of the early 1960s was that racial and religious discrimination persisted in many of the capital's swankier environs, although often it was vaguely masked by a studied politeness. When a member of the elite Metropolitan Club was turned away from its dining room at lunchtime because he had brought along a black guest, the resulting international publicity embarrassed the Kennedy administration.

Several members of the Cosmos Club, long regarded as Washington's haven for intellectuals, approached Rowan and asked him to apply for membership there. They promised him that approval was assured and said that his acceptance as the club's first black member would be "good for the country." Rowan reluctantly agreed to apply, since both he and his wife felt that they could ill-afford the club's hefty dues, but months went by without a reply. Finally he received word in January 1962 that two men on the club's twelve-man membership committee had blackballed him. One of the committeemen told Rowan's crestfallen sponsors that his blackball vote was unavoidable because his relatives "got physically ill in the presence of Negroes," Rowan recalls.

The blackballing got front-page play in the *New York Times* and around the world, since it also personally embarrassed President Kennedy, whose own application for membership in the Cosmos Club had yet to be acted upon. John Kenneth Galbraith,

Kennedy's ambassador to India and one of his sponsors at the Cosmos Club, solved the President's dilemma by resigning from the club, thereby voiding Kennedy's application. Many other prominent members resigned as well.

In his public response to the blackballing, Rowan was a model of restraint, but he seethed inside—and still does. He issued a public statement saying: "It's my understanding that this is Washington's club of intellectuals. If it is the intellectual judgment of the membership committee that I do not merit membership, I can do no more than note this judgment and wish the club well." Later, however, after the club quietly altered its policies and admitted blacks, he adamantly refused requests by several members that he apply again. "They never had the guts to say publicly that, yes, we had two racists on the membership committee, and as a result I've never set foot in the Cosmos Club to this day."

As head of the State Department's press operations, Rowan made an uneasy transition from journalism to public relations, as have many reporters before and since. He would tell gatherings of reporters and editors that he still considered himself one of them, which of course he could not be in the intense, high-stakes battle between Washington reporters and government officials. He was accused—as were many in the Kennedy administration, including the President—of trying to "manage" the news.

In a series of speeches, Rowan charged that the press was too "scoop-conscious," adding acidly: "This so-called concern for the public's right to know is really concern about the fourth estate's right to make a buck."

"You do not take an oath [to protect the nation's vital interests] and sit in Washington in a sensitive job very long without admitting to yourself that while the public does have a right to know, it also has a right *not* to know . . . ," he said.

A frequent visitor to Vietnam during the early days of the growing U.S. military involvement there, Rowan drafted a much-criticized "press guidance" memo for American officials in Saigon, telling them that "newsmen should not be transported to military activities of a type that are likely to result in undesirable stories" and should be persuaded not to engage in "trifling or thoughtless criticism" of the regime of Ngo Dinh Diem, the U.S.-backed South Vietnamese leader.

Rowan insists that he had no desire to stifle news coverage of the war and that in fact he tried to prevent the Kennedy administration from doing just that. The subsequent lambasting he received when his memo was leaked was, he says, "a perfect example of the press getting a tidbit of a story and getting it ass-backwards.

"The simple fact was that an Associated Press reporter . . . was let out on a helicopter mission and came back and wrote an article which made it clear—as was true—that Jack Kennedy was getting us more deeply involved in Vietnam. Well, when Kennedy saw this story, he hit the ceiling. Art Sylvester [an assistant secretary of defense for public affairs] and Pierre Salinger [then President Kennedy's press secretary, now an ABC News correspondent in Paris] got together, and they drew up a telegram of instruction to Saigon that in effect would have crippled the press operation.

"I went into the State Department on a Saturday morning, and I'm looking at the traffic, and I see this telegram. I called McGeorge Bundy [Kennedy's national security adviser] and I said: 'This is ridiculous. You *cannot* win by trying to muzzle the press this way. You're going to get your asses in a sling. I would like to say this to the President.' He said: 'I'll talk to the President and call you back.' He called me, I rode over to the White House, I walked into the Oval Office, and Kennedy's initial words were: 'Now Carl, isn't this a bunch of shit?' And we got into a hell of an argument. . . . [Both] Sylvester and Salinger weighed in to tell the President I was full of crap.

"I raised so much hell that Pierre, the President, and I agreed that I would go back to the State Department and would rewrite those regulations, and I wrote regulations that did spell out the pitfalls and possible dangers, but the regulations said: 'You are to give the press the maximum, feasible cooperation.'

"So what I did was to move in the *opposite* direction [and] I see myself accused of doing exactly the opposite of what I had done."

Rowan still believes, however, that there are times when the public does have "a right *not* to know" what its government is up to. "There are some things the public has a right not to know because it's in the public interest not to have national security damaged. I would say those [things] are very limited, though. . . . Every public official wants people to believe he's God's gift to public service, and he doesn't want any information out to the contrary. And any public official who doesn't feel that way is too dumb to be a public official. And therefore we must always have this civilized, adversarial relationship between the press and the people who do the public's business and spend the public's money. . . . The press *always* has to be zealous to look at these kinds of things, but that doesn't mean that I believe we ought to rush out and print whatever somebody tells us about U.S. weaponry that the Soviet Union might not know about."

To do so, Rowan believes, is cheap journalism. He was involved in the delicate negotiations in 1962 that led to the swap of Francis Gary Powers, the pilot of the U-2 spy plane downed by the Soviets in 1960, for imprisoned Russian master spy Colonel Rudolph Abel, and he has never revealed much of what he learned then. The United

States, he says, "was eager to make the trade [because] we knew that Powers knew certain things the Soviets had not gotten out of him yet, and we wanted to get him out of there before the Soviets beat, or bled, or otherwise got out of him certain information we didn't want them to know. I *still* have not written about the things that Powers did not tell that he could have told because I just don't believe that I need to do that to have a good reputation as a journalist."

In March 1963, Kennedy appointed Rowan as ambassador to Finland, making him the youngest envoy (at 37) in the diplomatic corps and the fifth black to attain ambassadorial rank. Official Finland, somewhat cool towards the United States because of its precarious geographical position abutting both the Soviet Union and Poland, was enthralled by the "chocolate brown" ambassador, as one Helsinki paper described Rowan, and his family. He lectured widely, traveling around the country more than any previous ambassador; he was blunt about U.S. racial strife, calling it a "national disgrace," but stressed the gains blacks had made in America; and he was enthusiastically athletic—something the Finns admired. He was photographed golfing, bowling, taking saunas, and playing baseball with his two young sons. He even took lessons every morning in Finnish, the grammar of which he found "a killer," and managed to insert a few Finnish phrases in his speeches, much to the astonishment—and delight—of his audiences.

Rowan's ambassadorship lasted only nine months, however. He was back in Washington for consultations in November 1963 and had the last appointment with Kennedy the night before the President left for Dallas, where he was assassinated. It was at this final, uneventful consultation that Rowan, who had never known why Kennedy had asked him to join the administration, casually asked the reason for his original appointment and learned of the unexpected

aftereffect of his 1960 articles. "I was so glad to have him tell me that story, because I had no idea why I all of a sudden became a federal employee," Rowan says.

Following Kennedy's death, Rowan was one of the first officials to meet with Lyndon Johnson, and two months later, when Edward R. Murrow resigned as head of the United States Information Agency because of lung cancer, Johnson appointed Rowan to the post, making him the highest-ranking black in the federal government and the first to sit on the National Security Council.

Johnson and Rowan had a rocky working relationship, one characterized by mutual respect but punctuated with frequent disagreements. When Johnson was Vice-President, chafing at the inconsequential nature of the job, Rowan, then still in the State Department's press office, accompanied him on a round-the-world trip, during which they clashed often. They did not reach an accord, Rowan recalls, until a stopover in India, where Johnson ignored Rowan's advice about the wording in a proposed communiqué to be issued jointly with Indian Prime Minister Jawaharlal Nehru. Nehru—as Rowan had predicted—angrily rejected the document, much to Johnson's embarrassment.

Having a new respect for Rowan's views, Johnson told him: "It don't never hurt to stand up for what you believe. You just go on. You'll get knocked down a few times but you keep standing up for what you believe." Pausing a moment, he added: "But you'd know that wouldn't you, 'cause you've been getting knocked down all your life." "I got along famously with Johnson after that," Rowan says.

Kennedy and Johnson were "vastly different men," Rowan observed, but he believes that Vietnam would have been as likely an Achilles heel for Kennedy as it proved to be for his successor. "Kennedy was a more stable personality in the sense that he was an intellectual and he had a great concern for justice. . . . [But] Kennedy was, I think, tough, and I've always believed that had he lived, he would have played one hell of a tough role in Vietnam. He wouldn't have gone the other way; we would have been in as deep or deeper in that war.

"Lyndon Johnson was a different kind of man, as complicated a man as I've every known in my life. There's nothing so good or so bad that you can say about Lyndon Johnson that it wasn't true at some time, and generally in the same day. I think were it not for the Vietnam War though, he would rank as one of the greatest presidents in this country's history because the man really did have deep inside him a social concern."

The country's growing involvement in the Vietnam War under Johnson also plagued Rowan's tenure as head of the United States Information Agency, and it led as well to a bitter rift between him and the Reverend Martin Luther King, Jr., an old friend from the early days of the civil rights movement who began to passionately denounce the war.

During his year and a half at the USIA, Rowan upgraded the agency by persuading Congress to grant foreign-service status to its employees, but critics of his stewardship complained that he neglected his administrative duties and became preoccupied with U.S. propaganda in Vietnam, either on his own initiative or at Johnson's insistence. Eventually all of the psychological warfare efforts in Vietnam were placed under Rowan's direction, and critics charged that by assigning over 100 members of the USIA's staff to Vietnam-related duties, he weakened the agency's activities elsewhere. It also was charged that the agency's Voice of America newscasters were being forced to present pro-Vietnam stories, thereby undermining the credibility of its reports. Voice of America's veteran director, Henry Loomis, quit in March 1965, complaining in a farewell address that commentaries on the radio network were made "to toe the administration line."

Rowan denied the accusations of news-doctoring, contending that Voice of America's straight news reports maintained the "same judicial balance" of favorable and unfavorable stories about the United States and its policies as any responsible newspaper would have. He insisted, however, that the station's commentaries, like a newspaper's editorials, were expressions of opinion and that Voice of America editorialists were supposed to express "the official opinion of the United States government."

When Rowan resigned from the USIA in July 1965, becoming the first top Johnson appointee to quit, there was speculation that he had been forced out, perhaps because his supposed administrative shortcomings had hobbled the agency or because his handling of Vietnam War propaganda did not satisfy Johnson. Rowan says that Vietnam had nothing directly to do with his departure from government. He wanted to leave because he had received a lucrative offer to write a column, and he took advantage of a relatively minor tiff with Johnson to make an abrupt exit.

Johnson had wanted another USIA transmitter placed in Southeast Asia, and after India refused to allow one on its territory, Rowan persuaded the foreign minister of Thailand, Thanat Khomen, to push for placement of a transmitter in his country. Rowan pledged that he would come to Bangkok to explain the importance of the new transmitter personally. When he later received an urgent telegram asking him to come to Thailand immediately to make his pitch, Rowan informed Johnson that he had to go to Bangkok to argue for the transmitter.

"Johnson . . . said: 'Oh, God, no!'" Rowan recalls, mimicking the Texas twang of LBJ, waiving his hands, and wailing. "'The moment you leave, the sons of bitches on the Hill will attack USIA and my administration, and you won't be here to answer it.' And I thought, 'This is bullshit.' I said to Johnson: 'I have never in my life shaken hands with a man and given him a commitment and walked away from it, and if I've got to walk away from my commitment to Thanat Khomen in order to work for you, then I don't work for you. I quit.' And I walked out of the administration."

What he walked into was a deal with the *Chicago Daily News* under which he would write three columns a week. (Since the *Daily News* folded in 1978, Rowan's flagship paper has been its surviving partner, the *Chicago Sun-Times.*) In addition to the *Daily News* deal, he signed a separate agreement with the Westinghouse Broadcasting Company for three weekly radio commentaries which alone paid him $30,000 a year, exactly what he had been earning at the USIA. He also signed an exclusive contract with the *Reader's Digest* to become a "roving editor" and write about four articles a year. He declines to discuss his current income ("There are a lot of jealous people," he says), but it clearly is substantial. He enjoys recalling that the first Red Chinese envoy to Washington once visited his home, looked around, and asked with wonder: "Are you a millionaire?" "I'm working on it," Rowan replied.

Regardless of the circumstances surrounding Rowan's departure from the Johnson administration, his former association with it did not exactly put a damper on his debut as a columnist. The *Daily News*'s syndicate, Field Enterprises, promoted its new star with old photographs of him chatting with LBJ (although Rowan had never interviewed Johnson for the column), and it boasted that Rowan's list of charter subscribers was the largest ever to sign up for a new commentator. Despite the passage of time, Rowan claims that his former government positions still give him special cachet, particularly when he travels overseas. "There is hardly a country in the world that I go to that the ambassador has not already said to the chief of state: 'See this man.'

There is hardly an embassy in the world that doesn't have somebody in it who used to work for me, either at the USIA or in the State Department. And this is a tremendous asset. I find that when you're in a foreign country, being in a position to meet the people who matter—often in social settings—is great."

Although he quit the Johnson administration in a huff, Rowan remained philosophically attached to LBJ's policies, including—for awhile—the war in Vietnam. He grew increasingly uneasy about the toll the war was taking on the American psyche and Johnson's Great Society program, but he and several other leading blacks were even more upset when Martin Luther King, Jr., began criticizing the war in what they thought was an inflammatory, counterproductive way. They were convinced—largely on the strength of behind-the-scenes contacts with Johnson and his emissaries—that King's antiwar rhetoric would harm the civil rights movement, and Rowan had what he believed was unsettling inside information suggesting that King's motives—and safety—were in question.

The late William Sullivan, then domestic intelligence chief for the Federal Bureau of Investigation, met with Rowan frequently, both when he was in the administration and afterward, and told him of the FBI's ongoing surveillance of King. According to David Garrow's 1981 book, *The FBI and Martin Luther King, Jr.*, Sullivan portrayed himself as a liberal counterbalance to the reactionary FBI director, J. Edgar Hoover, but in reality he despised King, writing in one memo that the civil rights leader was "the most dangerous Negro of the future in this nation from the standpoint of communism, the Negro and national security." Garrow uncovered evidence indicating that Sullivan in fact masterminded the surveillance of King, which included tapping his telephone, keeping track of his contacts with suspected communists, and bugging his hotel rooms. In an effort to destroy King's reputation, transcripts, recordings, and photographs of King (some of them indicating extramarital affairs) were offered surreptitiously to reporters from the *New York Times*, the *Los Angeles Times, Atlantic Constitution*, and the *Chicago Daily News*. In the case of the *Daily News*, the recipient was Mike Royko. None of the papers ever used the material.

Rowan still believes that Sullivan disapproved of the seamier aspects of the eavesdropping but was disturbed by some of the information he claimed it uncovered. "He told me of surveillance in Mexico of a guy King was seeing that they believed to be a Soviet agent. He told me of the plots to set up King, of the tappings of King's hotel rooms and so forth, and expressed to me his view that there were some dangers to King. He always left it vague. I never knew whether he was suggesting that Americans might want to get King or the Soviets might want to get him or whatever.

" . . . I had a very close relationship with Martin King, and I sat down and said to him, 'Martin, you must be more circumspect, in terms of the people you talk to, in terms of the people you let write your speeches.' [Urban League Director] Whitney Young and [National Association for the Advancement of Colored People President] Roy Wilkins talked to him—at Lyndon Johnson's request—about not getting the civil rights movement sullied with these attacks on the war in Vietnam. Johnson's argument was: 'I'm up there trying to move the Congress on housing bills, on public accommodation bills, on the voting rights act, and he [King] is making it very difficult for me to carry some of these guys along.'"

Black diplomat Ralph Bunche, Whitney Young, and Roy Wilkins all publicly urged King to tone down his criticisms of the war, Rowan recalls, and "there was a pledge, privately, from King that he would stop seeing certain people." King neither kept his

pledge nor cooled his rhetoric. In late March 1967, he led 5,000 demonstrators through Chicago's shopping district in his first antiwar march and told a crowd at the Chicago Coliseum that the war was "a blasphemy against all that America stands for." He accused the United States of "committing atrocities equal to any perpetrated by the Vietcong" and said that the United States was "left standing before the world glutted by our own barbarity. We are engaged in a war that seeks to turn the clock of history back and perpetuate white colonialism." A week later, at New York's Riverside Church, King urged all blacks and "all white people of goodwill" to boycott the war and become conscientious objectors. He called the U.S. government the "greatest purveyor of violence in the world today."

Rowan says that "reports came back" to him, Bunche, Young, and Wilkins that King secretly "was still talking to some people, [and when] I was told again that there was some danger, I said, Alright, I'm going to write a public article that I hope will shake Martin up to the point that he will think seriously about this." Less than a week later, Rowan wrote a column criticizing King, contending that he was "listening most to one man who is clearly more interested in embarrassing the United States than in the plight of the Negro or the war-weary people of Vietnam."

The following September, Rowan wrote a piece for the *Reader's Digest*, entitled "Martin Luther King's Tragic Decision," in which he accused King of becoming an egomaniac. Recounting his early contacts with King during the 1955 Montgomery bus boycott in the opening days of the civil rights movement, Rowan praised the young minister's "gift of articulateness, his apparent lack of personal ambition," but then questioned his developing "exaggerated appraisal of how much he and his crisis techniques were responsible for the race-relations progress that has been made."

Noting that Wilkins, Young, and other civil rights advocates had urged King to steer clear of foreign policy debates, Rowan posed the question, "Why did King reject the advice of his old civil-rights colleagues?"

Some say it was a matter of ego. . . . Others revived a more sinister speculation that had been whispered around Capitol Hill and in the nation's newsrooms for more than two years—talk of communists influencing the actions and words of the young minister. . . .

I report this not to endorse what King and many others will consider a "guilty by association" smear, but because of the threat that these allegations represent to the civil-rights movement. When King was simply challenging Jim Crow . . . [such accusations] had only limited impact. . . . But now that King has become deeply involved in a conflict where the United States is in direct combat with communists, the murmurings are likely to produce powerfully hostile reactions. They cannot help but imperil chances of passage of . . . civil-rights bill[s]. . . .

By urging Negroes not to respond to the draft or to fight in Vietnam . . . [King] has taken a tack that many Americans of all races consider utterly irresponsible.

This assault on King's antiwar crusade prompted one of his aides, Andrew Young (now mayor of Atlanta and formerly President Carter's ambassador to the United Nations), to issue a counterattack against Rowan, labeling him an "Uncle Tom." Rowan was unperturbed by Young's attack, believing that what he had written was in the long-range interest—and for the safety—of King, who he felt fully understood all the implications of the articles, although he never responded to them.

"Martin's wife [Coretta King] knows exactly what my motivations were. That's why she [later] would ask me to come to Atlanta to speak on Martin Luther King's birthday," Rowan says, "I never for a moment thought that Martin Luther King was a communist, but I also never had any doubt that if the Soviets could have used him in any way, they would. And one of the things . . . that was suggested to me was that the Soviets might want to kill him for the trouble this would produce. . . . Well, I don't know whether this was bullshit or not, but you have to also remember the magnitude of the cold war in those days, the dirty games that were being played."

Even though Rowan eventually opposed the Vietnam War, he never developed the moral passion against it which King had and which in retrospect does not seem unjustified. Rowan cannot pinpoint when the scales fell from his eyes on the war, although he says he had doubts about the quality of the military's intelligence information ever since the 1965 Gulf of Tonkin incident. He simply came to the conclusion that the war was "an unsustainable operation" militarily, economically, and politically. While he doesn't fault King for continuing his criticism of the war, he still believes that his rhetoric was unwarranted—and possibly fatal. "His words and his charges were so extreme as to intensify the hatred of him by the people, I think, who were behind his murder [in 1968]. I am convinced, in my own heart and mind, that there was a conspiracy involved in the killing of Martin Luther King," Rowan says, although he has no theory on who personally was responsible for King's assassination. He does believe, however, that "from the top of the FBI, far down, there were people trying to destroy" King. Rowan claims to have been the first columnist to have revealed the extent of the FBI's smear campaign against King, but it was not until 1969 revelations in a New York courtroom of the longstanding surveillance of King by the FBI that Rowan finally wrote a blunt column calling for Hoover's replacement. In June 1969 he wrote:

This society is in a lot of peril if we may judge from the public reaction—or lack of it—to [the] admission of a variety of illegal FBI wiretaps and buggings of homes and hotel rooms.

There is a not-too-flippant assumption in Washington that J. Edgar Hoover has been FBI director for 45 years because all the recent Presidents have assumed he knew too much about them to be replaced. . . . Hoover ought to be replaced as FBI director—immediately. . . .

If it is dangerous to have one man serve three full terms as President, it is far more dangerous to have one man take life-time possession of a powerful police-investigative agency that prods into the deepest secrets of the most prominent, most honored citizens and has the power to discredit, even destroy, almost everyone. . . .

Were Hoover a thoughtful man, or as concerned about the preservation of democracy and liberty as his speeches suggest, he would have resigned long ago.

Hoover, of course, did not resign, nor did President Nixon replace him. But, Rowan recalls with a smile that comes close to being a smirk, the old director could do little more than complain to other reporters about "that racist columnist Carl Rowan," because "he knew I had the goods. He knew that [as USIA director] I received the same top-secret documents about his buggings and wiretappings of King that Johnson received, and he never knew whether I still had the copies."

Did Rowan have the transcripts? "I had some," he says with a grim chuckle.

Many without Hoover's undisguised enmity are inclined to think of Rowan as, if not a racist, then simply a "black columnist," interested only in the concerns of fellow blacks. It is a label he rejects but is somewhat resigned to.

"It's obvious people know that I'm a columnist who happens to be black, and there are a lot of people who can't see past my blackness. There are a few editors who have this blind spot. But I am happy to say that most of the editors and publishers know that my claim isn't just to a knowledge about civil rights or social issues. Hell, I sat on the National Security Council and in the Cabinet, and I know how people can get misled by bogus intelligence information, I know how the personality of a president can impact upon decisions. . . . Well, when you see this and you know all these things, you develop some special perceptions that enable you to write about these kinds of things, and that's why I write a hell of a lot of columns about foreign policy and a lot of other things that have nothing to do with race."

In fact, a review of the topics covered in Rowan's column over a year shows that about a third of them deal with foreign policy. Rowan likes to recall with amusement that one editor in the Northwest discovered a few years ago that his columns on social issues transcend race. "He ran a front-page editorial saying that they were dropping my column and explaining . . . in so many words that I had been a too persistent critic of President Reagan and his economic recovery program, and spent too much time in my column wailing about the woes of poor black people.

"He was deluged with mail saying, What's wrong with you? Rowan's not talking about poor black people; he's talking about my uncle over there who just lost his auto dealership, my cousin who just lost his job in the timber industry, my cousin over there who's losing his farm, etc. The guy ran another editorial, front page, saying, I was wrong. The column is back in the newspaper.

"Well, I cite that simply to say that I don't view myself, when I talk about social programs or economic policy, as beating the drums just for poor blacks. I'm beating the drums for all kinds of people I know are going to get hurt."

Rowan admits, however, that the problems of the black community are a special, preeminent concern of his. "We have to be mindful of the fact that there is a special dimension where minorities are concerned. Unemployment *consistently* runs more than double that for whites in black America, and . . . there's got to be somebody who will talk about that. I feel a special responsibility, for example, to say to Americans who are propagandized about things like welfare, Wait a minute! Welfare is for poor people, and if you run your country in such a way that you have a lot of poor people, you're going to have a big welfare program. We aren't talking about some lazy bum or some chiseler. Basically we're talking about a lot of children, 8 million of them, and it is not to Carl Rowan's benefit, and it's no protection to Carl Rowan's children and what they inherit or own, to have 8 million youngsters grow up in poverty and hunger and misery and hostility toward this society."

But Rowan does not see his role as a journalistic emissary between the black and white communities as the only way of improving the lot of black Americans. As an impressive example himself of the bootstrap philosophy drilled into him by the teachers in the little Jim Crow school in McMinnville, he is a vigorous exponent of self-improvement in his columns and has little patience for those who won't work at it. In a memorable 1973 column, he angrily advised blacks, particularly young blacks,

to stop swallowing this malarky that styling your hair in 30 nappy plaits, with enough head skin showing to cane-bottom granny's rocker, is the epitome of "pride in racial heritage."

This is, to put it as decently as I can, pure nonsense. Black Americans can let their hair grow to the ground, they can shave till their heads outshine cue balls, they can straighten or tease or crocinole or curl or process, they can buy wigs till they run out of money (as a lot of Afri-

cans do in Nairobi or other African cities I have visited), but there isn't going to be any meaningful black pride until more black people are making solid achievements in competition with the white majority.

Nothing galls me more than a black dude who is cutting classes, or who never reads a newspaper or magazine or book, or won't hold onto a job, or won't give a dime to help some needy black, sitting around the barber shop or the pool hall or the student union talking about how his "rags" or his "fro" symbolizes black pride. . . . I don't give a damn how you style your hair; what bothers me is that you spend more time on your hair than on your physics or English class. . . .

Let's face reality: we don't have enough firepower to take this country; we don't have enough manpower to dominate it; we don't have enough dollar-power to buy it. And we'll be short of all these "powers" until we develop a lot more brainpower. In truth, that's the one power we can develop rapidly, with zeal, without scaring the dominant group to the point that it loads on new oppressions.

So, in the name of the souls of black folk, let's say to hell with this nonsense about hair. Let's face up to some tests of manhood and womanhood that are truly relevant to black uplift.

The column brought Rowan more mail than he had received for any other column up to that time, and not all of it was from "middle-aged black teachers and old 'slick-headed fuddy-duddies' like myself," he wrote a month later. "I have received scores of letters from young blacks, with at least 90 percent saying they can understand and applaud my call to excellence. . . ."

Rowan himself often puts in a seven-day work week. He writes practically all of his columns at the office he keeps in his home, and he is often at his desk by 6:30 or 7:00 A.M. "Sometimes I'll wake up at 2:00 A.M.

with an idea and I may have trouble going back to sleep," he says, sitting on a large, off-white sofa in the spacious, sparsely furnished living room of his home. "I have a rule: if I can't get back to sleep in an hour, I'll go to work. So I sometimes begin at 3:00 or 4:00 in the morning."

Five feet eleven inches tall and weighing 205 pounds, Rowan appears relaxed, almost languid, as he shows a guest around his home, pointing out gifts he received from foreign dignitaries. Casually attired in a pair of slacks and the kind of cream-colored, open-necked silk shirt one associates with South American plantation owners, he seems unhurried and serene. It is a deceptive pose.

In his first 17 years as a columnist, Rowan never missed a deadline, writing three columns a week regardless of overseas trips or "vacations." He complains of being overworked and says that in 1982 he finally allowed himself some time off, retreating to a home he and his wife bought in Boca Raton, Florida. It is a haven, he says, that "may add a few years to the old man's life, because I'm never so relaxed as when I'm there. There are no telephone calls."

In addition to his columns, Rowan records five four-minute radio commentaries a week for the Chrysler Corporation, which has set up its own network by purchasing air time on radio stations in 50 of the largest cities in the country. In addition to his salary for the commentaries, Rowan and his wife both are supplied with Chrysler cars. He also delivers up to 25 lectures a year at a fee of $4,500 "and up"; he produces and appears in television news specials for WDVM-TV, the CBS affiliate in Washington, and the Evening News Association; he writes up to four articles a year for *Reader's Digest,* often in collaboration with David Mazie, 51, a thin, engaging Iowan who was the Latin America correspondent for the *Minneapolis Tribune* before Rowan hired him as an assistant in 1968; and he has

appeared on "Agronsky and Company" since its debut in 1969.

On the Agronsky program, Rowan is a ready foil for conservatives James J. Kilpatrick and George F. Will and is "as articulate, and, some would say, as pompous, as a white person in that rapid-fire game of armchair commentary," a *Washington Post* reporter once observed. Other reporters have described Rowan as "brusque" or "charming when he chooses to be," implying that there are many times when his adolescent haughtiness reemerges. He gives few interviews; in fact, a member of his staff expressed surprise when he consented to being questioned for this book. "I guess it has something to do with the company he'll be keeping," the staff member said. Once the interview got under way, however, Rowan was courteous to a fault. When a tape recorder malfunction left an hourlong cassette completely blank, he smiled, shrugged, and graciously agreed to record the entire interview again.

Once an enthusiastic golfer and late-night card player (with poker pals such as Art Buchwald and Pierre Salinger), Rowan now limits his recreational activities to tennis, which he finds a more efficient means of exercise than golf, and swimming in his private pool. He despairs of his weight, wishing that he weighed 175 again, but is unable to resist the good food and drink at the many embassy lunches and dinners to which he is invited. He also is handy in the kitchen and at the backyard grill. Possessed of a pleasant tenor voice (he used to be mistaken on occasion for one of the Mills Brothers), Rowan loves singing and enjoys composing both lyrics and tunes, although he cannot read music or play an instrument. "That's the great regret of my life," he says. The lyrics he writes to the well-known songs of other composers are sung in the satirical show put on each year by the Gridiron Club for the journalistic and political powers in Washington.

Rowan has six other people on his staff besides Mazie, who also writes the scripts for most of his radio broadcasts and sometimes researches Rowan's columns. Two full-time and one part-time researcher, as well as three salaried interns from Howard University's School of Communications, work in a separate office he maintains in a three-story condominium townhouse several miles from his home. He keeps in constant touch with the office by telephone, sometimes making three or four calls in less than a half-hour, and the office personnel can transfer outside calls to him.

When Rowan selects a column topic, he will ask one of his staff to research the subject by clipping newspaper stories on it, accumulating other data, and assembling a file. Rowan himself will call sources to obtain additional background information. If he simply is commenting on the latest news, he says, he can write a column pretty quickly; if he is trying to be more analytical—or on some rare occasions, humorous—the column is harder to compose. "Once I've made up my mind . . . and I've got my material, I can do a column in 35 to 40 minutes. But it depends on what kind of column I'm doing. If I sit down to write a 'think' piece, that's another story. . . . That takes a lot more time."

Rowan, a swift and accurate self-taught typist, writes columns every Tuesday, Wednesday, and Friday morning, although he says that he may contemplate a particular subject three, four, or seven days in advance and that "everything I do all week is preparation for doing that column."

Rowan's knee may jerk to a liberal beat, but his exhortation to black youth to improve themselves could inspire amens from any conservative audience. He is an advocate of affirmative action programs, but in a 1959 article for the *Saturday Evening Post* he wrote:

What we want our children to really understand . . . is that social equality is something no Negro—or white man— can demand, either as a civil right or a moral right, for social equality is a relationship one wins by character, personality and achievement. Even the most militant Negro must forever insist that this remain a matter of choice. . . . We are warning our children that above all else they must be prepared to compete. . . . This is so because no court can, or should, declare more than equality of opportunity.

"I still believe that," Rowan says. "You cannot declare equality of results. I would not remotely insist that as a matter of law I have the right to go to somebody's private club. . . . But I do believe that in all of those other areas the court must be willing to move."

Curiously, with all that Rowan writes about social ills, racial problems, and foreign policy, the columns of his that have prompted the most mail in recent years were intensely personal ones dealing with, of all things, a durable toaster, a dying dog, and a deceased lyricist. The toaster, a venerable Sunbeam, is one of the few things in his elegant home that he and his wife have owned since the day they got married. His essay on "the little toaster that endured" brought a flood of mail, much of it from readers who boasted about even sturdier old appliances they owned, the rest from people who had a similar sentimental attachment to a mundane item. The article about his aged Doberman pinscher, and the uncanny instinct it had for sensing who was a welcome guest in the house and who wasn't, caused "the dog lovers of the world to rise up and send those letters in!" Rowan recalls with a laugh.

But the column he wrote in 1976 on the death of Johnny Mercer, his favorite lyricist, brought in perhaps the most mail and revealed a softer, more sentimental Rowan than readers had known. It since has been reprinted on a scroll in the Songwriters' Hall of Fame in New York and hangs in the

Johnny Mercer Theater in Savannah. Just as the motion pictures of the 1930s and 1940s contained the images that Russell Baker finds both inspiring and haunting, so the songs of the same period have a special meaning for Rowan, encapsulating, in a way, his basic philosophy of life. In most of his columns, Rowan is not much of a stylist. He writes in an unadorned, forceful manner that might be more colorful if newspapers permitted the occasional barnyard expletive with which he flavors his private conversation or if he allowed the wit that he freely employs in social settings to emerge more often in his columns. But in the Mercer piece, as in a few others, he was warm, humorous, even touching:

Ask me how I'd prefer to judge a society. By its preachers and politicians, its authors or architects? No, I'd first like a look at the output of those who write its popular songs.

In war or peace, hard times or good, it is the popular lyricists who tell us so much about the heart and soul of a nation.

That's why a little bit of me died the other day with the passing of Johnny Mercer. And I'm disappointed that a greater fuss wasn't made over this man who for more than four decades put magical words to tunes and touched, even helped shape, the lives of millions of us.

As a boy of 8 in Tennessee, wading barefoot in a creek looking under rocks for crawfish, I learned about "the work ethic" from Johnny Mercer.

I truly believed that he was telling me something when I sang lines from his "Lazybones":

"You'll never get your day's work done resting in the morning sun. You'll never get your cornmeal made sleeping in the noonday shade."

. . . It is almost incredible that from boyhood depression days in the early '30's, when I sang "Lazybones," right up till these days when I delight in crooning "Moon River," it has been Johnny Mercer psyching me up, making me a romantic, sending up warning signals about that other sex—yet always telling me that "we're after the same rainbow's end, waiting round the bend."

Johnny Mercer, thank you. I hope you make it to rainbow's end.

Why does Rowan think these atypical columns of his are the ones to which readers respond the most? "I think basically the average human being cares about the longer lasting verities of life: love, trust, having somebody to live with for just about all of your life. I think they would rather, if they could, get away from a world in which there's a PLO and an Israeli Army and a South Africa, and a people killing each other in Rhodesia and so forth. Unfortunately, we have to write about those things."

Rowan believes that the major purpose of his column "is to say to the American people some of the things I don't think they would hear, or some explanations I don't think they would get, or some insights I don't think they would get, if I weren't writing the column and if I weren't talking about what a college loan meant to a segment of America's population, or what food stamps mean to millions of families, or the relationship between poverty and mental retardation, and these kinds of things."

When Hodding Carter reviewed *South of Freedom* three decades ago, he described it as "the bitter report of a loyal and perhaps unquietly desperate American who will not find in his lifetime full acceptance as a first-class citizen everywhere in his country." Rowan thinks that Carter may have been wrong about him personally, but he is not certain that Carter's prediction was incorrect for blacks in general.

"I think he would say that he was wrong if he looked today and saw the degree of acceptance that I have personally. I rarely run into [discrimination]. But I am not so dumb as to think that this is a barometer of what exists in this society. The fact that Carl Rowan can call the best restaurant in Washington and get a table has really no bearing on the fact that there are thousands of black people out there who can't even get a job. It is only the nitwits, the dumb blacks, who are enamored of Reaganomics, who want to pretend that their success is an indication of what's happened for all black America."

Although Jim Crow largely is dead and the racial situation in this country is "night and day in some respects" from what it was 30 years ago, "we are far from being a fair and just society," Rowan says. "You still have a situation where a black child born in America today carries far greater handicaps than does a white child. . . . When you've got a situation where only 18 percent of all the black teenagers in America hold a job, you know that there is trouble down the road for many, many years to come. . . .

"So we've got a long way to go, and particularly it's discouraging in these times, when the civil rights movement is in limbo, because you've got people in power who don't understand these things and some who don't much give a damn. If I learned anything in four and a half years in government, it is that minorities make progress only in good times and only when they have people at the top level of government who are not hostile to their aspirations."

In his role as an advocate for those aspirations, Rowan—a print journalist for over 35 years—admits with chagrin that his television appearances have greater immediate impact than his columns. "Taxi drivers stop and honk, stick their heads out of the window and shout: 'Hey! When you gonna punch old Kilpatrick in the nose?' They

don't stop and honk and say: 'I read the column yesterday.' "

But the column has longer-lasting impact, he says, and whatever influence he may have he attributes to what he has written. "The fact is a column is something you can go back to again and again. And I am amazed as I go around the country to give speeches at the numbers of people who clip those columns and save them, who walk up to me at a speech and will open up a wallet and pull out . . . a column I did years ago. . . ."

It is his column, he believes, that has earned him the ire of politicians whom he criticizes, which perhaps is the only demonstrable measure of the influence any political commentator can have. "I get enough flak from people in the Reagan administration to know they're reading and listening. I've noticed that even when there are administrations that really detest what I'm writing, they still invite me to the White House for briefings and meetings and so forth. . . .

"I would go out in the days of Stokely Carmichael and Rap Brown, when they were supposed to be the great terrors of black America, and some kid at college would say: 'Carl Rowan, how do you describe yourself? You're not a militant. How would you rank yourself along with Stokely Carmichael and Rap Brown?'

"I would say: 'I don't engage in labels, but I'll call your attention to one thing: When Richard Nixon drew up his enemies list, Stokely Carmichael wasn't on it. Rap Brown wasn't on it. But Carl Rowan *was* on it.'

"Now what do you want to make of that?" he says with a laugh.

Mike Royko

Latter-day Dooley

He sits alone in a cramped, disorganized office, a morose man incessantly smoking unfiltered cigarettes, fumbling for matches, dribbling ashes on his turtleneck sweater and corduroy pants, drinking mug after mug of heavily sugared black coffee. Often, however, his brown, lizardlike eyes will squint with malicious merriment behind his thick aviator glasses, his thin lips will curl mischievously upward beneath his extravagant nose, and he will offer an observation that is blunt, incisive, and funny. Brutally funny. There is no whimsey in Mike Royko.

Royko, the Pulitzer Prize–winning columnist for the *Chicago Sun-Times,** is a great debunker. In the 1960s he demolished the myth that racism and segregation were exclusively southern by grimly reporting their presence in Chicago. He rabbit-punched the reputation Chicago once had as "the city that works" by detailing the blunders of its callous, shabby—and often corrupt—bureaucracy. He savaged the city's iron-fisted, five-term mayor, Richard J. Daley, considered by some the architect of Chicago's rebirth, by decrying his destruction of city neighborhoods and quoting exactly what the malapropism-prone mayor said.

*In January 1984 Royko joined the *Chicago Tribune.*

Royko is the latest—some would say the greatest—and perhaps the last in a long line of renowned Chicago columnists: Eugene Field, the gentle humorist of the 1880s; Finley Peter Dunne, the first great urban columnist and creator of the turn-of-the-century philosopher barkeep, Mr. Dooley; Ring Lardner, the sportswriter nonpareil; Ben Hecht, who with Charles MacArthur made the words *front page* synonymous with Chicago journalism in the 1920s—and for decades thereafter.

Not surprisingly, Royko questions Chicago's credentials as one of the country's best newspaper towns. "I'm not one of the people who buys that great romantic myth about Chicago as a great journalism town," he says in a low, raspy voice. "I've never worked anywhere else, so I have no way of comparing Chicago to anywhere else, but I would . . . doubt that it's any more competitive, say, than Washington journalism, where you've got thousands of reporters running around chasing down stories. Some of the best in the country are out there. I don't think we're any more competitive than New York."

In the 1950s, when Chicago had four newspapers—the now extinct *Daily News* and *American,* as well as the surviving *Sun-Times* and *Tribune*—and Royko, now 51, was a cub reporter, there may have been a more competitive atmosphere, he says. But he thought that the *Tribune* and the *Ameri-*

can were pretty awful, that the *Sun-Times* was not nearly as good a paper as he thinks it is today, and that the *Daily News,* his employer then, was "the only decent paper in town." The city was devoid of any evidence of journalistic excellence, he says, and many of the surviving veterans of Hecht and MacArthur's police-beat days were anything but sterling reporters.

"I knew a lot of the old-time police reporters, who still were active when I was a young reporter, and some of them were lazy; some of them were ignorant; some of them were corrupt; and most of them were just mouthpieces for the coppers. I can't say I was particularly impressed with any of them."

While debunking Chicago journalism myths, Royko also makes a stab at whittling down one which he had a substantial role in creating and which in times past he relished: the image of Mike Royko, "The Man Who Owns Chicago," as *Esquire* once called him; journalism's "tough guy," a mean drinker—and drunk—a man as quick with his fists in a barroom as he is with words at the paper.

A lot of what has been written about him is, in Royko's view, "bullshit." " 'The Man Who Owns Chicago,' for chrissakes, I mean that kind of crap is silly," he grouses.

He has never considered himself the voice of Chicago. "I sure as hell wasn't speaking for Chicago during the 1960s, when I was extremely pro–civil rights. My neighbors were throwing garbage on my porch. I lived in a blue-collar, middle-class neighborhood. I sure as hell wasn't speaking for them. I really don't think I have ever spoken for Chicago. I speak for myself."

He also disputes—mildly—"the legend of me being a barroom brawler," and says that his once-substantial consumption of liquor has diminished considerably in recent years. "I suppose most people haven't been in 8 to 10 fistfights in the past 15 years; that's probably more than the average for someone who's supposed to be civilized. But all

things considered, that's not a whole lot. Billy Martin's been in a lot more fights than I have," he says with a crooked, slightly sheepish grin.

"I guess if I added up my annual consumption [of alcohol] it'd be above the national average, but as I got older I discovered that you can't drink as much as you could when you were 30. Your body just doesn't recuperate as quickly. I'd love to sit down every night and drink a bottle of good wine and a couple of brandies, but then I'd walk around all morning cross-eyed. You can't do it. . . . You can't do your work and do all the things that are more fun.

"I don't drink as much as I once did, and as much as I drank then was exaggerated. I told somebody once that if I've managed to put out five columns a week, play softball— and I played on a serious level, 40, 50, 60 games a summer—and play handball, I'd have had to be the bionic drunk in order to keep that pace going."

Softball, handball, and some of the booze may have become casualties of Royko's middle age, but he still writes five columns a week, an output that many other columnists would find killing. "It hasn't killed me," he says with a shrug. "I've been doin' it since 1964."

Royko really doesn't try to debunk his image as a tough guy, which is borne out often enough by his unsparing columns. He uses words like well-aimed bricks, beaning the people and issues that anger him with terse volleys of sarcasm, invective, outrage, and scorn.

He emits epithets as casually as he does cigarette smoke. In his columns, the most common (and printable) ones are "jerk" and "slob," but in interviews for publication elsewhere he has dismissed Chicago's aldermen as "assholes"; called the new breed of money-conscious professional athletes "shitheads"; and characterized the sportswriters who cover the athletes as "shitheads" as well, because they take what they cover so seriously.

When it comes to diagnosing the characteristics that make someone an "asshole" or a "shithead," Royko is an expert, a Louis Pasteur. There are some—especially those who disagree with him—who think that he has contracted some of the symptoms he is so skilled at detecting in others and could join the ranks of aldermen, athletes, or sportswriters. Even a friendly interviewer once called him "mean, unfair, mocking . . . ; a lowbrow, a boor, ill-mannered, vulgar, the Philistine of the prairie." But Royko has never been sued by anyone he called a bum or a crook. "The people I call bums and crooks *are* bums and crooks," he once said.

Royko has labeled some women's liberationists "chauvinist sows" and called opponents of gun control "hair-trigger heroes." He was a bitter foe of the Vietnam War but loved John Wayne movies. He has ridiculed that "great moral leader" Jane Fonda, "who gives interviews in which she solemnly prattles about her concern for grave social problems, while also talking about how good her latest movie is," and written movingly about many of those things Fonda also professes to despise, such as the nuclear arms race. He knows, perhaps better than any other columnist, how to make people mad, which probably accounts for his above-average participation in fistfights.

There is another side to Royko, however, a sensitive, gentle side that loves classical music and opera, enjoys cooking (pasta dishes are his specialty), is fond of the quiet of the Wisconsin lake country. He is a lonely man, still striving to cope with the sudden death of his wife of 25 years, who had a stroke in 1979 at the age of 44. Much of the zest for his work is gone. "I used to think that was everything. It sure as hell isn't," he says.

Royko's complexity is reflected in his column—not by changes in his style, which is brisk and cryptic, but in tone. In most of his pieces he is brash and hard-nosed, regardless of the subject, but sometimes he is touching and warm, and sometimes—just enough to keep the reader off balance and intrigued—he is incredibly funny. Royko is not a humorist in the traditional sense. He is not as gag-oriented as Art Buchwald or Erma Bombeck, who pursue the reader's laugh with single-minded determination. But Royko's readers often find themselves laughing out loud at his irreverence and irony, and in his alter ego, the despicable Armitage Avenue urchin Slats Grobnik, he has created one of American journalism's great comic characters, an urban Huckleberry Finn.

Slats is not a nice person. He is a liar, a thief, a cheat, a "disgusting creep." "Who's perfect?" Royko asks with a grin. "You know, Tom Sawyer's a nice kid, but Huck Finn was a real nasty little shit. He was a liar, a cheat, and a thief—probably would have killed his father if he'd had a chance— a lazy ne'er-do-well." By comparison, Royko feels, Slats "is not a bad guy." At least he never tried to kill his father.

Slats Grobnik never cared much for Halloween.

It made him angry that all the kids in the neighborhood went around soaping windows, tipping over garbage cans, and leaping out of gangways to scare old ladies.

That's the way he acted all year, and it was no fun when everybody else did it. . . .

He did attend one party, though, because his mother insisted he accept an invitation from a kid in the nice neighborhood two blocks away, where some people owned their own houses.

"I want to wear a costume so nobody will recognize me," Slats said.

"All you gotta do is wash your face for that," his father said. . . .

He went to the party but didn't have a good time. When it was time to duck for apples, Slats plunged his head into the tub. The water turned a muddy color and he was thrown out.

Slats didn't go trick-or-treating, either. . . . [He] worked out a system that made walking the streets unnecessary. . . .

Slats would pull a nylon stocking over his head and face, turn out all the lights in the flat, and wait.

When there was a knock on the door, his little brother Fats would yank it open.

For a moment the little kids outside would see nothing.

Then Slats would click on a flashlight held to his chin. In broad daylight, Slats had a face that made some old ladies cross themselves. And with the stocking and flashlight in the dark, the effect was ghastly.

Most of the kids would scream, drop their bags of candy and run.

Then Slats and Fats would gather up the bags, take them inside, close the door, and wait for the next bunch.

Slats justified this practice by saying: "You don't see the alderman going door-to-door to get his; so why should I?"

Making only modest allowances for poetic license, one can learn the basics of Royko's youth from his tales of Slats, who he readily acknowledges is a composite of himself and several childhood friends. Like Slats, Royko learned his civics lessons on the streets or in one of the several blue-collar taverns his parents owned in Chicago's Polish neighborhood on the city's Northwest Side. As an infant, Royko, like Slats, was propped up on a barstool or pinball machine, given hard-boiled eggs, pepperoni, and small tumblers of beer, and was "the most contented child you ever saw. . . .

"By the time he was 3, the only way Mrs. Grobnik could persuade him to drink milk was to put it in a stein and say, 'Have a snort, little Slats. . . . ' "

His parents were divorced when Royko, his brother, and two sisters were children, and Royko, the youngest, moved back and forth between his father's Blue Sky Lounge, which had blue paper on the ceiling, and his

mother's Hawaiian Paradise, which featured a plastic palm tree in the window. What little time he spent outside taverns or off the streets was passed in a second-floor flat beside an elevated subway track or in a bowling alley, where he was a pinboy for seven or eight cents a game.

"I don't know what the labor laws were, but many of us started setting pins when we were about 12," he once wrote. "You could tell a pinboy by the joints on his first two fingers. Hoisting the pins between the fingers made them big. By the time Slats Grobnik was 15, the joints on his fingers were bigger than his brain."

By the time Royko was 15, he was an experienced bartender and dispenser of payoffs to the local police, city inspectors, and aldermen. Corruption, petty or grand, is so endemic to Chicago, Royko wrote in *Boss,* his best-selling biography of Daley, "that it has been suggested that the city slogan be changed from *Urbs in Horto*, which means 'city in a Garden,' to *Urbi Est Mea,* which means 'Where's mine?' "

He hated school and was a chronic truant. Eventually he was placed in a "social adjustment school," Montefiore (known as "Monty-fee"), where several of his classmates were already accomplished hoodlums who went on to become minor thugs and casualties in Chicago's mob wars. As soon as he reached 16, he dropped out of high school. "The best place for a child to play and learn is on the sidewalk," he wrote in one Slats column.

In many ways, Royko was little more than a juvenile delinquent. He hung around street corners perfecting his ability to spit through the space between his two front teeth; pitched pennies for hours on end; filched comic books and candy from the dime store; threw bricks through school windows. He was a relatively cautious delinquent, however.

"Most of the youths in my neighborhood had it drummed into their heads that just one arrest would result in a lifelong black mark that would make it impossible to get a job," he once wrote. "It became part of our street lore that even if we lied, an employer would somehow, some day find out and confront us with the evidence and a pink slip. . . . We never doubted that it was all true. And we were very careful about what we did. Not careful about staying out of trouble, but careful in planning what we did so we wouldn't get caught, which is the secret to success even today."

In *Boss,* Royko described the Chicago in which he and Daley grew up. It was much the same for both of them, despite the thirty years' difference in their ages, because, as Royko wrote,

Chicago, until as late as the 1950s, was a place where people stayed put for awhile, creating tightly knit neighborhoods, as small-townish as any village in the wheat fields.

The neighborhood-towns were part of the larger ethnic states. To the north of the Loop was Germany. To the northwest Poland. To the west were Italy and Israel. To the southwest were Bohemia and Lithuania. And to the south was Ireland.

It wasn't perfectly defined because the borders shifted as newcomers moved in on the old settlers, sending them fleeing in terror and disgust. Here and there were outlying colonies, with Poles also on the South Side, and Irish up north.

But you could always tell, even with your eyes closed, which state you were in by the odors of the food stores and the open kitchen windows, the sound of the foreign or familiar language, and by whether a stranger hit you in the head with a rock. . . .

The ethnic states got along just about as pleasantly as did the nations of Europe. With their tote bags, the immigrants brought along their old prejudices, and immediately picked up some new ones. An Irishman who came here hating only the Englishmen and Irish Protestants soon hated Poles, Italians and blacks. A Pole . . . arrived hating only Jews and Russians, but soon learned to hate the Irish, the Italians, and the blacks.

That was another good reason to stay close to home and in your own neighborhood town and ethnic state. Go that way, past the viaduct, and the wops will jump you, or chase you into Jew town. Go the other way, beyond the park, and the Polacks will stomp on you. Cross those streetcar tracks, and the Micks will shower you with Irish confetti from the brickyards. And who can tell what the niggers might do?

It would seem curious, then, that coming from a neighborhood in which anti-Semitism was a recreational activity and racism was unalloyed, Royko should have become an uncompromising opponent of segregation. One of his colleagues believes that Royko has had to overcome the built-in bigotry of his upbringing and an early environment in which "*nigger* was a part of his everyday vocabulary," but Royko claims that he cannot remember "when discrimination didn't bother me.

"I was always getting in arguments when I was 15, 16, 17 years old on the subject of racial discrimination. I can't even trace it to any one thing or any particular person, other than perhaps my mother, who never did understand discrimination. But . . . some chemistry kept me from acquiring the attitudes that were prevalent in the area I grew up in. So it was the way I've always thought. . . .

"I have very few memories of discussing blacks and Jews and things like that [at home]. It just wasn't something that I was really aware of. My father, I'm sure, had more conventional racial and ethnic attitudes, but it wasn't something that he carried around with him. He was too busy."

Perhaps advocating integration in a city as racist as Royko found Chicago to be was just another manifestation of his instinct for driving people up the wall.

After he dropped out of high school, Royko worked briefly as a stock clerk in a department store and as a theater usher, then went back to school and earned his high school diploma while still working full-time. He went to a junior college for a short time, found it no more congenial than high school, quit, and joined the Air Force in 1952. He was trained to be a radio operator and was sent to Korea.

While on a leave in 1954, he married his childhood sweetheart, Carol Duckman, who lived only a block or so from him in the old neighborhood. He then won a transfer to Chicago's O'Hare Field, where he was slated for an unenviable assignment as a military policeman. Repelled at the thought of being a cop, Royko did what came naturally to avoid it: he lied. He told the personnel officer that he had been a reporter for the *Chicago Daily News* and applied to become editor of the base newspaper, which happened to be without one.

Although one of the few things he enjoyed in high school had been writing—"I always found it very easy to put together a story," he says—Royko knew nothing about newspaper work. He wangled a three-day pass and went to the public library and read everything it had on newspapers, taking notes and copying prize-winning front-page layouts from journalism textbooks.

At first his superiors were impressed with the result, but when Royko gave himself a column and started spouting off, the fur began to fly. In his first column he pointed out that Air Force personnel had to follow a dress code and look snappy, so it was only right that officers' wives should not be permitted to show up at the base in hair curlers or looking disheveled. "I was sitting in the PIO office and the door burst open and a bunch of angry-looking women demanded to see the guy who wrote that thing," he once told an interviewer. "I said, 'He's on leave, a 30-day leave. He won't be back.'"

Undaunted, and naive, Royko later wrote a story about how the enlistment of the base's top softball pitcher had been quietly extended for one month so he could pitch in a tournament. He was astonished at the reaction. "The base adjutant who had arranged the extension was transferred to the Aleutian Islands. The first sergeant was shipped to Alaska. The base newspaper was shut down, and I was made, in effect, a hotel clerk for the last two months of my enlistment, " he recalled in a 1981 interview. "I didn't even know I had an exposé."

What he did know, however, was that there something he liked about newspaper work. "What power," he told a friend. "You could write 500 words and get people all excited."

One of his former colleagues on the base paper—an ex-reporter for the Associated Press—suggested that Royko give reporting a try when he got out of the service. Before the fling at newspapering at the base, Royko had vaguely considered using the GI Bill to get through law school, but he decided to follow his friend's suggestion. If things didn't work out, he thought, "there was time for me to shift gears."

He went to work for the Lerner newspapers, a group of suburban Chicago weeklies, in early 1956, and later that year he moved on to the City News Bureau, a metropolitan area wire service similar to the Associated Press or United Press International but covering only the city and surrounding Cook County.

He began, as most young reporters do, by covering the police beat. He then put in time at City Hall and on other beats before becoming the service's night city editor and then assistant day editor. In 1959 he joined the *Daily News,* long revered as a "writer's newspaper." It was considered one of the finest evening papers in the country, with a top-notch Washington bureau; a highly respected foreign service (the oldest in the country); numerous Pulitzers to its credit; and a distinguished roster of alumni.

Among those who had worked for the *Daily News* were Eugene Field, often credited with being the country's first daily columnist; Finley Peter Dunne; Carl Sandburg, who, among other things, did a brief, unimpressive turn as the paper's silent movie critic; and Ben Hecht, who fashioned much of *The Front Page* from grist he gathered as a *Daily News* reporter.

Now it had Royko, starting him out, predictably, on beats similar to the ones he had covered for the City News Bureau. By 1961, however, he began to feel restive. What he wanted, he says, was freedom. "I didn't like being under the control of editors, being told, This is what we want you to cover and this is how we want you to handle it. Not that I was being told to do things I felt were wrong; I just didn't want them shaping the story for me. I didn't like being assigned to dull stories. I didn't like the idea that I didn't know what I'd be doing, where I'd be going."

He had received an attractive offer from the *Daily News*'s competition, Hearst's *American,* and when he told the late Larry Fanning, the *News*'s editor, that he planned to quit, Fanning asked him what his ambitions were and how the *News* could keep him.

"I'd already written . . . a weekly column . . . , kind of a county government thing. Every beat man got to write a weekly column. They were supposed to be chit-chat columns . . . , stuff that really wasn't worth a whole story in itself. But I decided I would try to do more of an essay column. . . . I don't think the public noticed it, but it was well-received by the people at the paper. And I said if I can make this crap interesting from the county government, county politics, I can go beyond that. . . . I didn't have . . . any ambitions toward being an editor. I was in awe of the whole idea of being a city editor at the *Daily News*. I didn't think I'd be good enough. I thought I could handle writing a daily column."

On the strength of Fanning's promise to give him a shot at a column, Royko remained at the *Daily News*. A year and a half later he finally got his break. In September, 1963, his column began appearing three times a week, and on New Year's Day, 1964 (when another *Daily News* columnist quit), Royko became the paper's top local columnist, writing five times a week.

He was not an overnight success, but gradually the "little ripples" that his column made grew bigger and bigger. His exposés of petty bureaucratic bumbling and waste, the scathing assaults on Daley and his Machine, the unvarnished descriptions of Chicago mobsters and boodlers, the antic tales of Slats Grobnik and other Runyonesque characters from his old neighborhood, eventually became must reading for many Chicagoans. In 1966, *Time* magazine conferred national standing on Royko by printing a glowing profile of him, and by 1968 he had become the premiere interpreter of his city, the guru whose insights were sought by out-of-town colleagues trying to get a fix on Chicago and its redoubtable mayor.

"It is a strain for local newsmen, being interviewed by visiting writers, especially the scholarly ones. They always ask if the mayor has charisma. In the mayor's neighborhood, they could get punched for talking dirty," he wrote.

To assist visitors, I have prepared a primer on the mayor. Most of it isn't new to Chicagoans, but it might help others appreciate our most famous citizen. . . .

The key to Daley's success is the fact that he was born in a magical old neighborhood called Bridgeport. It has produced Chicago's last three mayors, their rule spanning thirty-seven years. All this political clout means nearly every family has got somebody on a government payroll. In the East, some families register a newborn son at Harvard or Yale. In Bridgeport, they sign him on with the city water department.

The Mayor's father was a sheet metal worker. As a kid, Daley worked in the stockyards. This convinced him there were better things than work, so he got into politics. . . .

Daley likes to build things. He likes high-rises, expressways, parking garages, municipal buildings and anything else that requires a ribbon-cutting ceremony and can be financed through federal funds.

He isn't that enthusiastic about small things, such as people. Daley does not like civil rights demonstrators, rebellious community organizations, critics of the mediocre school system, critics of any kind or people who argue with him. . . .

He has simple tastes. Nobody catches him chatting about literature, music or French cooking. He likes White Sox games, fishing and parades. He has led more parades than anyone since Rome fell apart. Hardly a Saturday passes when the mayor isn't hoofing down the middle of State Street with thousands of city workers behind him. It has been estimated he has paraded the distance from Chicago to Minsk. . . .

Whom will he support for the [presidential] nomination? The mayor will consider which candidate is the wisest, the noblest, the most inspiring, the best qualified. Then he will pick the one with the best chance of winning. In his parades, the politicians march up front. No matter how pretty they sound, the flute players walk behind the horses.

Ironically, although Royko had—and has—a formidable network of sources throughout the city government, he was forced to observe Daley from afar, just as State Department Kremlinologists or China-watchers pursue their quarry. Daley would never grant a one-on-one interview to a reporter—even one he liked—and literally banned Royko from his press conferences. Their rare encounters were accidental, brief, and unpleasant.

"I bumped into him a couple of times, and he always looked like he'd made the acquaintance of a snake. But he stayed away from me and wouldn't talk to me. I used to go to his press conferences, but his press secretary told me that if I kept showing up at his press conferences, he'd stop having them and that would be a disservice to the rest of the press. So I stopped going to his press conferences 'cause it bothered him so much."

It was no great loss for Royko, whose knowledge of Chicago and its politics is encyclopedic and was not likely to be honed at any tête-à-tête Daley had with the press.

Royko gained even greater recognition at the tumultuous 1968 Democratic Convention in Chicago, where Daley's ham-handed deployment of police crushed antiwar demonstrations in what later was termed a "police riot." Royko's coverage of the street battles and the convention won him the Heywood Broun Award of the American Newspaper Guild.

Partly in response to the heightened interest in Chicago and Daley, and partly to prove that he could do it, Royko began writing *Boss* shortly after the 1968 election. He did not reduce his output of columns but spent one year of weekends and vacations researching the book and another year of weekends and vacations writing it. When it was published in 1971 and received ecstatic reviews, he spent the rest of that year promoting it. "And after 3 years I was about 10 years older," he recalls.

He decided that trying to write books (other than compiling anthologies of his columns, of which there have been four) "just wasn't worth it." The column, in his view, was more important, and in fact the columns he wrote the year he was writing *Boss* were the ones that earned him the 1971 Pulitzer Prize for distinguished commentary. "If anything, I worked harder on the columns [that year] because I was very worried I might let the column slip, the book would distract me," he says.

It was, distraction or not, a remarkable

book, a classic, merciless dissection of big-city politics. It won praise from scholarly reviewers and fellow journalists alike, including a ringing endorsement from Royko's New York counterpart (and friend) Jimmy Breslin, who called *Boss* "the best book ever written about an American city by the best journalist of his time."

Royko described an implacable political machine and its uninspiring but crafty leader. Daley was personally incorruptible, Royko conceded, but he was unconcerned about the thievery and incompetence surrounding him. Daley's moral code, Royko wrote, was: "Thou shalt not steal, but thou shalt not blow the whistle on anybody who does." By condoning, if not openly encouraging or participating in, the mudslinging, corruption, and racism by which his machine thrived, Daley guaranteed that his "virtue remained as intact as his hypocrisy."

So cleverly venomous was Royko's description of Daley that one gets the impression that the only reasons he was elected five times—besides the muscle of his machine—were that he was faithful to his wife, liked ice cream, and went to Mass regularly. Otherwise, as one reviewer put it, Royko's tale of Daley was one of "autocracy, backscratching, nepotism, neanderthalism and bigotry all the way."

Daley ignored the book, just as he had ignored Royko's column, but the mayor's wife apparently did not. Royko learned that Mrs. Daley became furious when she saw paperback copies of *Boss* on sale at her supermarket and demanded that they be taken off the shelves. The store manager complied—as did all 200 stores in the National Tea Company chain. Royko reported the ban in his column and observed that the grocery firm had not responded so quickly in the past to customer inquiries about the freshness of its wares. "I have issued a directive to my wife that all National food products are to be removed from our shelves immediately and fed to a goat," he wrote. The supermarket chain

quickly returned *Boss* to its paperback racks.

Although the Daley book was a triumph, Royko found that he was becoming permanently linked in the public's mind—at least the public outside of Chicago—with Daley. It drove him nuts. "The fact is, after I did *Boss,* I was kind of all Daleyed-out. After years of writing about him and doing a book on him, I just found it painfully hard to sit down and write about the guy. I used to turn down magazines that wanted me to write about him. . . .

"When *Newsweek* started that contributing column they carry, 'My Turn,' they started out with great hopes of getting all the best-known journalists in America to do it, and the editor contacted us and I said, 'Yeah, I'll do one for you if you suggest the idea for me, because I've got to think of five columns a week. I haven't got time to think of something for you.' And what do they think of? A piece on Daley. I said the hell with it. I *am* capable of writing about other things."

When Daley died of a heart attack in December 1976, Royko bade him farewell with an unsentimental yet surprisingly gracious tribute:

If a man ever reflected a city, it was Richard J. Daley and Chicago.

In some ways he was Chicago at its best—strong, hard-driving, working feverishly, pushing, building, driven by ambitions so big they seemed Texas-boastful.

In other ways, he was this city at its worst—arrogant, crude, conniving, ruthless, suspicious, intolerant.

He wasn't graceful, suave, witty or smooth. But then, this is not Paris or San Francisco.

He was raucous, sentimental, hot-tempered, practical, simple, devious, big and powerful. This is, after all, Chicago. . . . If Daley was reactionary and stubborn, he was in perfect harmony with his town. . . .

Eventually Daley made the remarkable transition from political boss to father figure.

Maybe he couldn't have been a father figure in Berkeley, Calif., Princeton, N.J., or even Skokie, Ill. But in Chicago there was nothing unusual about a father who worked long hours, meant shut up when he said shut up, and backed it up with a jolt to the head. Daley was as believable a father figure as anyone's old man.

Royko says he was "offended when Daley died and people were saying, 'What is Royko going to write about?'" There were (and are) many other subjects: integration, gun control, the mob, hippies, feminists, Reaganomics, the proper usage of Chicagoese. All were suitable for enraging—or amusing—his readers.

Royko could, for example, assume the tone of a streetwise pedagogue and chastise erring users of a Chicago term he helped popularize nationally: "clout." Among the chief offenders, Royko wrote in a 1973 column, were self-important trend watchers and Washington-based columnists, including (horrors!) the meticulous David Broder himself.

In order to understand the Washington pundits, the rest of us have had to constantly absorb those words and phrases that become "in."

There was charisma, viable, input, low profile, opting, nitty gritty, game plan and keeping the options open.

So you would think they, in turn, would learn to use a Chicago word properly.

That word is "clout," and it has been part of the City Hall vocabulary for years. . . .

Now even someone of the stature of David S. Broder . . . has seized upon the word. And like the others, he uses it without knowing what it means. . . .

In trying to explain [U.S. Attorney (now Illinois Governor) James R.] Thompson's sudden prominence, Broder wrote:

". . . His sudden fame and reputation as the most feared wielder of that special Chicago commodity called 'clout' rests on his work in the field of public corruption. . . . What makes even skeptical politicians here take Thompson seriously as a threat to Daley's control of Chicago is the reputation for 'clout' he has developed."

No, no, no—NO!

If what Thompson has is "clout," then charisma is some kind of Spanish soup. . . .

What Thompson has is law enforcement power. And what "clout" is in Chicago is political influence, as exercised through patronage, fixing, money, favors and other traditional City Hall methods.

The easiest way to explain clout is through examples of the way it might be used in conversation.

"Nah. I don't need a building permit—I got clout in City Hall."

"Hey, Charlie, I see you made foreman. Who's clouting for you? . . ."

"My clout sent a letter to the mayor recommending me for a judgeship. Maybe I'll enroll in law school."

Get the idea? Clout is used to circumvent the law, not to enforce it. It is used to bend rules, not follow them. . . .

Royko is not easily classifiable as either liberal or conservative. In some of his columns he speaks with the voice of the middle-class, blue-collar neighborhood in which he grew up and lived until a few years ago. He despised hippies, ridicules social workers and feminists, supports the death penalty. But he also has been a persistent critic of the gun lobby, an opponent of the Vietnam War, a foe of segregation, and a defender of the rights of nonconformists.

Some might see the conflicting views

expressed in his columns as evidence of philosophical schizophrenia, but Royko actually is guided by a hard, unwavering principle: he hates phonies, liars, bullies, and bureaucrats, whatever their political stripe. A case in point was Jerry Rubin, once a highly visible yippie and leader of the Chicago Seven antiwar protesters, now a New York stockbroker.

"Jerry Rubin always said he was afraid of me . . . back in the sixties because he said he had this eerie feeling that I was reading his mind," Royko says. "He knew what a phony he was, but he didn't realize that anyone else knew what a phony he was—except *I* knew what a phony he was. And that really bothered him.

"If I think Jerry Rubin or Abbie Hoffman were a couple of vaudevillians posing as social reformers, I was going to say so. At that time I may have believed in everything they said they believed in, but that didn't mean I had to believe in them.

"So maybe that's where I become schizo. I never bought a lot of the sixties values. I knew a lot of young reporters . . . who were caught up in the revolutionary fervor of the sixties, who really thought a bunch of upper-middle-class suburban kids from Milwaukee were going to run around with clenched fists and lead the working class out of the factories and into the streets. I figured if the working classes ever came out of the factories and into the streets, it would be to *hang them.*"

Similarly, while Royko complained about taverns' adopting "the bad practice of admitting women, which leads to wall signs that prohibit swearing and other simple pleasures," he also zapped anti-feminist Phyllis Schlafly for opposing stronger federal laws protecting women from sexual harassment on the job.

Royko has written that "97.2 percent of all Chicagoans are bigots in one way or another," and when Martin Luther King, Jr., was assassinated in 1968, Royko's indict-ment of the racism that led to King's murder covered the whole country:

FBI agents are looking for the man who pulled the trigger and surely they will find him.

But it doesn't matter if they do or don't. They can't catch everybody, and Martin Luther King was executed by a firing squad that numbered in the millions.

They took part, from all over the country, pouring words of hate into the ear of the assassin.

The man with the gun did what he was told. Millions of bigots, subtle and obvious, put it in his hand and assured him he was doing the right thing.

It would be easy to point at the Southern redneck and say he did it. But . . . what about the northern mayor who steps all over every poverty program advancement, thinking only of political expediency, until riots fester, whites react with more hate and the gap between races grows bigger?

Toss in the congressman with the stupid arguments against busing. And the pathetic women who turn out with eggs in their hands to throw at children. . . .

And behind them were the subtle ones, those who never say anything bad but just nod when the bigot throws out his strong opinions.

He is actually the worst, the nodder is, because sometimes he believes differently but he says nothing. He doesn't want to cause trouble. . . .

The bullet that hit King came from all directions. Every two-bit politician or incompetent editorial writer found in him, not themselves, the cause of our racial problems. . . .

Hypocrites all over this country would kneel every Sunday morning and mouth messages to Jesus Christ. Then they would come out and tell each other, after reading the papers, that somebody should string up King, who was living

Christianity like few Americans ever have. . . .

We have pointed a gun at our own head and we are squeezing the trigger. And nobody we elect is going to help us. It is our head and our finger.

As sympathetic as he is to the cause of civil rights, Royko has no patience with members of minority groups who fail to exercise the rights they have and think they "deserve" representatives in government without going to the polls to elect them. "In politics, you can't say you deserve anything unless you win. And you don't win unless you get more votes than the other guy. And if you don't do that, you don't deserve to win," he wrote in a 1981 column that advised Chicago blacks that they did not yet "deserve" a black mayor.

When Chicago's blacks did come out in huge numbers to elect Harold Washington mayor in 1983, they supported a man whose history of legal and professional problems puzzled and disturbed Royko, as did the tolerance Washington's followers apparently had for his failure to file income tax returns or perform legal services for clients who had paid him. "I can't conceive of a white candidate with that in his background being slated," Royko says. "The reasons why the blacks slated him and why he was accepted despite this are pretty complicated, I suppose, having to do with different attitudes toward that type of thing by whites and blacks. And it's a real tricky area to get into without sounding racist.

"But there are different attitudes about that. I've had a lot of blacks say, look, no black man from his generation is going to make it through without getting in some kind of trouble because, you know, there are just so many booby traps and land mines set up for us that aren't set out there for you. And that may be so, I don't know."

In general, Royko feels that more often than not Chicago's voters—black, white, or whatever—make some awfully dumb choices. "I would say it's pretty hard not to conclude that there are a lot of assholes out there when generation after generation you get thief after thief being elected," he says, propping his large feet up on his paper-strewn desk.

"We've had an awful lot of thieves and an awful lot of clods in the City Council, and they reflect, if anything, the indifference on the part of the public. Whether the indifference is brought on by not caring, or [by being] too troubled with your own problems, whatever it is, it's not a very good excuse. It just isn't. I've seen an awful lot of good people run for office in Chicago and be really ignored, and when that happens people wind up with some real baddos, and it's their own fault."

Royko even has some sympathy for the politicians he often lambastes. "I don't think public service is that good a deal. I don't know that being a congressman, when you run every two years—especially in a district where you might have to bust your tail to get reelected—is really that great. A lot of those guys are bright enough to be out making damn good livings at something else. But the public dumps all over them.

"People expect too damn much of government. They expect too much in the way of public service. The American electorate . . . chooses to remain just about as ignorant as it can about what's going on and what the real reasons are for different problems. . . . It's very easy to turn around and say, Ah-h-h, the mayor ain't doin' this, the mayor ain't doing that, while you are sitting home, flipping on your TV set at 5:00 and sitting in front of it until 10:30 at night. I have found that even as bad as Chicago politicians are, they are at least as good as the people who elected them."

Royko's rage is frequently enhanced by sarcasm, and blended with the rage and sarcasm in his columns is his humor. It is sometimes subtle and nostalgic, but more often it is rough and even malicious. It is rarely off the mark.

It was an unkind thing that Ald. John Hoellen said a few days ago.

He was making a plea for overtime pay for policemen and firemen. This was a nice thing to do.

But he couldn't leave it at that. He had to emphasize his point in an unsportsmanlike way. He said:

". . . Neither the policeman nor the fireman receives time and one-half for overtime—even though the garbage truck driver does."

. . . For years teachers, policemen, firemen, social workers and others have gone before legislative bodies to ask for more money. And one of their favorite arguments has been:

"Do you realize that we earn less (or the same as, or hardly any more) than garbagemen—GARBAGEMEN!"

. . . I don't know what Hoellen thinks garbagemen do all day. Maybe somebody told him that they toe-dance down the alleys, sniffing backyard roses and listening to transistor radios.

But for his information, they spend all day messing around with garbage— G-A-R-B-A-G-E. . . .

Day after day, they empty the cans. . . . They work in the heat and the cold. . . .

And what do we do? Do we ever thank them? Do little old ladies, frightened by social changes, ever write letters to the editor saying: "God bless our garbagemen. They deserve our support. Wake up, America!"

. . . No. When they empty the cans we just fill them up again.

. . . The only time they hear themselves mentioned is when someone comes along and says:

"We earn less than garbagemen. . . ."

I have never heard a garbageman point out that the only time an alderman lifts something heavy and disposable is when he gets up and goes home. . . .

Royko says his use of humor is both natural and calculated. "I find it a natural thing for me to try to show the irony of something by telling a story. And it's partly just a calculated thing on my part. I can get the reader to read about a more serious subject sometimes if I've injected some humor in it, or if the reader knows that if I'm serious today I might be funny tomorrow, and I can get him to come back. Part of it is just a device."

Once it was a device with unexpectedly long-lasting results. In 1970 he wrote a column about his unwilling receipt of four stray cats, which one of his two tender-hearted sons had brought home one at a time. Three cats were bad enough, Royko wrote, but four were impossible.

I was raised to believe that only a mad old recluse, who saved tons of old newspapers in the parlor, and concealed damp wads of money in rusty cans under the dusty bed, would own four cats. . . . I refuse to be pointed out as a mad old recluse.

So the fourth cat must go. . . .

A friend of mine keeps a tank full of piranhas, those little razor-tooth cannibal fish from the Amazon River. Admittedly, they are strange pets, and he really doesn't like them. It's just that his landlord won't let him keep a python.

He says I may, if I wish, throw my surplus cat into his fish tank.

I know this might offend kindly old ladies and sensitive children, so I'll tell you what I'll do.

I'll hold off feeding the cat to the piranhas for a day or two. It's only about three months old, and my friend says it could use some fattening up anyway.

That will give anyone who wants to rescue it from the snapping jaws an opportunity to take it off my hands. It is Calico, by the way, and seems good-natured.

So if any little children happen to be

reading this, you run to mommy and daddy and tell them they must do something to save the nice little Calico kitty from the mean man in the newspaper.

All mommy or daddy has to do is pick up the phone and call me at 321-2198 and make arrangements to get the cat before the hungry piranhas do.

Because if somebody doesn't, little children, it will be snap, snap, gobble, gobble, right down to his curly tail.

(I swear, I could write great TV toy commercials.)

That column had more lives than the Calico kitty. It was reprinted in one of Royko's anthologies, and he received telephone calls about it for years. "I'd get a call from California or someplace: 'Are you the guy who's going to feed the cat to the piranha?'" he says, imitating the whine of a terror-stricken child and then laughing. He could report that the cat was indeed saved by "some nice young flower children couple [who] came over and got it. For all I know they ate it."

Royko's column continues to prompt a steady flow of reader reaction—up to 400 letters a week—but the fun he once had in stoking their interest and anger is largely gone now. What many consider his most impressive feats of opinion-molding occurred in the late seventies, when columns he wrote favoring (but not actually endorsing) the candidacies of Jane Byrne for mayor of Chicago and Senator Charles Percy for reelection were credited with helping them win. During the same period, however, Royko himself suffered staggering losses. When the *Daily News* folded in March 1978, he lost more than just a work place; he lost a home. And when his wife died of a stroke in September 1979, "a lot of Mike Royko died," Jimmy Breslin has said. "That was a very special relationship. You don't see many men who care so deeply for a woman or need her so badly," Breslin told an interviewer.

"We met when she was six and I was nine," Royko wrote a few weeks after his wife died. "Same neighborhood street. Same grammar school. So if you ever have a nine-year-old who says he is in love, don't laugh at him. It can happen."

People who saw her picture in this paper have told me how beautiful she appeared to be. Yes, she was. As a young man I puffed up with pride when we went out somewhere and heads turned, as they always did.

But later, when heads were still turning, I took more pride in her inner beauty. If there was a shy person at a gathering, that's whom she'd be talking to, and soon that person would be bubbling. If people felt clumsy, homely and not worth much, she made them feel good about themselves. If someone was old and felt alone, she made them feel loved and needed. None of it was put on. That was the way she was.

I could go on, but it's too personal. And I'm afraid that it hurts. Simply put, she was the best person I ever knew. And while the phrase "his better half" is a cliche, with us it was the truth.

Anyway, I'll be back. And soon, I hope, because I miss you too my friends.

In the meantime, do her and me a favor. If there's someone you love but haven't said so in a while, say it now. Always, always, say it now.

Without his wife, Royko says, his life is "chaotic." His eyes tend to glaze over a bit as he describes his daily routine—or lack of it. "I'm disorganized. . . . I've had a lot of trouble adjusting to being single. I never used to have to worry about paying all the monthly bills, taking care of all the legal matters that come with owning a house, all of the legal crap you have to deal with. Just getting by from day to day," he says with a sigh, fumbling with a cigarette pack. "I've never been a really well-organized person, and it's just become worse and worse."

Royko has no such thing as a typical work day, he says. "It's just too goofy. I used to be able to say my typical work day is like this or that, but . . . when you wind up being a columnist and a celebrity at the same time, you have so goddamn many different things pulling at you that I spend a certain part of every day fending off people who want me to bowl in a charity tournament, or do this or do that, or make a speech, and I get so many phone calls and spend so damn much time talkin' on the phone. . . .

"I used to have a much better-organized life. I was able to have much greater discipline—you know, get the hell out of here by six o'clock. My work day could be organized. Now my work day is just when I get the job done. It could be late at night, it could be early in the afternoon, it could be anytime."

In the early years of his column, Royko worked alone, practically living at the *Daily News* and at the Billy Goat Tavern, a favorite newspaper hangout nearby. His wife became a widow to the column, friends said, and Royko became known as a combative drunk. He got in one tavern fight that resulted in his arrest for disorderly conduct and enough embarrassing publicity to persuade him that he had lost his credibility and should resign from the paper. His resignation was not accepted, and the incident blew over. The five-days-a-week pressure got to be too much, however, and Royko cut back briefly to three columns a week, offering to resume the five-a-week pace if the paper gave him help to answer the phone and run down leads. He got an assistant.

There are many who think that Royko's column alone sold the *Daily News* in its declining years, and Royko is not shy about claiming a similar power at the *Sun-Times*. He reportedly earns $250,000 a year and thinks he is worth every penny. "You take a television anchorman who is worth a point or two in the ratings, and he'll make a half-million dollars. I am just as important in

selling the *Chicago Sun-Times* as that anchorman is in selling the 10:00 news," he once told the *Washington Journalism Review*. "If I went to the *Tribune*, I would take 50,000 readers with me. If you take 50,000 readers away from the *Sun-Times* and give them to the *Tribune*, that's a 100,000 spread. End of ballgame."

The *Tribune* has made overtures to Royko in the past, and he has considered them seriously enough to have held a pen over a proposed contract, he says, but the thought of working for the once-reactionary and still very conservative Republican broadsheet makes the hair stand up on the back of his neck. He also has many friends still at the *Sun-Times*, although it is simply a work place for him now, not the home the *Daily News* was. It is peopled with familiar faces, not the "strangers" he says he would encounter at the *Tribune*.*

Royko has been lured into making a number of appearances on Chicago television talk shows and serving as an occasional television commentator. He even made a stab at hosting his own program in 1981. Called "Royko On Tap," the program featured Royko and several guests sitting in a bar

---

*As uncomfortable as Royko once was at the thought of working at the *Tribune*, the November 1983 purchase of the *Sun-Times* by Rupert Murdoch, the ultra-conservative Australian press baron, made him even more uneasy about the future character of the *Sun-Times*. Murdoch's publishing empire includes some of the tawdriest periodicals in the English-speaking world as well as such prestigious publications as the *London Times*. Royko feels the true tone of Murdoch's papers is exemplified by the *New York Post*. "No self-respecting fish would want to be wrapped in Murdoch's publications. He puts out trash," Royko said when he took a "vacation" from the *Sun-Times* in December 1983. When Murdoch's purchase of the *Sun-Times* became final in January, Royko walked into the *Tribune* and was hired on the spot. How many readers does he now think he'll bring with him? "We'll pick up my [two] sisters," he told a press conference. The new owners of the *Sun-Times* apparently think their losses might be greater, and as this book goes to press, Royko's move to the *Tribune* is the subject of litigation.

(where else?) and chatting, as well as a comic sequence in which he had himself fitted for a hairpiece. The show, which was touted as a possible regular feature, received fairly good reviews—better in the *Sun-Times* than in the *Tribune,* predictably—and got great publicity, but it was never repeated. He has a low opinion of both the people who work in television and their product. Station managers and program directors all belong in "loony bins," he says, and "before television I'm sure they all would have been managers of used car lots. That's how creative they are. . . .

"Television commentary's not for me because the secret of television commentary is to take one thought and that's it. One thought for one commentary. If you try to go beyond one thought, if you sidetrack a little bit, if you ramble a little bit as you can do in an essay . . . , you're going to lose the viewer.

"You've got to say: 'Dick and Jane ran. Dick and Jane ran fast. Dick and Jane ran home fast,' and keep up that one theme over and over again. . . . You can't take anything that really makes people [think]. Andy Rooney, you know: 'You ever notice when the sun goes down it always gets dark?' 'You ever notice that when you stand out in the rain you get wet?' It's the most inane crap I've ever seen! This guy is the biggest commentator on television. I can't do shit like that."

Royko also has little patience with the Washington- or New York-based panjandrums in journalism who fret about the nation's press. The hand-wringing following the discovery that the *Washington Post* had been awarded a Pulitzer Prize for a fake story missed the point, he felt, and left him cold.

Some [columnists] have written that every journalist in America is somehow tainted by this shabby affair.

Nuts. Only the *Washington Post* is tainted by this shabby affair. After all, when Bradlee, Woodward, Bernstein, and the *Post* became national idols because of Watergate, they didn't say that the rest of us were also national idols. Now that they're bums, they can keep that distinction for themselves, too.

And there's been much written about the credibility of the press being endangered because of the faked story, and how the press must be even more alert to this danger.

More nonsense. The credibility of the press is most often questioned by people who find that their particular prejudice is being punctured. . . .

When the *Post* dug up Watergate, millions of Republicans said the "credibility" was no good because they just didn't want the truth coming out. . . .

And there is no way the press can say this must not be permitted to happen again. . . . Who can guarantee that out of thousands of reporters in this country, another one won't get carried away by blind ambition?

But there is one aspect of this fiasco that bothers me [and] any editor involved in approving that faked story should be fired. And not because it turned out to be faked, either. Here's why.

The story was about an eight-year-old boy who was being turned into a heroin addict by the mother's boyfriend.

The reporter [said] she couldn't use names because she had promised the mother that everyone would be kept anonymous. Also, the boyfriend had threatened her life if she revealed who he and the others were. . . .

That editor and others went along with it [and] even when the police commissioner and the mayor demanded the name of the kid, the *Post* refused to tell the reporter to divulge it.

They talked about protecting sources, the role of the press and all the things editors love to get somber about. . . .

They were talking about the life of a child. Or at least they thought they were, the editors not knowing that the story was a fake.

How could they sit there and say, yes, we will keep our word to a mother who is letting her child be slowly destroyed? How could they say that we will protect the identity of a man who is slowly murdering a child?

. . . That's what's really wrong with the *Post* story. It was rotten from the inception because the *Washington Post* acted as if it were protecting a government source who had leaked a secret report the public should know about, when it was protecting a child murderer. . . .

Although he is appalled by television commentary and is a perceptive critic of his own profession, Royko says he does not spend much time worrying about the future health of newspapers. "I figure at my age I'll be gone before they are. I don't worry about the future of the world or the future of newspapers." He does worry—constantly—about his column. When he wakes up in the morning, the first thing Royko thinks about is his column, he says.

In 1981 Royko sold the house he, his wife, and sons had lived in and moved to a North Side high-rise apartment overlooking Lake Michigan. He received some twitting from local commentators for abandoning his middle-class Northwest neighborhood to become a resident of the city's ritzy lakefront, but he says it is a bum rap. There is not much glitter for him in the Gold Coast. "I felt much safer where I lived before. I could walk out of the building where I'm now and walk one half-block inland, and I enter [an area of] a much, much higher crime rate than I've ever lived in in my life.

"I have to laugh when people talk about 'Boy, you now live near the lake.' Yeah, I live near the lake; there're more goddamn murders within one block of where I live near the lake than there were in the entire ward where I lived before. . . . For chris-

sakes, there're hookers all around me. Hookers, bums, dope peddlers. . . . It's very nice. I can look out of my window and see the lake. If I look straight down from my window I'm liable to see some guy getting his head bashed in."

On rare occasions when he has the time (and perhaps the courage), Royko will walk the three miles from his apartment to the *Sun-Times* building, where from the window in his cubicle office he can see the muddy waters of the Chicago River. He arrives at the paper most mornings around 9:00 and confers with his secretary and current assistant. Over the past 18 years he has had 9 assistants, 2 of whom worked for him a second time after they lost their jobs as reporters when the *Daily News* folded. Royko calls them his "Dr. Watsons, Igors, Tontos, and most valued friends," and they all have considered their apprenticeship under him invaluable, if nerve-racking. He is a difficult boss, rarely giving clear assignments or praise for a job well done.

Technically, Royko's deadline is 10:30 A.M., but he tries to write his column the day before it is due so he does not run up against the clock. His assistants—generally recent college graduates or alumni of the City News Bureau—do most of his "basic reporting," since he has become bored with it and finds that his celebrity can get in the way.

"If I hear a judge in traffic court is doing some strange things, ordering people to get haircuts or making crazy decisions, if I go over there, he'll call a recess and invite me in chambers and say, 'What can I do for you?' That's one of the problems.

"But it's all outweighed by the benefits. If people want to phone the newspaper with something they've seen that they think might be newsworthy, 99 percent of the time it isn't, but that 1 percent can result in a good story [and] they prefer to call somebody that they think they know. So I get information they [the city desk] don't get. It's the same thing in Washington. If a guy calls and says 'I'm from the *Peoria Journal*,' his chances of getting information from some under secretary of this or that are not nearly as great as when Carl Rowan calls, or George Will, or somebody like that."

Royko does not keep a reserve file of columns to use in case some story he is working on turns out to be a dud. Most days he begins writing by three or four in the afternoon, working steadily but not swiftly on a computerized terminal behind his desk. When he has a good story to tell about some small victim of an unfeeling bureaucracy, the column comes easily. When he is writing a comic or reflective piece, the words come more slowly. He usually is finished by seven or eight at night.

Royko used to polish his columns more, but now he thinks that there are days when what he writes is "barely good enough to get in the paper." About one column out of four is potentially good enough for one of his anthologies, he says, which is a pretty remarkable batting average, considering the number of columns he has written in the past 20 years.

"It would increase my work day considerably if I played around with columns that much. I work pretty hard on them [but] I may have polished them a lot harder . . . when I first started the column. I think it's natural when you first start out [to] work with each one harder. When I reach a point [now] when the column says what I want it to say, I'm willing to let it go at that."

But Royko is not complacent about the column and will not undertake anything that might lessen his attention to it. "I don't do a lot of things that other columnists do. I don't fly around the country giving speeches. . . . I'm not going to do that because you've got to give something up, and I imagine what you give up is the amount of time you can spend on your column. . . . It must be very easy to start thinking, 'Well, if I wrote it, it must be good 'cause everybody's still printing it.' I

don't see that [speeches are] worth it, although you get the immediate gratification of an audience full of attentive faces and applause. It's really not worth it if it's going to take away from what your main work is.

"So I don't do the books. I don't do the speeches. I do very little television. And I don't run around the country a lot. There are columnists who . . . still get an ego trip from having an out-of-town dateline or a foreign dateline, and I don't think the readers give a shit. . . . I don't do a lot of things because they cut in on the time I can spend on the column. That's what I do."

Independent Press, the supplemental news service of the *Sun-Times*, syndicates Royko's column, which appears on page 2 of the Chicago paper Tuesday through Friday and on Sunday.* About 200 papers around the country receive it and use it often enough to give him a national following. In 1981 the Baltimore Sunpapers accorded him an honor that echoed his 1971 Pulitzer by presenting him with its first H. L. Mencken Award, citing his "witty, biting, irreverent, stylistically graceful" work in the spirit of Mencken, another provincial writer appreciated far beyond the borders of his city.

Royko has not exactly mellowed in recent years, but he displays a greater tolerance, perhaps, for petty bureaucratic thievery and the failures of Chicago's mayors. He has given former Mayor Jane Byrne, who is married to an old newspaper chum of his, and Mayor Harold Washington an easier time than he ever gave Daley.

"I'd rather attack," he says, "[but,] to use a phrase I guess that's 2,000 years old: 'The eagle does not hunt flies.' I don't want to spend my time pickin' on some precinct captain or some lowly building inspector. . . . I don't know that I want to go around looking for somebody to 'hit' all the time. I probably was more inclined to do that when I was a lot younger."

*That is, until his move to the *Tribune*.

He once told an interviewer that he has "given a surprising number of people a pass in my column—people I could have destroyed," and he says that some small bribes—$200 here or there to a minor functionary—are not so bad if they grease bureaucratic gears and guarantee good service.

He claims that he once caught a building inspector taking a bribe but let him off the hook—provided he return the money. "If I was the city editor and a reporter came to me with a story like that, I would tell the reporter to get the facts and write the story. That's the way it should be. But I am not the city editor. This is a personal column. I make my own rules. My rules are that I can play God if I want to," he told one interviewer.

Royko also candidly admits that at the outset of her administration he gave a pass on occasion to Byrne, a one-time protégé of Daley who broke from his machine and defeated Daley's nondescript successor, Michael Bilandic, in 1979. Byrne's election, Royko crowed in a column the day after, made him "feel prouder to be a Chicagoan than I ever have in my life." The honeymoon was short-lived, and his approval of Byrne's efforts was spotty, but he says there is no question that he was "easier on Jane Byrne that I was on Daley, and that's easily explainable.

"When I started my column . . . Daley had been mayor for nine years. I watched him for most of those years, in one way or another, as a reporter covering this town. Daley had a record that was already established; Daley had an approach that was established; he had attitudes that were established. . . . Jane Byrne came into office as an unknown factor. There was really nothing I could do unless I wanted to take what I recognized as a lot of growing pains . . . of her administration and treat these as what she really represented, and I couldn't be sure."

Byrne may have been an "unknown factor" politically, but she was hardly unknown to Royko, whose good friend Jay McMullen, a former *Daily News* political reporter, had married her before she was elected mayor and became her administration's major-domo. While Royko may have treated Byrne lightly where he would have pummeled others—not slamming her, for example, for backing the 1980 presidential bid of Senator Edward M. Kennedy, whom Royko loathes—he did not give her or McMullen a free ride by any means. He even took to referring to her as "Mayor Bossy."

Royko's tolerance for Byrne had evaporated by early 1982. She had disappointed those (himself included) who thought that she was interested in reform, he wrote, and she had lost the better people in her administration, replacing them with "guys who should be permanently wired for lie-detector tests."

"She's bounced back and forth between being Good Jane and Bad Jane so much that to a majority of Chicagoans there is only one Jane—Wacky Jane," he wrote.

Royko would have welcomed a reasonably acceptable alternative to Byrne. He did not get what he thought was one, and by the end of the brutal 1983 primary- and general-election campaigns his blunt columns had infuriated both sides. Early in his campaign, Harold Washington branded Royko a racist, and towards the end of the campaign Republican Bernard Epton called him "slime." Epton later vowed that he would buy the *Sun-Times* just to fire Royko.

Shortly after Washington declared his candidacy for the mayoral nomination, urging Chicago Democrats to examine "my record and my background," Royko drew his ire by doing just that and writing a column that highlighted Washington's 1971 conviction for failing to file income tax returns for four years and his suspension from the practice of law on two occasions.

Washington has never satisfactorily explained why he didn't file income tax returns, other than to say that he was very busy and forgot and that he had been prosecuted for political reasons.

Well, many of us are very busy and we still file our returns. And people who aren't politicians are prosecuted on tax charges every day. So these excuses don't actually clear the air. . . .

. . . Washington did things that even charitably would have to be called stupid.

Now he wants to be mayor of the second biggest city in the United States. And he says that of all the candidates, only he has the skill to make this city run properly.

Maybe so. But I have to wonder how a lawyer, who couldn't manage his own law practice, and a lawmaker who couldn't obey the income tax laws is going to administer something as huge, troubled and complex as the government of Chicago. . . .

When Royko also wrote a column describing how Chicago's white ward leaders were predicting a large white registration drive to counter Washington's candidacy, Washington lashed out by brandishing a copy of the *Sun-Times* and declaring: "If this campaign becomes racially polarized, I think we can look back . . . and point to Mr. Royko."

Royko later wrote that Washington's anger was puzzling and a bit misplaced. Black leaders had waged "a massive black voter registration drive for years," he pointed out.

They were quite open about their goal—to elect a black mayor—and nobody said they were being racist.

Washington himself had said that he expected every black voter in Chicago to support him, which sounded like racial polarization to me. But nobody criticized him for injecting race as a campaign issue. . . .

As I've said before, it's unfortunate, even tragic, that so many Chicagoans vote along racial or ethnic lines. But the reality is that they do—especially whites.

Royko predicted that Washington had little chance to defeat Byrne or her archrival, Cook County State's Attorney Richard M. Daley, the son of the late mayor. Byrne had amassed a staggering reelection campaign fund of over $9 million, Royko pointed out in one column, figuring that she would have had to stuff $1,265 into her campaign purse each hour since she took office four years earlier in order to accumulate that much. "She must have a purse the size of a Streets and Sanitation truck," he wrote. On the other hand, Daley apparently had more solid political support. "Politicians are like house dogs," Royko wrote. "They give their love and loyalty to the person who fills their bowl." Daley appeared to have more political puppy chow.

When Byrne and Daley split the white vote and Washington won the Democratic nomination with 36 percent of the tally, Royko—like political observers around the country and national Republican power brokers—took a close look at the hitherto ignored GOP candidate, Bernard Epton, a wealthy ex-legislator with a record as a liberal Republican. Despite an unctuously self-congratulatory style, Epton had a shot at being elected, Royko wrote, because he had "a quick wit, political experience and a good record as a legislator," as well as the potential support of thousands of life-long Democrats who couldn't stomach the thought of a black mayor.

When Epton's campaign managers played on those fears—adopting the slogan "Epton—before it's too late"—and Epton attacked "the media" for exacerbating racial tensions that many of his supporters were enflaming, Royko wrote that the Republican candidate could "now add hypocrisy to his other noticeable flaws."

"The press in this city would have been content to cover the issues if Epton had decided that the campaign should be based on issues.

"But he didn't. He or his staff decided that his only hope of winning was to make it a campaign based on personal attack. And that was what encouraged the . . . outright racism."

Royko wrote over 50 columns about the Byrne-Daley-Washington-Epton campaign, and at its close he remained as he was at the beginning: a weary, even-handed realist, dismayed at the caliber of the candidates, disgusted by their campaigns, and undecided as to how he would vote.

"It's a tough choice," he wrote. "Epton's supporters call Washington—because of his tax problems—a crook. Washington's supporters call Epton—because he visited shrinks—a kook.

"A kook or a crook?

"And the voters turned down a two-for-one deal in Jane Byrne."

Although he had been among the first to rehash Washington's legal problems, Royko felt after the campaign was over that he had treated Washington far more gently than he would have a white candidate with a similar record. "I didn't consider it, keeping it in perspective, a corrupt thing. You know, he was not out there rezoning places and taking bribes and stuff like that. It was more of a careless, stupid thing he did. I think I went easier on him than I would have on a white politician, because I think that maybe there is some truth in the attitude that things were more difficult for him than if he had been a white lawyer."

Royko readily confesses to being bored with his column, even if his readers are not. "Oh, hell, I was tired of the column ten years ago." He would like to retire, perhaps as he has retired Slats Grobnik, who only makes an occasional cameo appearance in the column now. "I didn't want to turn Slats into an aging philosopher or anything."

What would he rather do? "Nothing. I would rather do nothing. Give it a whirl, you know? Ever see a movie with Walter Matthau called 'New Leaf'? I'd like to live Walter Matthau's life—tool around in a Mazerati and ride a horse through the park and fly an airplane and be a playboy. I've never tried to do nothing. I would like to try it before I got too old to enjoy it. If I didn't have to work for the money, I wouldn't be working."

He would be missed. It is not unusual in Chicago for drivers to slam on their brakes, roll down their windows, and shout compliments to Royko if they see him walking down Michigan Avenue. He is recognized throughout the city—at bars, restaurants, theaters—and more often than not is greeted warmly. He encounters boors, nuisances, and jerks, of course, but he finds most people "civilized, nice . . . , and you never know when somebody's going to mention something that's going to lead to a column." The contests he sponsors in his column—the penny-pitching, pierogie-eating, or rib-cooking championships—are civic events; his on-again, off-again love affair with the Cubs is followed closely. He once gave up the Cubs, calling them "petulant jerks," and swore allegiance to the White Sox by stomping to the pitcher's mound at Comisky Park and taking an oath on the wooden leg of Sox owner Bill Veeck.

He has spurned some employment feelers from Washington—although the most serious one, from the *Post*, was for a job as a sportswriter, which he considered absurd. "Washington is where they talk about the problems," Royko says. Chicago is where people live them. "You don't have to go anywhere else in the country today to find the fruits of Reaganomics as vividly shown as here. Generally, whatever the country's problems are, you'll find them cropping up here." Royko may not own Chicago, but he belongs to it.

"It's a lot easier for me now than it was,

say, 10 or 12 years ago. Now I'm very popular. I don't have people throwing rocks through my windows. The number of hostile people is far outweighed by the number of friendly people. I don't know, maybe I've been around so goddamn long now. The column really hasn't changed, but I just don't run into many antagonistic people, and I generally walk away from them if I do. It's much easier to be liked."

Perhaps Royko has become—as uncomfortable as he may be with the title—the elder statesman of the Chicago press. Chicagoans may realize that what once was written about Finley Peter Dunne applies just as well to Royko:

"He was a pragmatist. . . . He was not a devotee of the single cause nor a propagandist for the single solution. . . . He believed that the philosophy of diversity was the foundation stone of our national virtue.

"He was a libertarian. He resented all invasions of personal liberty, whether the invading power was government, business or plain bigotry. . . .

"Last and most important, he was a democrat in the purest sense. He was one of those rare souls who really believe in the absolute equality and the absolute brotherhood of man. His first and last allegiance was always to humanity."

George F. Will

"An Interesting Tory Mind"

he contents of a person's bookcase are perhaps as much a mirror of one's personality as the eyes are said to be a window on the soul. The large, eclectic collection of volumes packed in George F. Will's small, comfortable study are a case in point. On the heavily laden shelves, which stretch from floor to ceiling, can be found numerous biographies of politicians, both practical and philosophical: Abraham Lincoln and Winston Churchill, two of Will's idols; Karl Marx and Leon Blum, whose philosophies he disputes; Huey Long and Alger Hiss, about as disparate a pair of personalities and lives as can be imagined. There are novels by Steinbeck and Bellow, Drury and Wambaugh; essays and mysteries by G. K. Chesterton; comic tales by P. G. Wodehouse. A tiny photograph of Queen Victoria, sitting in the shade of an Indian tent and working on her correspondence with the aid of a typewriter (of all things), rests near a decorative China plate devoted to the memory of William McKinley. Similar treasures flank a rare, four-volume first edition of George Eliot's *Middlemarch,* printed in 1871.

But wait. On the shelf adjacent to *Middlemarch* rest seven autographed baseballs, including one inscribed by all the Baltimore Orioles, and a dark blue cap from the Chicago Cubs. There is a book on the his-

tory of the American passion for hamburgers, and several shelves are given over to collections of editorial cartoons and comic strips. A multibuttoned telephone on Will's antique desk rings constantly—although its bell is muffled discreetly—and two young boys and their tiny sister rush in and out of the study, alternately harassing and delighting him. This is no cloister of an otherworldly pedagogue, but the home, as well as the office, of a political analyst and philosopher who, at 43, is perhaps the most eloquent exponent of conservatism in the country.

The decor in Will's study is similarly instructive. On the walls are several delicate etchings depicting Princeton University by day and the U.S. Capitol by night, aglow in its spotlight. Beside a nineteenth-century Morris armchair, the first designed to recline, sits a polished World War I brass artillery shell, powerful evidence, says Will—one of the Pentagon's most uncompromising advocates—of the extravagant waste of war. It now contains a handsome, and much used, collection of antique walking sticks. There is a large, somber painting of a prairie wheat field, thunderclouds darkening the sky; in the foreground, a telephone pole, devoid of wires, sports some tattered campaign posters and serves as a landmark on an empty crossroads.

Will sprang from prairie country not unlike that in the painting on his study wall.

239

He was born in Champagne, Illinois, the progeny of "word people from way back." His father was a professor of philosophy at the University of Illinois; his mother was a high school teacher and editor of a children's encyclopedia; and one of his grandfathers was a peripatetic Lutheran minister who sought to uplift fallen souls in tiny towns scattered throughout Pennsylvania and Maryland.

But Will was not born with a thesaurus in one hand, a pen in the other, and an appropriate literary allusion or historical quotation in his mouth. He was, in fact, a frustrated athlete as a youngster, uninterested "in anything except the National League until my senior year in college," he once confessed.

"As an athlete, I was a diligent underachiever," he wrote in a 1980 column. "I was one of those people whom a coach calls 'huggers': benchwarmers you keep around 'so you can hug 'em after you win, instead of having to hug the guys who play and sweat.' "

With tongue only slightly in cheek, Will contends that his first, most enduring, and certainly most futile philosophic and moral attachment was to the Chicago Cubs, who haven't won a pennant since 1945. He even put his money where his heart was. A single, framed share of stock in the Cubs is displayed in his study, along with a document certifying his attendance at the team's 15,000th game in 1978. Although he wrote in 1974 that his "gloomy temperament received its conservative warp from early and prolonged exposure" to the Cubs, the ascendance of a conservative administration more in tune with his beliefs has evidently persuaded him that the realm of lost causes does not need to be his permanent haven. He has become disillusioned with the Cubs, he admits. "They don't even try any more," he says, wrinkling his nose. Now he roots for—and writes about—the Orioles.

Columns such as the ones Will writes about baseball, his own athletic failures,

and a diverse variety of subjects can make confirmed Will readers out of even the staunchest liberals. He has not only an incredible range of interests but something all too many conservatives lack: a sense of humor. "Conservatives have tended to go through life with an awful moral squint and their lips pursed," he once told an interviewer. Although Will can be, and often is, as serious—even grim—as any of his colleagues on the right side of the Op Ed page, he leavens his sourdough with a blend of wit and lightness that makes it palatable and intellectually nourishing to a much broader readership.

"A pleasant meal," Will once wrote, "should include sherbet as well as meat," and the tangy touches he adds to his discourses almost guarantee that the columns beneath his by-line will be interesting and lively. He writes about everything from the principles of conservatism as he interprets them to the questionable pleasures of camping with small children to the hamburger advertising wars of fast-food franchisers. Some of Will's most memorable columns, his colleague and friend David Broder believes, describe his reactions "when he confronts popular culture—or rather, when popular culture confronts George Will." In that confrontation, Will often depicts himself as a bespectacled Buster Keaton: solemn, intrigued, perplexed, horrified. For example, he is appalled by what he finds in fast-food eateries—not so much by what they serve as by how they describe it:

The flavor list at the local Baskin-Robbins ice cream shop is an anarchy of names like "Peanut Butter 'N Chocolate" and "Strawberry Rhubarb Sherbert." These are not the names of things that reasonable people consider consuming, but the names are admirably business-like, briskly descriptive.

Unfortunately, my favorite delight (chocolate-coated vanilla flecked with nuts) bears the unutterable name "Hot Fudge Nutty Buddy," an example of the plague of cuteness in commerce. There are some things a gentleman simply will not do, and one is announce in public a desire for a "Nutty Buddy." So I usually settle for a plain vanilla cone.

Not all modern developments distress Will. He finds that some, such as the Sony Walkman and tape-recorded books, can help ameliorate the bleakness of modern life, as well as encourage old-fashioned virtues:

Listening to tapes during otherwise barren time—there is a lot of it in life: shaving, vacuuming, riding in taxis, walking dutifully for exercise—you can consume a novel in four days. The cost is less than $1 an hour.

Of course, listening to Somerset Maugham's description of Charles Strickland's leprosy in "The Moon and Sixpense" can steal the charm from a bowl of Cheerios at 6:30 A.M. Unhappy suburbanites commuting to boring jobs are not advised to listen to George Orwell's "Coming up for Air." They might do something reckless. And no gentleman should listen to Anais Nin's "Delta of Venus," unless he does not mind walking down the street blushing the color of a beet that is out of breath. But imagine being in a taxi, and instead of hearing the driver's opinion of Paul Volcker, you are hearing Virginia Woolf's "A Room of One's Own."

The pleasure is not just in the particular books. It also is in learning to listen. . . .

Listening to a book—not just following the plot but following the syntax of Nineteenth-Century sentences rich in semicolons and parenthetical clauses—requires a special kind of concentration, and it exercises segments of my brain that have been unexercised since my father read me the exploits of Horatio Hornblower. . . .

Each of Will's columns—whether it is an exhortation against the Soviet Union in the most implacable cold-war rhetoric or praise for an unsung hero who walked out of a Burger King rather than call a ham and cheese sandwich a "Yumbo"—has a firm, underlying moral.

"Everything I write, especially some of the so-called lighter pieces, reflects a carefully, protractedly developed view of the world," Will says. It is the view of a rigorously polite, stern yet sensitive man who, schooled in many political philosophies, adopted "an authoritarian, strong-government conservative" outlook. However consistently Will may adhere to that view, he tempers it with a keen sense for the practicalities of life, politics, and governance. Quoting Chesterton, one of his favorite authors, Will declines to lock himself away in "the clean, well-lit prison of one idea."

While the refrains in Will's pieces all come from one philosophic symphony, he is an adept orchestrator. He captures the readers' interest by supplying them with wide-ranging, often unexpected variations on his theme.

"There is nothing in the world more optional than reading a column," Will says. "You have to read the front page; you have to read the sports page if you're going to be conversant with the essence of American life, but you don't have to read 'opinion journalism'. . . . The people read a columnist because they like the play of his mind on reality, not because they agree with him always, or even ever, but because—and I'm putting it baldly to make a point—because it's fun. And I don't mean 'fun' in any low sense of entertainment, but because it is an enjoyable experience—and it *better* be enjoyable or they're not going to do it, which is why, among other good reasons, care should be taken to style."

Will, a lapsed academician, was trained to engage the wandering minds of undergraduates in the ponderous subject of political philosophy. Since the Op Ed pages of the nation's newspapers are supposed to contain as many viewpoints as one may find on the faculties of most universities, he is, perhaps, as well equipped as any commentator to snare the roving eye of readers. But he quickly admits that he never would have prospered in journalism—or even entered it—had he been required to go the traditional route of apprenticeship: police beat to general assignment to political coverage to punditry. Although Will prefers a social order bound by strict rules, the rapid development of his own career suggests that in some cases the abrupt elimination of certain stages of professional development can be salutary—and potentially hazardous.

By starting his journalistic career at the top and never having been a reporter, Will has been unschooled to some degree in the subtleties of a profession in which observers and subjects must be both intimate and apart. Because of his prominence, his occasional lapses in judgment—which have been serious but not fatal—have sparked a national debate among his peers. His performance in that debate has been uncharacteristically awkward and unpersuasive, but "the play of his mind" on other topics remains intriguing and enjoyable.

After attending public grade school in Champagne and the University of Illinois's small, select high school, Will went to Trinity College in Hartford, Connecticut, a liberal arts institution affiliated with the Episcopal Church. His political awakening at Trinity—symbolized by his switch from sports editor on the campus newspaper to its editor—was sparked in part by the presidential candidacy of John F. Kennedy. He headed the Students for Kennedy organization at Trinity and was appropriately "liberal."

"I was quite taken by Kennedy and no doubt would have voted for him," Will says, had he been old enough to vote in 1960. In retrospect, his attraction to Kennedy was not as ironic as some might think. "Remember, Kennedy's inaugural address is now cited as the rankest cold-war rhetoric," Will points out, "so . . . the Democratic party was still part of the postwar, cold-war consensus."

Trinity was an all-male school when Will attended it, but he compensated for the absence of coeds by becoming friendly with the daughter of a local restaurant owner whose establishment he patronized regularly. The restaurateur's daughter, Madeleine Marion, became his wife in 1967.

Following his graduation from Trinity in 1960, Will went to Magdalen College at Oxford University in England, where he studied philosophy, politics, and economics and where his "genetic Republicanism" ultimately triumphed over his brief flirtation with college liberalism. During his two years in England, Will says, he was "very struck by the suffocation of social energy" there by "an irrationally expansive public sector," and the views of libertarian economists such as Chicagoan Milton Friedman— better known then in England than in the United States—greatly influenced him. He also made several trips to Berlin, then the epicenter of the cold war, saw the Berlin Wall, and helped an East Berliner escape to the West.

"I went to visit some friends of a friend in Berlin, and I went over to East Berlin and I met a kid there. And we'd talk and I'd go back and I'd do a lot of extremely foolish things, smuggling in newspapers and Guenter Grass paperbacks, all of which can get you three years. Just a terribly foolish thing to do.

"Then I asked him if he wanted to escape, and he said yeah, and I figured out how to do it, which was to get an Air Force uniform in and have him walk out . . . , [since] one of the last vestiges of four-power . . . rights in Berlin was that our military could pass in and out without dealing with the East Germans. . . . So I got a uniform—the wrong kind, but he could walk through—and they didn't catch him."

It was the kind of experience, Will has said, that "really concentrated my mind on the Cold War and what the stakes of 20th Century politics really are." He cast his first presidential ballot for Barry Goldwater.

Will obtained a second bachelor's degree

and a master's degree at Magdalen, where his father had once taught as a visiting professor, and then chose Princeton University's graduate school in philosophy because—he once claimed in a column—it was located midway between two National League cities, New York and Philadelphia, thereby permitting him to indulge his "cruel addiction" to the exploits of the hapless Cubs.

At Princeton, Will soon switched his field from philosophy to politics and wrote what he now describes as a "sprawling, undisciplined, garrulous" doctoral dissertation on "tolerance," arguing—as he still does, but more succinctly—that "there is too much of it."

"I'm not against tolerance," he explains, "I never was against tolerance. I'm against tolerance as the central social value. I'm against tolerance advocated on the grounds that we can't tell truth from falsehood anyway, or trash from art. What I said in my doctoral dissertation is that more dangerous than pornography, for example, are the reasons given for tolerating it. We can stand pornography; what we cannot stand is the Supreme Court of the United States teaching through the opinions of its justices such as William O. Douglas that we must . . . tolerate *Hustler* [magazine] because if we censor *Hustler,* we will not know where or how to stop.

"Well, I know where and how to stop. People more discriminating than Justice Douglas do. They understand that life is not quite that random and standards are not as capricious. . . . [Douglas] was a Holmesian. I'm a great anti-Holmesian. [Justice Oliver Wendell] Holmes was a great teacher of bad doctrine when he said that the best test of the truth of a proposition is its ability to get accepted in the marketplace of ideas. That does not test 'truth' at all; that tests popularity. Popularity isn't truth, but it's the way you talk if you don't think there are standards of truth."

Will received his Ph.D. in 1967, and from then until late 1969 he taught political philosophy, first at Michigan State University in East Lansing, then at the University of Toronto. Despite an upbringing in its groves, he did not find academe particularly appealing. "I was exasperated with the academic climate," he recalls, and when an opportunity arose to work in Washington, a city where politics is the main industry, he found it had a "certain charm."

Will became an aide to Senator Gordon Allott of Colorado, a conservative Republican who had been named chairman of the Republican Policy Committee following the death of Everett McKinley Dirksen, the GOP's colorful Senate leader. Receiving allocations for a larger staff when he obtained the leadership post, Allott began searching for a "Republican academic" to do some writing for him. A friend he consulted in Denver had been at Princeton with Will and recommended him to Allott.

"I was at the American Political Science Association convention in New York when Gordon Allott first tried to reach me . . . and it was the day Ho Chi Minh died, I remember, because the idiot political scientists were doing the sort of thing that made me want to leave teaching at that time. They were arguing about whether to have a memorial service for him and pass resolutions in praise of the old butcher."

Then came the call offering sanctuary in Washington. Will thought he would spend only a short time in the capital, but "once I got down I just never looked back."

The conclave of political scientists had another fateful and beneficial side effect for Will: the trip to New York gave him an opportunity to meet William F. Buckley, Jr., for whom Will had done his first piece of journalistic writing, an analysis of the 1968 presidential election which appeared in the *National Review.* When Will later decided to leave his Senate job, Buckley opened the door to a full-time career in journalism.

From 1970 to 1972, when Allott lost his bid to become Colorado's first four-term senator, Will wrote speeches for him, did legislative work, and "just sort of wandered around the landscape," a political zoologist happily set loose in his subjects' native habitat. "You have to learn not just the vocabulary of politics, but certain mental circuits have to develop in your head. And I think now, 14 years on from when I came to Washington, I really think it was the best possible way for me to have approached journalism, because I do think that I learned how to think politically a good bit there, in a way that I think some other journalists have never had to."

Most Washington columnists understand how backs are scratched, egos are massaged, and compromises are made in order to construct the coalitions that enable a government to function, but what particularly distinguishes Will from some of his dogmatic conservative brethren is his acceptance of the accommodations inherent in politics. Occasionally he becomes a prim ideologist, but more often he refuses to join those conservatives who find it "much more fun to be in this splendid isolation . . . , which is where they live."

"All politics takes place on a slippery slope," Will wrote in his 1983 book, *Statecraft as Soulcraft*.

The most important four words in politics are "up to a point." Are we in favor of free speech? Of course—up to a point. Are we for liberty, equality, military strength, industrial vigor, environmental protection, traffic safety? Up to a point. (Want a significant reduction of traffic deaths? Then ban left turns. You say that would be going too far? Then you are for improving traffic safety—but only up to a point.) Those four words may seem to lack intellectual rigor or heroic commitment. . . . But "Up to a point" is one answer to many political questions. Political argument often, perhaps usually, is about degree. It is about the point up to which we want to

go in pursuit of a good that may, at some point, conflict with other goods. . . . There is only one political good that we should not speak of wanting only "up to a point." It is the central political value, justice. But then, justice consists of pursuing other political values—such as freedom and virtue—only up to appropriate points.

Since Will planned to leave the Senate after the 1972 election regardless of the outcome, he telephoned Buckley and asked if the *National Review* needed a Washington editor, a post then vacant. When Buckley offered him the job and word began circulating that Will soon would join *National Review*'s staff, "there was a big brouhaha in a wing of what we shall smilingly call the conservative community—'conservative' it's not very . . . , and 'communal' they are not—which sent a lot of letters to Buckley saying 'You're letting in a left-winger,' and all that stuff," Will recalls.

The fears of the anti-Will wing were soon confirmed—in spades. "The problem was, of course, that almost simultaneously with my coming aboard the *National Review* [in January 1973], Watergate began to unravel," Will says. "I was . . . as quick to decide that Nixon was guilty as anyone, and I think quicker than any journalist writing to say he ought to be impeached. I can tell you the date: it was the fifth of July 1973 . . . I said on the Agronsky program that the failure to superintend subordinates was a Madisonian ground for impeachment and that to search for further 'smoking guns' was unnecessary."

"Mental whiplash is an occupational hazard of reading Nixon's statements these days . . . ," Will wrote in the next issue of *National Review*.

And this whiplash is a matter of historic importance now that Nixon's reputation rests on a fraying web of claims—his and others—that require a willing suspension of disbelief.

Nixon's Watergate statements, considered separately, are . . . dizzying. But they cannot be taken separately, and consumed together they are like sauerkraut ice cream, an indigestible mess. . . .

Such commentary did not endear Will to the readership of *National Review*. Like all magazines, it makes a running survey of its mail. "They had a section called 'Subscription Cancellations and George Will.' They were all together," Will recalls.

Ironically, a few months earlier Will had almost joined Nixon's staff. When Nixon's two top aides, John Ehrlichman and H. R. Haldeman, had been forced to resign in April 1973 because of the spreading scandal, Will's friend General Alexander Haig had become the White House Chief of Staff. He had immediately called Will and asked him if he would go to work at the White House, and Will admits with a nervous chuckle that he "might have gone and done it" had Haig not "delayed a little too long" in pressing the request.

By then Will was a weekly contributor to the *Washington Post*'s Op Ed page. A few weeks after Haig's initial offer of a White House job, "one of his aides called on a Saturday from Camp David and said, 'The General wants to see you on Monday,' and I said, 'You'd better read what's in tomorrow's Sunday *Post*—my views on Watergate—before he commits himself to seeing me,' " Will recalls. "And that was the last I heard of that."

Back in the waning days of Will's career as a Senate aide, and when his impending move to the *National Review* was generally known in Washington's journalistic circles, he met Meg Greenfield, then deputy editor of the *Post*'s Op Ed page, at a conference at Kenyon College. Impressed with his contributions to the conference's discussions,

Greenfield suggested that Will send the *Post* some of his efforts when he began working at the *Review*.

Spiro Agnew was then riding high as the Nixon administration's point man against the press. American newspapers have been overwhelmingly Republican in editorial philosophy for most of this century, but the leading papers nevertheless were acutely discomfited by the administration's charge—alliteratively argued by Agnew—that their commentary was produced by an inbred, isolated elite of Eastern-educated liberals. The two reigning monarchs of the Eastern press, the *New York Times* and the *Washington Post*, began searching for conservative commentators they could call their own. The *Times* went to the source of its discomfort and hired William Safire, a Nixon speechwriter, and in Will the *Post* found what it wanted—it thought.

A year after Will began writing his column, he told *Newsweek* that the *Post* had hired him because it was "looking for someone of my disposition, but I'm not sure they knew what it was." Greenfield, a liberal for whom Will has unalloyed admiration, has said that she finds herself often agreeing with his columns, as do other, somewhat surprised liberals. "He's got an interesting Tory mind," Greenfield said.

Will began writing a thrice-weekly column for the Washington Post Writers Group in September 1973. It appeared initially in 84 newspapers, and within three years it was syndicated in 274 papers. He then trimmed his newspaper contributions to two a week and began a separate, biweekly column for *Newsweek*, which is owned by the *Post* and once printed Walter Lippmann's analyses on its closing page, now alternately occupied by Will and Greenfield, who has since become the paper's editorial page editor. In 1977, at the age of 35, Will won the Pulitzer Prize for commentary. He has led, he says, a "charmed life" in journalism—all too "charmed," in the view of his some of his fellow conservatives and journalists.

Maintaining a siege mentality, some right-wing conservatives consider success of any sort as proof that unseemly compromises were made. Will has failed this and several of their other litmus tests and is deemed suspect. With his refined political philosophy, polished literary style, and academic background, Will might not exactly be a liberal, they concede, but his head is distinctly egg-shaped and perhaps even pointy. He will not abide what he believes are political and moral grotesqueries, even if they come stamped with a right-wing imprimatur. For example, he vigorously supports the (gasp!) welfare state. "The political system must . . . incorporate altruistic motives," he wrote in *Statecraft as Soulcraft*.

It does so in domestic policies associated with the phrase "welfare state." These are policies that express the community's acceptance of an ethic of common provision. It would be misleading were the term "altruistic" to obscure the practicality of such policies. Altruism—principled regard for others—is not optional. It is necessary for strengthening the sense of community that the theory and practice of modern politics attenuates. . . .

For conservatives to doubt the strength and durability of [the welfare state] is intellectually idle and politically feckless. . . .

Such deviations from the right-wing catechism have prompted some prominent conservative commentators to say unpleasant things about Will. Kevin Phillips, a widely syndicated conservative columnist, once called Will the *Washington Post*'s "creature," and Allan H. Ryskind, writing in the periodical *Human Events*, contended that Will "sails under false colors."

If some right-wingers find Will distasteful, the Soviets clearly despise him, and he considers their disgust a badge of honor. They have nominated him, he noted proudly in a 1980 column, for their "gallery of slanderers."

The *Soviet Literary Gazette* has honored me with an attack that is, so experts tell me, remarkably coarse, even considering the source. To its calumny I reply: Sticks and stones may break my bones, but words will never hurt me— although when a Communist says I once was a "run-of-the-mill" professor, he goes beyond what is permissible even in the death-struggle with capitalism.

And Will, of course, is more than capable of giving back much better than he got. In 1978 he wrote:

Since November 8, 1917, every assumption adopted, every premise clung to by people eager to rationalize a policy of accommodation toward the Soviet Union has been shredded by events. Today, the Soviet regime is so grotesquely ignorant and arrogant, so boorish and bullying, that its cruelty and recklessness may awaken Americans from their dogmatic slumber.

He is perhaps the Pentagon's favorite columnist, enthusiastically supporting practically every request the military makes for more weaponry. He believes that for "those who today say that polls prove (in words hurled at Churchill) there is 'no mandate from the people' for more defense spending, Churchill's reply remains unanswerable: 'The prime responsibility of any government for the public safety is absolute and requires no mandate.' " Will is convinced that the atomic megatonnage at the command of America's military is an insufficient deterrent, and he is not persuaded that a nuclear war would obliterate civilization.

"It might. I don't know. We are in a terribly frightening, unexplored landscape.

Look what happened when someone shot the Archduke [Franz Ferdinand of Austria in 1914]: a mechanism of mobilization took hold in Europe, and you had four years of unprecedented carnage. Who knows whether you could stop a nuclear exchange from being general? You certainly don't want to get into a position where you find out. And the only way is to deter. . . . [U.S. arms are] demonstrably not sufficent to deter some things and are getting weaker and weaker.

"Look, if I spend all this money . . . for the Pentagon and I'm wrong, I've wasted some money. If the other guys don't spend it and they're wrong, we lose our freedom. I'd rather waste money."

Not surprisingly, Will ridiculed the policy of détente under both Nixon and Ford. Establishing greater commercial ties to Russia did nothing to curb its aggression in Afghanistan, Africa, Central America, or elsewhere, he contends, and establishing diplomatic relations with Communist China at the expense of Taiwan has produced little or no benefits.

Jimmy Carter, needless to say, never gained Will's approval, in either domestic matters or foreign policy. "A President is disarmed unless he can seize the nation's moral imagination," he wrote in 1978.

Carter cannot seize it with his rhetoric: remarkably, fifty-three years with the King James Bible has not given him a flair for stirring cadences. So he needs all the help he can get from what remains of the nation's reverence for the Presidency. After an Administration of Prussian arrogance and Sicilian corruption, it was fine for Gerald Ford to invite the networks to watch him toast muffins. But in other times, the Presidency should be clothed in majesty, not denim.

Although some of Will's detractors consider him the kept columnist of the Reagan administration, the truth is that he has never

been an uncritical Reagan admirer and would have preferred Tennessee Senator Howard Baker as the Republican candidate in 1980. "He was my first choice," Will says. "I may have been wrong, by the way, in two senses. I may have been wrong [since] the first object in 1980 to me was to change Presidents. I thought Jimmy Carter was unsatisfactory. And I think Baker would have beaten him, but I'm not sure of that. . . . Ronald Reagan had a power to attract Democrats that is rare among Republicans. Any Republican who wins has to attract a fair number of Democrats, but Reagan really was astonishingly good at that. And he's been a good President, all things considered."

Far more controversial—at least among other journalists—than anything Will has written about Reagan has been what he has done, and written, for him. In advance of Reagan's debate with Carter late in the 1980 campaign, Will agreed to a request from the Reagan camp that he help prepare the Republican candidate for the confrontation by asking him some questions at a trial-run session. "They said, 'Come down and ask some questions,' " Will recalls, adding in a strained and not quite persuasive analogy that he does not see any difference between his willingness to do so and the willingness of some other journalists to respond to a presidential request that they participate in what Will calls Carter's "seance" at Camp David prior to his speech lamenting the country's "malaise" in the summer of 1979.

After assisting Reagan in preparing for the debate, Will subsequently "analyzed" Reagan's performance in it for ABC-TV's "Nightline," finding—not surprisingly— that Reagan appeared "more confident, less nervous, and less defensive" than Carter. Will added that he had witnessed Reagan's preparation for the debate "as an observer"; a more candid admission would have revealed his active participation in the rehearsal.

Although Will's presence at Reagan's

debate rehearsal was known at the time, the extent of his role in the trial runs was not. When that was revealed during the controversy over the Reagan campaign's use of pilfered Carter briefing documents, the firm, anti-Holmesian for whom standards are not capricious discovered that many of his fellow journalists thought he had seriously violated the prevailing ones of their profession. (In the immediate aftermath of the brouhaha, seven newspapers, including the conservative *New York Daily News*, dropped Will's column.) Other Will contacts with Reagan also have been questioned by Will's colleagues, and the testy and aloof manner in which he responded to their inquiries and criticisms—he told the *Wall Street Journal* that he thought it "beneath the dignity" of the paper to question his actions—did not enhance his reputation.

Shortly after the 1980 election, Reagan came to Washington to meet with congressional leaders, and in the course of the visit he had dinner at Will's home, along with Vice-president–elect Bush and a number of the capital's elite, including then-Democratic Chairman Robert Strauss and Washington Post Chairman Katharine Graham. Reagan since has returned to the Will home a second time for dinner, when the guest list again included a number of prominent Democrats, and has reciprocated by having Will to dinner at the White House on a number of occasions, sometimes in small, private gatherings with other presidential friends and advisers. And when Reagan was accorded the honor of addressing the British Parliament in 1982, his then-national security adviser, William Clark, sent Will a copy of the State Department's draft of the speech and asked him to try polishing it up. Dismayed at the prose from Foggy Bottom, Will wrote his own speech for Reagan and sent it back to the White House. In 1983, Reagan appointed Will to the nonpaying Board of Visitors of the U.S. Naval Academy and gave Madeleine Will a $68,000-a-year job as an assistant secretary of education.

Among the critics who have scored Will for his presidential hobnobbing and speech writing are cartoonist Gary Trudeau, who devoted two weeks of "Doonesbury" to ridiculing the pre-Inauguration dinner Will gave for Reagan; Mike Royko, who attacked Will for drafting Reagan's address to Parliament; and Jimmy Breslin, who has dubbed him "Will the Shill."

In "Doonesbury," Trudeau had Will describing himself to Rick Redfern, the *Post*'s member of the "Doonesbury" crew, as "just a guy who likes to chow down and chew the fat with the President-elect." In the comic strip version of the dinner, Reagan slips away in the middle of the meal to take a nap but then returns to offer a toast—and a job—to his host: "There are few journalists who would feel it was their duty to help us meet the players in this town. Both Nancy and I are most grateful and, we hope, George, that you will honor us by accepting the post of transition team social director." "What? Oh, no Governor, I couldn't," Trudeau had Will reply, while another dinner guest shouts: "Go for it, George!"

Royko did not pointedly criticize Will for supplying presidential victuals. He himself has been known to break bread and bend elbows with politicians now and then and even has been photographed having lunch with a Chicago alderman. But supplying words for a politician to speak is a much graver matter, in Royko's view.

"Let's say that Mayor Jane Byrne of Chicago has written a speech, but she's not sure about it," Royko postulated in a July 1982 column.

Because I frequently write about Chicago government and politics, let's also say that she asked me to look at it.

Let's say I don't think it is a good speech. So I sit down and write one for her.

Then let's say, she uses my speech, or parts of it.

What's wrong with that? Nothing, now that George Will has explained it.

After all, she is the leader of my city, and am I too grand as a journalist to help a mayor? Am I too noble to perform a service for a mayor?

As Will says, that's silly.

I suppose somebody might ask how I could be an objective observer of the Byrne administration if I were, in effect, part of her administration.

They might say: "Hey, how can I trust what this guy writes about her in his column if he's writing speeches for her on the side?"

My answer—now that Professor Will has shown us the way—would be: "That's silly."

But I'm not sure how that would go over in Chicago. The journalistic tradition in Chicago is that newspapermen try to act like watchdogs.

In Washington, it appears, some are more like lap dogs.

To brand Will a "lap dog" of Reagan is unfair, since he has hardly been an unswerving apologist for Reagan, his policies, or his administration. He has opposed Reagan's call for constitutional amendments to permit prayer in public schools and require a balanced budget; ridiculed the "creative semantics" with which Reagan has sought to disguise tax increases as "user fees" or "revenue enhancers"; decried the administration's refusal to admit that its cuts in social services will cause pain; called for national handgun control, something Reagan opposes; chided the administration on its environmental protection policies; and taken it to task for—believe it or not—being too soft on the Soviets, arguing that the administration "loves commerce more than it loathes communism."

But the issue of journalistic ethics that Royko raised in his typically punchy fashion

is one that bothers many of Will's Washington-based friends and colleagues, too, and Will's reaction to their concern has been unpleasantly flavored with sanctimony and condescension. "George is filled with wit and . . . self-righteousness," Ben Bagdikian has observed. "He thinks he's smarter than anyone else and, therefore, purer than anyone else. But he's neither."

There is no neatly printed, leatherbound, universally accepted journalistic code of ethics to which reporters or columnists can refer for instruction, and the unwritten rules of procedure have changed over the years. While Arthur Krock was on the *New York World* in the 1920s and later while he was at the *Times* he apparently received stock tips in return for serving as a public relations adviser for financier Bernard Baruch, the self-proclaimed "advisor to Presidents"; he also served as a public relations adviser to the banking firm of Dillon, Read. As World War II was drawing to a close in early 1945, both Walter Lippmann and James Reston—working for rival newspapers—believed it was crucial to persuade leading Republicans to abandon their prewar isolationism and support the concept of the United Nations. To do so, they sweet-talked Republican Senator Arthur Vandenberg—a man they both thought vain and pompous—into supporting the United Nations and drafted a statesmanlike speech for him to deliver in the Senate. After Vandenberg, who yearned to be the Republican candidate for President in 1948, used their speech to proclaim his new-found devotion to internationalism, both Lippmann and Reston praised him in print for his wisdom. On other occasions, both before and after the Vandenberg incident, Lippmann served as a behind-the-scenes adviser to a number of presidential candidates. Numerous similar examples could be cited of close personal—and unofficial working—relationships between journalists and politicians in the past.

As is the case in other fields, journalism

has seen its mores change with the times. While even in earlier days some reporters believed that the only way to view politicians was with contempt, now it is generally accepted that an adversary relationship—on a cordial basis if possible; on a cooly correct one if not—is the proper way for the press and government officials to relate. When they were interviewed for this book, both David Broder and James J. Kilpatrick expressed discomfort with the idea that journalists should do anything other than keep a respectful distance from the politicians they cover or comment upon.

"Look, I am not an ethics committee for anybody," said Broder. "I would not do that [help rehearse a candidate or draft a speech]. I think there needs to be a kind of arm's-length relationship with people that you're writing about. It's not easy to maintain that because there are all kinds of human sympathies and shared interests and enthusiasm and so on that reporters and politicians have, but the fact of the matter is that we have very different functions and roles to play. Personally, I'm much more comfortable with that kind of professional relationship. I don't think that people who have a significant role as journalists ought to be campaign advisers, strategists, writers, planners. I think you can do one or the other. . . . But I do think you've got to make a choice."

Kilpatrick, whose experience as a political reporter goes back 40 years, similarly believes that "as a general rule," journalists should not serve as behind-the-scenes advisers to politicians. Although when he was interviewed, Kilpatrick said he preferred to "preserve a diplomatic silence" on the controversy over Will's speech-drafting work for Reagan, he observed with a chuckle: "I haven't written any speeches for Reagan or any other Republican in national office. Years and years ago, when I was editor of the *Richmond News-Leader,* I had a hand in writing an inaugural address for a Virginia

governor, and I later regretted it—although it was a hell of a lot better speech when I got through with it than the one he intended to deliver!"

Later, when the controversy arose over Will's role in assisting Reagan prepare for the debate with Carter, Kilpatrick was sterner in his assessment. On the Agronsky program he bluntly told his friend: "I think it was a mistake, George. I think we should be up in the press box and not down on the field," he added, finding himself in unaccustomed agreement with both Agronsky and Carl Rowan. (Hugh Sidey found nothing wrong with Will's actions.)

Will was not impressed with the doubts expressed over his future ability to maintain a detached, critical eye on Reagan's administration because he invited the President-elect over to his house to have lobster, veal, and raspberry soufflé. The criticisms raised over his subsequent foray into speech drafting left him similarly unmoved, and he has only half-heartedly conceded that it may possibly have been wrong for him to take part in Reagan's debate preparation.

"Is journalistic duty compatible with feelings of friendship between journalists and those political people who do the work of democracy? And will this columnist be as critical of Reagan's Administration as he was of Carter's?" he asked rhetorically in a *Newsweek* piece just prior to Reagan's inauguration.

The answers are: yep, and I certainly hope not. I am moved to expand upon these answers only because journalism (like public service with its "conflict of interest" phonetics) is now infested with persons who are little "moral thermometers," dashing about taking other persons' temperatures, spreading, as confused moralists will, a silly scrupulosity and other confusions.

We all have our peculiar tastes. Some people like Popsicles. Others like Gothic novels. I like politicians. A journalist once said that the only way for a journalist to look at a politician is down. That is unpleasantly self-congratulatory. A journalist's duty is to see politicians steadily and see them whole. To have intelligent sympathy for them, it helps to know a few as friends. Most that I know are overworked and underpaid persons whose characters can stand comparison with the characters of the people they represent, and of journalists.

Friendship between journalists and politicians offends persons who consider a mean edge the only proof of "candor" in writing about politicians. . . . But friendship, including relaxation in social settings, reduces the journalist's tendency to regard politicians as mere embodiments of ideas or causes, as simple abstractions rather than complicated human beings. The leavening of friendship may take some of the entertaining savagery from our politics, but, then, politics has not recently suffered from an excess of civility. . . .

Will predicted, correctly, that the Reagan administration would be incapable of "unflagging worship at the altar of Will's creed" and therefore would get some lumps from him. He cited with approval the examples of Reston and Lippmann's "public-spirited involvement" in the affairs of presidents and senators, writing that "Lippmann was, Reston is, a citizen too: a citizen first." The chastising he received from Royko and others because he worked on Reagan's Parliamentary address seems to Will to ignore his own rights—and obligations—as a "citizen first."

"[The White House] sent me . . . a copy of a speech that would have been a national embarrassment," he says. "It was a classic State Department piece of work. So I called back and said I can't help you with this, [but] I could write you another speech. I said I'll write a speech that I would like to

see given on a great state occasion, not a partisan occasion. It would have been different if he'd been out attacking Democrats. This was a signal honor; [Reagan was] only the second non-Briton in history invited to address the Commons. So for a state occasion I saw no problem, and I still don't. . . . It would seem to be a moral problem if you believe that journalists should be hermetically sealed from all civic concerns. That's perfect rubbish. I mean, to state the problem is to see it's no problem."

Will objects to what he considers the unwarranted belief among many members of Washington's press corps "that journalists are not only custodians of the country's virtue but are themselves singularly virtuous and that they are in this relentless adversary posture toward the civil arrangements of the government, which is presumed to be the reverse; that is, it is presumed to be basically vicious, duplicitous [and] of a lower moral order." He thinks talk about an "adversary relationship" between reporters and politicians is "adolescent."

"It's sort of a hairy-chested view of journalism," he says. "Second it's awfully self-flattering in the end; it makes journalism more heroic than it ought to want to be. It's not heroism doing what we do. It's a profession like a lot of others . . . [and] unlike most others, in that it doesn't have a professional education; it doesn't have a clear professional standard of ethics. There's a sense in which we're not a profession, I suppose. We're a craft."

Regardless of whether the graduates of the journalism schools at Columbia, Northwestern, Missouri, and numerous other universities and colleges around the country have been taught a craft or a profession, they would undoubtedly agree with Will that they did not surrender their citizenship papers when they accepted their journalism degrees. But many of them also have been taught to believe that their most valuable service as citizens is rendered when they perform their critical, skeptical, and detached work as journalists with the sort of "scrupulosity" that Will does not find silly when it is applied to precepts of which he approves and which he more often than not employs himself in his commentary.

Ironically, Will notes that much of the Parliamentary speech that he wrote for Reagan ended up on the cutting room floor. "In the end, he didn't take my advice," Will says with a shrug. What did remain were a few (naturally) appropriate quotations from Winston Churchill; some eloquent historical citations; and stirring praise for the courage of Poland and its Solidarity movement— sentiments that Polish-American Mike Royko probably would be proud to have a President of the United States express.

A corollary to Will's disdain for the homage paid to the adversary relationship between the press and politicians in Washington is his dismay over the practice government bureaucrats have of leaking information to the press in order to promote their side in policy debates. He expresses sympathy with the frustration over leaks expressed by Reagan—who he says was used to a more genteel atmosphere in Sacramento. In taking the President's side over leaks, Will almost assumes the awkward position of an anti-journalist journalist, a Washington commentator who spurns the procedure by which so much news in the capital is generated and which the White House itself employs when it suits its purposes. As David Broder observed:

Time after time, in administration after administration, colleagues and I have sat in the office of some senior official who, promised anonymity, has divulged the substance of, or even read from, highly classified documents. The purpose, in almost every case, was to advance the President's policy line—in Vietnam, in some international negotia-

tion, or in dealing with a domestic political fight. No President that I can recall ever has gotten sore about the resulting stories, which used classified information to buttress the argument the President wanted publicized.

The bureaucratic wars that are fought with leaks "make for good journalism," Will says, but he believes that journalists are "being used" in the process. "The way our government operates is sufficiently carnivorous and ruthless in its internal struggles that is seems to me the first worry for a citizen— and the constant point is that you have to think as a citizen at all times—is that it is more important to have orderly, civilized, candid, and reasonable government than it is to have entertaining journalism."

The case of a reporter burrowing into the bureaucracy and sniffing out a story "is not the same thing as bureaucrats who are losing a battle leaking [information] to carry the battle into the public arena, using the front page of the *Washington Post* as a bulletin board. That's not the same thing," Will says.

"It seems to me in government you have two things: you have to have the ability to have privacy, so that people will speak their minds without fear that it's going to appear in print; then you have to have due process. There has to be a way of making decisions and once the decisions get made, they stick; that you don't lose and say, 'Well, that's the end of Phase One, now we'll fight it out in a new kind of guerrilla welfare.' That's extremely sapping to the collegiality of government, to the sense of orderliness in government."

But Will also finds himself bothered by some of the Reagan administration's more draconian efforts to stem the flow of leaks. When the President signed an executive order requiring hundreds of thousands of federal employees with security clearances to submit to lie detector tests in any investigation of leaks or face "adverse consequences," Will dissented.

"No one needs to be for leaks to be opposed to this policy," he said the following Sunday on ABC's "This Week With David Brinkley." "The problem with lie detectors is (a) they're unreliable; (b) they're an indignity. The trouble with leaks is they destroy the atmosphere of trust in government, and a lie detector system is going to do the same thing."

Even if lie detectors were infallible, Will doubts that he would favor such a practice, in part because he does not think it would be applied without fear or favor. The most devastating leaks, he readily agrees, almost never come from lower-level functionaries. "The ship of state, it has been said, leaks from the bridge. One of the things I want to know is if [Reagan's top aides] are going to be strapped up to these machines in the event of embarrassing leaks," he said with a skeptical laugh.

Will has a penetrating, intimidating intellect. Even during relaxed, friendly conversations, he can fix a companion with the gimlet gaze of his pale blue eyes, made smaller and cooler by thick eyeglasses, and speak in a manner that an interviewer once described as "erudite, opinionated, irritating, witty, appealing and stunningly blunt."

It is natural, of course, for Will or any other columnist to be "opinionated." Opinions are what they are paid to have and express. But Will has a way of expressing his opinions that many find awe-inspiring, a bit chilling, and occasionally annoying. There is a touch of arrogance in his tendency to preface an observation by saying that when an issue or concept is "properly understood," it should be viewed as he sees it. Somehow that implies that those who disagree with him may either be slightly stupid or willful nincompoops.

Will is not likely to change his mannerisms, but he quickly acknowledges that there are many honorable views other than

his own. "I write about the difficulties and complexities of issues," he points out. "When I take a position, I have a premise that I try to make clear, and I try to make clear the steps by which I go from the premise to the conclusion—and I'm not going to adopt an 'Aw, shucks, I stepped on my shoelaces' attitude. . . . Some people have said I talk in paragraphs. When I talk, it comes out clearly, and I think that sometimes people confuse that; that sort of gives me, they think, an aura of unbecoming certainty—for which I do not apologize."

There is much in Will's writing that appeals to readers who would not classify themselves as "conservative" and much that makes right-wing Americans apoplectic. Conservatives, he says, rapping his desk top with his fist, "have got to quit *yimmering* the way they do, in this kind of Yahoo way, about 'big government' and regulations are always wrong and government should never intrude and all that. Those are not useful governing axioms. . . . As Gary Hart said, you cannot love your country if you hate your government. He's right. Government is, in many ways, the embodiment of collective aspirations, the codification of ongoing national values. It's not ugly!

"I don't know what conservatives think [in the spring] when the school buses start arriving, and you see them parked like a great, colorful snake all the way around the Capitol and down Pennsylvania and Constitution avenues; and you see all summer long as Mom and Dad in their Bermuda shorts and Hush Puppies, and the kids with their cameras over their shoulders, come to Washington. They don't come here as to a hostile province, and they don't come here to look at the enemy; they come here as on a pilgrimage. They come here with their eyes full of wonder and pleasure and awe and respect. *Americans don't hate their government*."

Some may think such talk implies that

Will is more moderate politically than they previously thought. They would be wrong. "I'm more conservative than a lot of people think, also," he says. "What looks to you like moderate is, I'm tellin' ya, true conservatism. On national security policy and defense, I'm well to the right; on the welfare state, I think I'm where conservatives are. I do not think it's conservative to oppose the welfare state. But I'm not far away from where the country is, as a matter of fact, right now. . . ."

Will, perhaps more than any columnist since Walter Lippmann, is a political philosopher, bred and trained. In the view of James J. Kilpatrick, he may be the only journalist capable of filling the rarefied position Lippmann once held in public and political esteem. Will's aim is not just to comment on and elucidate current affairs; he would prefer nothing less than "to change . . . the vocabulary of contemporary politics."

At the core of Will's political philosophy is the conviction that the only way this nation can survive is by, in Lincoln's words, "the best cultivation of the physical world, beneath and around us, and the intellectual and moral world within us." We have cultivated the physical world with unrelenting zeal, Will says, but have dangerously neglected the "moral world."

I t will be said, instantly and energetically and broadly, that "sentiments, manners and moral opinions" are none of the government's business. Are they not "private" and properly beyond the legitimate concern of public agencies? No, they are not.

Keats said the world is a "vale of soul-making." I say statecraft is soulcraft. Just as all education is moral education because learning conditions conduct, much legislation is moral legislation because it conditions the action and the thoughts of the nation in broad and important spheres of life.

It is generally considered obvious that government should not, indeed cannot legislate morality. But in fact it does so, frequently; it should do so more often; it never does anything more important. By the legislation of morality I mean the enactment of laws and implementation of policies that proscribe, mandate, regulate, or subsidize behavior that will, over time, have the predictable effect of nurturing, bolstering or altering habits, dispositions and values on a broad scale. . . .

The aim of government is justice, which is more apt to come about if government is more aware of, and forthright about, the fact that statecraft is, inevitably, soulcraft. Therefore it is odd, though explicable, that so many intelligent people say government cannot or should not do what, in fact, it does in manifest and manifold ways.

Will instructs those conservatives who fume at the intrusion of the welfare state in their lives that two nineteenth-century conservatives, Disraeli and Bismarck, "pioneered the welfare state, and did so for impeccably conservative reasons: to reconcile the masses to the vicissitudes and hazards of a dynamic and hierarchical industrial economy. . . . A welfare state is implied by conservative rhetoric. A welfare state can be an embodiment of a wholesome ethic of common provision."

One of the questions that concerns Will most is whether American conservatives—who may be gathering more political strength now than in 50 years—will be able to "come to terms with a social reality more complex than their slogans." In *Statecraft as Soulcraft* he wrote:

F or nearly half a century, conservatism was, or felt itself to be, in the political wilderness. Although there were some conservative Presidents and some conservative legislating majorities in Congress during this period, conservatism generally was a doctrine in, and of, opposition. During this period it became cranky and recriminatory. Therefore, the question posed by the coming to power of self-conscious conservatism is: Can there be conservatism with a kindly face?

In private dealings, and on many public issues, Will himself has a "kindly face," although his external expression often is thin-lipped and priggish. For example, he has written movingly of a Catholic charity group in Chicago that aids the elderly (and urged his readers to contribute to it); a Nevada home for abused children; and the struggles of the doctors and institutions that try to minister to disabled Americans, as well as the internal struggles their patients face every day:

W̲ere Americans to curtail handguns and limit drunk driving substantially, the burden on rehabilitation resources would be vastly reduced. . . . A walk through the [Rehabilitation Institute of Chicago's] physical-therapy rooms is an antidote to sterile libertarian arguments against passive restraints in automobiles (airbags, for example) or laws requiring seat belts. Such laws, common in Europe, would . . . contribute more than any other single measure to reducing the soaring expenditure on rehabilitative medicine. . . .
Children in the institute are disproportionately black. Being conceived in the ghetto is hazardous to your health. Unhealthy factors can include your mother's diet, your pre- and postnatal care, the lead contents in your home's interior paint and the ambience of the street and other places of play. In allocating risks, life is severely regressive. . . .
Most of our lives are as soft as soufflés. It is hard for the hale to realize that even the strongest body is a twig easily broken by the sharp edges of life. Charles Dickens, who had the painful gift of

empathy and a genius for awakening empathy in others, wrote: "There are many lives of much pain, hardship, and suffering, which, having no stirring interest for any except those who lead them, are disregarded by persons who do not want thought or feeling, but who pamper their compassion and need high stimulation to rouse it." The institute's work, like Dickens's fiction, is such a stimulant.

Will is, behind his small, impassive *Gioconda*-like grin, a person with the rare talent to feel the insecurity, fear, and distress of others. As Carll Tucker, of the *Saturday Review*, noted, while Will "would have one perceive him as a misanthrope, an owlish, cranky relic of some simpler era," his columns actually reveal "a decent, gentle, companionable man, aware of the complexity of events and pained by the pain of others":

T̲he world's most serious shortage is, we are told, energy. Or protein, Or democracy. Or something. Most nominees for the title of Most Serious Shortage are arguable, but my nominee is better. It is imagination. I mean imagination of a particular kind: the kind that produces social sympathy—the ability to comprehend, however dimly, how other people live. I don't mean just people in other cultures or neighborhoods, but also neighbors who have sick children and other private worries. . . .
I know perhaps six adults really well; I am endlessly surprised at their depths, mysteries and courage. And surely there comes a moment when every parent rocks back on his or her heels, figuratively speaking, and exclaims, "What a complicated creature a four year old is!" It is extraordinary how extraordinary the ordinary person is.

Those readers—and assuredly there are many—who are tempted to dismiss Will as the child of a moderately affluent family;

untempered by war (he was never even drafted); accustomed to the high-perk life in Washington; and all too comfortably settled into his conservatism because the harsh realities of life have not touched him would be wrong.

In April 1980, Will wrote a searing piece for *Newsweek* about the case in California of a retarded child with Down's syndrome, a chromosomal defect commonly called Mongolism, whose parents refused to permit heart surgery that would save the youngster from a slow, painful, premature death. The parents, who had institutionalized the child since its infancy, convinced the courts that the boy, named Phillip, should not be subjected to a "risky" operation, since it might kill him or, worse yet, save him. If he outlived them, he might receive inadequate care, they argued, and extending his life was useless, since it was inherently not worth living, they said.

Just when society is beginning to acknowledge an obligation to nurture the significant fulfillment of even the limited potentialities of retarded citizens . . . , [this] case works to cast those citizens into legal limbo as less than persons with a full right to life.

My aim is not to demonstrate the demonstrable: that respect for parental sovereignty has here been carried to absurd, not to mention lethal, lengths, unthinkable were Phillip not retarded. . . . My aim is to stress this: the idea that the value of human life varies with intelligence is an idea at war with our civilization's core belief in the intrinsic and equal value of lives. . . .

It is often said that someone "suffers" from Down's syndrome. But Down's people lead happy lives when parents and other friends allow their lives to be enriched by loving and being loved by them. . . .

The Down's child I know best is 7. He is learning to read but prefers "Happy Days," the Washington Bullets and the

Baltimore Orioles. These impeccable tastes help explain why neighborhood children treat him as what he, like Phillip, is: a boy.

A few weeks later, a *Newsweek* reader in Denver wrote the magazine: "Will's column was a simplistic comment on a very complex problem. To assume that raising a child with abnormal brain capacities is enriching is rather idealistic. . . . Unless you have experienced the crushing responsibility of a 24-hour-a-day job, you have no idea of the emotional and physical drain placed on a family."

But Will does know. A year and a half later, after surrogate parents had won custody of the retarded boy in California and the child's natural parents had sued Will (and others who reported the story) for libel, he concluded a follow-up column about the case by revealing the identity of "the Down's child I know best":

"Jonathan Will, 9, trout fisherman and Orioles fan, has Down's syndrome."

In Will's study, the quiet tintinnabulation of the bell on his telephone serves as a constant counterpoint to the music from his stereo set. Having been reared in an academic family in which his father regularly worked at home, Will says that following the same procedure always seemed natural to him. "I save a full working day a week by not commuting and by not having Washington lunches," he says. Abstinence from those renowned midday rituals of the capital also enables Will to keep his 5-feet, 11-inch frame at a relatively trim 154 pounds.

The only persons who can regularly command his attendance at lunch are his children, Jonathan, now 12, Geoffrey, 10; and Victoria, 3, named in honor of the queen whose era Will reveres. "My philosophy of life can be put in five words: 'The world needs another Victoria,'" he likes to say—and he is unabashedly proud of having provided it with one. Will and his children usually go out to lunch on Saturdays, patronizing the same fast-food emporia which have provided fodder for his column. He has one of the finest traits a parent can possess: an understanding of his children's sense of wonder, combined with a refusal to talk down to them. "The age of reason comes early to my children," he says.

The home in which Will works is a large, rambling, 83-year-old house that began as a small cottage in what then were the rural outskirts of Washington, in Chevy Chase, Maryland. It since has grown prodigiously, like the enterprises of its current owner.

Will is up before dawn and works every day. He described himself in a column as a classic "Type A" person who is always " 'thinking of or doing two things at once' (Only two?)" and plays "nearly every game to win, even when playing with children." Until a few years ago, Will did not even employ a secretary but used numerous "electronic gadgets, all of which in theory I disapprove of." These still include a machine that answers the telephone when he is out and a Betamax that tapes the network news programs so he can watch them at his convenience. He answered all of his own calls and would curtly, indeed waspishly, cut short unproductive conversations and turn down speaking engagements. He would say by way of apology: "Most people don't answer their own telephones, and they have secretaries to tell people these abrupt things. But I do it myself."

Now he has an assistant, Dusa Gyllensvard, a British-trained secretary who does research for him and politely but firmly handles the telephone and tells callers "abrupt things" on Will's behalf. His wife Madeleine has her own secretary and is just as busy. Until her appointment to the post in the federal department of education, she lobbied for the Maryland Association of Retarded Citizens, and in that capacity she was, Will once wrote, "what Boss Tweed would have been if he had really meant business."

The telephone is both Will's master and his servant. "The telephone is the clearest confirmation of Thoreau's belief that we become the tools of our tools," he says, confirming in turn that his conversation is as sprinkled with literary references as his column. "But without the telephone I couldn't work at home." Nor could he work as efficiently. Sources who call and ask to meet him for lunch are quizzed on the telephone instead. "If they'd take two minutes on the telephone instead of two hours at lunch, they'd get all their information out," Will says.

One Friday afternoon, Will was chaffing at the prospect of having to submit to one of the indignities of celebrity: he had been "auctioned off by the Opera Society" during a fund-raising campaign and had not only to go to a Washington lunch but to consume it with total strangers. He had no idea how much he fetched as a trophy and rather wished he had an opportunity to give the opera fund the money himself.

A source called and—predictably—wanted to have lunch with him. "Buy me," Will replied.

As he chatted with one caller and then another, Will rummaged through clippings from the *Post*, the *New York Times*, and the *Wall Street Journal*, stacked with a semblance of neatness on his desk, and jotted down notes on a yellow legal pad with a large, gold-pointed Mont Blanc fountain pen christened "The Diplomat" by its West German manufacturer.

With one caller he digresses: What is the "real, essential George Will car?" Le Car by Renault. "It's dumb, dumpy. That's me," Will says with a chuckle. He admits that the cornerstone of American capitalism, the automobile industry, receives little support from him. He kept his last car until it was 13 years old. This, he insisted in a column, was only in keeping with "a Will tradition. My father drove a Model A until 1953, when I betrayed embarrassment by asking him to let me out a block from the Little League field."

After the telephone calls and the note-taking, periodically interrupted by visits from his children (one of whom insists on sitting upon his lap during part of his conversation with an acquaintance), Will hopped in a cab and went to meet his owners-for-the-day from the Opera Society. Following lunch, Will hustled over to the northwest Washington television station owned by the *Post*, WDVM, where he and three other Washington-based columnists tape "Agronsky and Company," the popular discussion program chaired by Martin Agronsky, an old Washington hand of pronounced liberal persuasion, with whom Will exchanges good-natured but pointed banter.

On Friday mornings, Agronsky may talk on the telephone with Will and the other regulars on the program—James J. Kilpatrick, Carl Rowan, and Hugh Sidey, Washington bureau chief for *Time*—in order to decide what topics will be covered at that afternoon's taping. But basically the subjects are confined to the news of the week, "and we all know what that is," Will explains.

Despite the informality, Will prepares for the show like a graduate student priming for oral examinations. Anticipating a discussion of taxes, Will made an effort before lunch to talk with a Republican senator well versed in such measures; the senator and he finally chatted over the phone hurriedly as Will sat in a communal dressing room at the television station just prior to the taping session. The results of the cramming session were mixed. Will cited some statistics with characteristic certitude at one point, then realized he had botched them and had to backtrack to correct the errors. He was furious with himself after the show.

Will also is an analyst for ABC News and appears every Sunday morning on its program "This Week with David Brinkley." Frequently the language Will uses in discussing the weekly topics on the Brinkley and Agronsky programs will bear a marked resemblance to his recent columns, which should come as no surprise. The points and phraseology in the columns are the products of slow, meticulous craftsmanship, and once a phrase is well-wrought, little can be gained by reworking it. Briefness and precision are an asset on television, too.

Will spends a full day writing his 750-word newspaper columns and a day and a half composing his slightly longer pieces for *Newsweek*. He writes in a scrawling longhand with his fountain pen, counting the words when he's done and trimming with a vengeance if necessary. He writes with a fountain pen "for the fun of feeling thoughts become sentences," and he considers "the rushing typewriter, with its clackety-clack rhythm . . . , an enemy of well-crafted sentences." When he has finished filling several sheets of yellow legal paper with the wavy lines of black ink that pass for his handwriting, he will type the finished product.

At first, Will's columns in the *Post* were printed in a space that could accommodate 1,200 words. "When the column was syndicated, I resented—intensely and wrongly and briefly—being urged to adopt a 700-word limit," Will recalls. Although he has "no solid empirical basis for my opinion," he now believes that "700 words fit the attention span of busy newspaper readers. And I know that 700 words carefully chosen can do the work of 1,200 words not so carefully chosen."

Will now writes a 750-word column because "almost everyone else does" and it is "more fun." But higher than that he won't venture. Will greatly admires *Newsday*'s resident liberal, Murray Kempton, "the first hero I had as a columnist, and probably the last," who produces "elegant and satisfying" pieces in a spartan 650 words. "It's the old story of Pascal, who said, 'I'm sorry about the long letter. I didn't have time to write a short one.' It's much harder to write [less] and get the job done."

Will's columns often do not conform to the traditional pattern of Washington commentary. Early in his career as a column writer, his eye settled on an article in the *Post* that smacked of "the pop sociology they periodically fall into" and dealt with "a young couple with no children, both of them working, living in Reston, Virginia, and 'making do' on $30,000 a year in suburban Washington—one of those things.

"So I just sat down and dashed off a light-hearted column about what would happen if Dave Broder drops by to see how things are going with George and Madeleine Will in this less glamorous setting. And I sent it in, and Meg put one of her inspired headlines on it, called 'At Home with George and Madeleine,' and my phone rang off the hook all day.

"It was the first time I'd had any significant response to a column—this was in May of '73—and people said, 'Gosh, we're passing it around the State Department, this is terrific fun,' and it struck me that people want to read about a lot of things other than the conversation of the capital.

"That is how most columnists through the ages have viewed the Washington columnist's job, which is to reflect—promptly—the conversation of the capital. I believe that most of the conversation of the capital should never have taken place in the first place, and certainly should not be preserved, and thirdly is far too perishable to last even four or five days to get into a column. And besides, people should not be encouraged in this monomania about Washington politics that we in Washington suffer from but, infectious diseases spreading as they do, the whole country's apt to suffer from sooner or later."

As a consequence, Will finds his subject matter in "not what is secret, but what is latent, the kernel of principle and other significance that exists, recognized or not,

inside events, actions, policies and manners. By manners I mean 'conduct in its moral aspect,' the way people address one another in conversation and through culture, the way they rear children and educate, inform, and entertain themselves. The agreeableness of a society, and of the people who bear its impress, depends as much on the manners that prevail as on the politicians who prevail," Will wrote in the introduction to the first collection of his columns printed in 1978. (A second anthology was published in 1982.)

Like any gifted teacher, Will has the ability to make supposedly dry subjects sparkle by the application of wit and erudition, including an astonishing (and occasionally overused) reservoir of appropriate quotations from sources as diverse as Yogi Berra, Oscar Wilde, Bertrand Russell, and the Bible. Unlike the essentially perishable work of many columnists, most of Will's essays age gracefully. The passage of time does little to dull their edge, and many of the pieces "read as well after the heat of events as during. Sometimes better," observed Carll Tucker of the *Saturday Review*.

Readers often seek to compliment Will by telling him that what they like best about his wide-ranging columns is their "unpredictability." It is a sentiment that he appreciates but does not accept. "If they knew the mind of an 1842 Oxford Movement Tractarian,*

*In case the gentle reader, like the gentle writer, was absent from school the day the Oxford Movement was discussed, brief recourse to an encyclopedia or two would reveal that its members sought to revive the early Catholic ideas underpinning the Church of England, which they believed had become too "popularly" Protestant. The movement's precepts were most eloquently delineated in a series entitled *Tracts for the Times*, written by John Henry Newman, an Anglican cleric who eventually converted to Catholicism and became a cardinal. Newman, a gifted poet and essayist, is one of Will's "pinups"; his portrait is hung on a wall facing Will's desk.

not a thing about me would be unpredicta-
ble. That is, if you say a thinker is unpre-
dictable, you're saying he's random, that he
just sort of gets up in the morning and has
no firm foundation, no roots driven into the
soil of philosophic understanding.

"I'm not that. . . . After all, I spent nine
years in institutions of higher learning being
educated at tremendous cost of other people's money and my time and with a specific
direction toward political philosophy, so
I'm—for better or ill—philosophically
inclined."

There is a distinct difference in Will's
view between being a "predictable" columnist and a "tired" one. "To be 'predictable'
is one thing; what people complain about
when they say someone's 'predictable' is
that either there's no subtlety to the philosophic lens through which he refracts the
world or that there's no reflection on his part
at all, there's something visceral or instinc-
tive—hence the use of the word *knee-jerk*,
which refers, after all, to a reflex that by-
passes the brain. . . . And I don't think
I'm like that. In some ultimate sense, any
self-respecting thinker has to insist that he's
predictable."

Being "tired," however, is an entirely different matter, and an occupational hazard all
columnists face. "This is a terribly difficult
job," Will says. "It's the easiest thing in the
world, probably, to write a 750-word,
grade-B column day after day. But I don't
write grade-B columns, I'm just going to
insist. It's very awkward to talk this way but
I must. Pride is my favorite of all the cardinal sins. Pride is the best, because it has
some socially useful consequences in some
of its forms. You can't put as much as I put
in front of as many people as I put it and
have any pride unless you work at it very
hard. When people get tired, the evidence is
that they don't know what to write about,
that they're the slave to the march of
events."

Will's columns don't "follow the news in

lock step," and he appears to have an inexhaustible supply of column ideas. "I keep a
list in my desk of topics I want to write
about, and the list gets longer and longer
and longer. I genuinely wish I wrote in
Newsweek every week and wrote three
columns a week for the newspapers . . .
because there're so many things to write
about."

And writing itself—the agony part of the
creative ecstasy that so many writers
dread—is for Will pure joy. "I can't imagine becoming tired of writing. . . . I love to
write. When I get on an airplane in Los
Angeles heading east, before the plane's
over Nevada, I've put aside my book and
turned the movie off and I'm writing. It's
fun to me; it's what I'd choose to do on my
vacation if my wife would let me."

Will revels in his work because he
believes he has the best job in the world—or
at least the fourth best. "There are three
better jobs. One is Chief Justice of the
Supreme Court; one is Pope; and the other
is President. The President's third because
you can't keep it as long. The people can
change a President; only God can change
Chief Justices and Popes. But I have the
fourth best job. I'm paid to think and read
books and talk to people who interest me
and do things that interest me in my own
time, in my own place. It's fantastic."

Several prominent Republicans in Maryland, wishing to revitalize the nearly mori-
bund Republican party in their state, sought
to persuade Will to run for the Senate in
1982. He turned them down largely for
practical reasons. Maryland is as predomi-
nately Democratic as any state in the Union,
and Will is convinced that the name recognition he has earned by virtue of his column
and television appearances would not be
enough to overcome the antipathy many
Maryland voters would have to any Republican running for office. In addition, a number of Will's friends in the Senate told him
that he'd be crazy to relinquish the power he

has as a columnist just to become one of 100 senators.

"I think politicians generally tend to exaggerate the influence of columnists and journalists, but one [Senator] did say that 90 of them would trade places with me tomorrow," Will says with a slight smile.

But Will has not ruled out running for office sometime, and the Senate, in which he loved working as an aide, has a special appeal. "This comes back to what I said about journalists in general: you are a citizen first, and who in the world is going to say he's too grand or too comfortable or too important or too influential to serve in public office, to help write the laws for a free people? That's not the way anyone ought to talk.

"On the other hand, it's equally unbecoming for someone to sit around and say—which I want to emphasize I'm not sitting around and saying—that there's any ground

swell urging me to get out of what I'm doing and into something else," he adds with a chuckle. "I'm a journalist and intend to remain one."

For now, it appears that few things, if any, could tempt Will to abandon his idyllic calling, save one of the three better positions that precede it in his estimation. But since he is an Episcopalian and lacks a law degree, Pope and Chief Justice seem beyond his grasp. The Senate, he has written, is a hothouse of Presidential ambition, so is it possible that his ultimate aim is the White House? He sets predictably strict requirements.

"If, in the nineteenth-century manner, a convention sends a delegation to my house and asks me to be their presidential nominee, I will accept. But they'll have to come to my house," he says with a laugh, "as everyone else does."

Afterword

He knew Harding. He knew Coolidge. He knew Hoover. He was one of that small, fortunate fraternity of journalists who clustered around Franklin D. Roosevelt's trinket-cluttered desk to question and trade quips with the jaunty squire from Hyde Park. He was jostled and parboiled on the train carrying Harry Truman on his give-'em-hell whistlestop campaign. He knew Eisenhower, both as General and President. He knew Kennedy (hell, he'd known his father). He knew Johnson from his days as a young, New Deal congressman. He knew—and thoroughly disliked—Nixon. He covered the pleasant Gerald Ford and the curious Jimmy Carter. Now he is squirming in his front-row, reserved seat on the Reagan administration, the 12th sequel to a show he has been reviewing for over 60 years.

He was, as self-described, "the oldest living columnist," and most of his readers didn't even know his name. It is Richard L. Strout, but from 1943 to 1983 his crisp, fuming observations of chief executives and Congresses were syndicated by the *New Republic* under the nom de plume "TRB."

The origins of the pseudonym are vague. When the column began in 1925, it was the work of several reporters who wished to remain anonymous. Some say the title was created from the initials of a well-known typeface, Times Roman Bold; others argue that it is a transposition of the initials of a New York subway system; another theory is that it stands for The Rover Boys, characters in a series of juvenile adventure stories to whom the early writers of the column were jokingly compared.

No matter, really. For 40 years it was an open secret in Washington that TRB was Richard Strout, a perennially enraged, compassionate, devoutly liberal foe of cant, injustice, and stupidity, whether in government or society. Contrary to the stereotype of an aging liberal, his views becoming constricted and rigid as his arteries harden, Strout remains quintessentially—indeed pugnaciously—progressive. "I just want to preserve our democracy," he says simply.

Strout chugged into Washington in a Model T Ford in 1923, a lean six-footer with a bachelor's and a master's degree from Harvard and four years as a reporter in England and Boston under his belt. He was being dispatched to the Washington bureau of the *Christian Science Monitor*, a respected, Boston-based international paper which he had joined in 1921. The column writing for the *New Republic* became a sideline 20 years later and always remained one. He still reports on Washington for the *Monitor*, rapidly tapping out stories on an old typewriter beside his original rolltop desk, which now is located in a small cubicle inside the paper's modern office a few blocks from the White House. Although he says he has "shrunk" with age, Strout exhibits only a slight paunch and stoop. He has the snowy eyebrows and clipped mustache of an elderly British guardsman. At 86, he retains the fire—if not, perhaps, the fleeting feet—of a young reporter. In a 1975 address to the National Press Club, Strout sternly advised his colleagues: "When the adrenaline runs low, when the little flame of anger flickers out, I think it is time for the reporter to think about going into some more remunerative form of work!"

Like all reporters, Strout has his favorite anecdotes about his beat. He likes to recall his first presidential press conference, with the affable Harding, snappily attired in knickers, standing behind his desk in the Oval Office and imploring the reporters to treat him gently because he wanted to go out and play golf. Strout attended practically all of Roosevelt's 998 press conferences and most of his major speeches and considers FDR the greatest chief executive of the twentieth century. He recalls places and events as well as people. One indelible image, which often recurred in Strout's columns about national crises, is of the stunned, worried crowd gathered outside the south gate of the White House on the chill, moonlit night following the Japanese attack on Pearl Harbor. They tried to sing "America the Beautiful" but couldn't. He also speaks of the scene on D-day, when he stood aboard the USS *Quincy* and watched troops wading onto the Normandy beaches.

As he teetered back and forth on his swivel chair, Strout's mind drifted back to another, much earlier event that he covered which seemed innocuous enough at the time but has had just as profound an effect on our lives. He recalls accompanying Herbert Hoover, who then was the Secretary of Commerce, to a small brick building at 1208 H Street in northwest Washington on April 7, 1927, for the first public demonstration of television.

On a tiny screen "we saw a little man about the size of a picture postcard who was speaking to us from New York, and Hoover was returning the call," Strout remembers. The next day the *New York Times* carried a front-page story headlined: "Far-Off Speakers Seen As Well As Heard Here In A Test Of Television." But there was a subheadline that Strout recalls with special relish. It read: "Commercial Use In Doubt." "It's ironic, isn't it?" he says with a grin.

Many newspaper people and columnists probably wish Strout had used the heel of his shoe to kick in the tiny screen and kill the monster in its cradle. Their anger over the role television has played in the decline of newspapers may be justified, but the fears some have expressed about the future of their medium may be unwarranted. Videotex, teletext,* cable, and computer systems may take over the delivery of some information now carried in newspapers, but it is likely that newspapers will remain an important means of news distribution and analyses and that syndicated columnists will continue performing their crucial task as interpreters of events. Fewer national "stars" may emerge from their ranks, syndicate chiefs and media analysts say, but the significance of those who do attain that status should not diminish.

Prognostication is a dicey business, especially in a field where the use of new technology still is in the experimental stage and the industry itself is in transition. During 1982, 11 daily newspapers folded, 9 merged, and 4 became weeklies. Across the

---

*Videotex is a system in which the viewer's home computer terminal is connected directly to a central computer system, which theoretically can supply or receive an unlimited amount of information. It is a two-way system. Teletext is a system whereby a more limited choice of information and services is conveyed to the home through a conventional television signal, which is decoded by a device attached to the television. It is a one-way system.

country, an estimated 300,000 homes were wired for cable television each month. The average American watches five and one-half hours of television a day, and two-thirds of our population say they now rely on television as their main source of news. Yet more newspapers have gained circulation than lost, with major metropolitan dailies growing an average 8 percent on weekdays and 5 percent on Sundays, and the number of papers in the country remains about what it was 25 or 30 years ago, despite the foldings and mergers. The dazzling promises of cable TV—with its multiple channels and a cornucopia of offerings—remain as yet unfulfilled. The potential of videotex, teletext, and home computer services as means of conveying in-depth news is difficult to predict. "It is possible to provide lengthy stories on a video screen," one industry analyst noted, "but it is enervating to read them."

Nevertheless, media giants are experimenting with—and investing heavily in—new technologies. CBS, Inc., and AT&T have joined forces in an experimental electronics publishing enterprise; NBC, Time Inc., Knight-Ridder, Times Mirror, and Taft Broadcasting all are delving into the business of transmitting information into the home either by cable or telephone lines or by latching onto an existing broadcast television signal. Major newspapers are exploring the opportunities for either supplying the new services with information or transmitting it themselves.

What will be the future for our syndicated wits and sages? According to one syndicate chief, 1982 "was a dreadful year for the syndicate business, presumably the worst in history, and it was because the papers were imploding, there was a recession, they had less white space because they had less advertising to support it. I was told by a few people that some of the syndicate people were saying 'Business is dead,' and they were looking for other jobs, particularly the

young people who were looking for a future. . . . They were taking terrible baths. I mean, papers were canceling features en masse."

Other syndicate heads painted a less dismal picture (and even the one who relayed the gruesome tales thought they were exaggerated). One syndicate editor spoke of 1982 as his firm's "best year in terms of feature billings," and most syndicate chiefs were bullish on the prospects for their comic strips. They spoke more hesitatingly about their public-affairs columnists.

New technology and ever-intensifying competition already are causing changes in the way syndicates do business. For example, there is greater competition against the syndicates from the supplemental wire services of large news organizations, such as the *Los Angeles Times,* the *Washington Post,* and the *New York Times.* Newspapers that subscribe to these services receive a great deal of feature material as part of the package, cutting into the need they once had for syndicated features. Territorial exclusivity, the hoary practice by which a large newspaper could demand—and had to pay for—exclusive rights to a column, is being whittled away slowly. In past years, papers such as the *Des Moines Register and Tribune,* the *Portland Oregonian,* the *Minneapolis Tribune,* the *Milwaukee Journal,* and the *Louisville Courier Journal* could claim their entire state as the area in which they had exclusive rights to print a column or comic strip. Court rulings and the efforts of some syndicates have begun to shrink the areas of exclusivity, so syndicates now are able to offer their best material to more papers. (The syndicates are not interested in seeing exclusivity disappear altogether, however, since they can charge higher prices for a feature when they offer it exclusively to a paper.) On the technological front, a rapidly increasing number of newspapers have stopped receiving columns by mail and have begun getting them over the high-speed wires of the Associated Press and United Press International. The wire services lease time on their facilities to the syndicates, and in some cases the syndicates charge the newspapers more for the wire delivery of a column—say, $5.50—than they charge for the column itself. The high-speed wires, which can transmit up to 1,200 words a minute over telephone lines or by satellite, enable the syndicates—and the columnists—to provide the papers with fresher material that can go directly into their own computer systems.

The syndicates are exploring other opportunities in the new technologies as well, albeit tentatively. Some of their features lend themselves readily to the new media. For example, King Features Syndicate already has its household "Hints From Heloise" and advice from Dr. Joyce Brothers available on floppy discs for home computers. Some other syndicates say that they are readying new print features or are looking into the feasibility of electronic spin-offs of the ones they have now. Whether what is written by their public-affairs columnists is similarly adaptable to computer, teletext, or videotex is less certain.

Some syndicate heads expect to see the work of their opinion columnists transferred to—or at least made available for—the new systems. "It's information that people want," said one syndicate editor. "Folks are paying good money to buy it now. The medium into which they put it is less important than the message, if you will. . . . That type of information, that kind of look at important things in the news, I think will be needed as long as people want more than to simply read a bare account of what happened."

"There's certainly going to be a market for [the columnists'] information," said another syndicate chief, "and the technology of it really doesn't matter."

"I don't think anybody, myself included, knows the answer to these things," said the head of one of the largest syndicates. "There's hundreds of millions of dollars being invested and gambled in these new areas, and no one knows how it's all going to settle down. Ultimately, it's going to be a very simple answer, and that's, what does the public want? And the public will be uninterested in the technology. They will have no interest in the miracle of this thing. It's like people are not interested in the miracle of the phone; they just want to know if it's good news or if it's bad news and does it work. And that, I think, will be exactly the same attitude [about columnists]. They're not going to be interested in whether they get George Will via satellite. . . . The habits . . . won't be changed by the technology."

Market research suggests, however, that the people who will use the new electronic systems also are those who tend to buy and read newspapers. Videotex and its technological siblings "will not be much competition for serious newspaper readers," according to one industry stock analyst, and these are precisely the audience most columnists address. "I kind of doubt the columnists will be much of a factor in the videotex systems—or much affected by them."

One syndicate director agrees, believing that the commentary of the columnists is essentially a print form. "I think they're a newspaper or a print medium, because if you're going to look at teletext, I think you're going to be looking for bulletin-type news and specific kinds of information, like a want ad, a classified ad, or a sports score. Opinion is still best read in a particular kind of setting, not sitting in front of a machine."

Fewer columnists, however, may attain quick and lasting national prominence. Gone are the days when syndicates could launch a new columnist with a reasonable assurance that there would be editors willing to give the writer a chance—or bid up the price for a column to keep it from the competition. Now there are only 23 markets in the country that support rival newspapers.

"Part of the reason that syndicates were so successful is that they went into competitive markets and by the use of fear—the fear that the paper that was first offered a feature might lose out and be embarrassed later that it didn't have Walter Lippmann—would get the paper to buy the feature, even if it never used it," explained one syndicate chief.

Many columnists also write less frequently now than did their predecessors. Twenty or thirty years ago, it was not uncommon for a columnist to write four or five columns a week; now many columnists only write twice a week. In the view of one syndicate director, the reduced writing has diminished the columnists' impact. "They're on the pages less often in the papers. Because the prices are low, the bigger papers tend to take a lot of columns and run them less frequently, so it's hard for the guy to have a lot of impact when maybe on an average he's showing up only once or twice a week."

More than a half-century ago, Damon Runyon advised his fellow columnists: "Keep your byline in there every day. Otherwise, your readers might miss it—or worse yet, they might not."

Since the early and mid-seventies, no new columnist "stars" have experienced the meteoric ascensions enjoyed by George Will and Ellen Goodman. It is possible—in fact, likely—that in this respect at least the "golden age" of column writing may be over. "I would say it's unlikely you'll have the huge superstars in the future," said one syndicate editor, "because, ironically, as there are fewer big city newspapers, there are far more columnists that have entered the field. There are more local columnists. Some papers have opened their Op Ed pages to an increasing number of local experts, which makes good journalistic sense."

On the other hand, another syndicate chief declined to foreclose the possibility that some new columnist, spearheading a trend or providing a viewpoint that papers are anxious to have, might not skyrocket to prominence. "I just don't know where he or she is going to come from," he said.

Knitting his wispy white eyebrows and peering into the future, Richard Strout says emphatically: "Newspapers are obviously in trouble. When I came to Washington, there were, for example, about a dozen daily newspapers from New York that had reporters here. That was 60 years ago. Now, I guess there are only about three or four. . . . So newspapers are in trouble . . . but there will always be the need for interpretive journalism. . . . People will always want to know not merely the bulletin but what's behind it."

Just as everything else in the field of editorializing is a matter of opinion, views differ on the influence, power, and importance of columnists, as well as on the manner in which syndicates will market their judgments in the future. I believe that the role today's columnists and their successors will play remains a vital one. As the *Washington Post*'s Colman McCarthy once observed, "The wealth of a community is the breadth of its citizens' ideas"; and columnists broaden the presentation of ideas in whatever medium they appear.

"In this and like communities, public sentiment is everything," Abraham Lincoln told the good people of Ottawa, Illinois, during the first Lincoln-Douglas debate in August 1858. "With public sentiment, nothing can fail. Without it, nothing can succeed. Consequently, he who moulds public sentiment goes deeper than he who enacts statutes or pronounces decisions."

As synthesizers, analysts, and sometimes jesters of the news, the wits and sages of the nation's press help define, explain, reinforce, and mold public sentiments in an age more complex and perilous than Lincoln's. Their voices are needed and are unlikely to be stilled.

PERMISSIONS

JACK ANDERSON:

Columns are copyrighted by United Features Syndicate and excerpts are reprinted with permission.

RUSSELL BAKER:

Columns are copyrighted © 1975/80/81/82 by The New York Times Company. Reprinted by permission. Excerpts from *Growing Up,* published in 1983 by Congdon & Weed, Inc., are reprinted with the approval of the author.

JIMMY BRESLIN:

Column excerpts on pp. 85, 86, 87, and 93 are reprinted by permission of the Tribune Company Syndicate, Inc.

ERMA BOMBECK:

Columns are copyrighted by the Field Newspaper Syndicate and excerpts are reprinted with permission.

DAVID BRODER:

Columns are copyrighted by the Washington Post Writers Group and excerpts are reprinted with permission.

ART BUCHWALD:

Columns are copyrighted by Art Buchwald and excerpts are reprinted with permission.

WILLIAM F. BUCKLEY, JR.:

Column excerpts on pp. 147–148 and 155 are copyrighted © 1981 and 1982 by the Universal Press Syndicate and are reprinted with permission. All rights reserved. Excerpt on pp. 156/57 reprinted with permission from *The New York Review of Books.* Copyright © 1983 Nyrev, Inc. Earlier columns and books by William F. Buckley, Jr., are copyrighted by William F. Buckley, Jr., and excerpts are reprinted with permission from the author.

ELLEN GOODMAN:

Columns are copyrighted by the Washington Post Writers Group and excerpts are reprinted with permission.

JAMES J. KILPATRICK:

Column excerpts on pp. 180 and 187 are copyrighted © 1980 and 1981 by the Universal Press Syndicate and are reprinted with permission. All rights reserved. Articles from *National Review* are copyrighted © 1968 and 1974 by *National Review* and excerpts are reprinted with permission.

CARL T. ROWAN:

Columns are copyrighted by the Field Newspaper Syndicate and excerpts are reprinted with permission.

MIKE ROYKO:

Columns are copyrighted by Mike Royko and excerpts are reprinted with permission.

GEORGE F. WILL:

Columns are copyrighted by the Washington Post Writers Group and excerpts are reprinted with permission. *Statecraft As Soulcraft* is copyrighted © 1983 by G.F.W., Inc., A Maryland Corporation; excerpts are reprinted by permission of Simon & Schuster, Inc.

The Johns Hopkins University Press

WITS & SAGES

This book was composed in Times Roman and American Typewriter by BG Composition Inc., Baltimore, Maryland, from a design by Gerard A. Valerio.

It was printed by offset lithography on 55-lb. Antique paper and bound in Holliston Kingston cloth by The Maple Press Company, York, Pennsylvania.